Lecture Notes in Computer Scie

T0250738

Commenced Publication in 1973
Founding and Former Series Editors:
Gerhard Goos, Juris Hartmanis, and Jan van Leeuwen

Peter Van Roy (Ed.)

Multiparadigm Programming in Mozart/Oz

Second International Conference, MOZ 2004
Charleroi, Belgium, October 7-8, 2004
Revised Selected and Invited Papers

 Springer

Volume Editor

Peter Van Roy
Université catholique de Louvain
Department of Computing Science and Engineering
Place Sainte Barbe, 2, B-1348 Louvain-la-Neuve, Belgium
E-mail: pvr@info.ucl.ac.be

Library of Congress Control Number: 2005921638

CR Subject Classification (1998): D.3, F.3, D.2, D.1, D.4

ISSN 0302-9743
ISBN 3-540-25079-4 Springer Berlin Heidelberg New York

Springer is a part of Springer Science+Business Media

springeronline.com

© Springer-Verlag Berlin Heidelberg 2005
Printed in Germany

Typesetting: Camera-ready by author, data conversion by Scientific Publishing Services, Chennai, India
Printed on acid-free paper   SPIN: 11398158   06/3142   5 4 3 2 1 0

Foreword

To many readers, Mozart/Oz represents a new addition to the pantheon of programming systems. One way of evaluating a newcomer is through the eyes of the classics, for example Kernighan and Pike's "The Practice of Programming," a book that concludes with six "lasting concepts": simplicity and clarity, generality, evolution, interfaces, automation, and notation. Kernighan and Pike concentrate on using standard languages such as C and Java to implement these concepts, but it is instructive to see how a multiparadigm language such as Oz changes the outlook.

Oz's concurrency model yields simplicity and clarity (because Oz makes it easier to express complex programs with many interacting components), generality, and better interfaces (because the dataflow model automatically makes interfaces more lightweight).

Constraint programming in Oz again yields simplicity and clarity (because the programmer can express what needs to be true rather than the more complex issue of how to make it true), and offers a powerful mathematical notation that is difficult to implement on top of languages that do not support it natively.

Mozart's distributed computing model makes for improved interfaces and eases the evolution of systems. In my own work, one of the most important concerns is to be able to quickly scale up a prototype implementation into a large-scale service that can run reliably on thousands of computers, serving millions of users. The field of computer science needs more research to discover the best ways of facilitating this, but Mozart provides one powerful approach.

Altogether, Mozart/Oz helps with all the lasting concepts except automation, and it plays a particularly strong role in notation, which Kernighan and Pike point out is an underappreciated area. I believe that providing the right notation is the most important of the six concepts, one that supports all the others. Multiparadigm systems such as Oz provide more choices for notation than single-paradigm languages.

Going beyond Kernighan and Pike's six concerns, I recognize three more concerns that I think are important, and cannot be added on to a language by writing functions and classes; they must be inherent to the language itself.

The first is the ability to separate concerns, to describe separate aspects of a program separately. Mozart supports separation of fault tolerance and distributed computation allocation in an admirable way.

My second concern is security. Sure, you can eliminate a large class of security holes by replacing the `char*` datatype with `string`, but strong security cannot be guaranteed in a language that is not itself secure.

My third concern is performance. David Moon once said, in words more pithy than I can recall, that you can abstract anything except performance. That is, you can add abstraction layers, but you can't get back sufficient speed if the underlying language implementation doesn't provide it. Mozart/Oz has a 10-year history of making choices that provide for better performance, thereby making the system a platform that will rarely run up against fundamental performance problems.

We all look for tools and ideas to help us become better programmers. Sometimes the most fundamental idea is to pick the right programming environment.

Peter Norvig
Director of Search Quality, Google, Inc.
Coauthor, *Artificial Intelligence: A Modern Approach*

Preface

Multiparadigm programming, when done well, brings together the best parts of different programming paradigms in a simple and powerful whole. This allows the programmer to choose the right concepts for each problem to be solved. This book gives a snapshot of the work being done with Mozart/Oz, one of today's most comprehensive multiparadigm programming systems. Mozart/Oz has been under development since the early 1990s as a vehicle to support research in programming languages, constraint programming, and distributed programming.[1] Since then, Mozart/Oz has matured into a production-quality system with an active user community. Mozart/Oz consists of the Oz programming language and its implementation, Mozart. Oz combines the concepts of all major programming paradigms in a simple and harmonious whole. Mozart is a high-quality open source implementation of Oz that exists for different versions of Windows, Unix/Linux/Solaris, and Mac OS X.[2]

This book is an extended version of the proceedings of the 2nd International Mozart/Oz Conference (MOZ 2004), which was held in Charleroi, Belgium on October 7 and 8, 2004. MOZ 2004 consisted of 23 technical talks, four tutorials, and invited talks by Gert Smolka and Mark S. Miller. The slides of all talks and tutorials are available for downloading at the conference website.[3] This book contains all 23 papers presented at the conference, supplemented with two invited papers written especially for the book. The conference papers were selected from 28 submissions after a rigorous reviewing process in which most papers were reviewed by three members of the Program Committee. We were pleasantly surprised by the high average quality of the submissions.

Mozart/Oz research and development started in the early 1990s as part of the ACCLAIM project, funded by the European Union. This project led to the Mozart Consortium, an informal but intense collaboration that initially consisted of the Programming Systems Lab at Saarland University in Saarbrücken, Germany, the Swedish Institute of Computer Science in Kista, Sweden, and the Université catholique de Louvain in Louvain-la-Neuve, Belgium. Several other institutions have since joined this collaboration. Since the publication in March 2004 of the textbook *Concepts, Techniques, and Models of Computer Programming* by MIT Press, the Mozart/Oz community has grown significantly. As a result, we are reorganizing the Mozart Consortium to make it more open.

Security and Concurrency

Two important themes in this book are security and concurrency. The book includes two invited papers on language-based computer security. Computer secu-

---

[1] In the early days before the Mozart Consortium the system was called DFKI Oz.
[2] See www.mozart-oz.org.
[3] See www.cetic.be/moz2004.

rity is a major preoccupation today both in the computer science community and in general society. While there are many short-term solutions to security problems, a good long-term solution requires rethinking our programming languages and operating systems. One crucial idea is that languages and operating systems should thoroughly support the principle of least authority. This support starts from the user interface and goes all the way down to basic object invocations. With such thorough support, many security problems that are considered difficult today become much simpler. For example, the so-called trade-off between security and usability largely goes away. We can have security without compromising usability. The two invited papers are the beginning of what we hope will become a significant effort from the Mozart/Oz community to address these issues and propose solutions.

The second important theme of this book is concurrent programming. We have built Mozart/Oz so that concurrency is both easy to program with and efficient in execution. Many papers in the book exploit this concurrency support. Several papers use a multiagent architecture based on message passing. Other papers use constraint programming, which is implemented with lightweight threads and declarative concurrency. We find that both message-passing concurrency and declarative concurrency are much easier to program with than shared-state concurrency. The same conclusion has been reached independently by others. Joe Armstrong, the main designer of the Erlang language, has found that using message-passing concurrency greatly simplifies building software that does not crash. Doug Barnes and Mark S. Miller, the main designers of the E language, have found that message-passing concurrency greatly simplifies building secure distributed systems. E is discussed in both of the invited papers in this book.

Joe Armstrong has coined the phrase *concurrency-oriented programming* for languages like Oz and Erlang that make concurrency both easy and efficient. We conclude that concurrency-oriented programming will become increasingly important in the future. This is not just because concurrency is useful for multiagent systems and constraint programming. It is really because concurrency makes it easier to build software that is reliable and secure.

Diversity and Synergy

Classifying the papers in this book according to subject area gives an idea of the diversity of work going on under the Mozart banner: security and language design, computer science education, software engineering, human-computer interfaces and the Web, distributed programming, grammars and natural language, constraint research, and constraint applications. Constraints in Mozart are used to implement games (Oz Minesweeper), to solve practical problems (reconfiguration of electrical power networks, aircraft sequencing at an airport, timetabling, etc.), and to do complex symbolic calculation (such as natural language processing and music composition). If you start reading the book knowing only some of these areas, then I hope that it will encourage you to get involved with the others. Please do not hesitate to contact the authors of the papers to ask for software and advice.

The most important strength of Mozart, in my view, is the synergy that comes from connecting areas that are usually considered as disjoint. The synergy is strong because the connections are done in a deep way, based on the fundamental concepts of each area and their formal semantics. It is my hope that this book will inspire you to build on this synergy to go beyond what has been done before. Research and development, like many human activities, are limited by a psychological barrier similar to that which causes sports records to advance only gradually. It is rare that people step far beyond the boundaries of what has been done before. One way to break this barrier is to take advantage of the connections that Mozart offers between different areas. I hope that the wide variety of examples shown in this book will help you to do that.

In conclusion, I would like to thank all the people who made MOZ 2004 and this book a reality: the paper authors, the Program Committee members, the Mozart developers, and, last but not least, the CETIC asbl, who organized the conference in a professional manner. I thank Peter Norvig of Google, Inc., who graciously accepted to write the Foreword for this book. And, finally, I give a special thanks to Donatien Grolaux, the local arrangements chair, for his hard work in handling all the practical details.

November 2004   Peter Van Roy
Louvain-la-Neuve, Belgium

Organization

MOZ 2004 was organized by CETIC in cooperation with the Université catholique de Louvain. CETIC asbl is the Centre of Excellence in Information and Communication Technologies, an applied research laboratory based in Charleroi, Belgium.[1] CETIC is focused on the fields of software engineering, distributed computing, and electronic systems. The Université catholique de Louvain was founded in 1425 and is located in Louvain-la-Neuve, Belgium.

Organizing Committee

Donatien Grolaux, CETIC, Belgium (local arrangements chair)
Bruno Carton, CETIC, Belgium
Pierre Guisset, director, CETIC, Belgium
Peter Van Roy, Université catholique de Louvain, Belgium

Program Committee

Per Brand, Swedish Institute of Computer Science, Sweden
Thorsten Brunklaus, Saarland University, Germany
Raphaël Collet, Université catholique de Louvain, Belgium
Juan F. Díaz, Universidad del Valle, Cali, Colombia
Denys Duchier, INRIA Futurs, Lille, France
Sameh El-Ansary, Swedish Institute of Computer Science, Sweden
Kevin Glynn, Université catholique de Louvain, Belgium
Donatien Grolaux, CETIC, Belgium
Seif Haridi, KTH – Royal Institute of Technology, Sweden
Martin Henz, FriarTuck and the National University of Singapore
Erik Klintskog, Swedish Institute of Computer Science, Sweden
Joachim Niehren, INRIA Futurs, Lille, France
Luc Onana, KTH – Royal Institute of Technology, Sweden
Konstantin Popov, Swedish Institute of Computer Science, Sweden
Mahmoud Rafea, Central Laboratory for Agricultural Expert Systems, Egypt
Juris Reinfelds, New Mexico State University, USA
Andreas Rossberg, Saarland University, Germany
Camilo Rueda, Pontificia Universidad Javeriana, Cali, Colombia
Christian Schulte, KTH – Royal Institute of Technology, Sweden
Gert Smolka, Saarland University, Germany
Fred Spiessens, Université catholique de Louvain, Belgium
Peter Van Roy, Université catholique de Louvain, Belgium (Program Chair)

---

[1] See www.cetic.be.

Table of Contents

Distributed Programming

Grammars and Natural Language

Constraint Research

Constraint Applications

The Development of Oz and Mozart

Gert Smolka

Saarland University
Saarbrücken, Germany
smolka@ps.uni-sb.de

In this talk I will review the development of the programming language Oz and the programming system Mozart. I will discuss where in hindsight I see the strong and the weak points of the language. Moreover, I will compare Oz with Alice, a typed functional language we developed after Oz.

The development of Oz started in 1991 at DFKI under my lead. The initial goal was to advance ideas from constraint and concurrent logic programming and also from knowledge representation and to develop a practically useful programming system. After a number of radical and unforeseen redesigns we arrived in 1995 at the final base language and a stable implementation (DFKI Oz). In 1996 we founded the Mozart Consortium with SICS and Louvain-la-Neuve. Oz was extended with support for persistence, distribution and modules and Mozart 1.0 was released in January 1999.

P. Van Roy (Ed.): MOZ 2004, LNCS 3389, p. 1, 2005.

The Structure of Authority: Why Security Is Not a Separable Concern

Mark S. Miller[1,2], Bill Tulloh[3,**], and Jonathan S. Shapiro[2]

[1] Hewlett Packard Labs
[2] Johns Hopkins University
[3] George Mason University

Abstract. Common programming practice grants excess authority for the sake of functionality; programming principles require least authority for the sake of security. If we practice our principles, we could have both security and functionality. Treating security as a separate concern has not succeeded in bridging the gap between principle and practice, because it operates without knowledge of what constitutes least authority. Only when requests are made – whether by humans acting through a user interface, or by one object invoking another – can we determine how much authority is adequate. Without this knowledge, we must provide programs with enough authority to do anything they *might* be requested to do.

We examine the practice of least authority at four major layers of abstraction – from humans in an organization down to individual objects within a programming language. We explain the special role of object-capability languages – such as *E* or the proposed Oz-E – in supporting practical least authority.

1 Excess Authority: The Gateway to Abuse

Software systems today are highly vulnerable to attack. This widespread vulnerability can be traced in large part to the excess authority we routinely grant programs. Virtually every program a user launches is granted the user's full authority, even a simple game program like Solitaire. All widely-deployed operating systems today – including Windows, UNIX variants, Macintosh, and PalmOS – work on this principle. While users need broad authority to accomplish their various goals, this authority greatly exceeds what any particular program needs to accomplish its task.

When you run Solitaire, it only needs the authority to draw in its window, to receive the UI events you direct at it, and to write into a file you specify in order to save your score. If you had granted it only this limited authority, a corrupted Solitaire might be annoying, but not a threat. It may prevent you from

---

** Bill Tulloh would like to thank the Critical Infrastructure Protection Project at George Mason University for its financial support of this research.

P. Van Roy (Ed.): MOZ 2004, LNCS 3389, pp. 2–20, 2005.

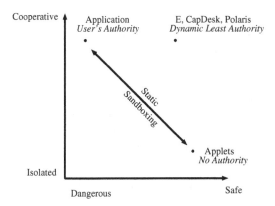

Fig. 1. Functionality vs. Security?

playing the game or lie about your score. Instead, under conventional systems, it runs with all of your authority. It can delete any file you can. It can scan your email for interesting tidbits and sell them on eBay to the highest bidder. It can install a back door and use your computer to forward spam. While Solitaire itself probably doesn't abuse its excess authority, it could. If an exploitable bug in Solitaire enables an attacker to gain control of it, the attacker can do anything Solitaire is authorized to do.

If Solitaire only needs such limited authority, why do you give it all of your authority? Well, what other choice do you have? Figure 1 shows your choices. On the one hand, you can run Solitaire as an application. Running it as an application allows you to use all the rich functionality and integration that current application frameworks have been built to support; but at the price of trusting it with all your authority. On the other hand, you could run it as an applet, granting it virtually no authority, but then it becomes isolated and mostly useless. A Solitaire applet could not even offer to save its score into a file you specify.

Sandboxing provides a middle ground between granting a program the user's full authority, and granting it no authority. Most approaches to sandboxing enable you to configure a static set of authorities (as might be represented in a policy file) to be granted to the program when it is launched. The problem is that you do not know in advance what authorities the program actually needs; the least authority needed by the program changes as execution progresses [Schneider03]. Or it might allow you to add authority incrementally, so you can trade away your safety piecemeal for functionality, but only by suffering a torrent of annoying security dialog boxes that destroy usability.

In order to successfully apply the *principle of least authority* (POLA), we need to take a different approach. Rather than trading security for functionality, we need to limit potential abuse without interfering with potential use. How far out might we move on the horizontal axis without loss of functionality or usability? Least authority, by definition, includes adequate authority to get the job done. Providing authority that is adequate means providing it in the right amount and at the right time. The key to putting POLA into practice lies in the dynamic allocation of authority; we must provide the right amount of authority just-in-time, not excess authority just-in-case.

In this paper we explain how narrow least authority can be practically achieved. We report on recent experience in building two working systems that put POLA into practice, and that demonstrate the potential for building secure systems that are both useful and usable. CapDesk is an open source proof-of-concept secure desktop and browser built from the ground up using the E language. Polaris is an experimental prototype from HP Labs that shows how the benefits of POLA can be applied to legacy applications.

1.1 How Much Authority Is Adequate?

How do we know how much authority a program actually needs? Surprisingly, the answer depends on architectural choices not normally thought to be related to security – the logic of designation. Consider two Unix shell commands for copying a file. In the following example, they both perform the same task, copying the file foo.txt into bar.txt, yet they follow very different logics of designation in order to do so. The result is that the least authority each needs to perform this task differs significantly.

Consider how cp performs its task:

```
$ cp foo.txt bar.txt
```

Your shell passes to the cp program the two strings "foo.txt" and "bar.txt". The cp program uses these strings to determine which files it should copy.

By contrast consider how cat performs its task:

```
$ cat < foo.txt > bar.txt
```

Your shell uses these strings to determine which files you mean to designate. Once this is resolved, your shell passes direct access to the files to cat, as open file descriptors. The cat program uses these descriptors to perform the copy.

Now consider the least authority that each one needs to perform its task.

With cp, you tell it which files to copy by passing it strings. By these strings, you mean particular files in your file system – your namespace of files. In order for cp to open the files you name, it must already have the authority to use your namespace, and it must already have the authority to read and write any file you might name. Given this way of using names, cp's *least authority* still includes all of your authority to the file system. The least authority it needs is so broad as to make achieving security hopeless.

With cat, you tell it which files to copy by passing it direct access to those two specific files. Like the cp example, you still use names in your namespace to say which files you wish to have cat copy, but these names get evaluated in your namespace prior to being passed to cat. By passing cat direct access to each file rather than giving it the file name, it does not need broad authority to do its job. Its least authority is what you'd expect – the right to read your foo.txt and the right to write your bar.txt. It needs no further access to your file system.

Currently under Unix, both cp and cat, like Solitaire, run with all your authority. But the least authority they require to copy a file differs substantially. Today's widely deployed systems use both styles of access control. They grant authority to open a file on a per-user basis, creating dangerous pools of excess authority. These same systems dynamically grant access to a file descriptor on a per-process basis. Ironically, only their support for the first style is explained as providing a form of access control.

2   Composing Complex Systems

In order to build systems that are both functional and secure, we need to provide programmers with the tools, practices, and design patterns that enable them to combine designation with authority. We can identify two main places where acts of designation occur: users designate actions through the user interface, and objects designate actions by sending requests to other objects. In both places, developers already have extensive experience with supporting such acts of designation. User-interface designers have developed a rich set of user-interface widgets and practices to support user designation [Yee04]. Likewise, programmers have developed a rich tool set of languages, patterns, and practices to support designation between objects.

That the tools for separating and integrating actions (and potentially authority) already exist should not be too surprising. Programmers use modularity and abstraction to first decompose and then compose systems in order to meet the goals of providing usability and functionality. By combining designation and authority, the same tools can be applied to meeting the goals of providing security.

2.1   The Object-Capability Model: Aligning Rights with Responsibilities

Object-oriented programming already embodies most of what is needed to provide secure programming. We introduce the object-capability model as a straightforward extension of the object model. Computer scientists, usually without any consideration for security, seeking only support for the division and composition of knowledge by abstraction and modularity, have recapitulated the logic of the object-capability model of secure computation.

In the object model, programmers decompose a system into objects and then compose those objects to get complex functionality. Designers use abstraction to carve a system into separate objects that embody those abstractions. Objects package abstractions as services that other objects can request. Each object is responsible for performing a specialized job; the knowledge required to perform the job is encapsulated within the object [Wirfs-Brock02].

Objects are composed dynamically at run-time through objects acquiring references to other objects. In order for an object to collaborate with another object, it must first come to know about the other object; the object must come to hold a reference that identifies a particular object that is available for collaboration. Objects must also have a means of communicating with these potential collaborators. References create such paths of communication. Objects can send messages along these references to request other objects to perform services on their behalf.

In the object-capability model references indivisibly combine the designation of a particular object, the means to access the object, and the right to access the object. By requiring that objects interact *only* by sending messages on references, the reference graph becomes the access graph. The object-capability model does not treat access control as a separate concern; rather it is a model of modular computation with no separate access control mechanisms.

By claiming that security is not a separable concern, we do not mean to suggest that no degree of separation is possible. Dijkstra's original modest suggestion – that we temporarily separate concerns as a conceptual aid for reasoning about complex systems [Dijkstra74] – is applicable to security as it is to correctness and modularity. What we wish to call into question, however, is the conventional practice of treating access control concerns – the allocation of access rights within a system – separately from the practice of designing and building systems. One cannot make a system more modular by adding a modularity module. Security, again like correctness and modularity, must first and foremost be treated as part of the process of de-composing and composing software systems. Access control in the object-capability model derives from the pursuit of abstraction and modularity. Parnas' principle of *information hiding* [Parnas72] in effect says our abstractions should hand out information only on a *need to know* basis. POLA simply adds that authority should be handed out only on a *need to do* basis. Modularity and security each require both.

2.2   The Fractal Locality of Knowledge: Let "Knows-About" Shape "Access-to"

What the object model and object-capability model have in common is a logic that explains how computational decisions dynamically determine the structure of knowledge in our systems – the topology of the "knows-about" relationship. The division of knowledge into separate objects that cooperate through sending requests creates a natural sparseness of knowledge within a system. The object-capability model recognizes that this same sparseness of knowledge, created in pursuit of good modular design, can be harnessed to protect objects from one another. Objects that do not know about one another, and consequently have no way to interact with each other, cannot cause each other harm. By combining designation with authority, the logic of the object-capability model explains how computational decisions dynamically determine the structure of authority in our systems – the topology of the "access-to" relationship.

What we typically find in computational systems is a hierarchical, recursive division of responsibility and knowledge. Computation, like many complex systems, is organized into a hierarchic structure of nested levels of subsystems. We can identify four majors layers of abstraction: at the organizational level systems are composed of users; at the user level, systems are composed of applications; at the application level, systems are composed of modules; at the module level, systems are composed of objects. Each layer of abstraction provides a space where the subsystems at that level can interact, while at the same time significantly limiting the intensity of interaction that needs to occur across these layers.

Computer scientist and Nobel Laureate in Economics, Herbert Simon, argues that this hierarchic nesting of subsystems is common across many types of complex systems [Simon62]. Complex systems frequently take the form of a hierarchy, which can be decomposed into subsystems, and so on; "Hierarchy," he argues, "is one of the central structural schemes that the architecture of complexity uses." Simon shows how this nesting of subsystems occurs across many different types of systems. For example, in the body, we have cells that make up tissues, that make up organs, that make up organisms. As Simon notes, the nesting of subsystems helps bring about a sparseness of knowledge between subsystems. Each subsystem operates (nearly) independently of the detailed processes going on within other subsystems; components within each level communicate much more frequently than they do across levels. For example, my liver and my kidney in some sense know about each other; they use chemical signals to communicate with one another. Similarly, you and I may know about each other, using verbal signals to communicate and collaborate with one another. On the other hand we would be quite surprised to see my liver talk to your kidneys.

While the nesting of subsystems into layers is quite common in complex systems, it provides a rather static view of the knowledge relationship between layers. In contrast, within layers we see a much more dynamic process. Within layers of abstraction, computation is largely organized as a dynamic subcontracting network. Subcontracting organizes requests for services among clients and providers. Abstraction boundaries between clients and providers enable separation of concerns at the local level. They help to further reduce knows-about relationships, not just by thinning the topology of who knows about whom, but also by reducing how much they know about each other [Tulloh02]. Abstraction boundaries allow the concerns of the client (the reasons why it requests a particular service) to be separated from the concerns of the provider (how it implements a particular service). Abstraction boundaries, by hiding implementation details, allow clients to ignore distractions and focus on their remaining concern. Applied to authority, abstraction boundaries protect clients from further unwanted details; by denying the provider authority that is not needed to do its job, the client does not need to worry as much about the provider's intent. Even if the intent is to cause harm, the scope of harm is limited.

Simon's fellow Nobel Laureate in Economics, Friedrich Hayek, has argued that the division of knowledge and authority through dynamic subcontracting relationships is common across many types of complex systems [Hayek45, Hayek64]. In particular, Hayek has argued that the system of specialization and exchange that generates the division of labor in the economy is best understood as creating a division of knowledge where clients and providers coordinate their plans based on local knowledge. Diverse plans, Hayek argues, can be coordinated only based on local knowledge; no one entity possesses the knowledge needed to coordinate agents' plans. Similarly no one entity has the knowledge required to allocate authority within computer systems according to the principle of least authority. To do this effectively, the entity would need to understand the duties of every single abstraction in the system, at every level of composition. Without understanding the duties of each component, it's impossible to understand what would be the least authority needed for it to carry out these duties. "Least" and "duties" can only be understood locally.

3   The Fractal Nature of Authority

The access matrix model [Lampson74, Graham72] has proven to be one of the most durable abstractions for reasoning about access control in computational systems. The access matrix provides a snapshot of the protection state of a particular system, showing the rights (the filled-in cells) that active entities (the rows) have with respect to protected resources (the columns). While not specifically designed for reasoning about least authority, we adapt the access matrix model to show how the consistent application of POLA across levels can significantly reduce the ability of attackers to exploit vulnerabilities. We show how POLA applied at the four major layers of abstraction – from humans in an organization down to individual objects within a programming language – can achieve a multiplicative reduction in a system's attack surface.

The access matrix is normally used to depict only permissions – the direct access rights an active entity has to a resource, as represented by the system's protection state. Since we wish to reason about our overall exposure to attack, in this paper access matrices will instead depict authority. Authority includes both direct permissions and indirect causal access via the permitted actions of intermediary objects [Miller03]. It is unclear whether Saltzer and Schroeder's famous "principle of least privilege" [Saltzer75] should be understood as "least permission" or "least authority". But it is clear that, to minimize our exposure, we must examine authority. To avoid confusion, when we wish to speak specifically about the structure of permissions, we will instead refer to the "access graph" – an alternate visualization in which permissions are shown as arcs of the graph [Bishop79].

Howard, Pincus and Wing [Howard03] have introduced the notion of an attack surface as a way to measure, in a qualitative manner, the relative security of various computer systems. This multi-dimensional metric attempts to capture the notion that system security depends not only on the number of specific bugs found, but also on a system's "process and data resources" and the actions that can be executed on these resources. These resources can serve as either targets or enablers depending on the nature of the attack. Attackers gain control over the resources through communication channels and protocols; access rights place constraints on which resources can be accessed over these channels.

They define the attack surface of a system to be the sum of the system's attack opportunities. An attack is a means of exploiting a vulnerability. Attack opportunities are exploitable vulnerabilities in the system weighted by some notion of how exploitable the vulnerability is. By treating exploitability not just as a measure of how likely a particular exploit will occur, but as a measure of the extent of damage that can occur from a successful attack, we can gain insight into the role least authority can play in reducing a system's attack surface.

We can use the area of the cells within the access matrix to visualize, in an abstract way, the attack surface of a system. Imagine that the heights of the rows were resized to be proportional to the likelihood that each active entity could be corrupted or confused into enabling an attack. Imagine that the width of the columns were resized to be proportional to the damage an attacker with authority to that asset could cause. Our overall attack surface may, therefore, be approximated as the overall filled-in area of the access matrix. (In this paper, we do not show such resizing, as the knowledge needed to quantify these issues is largely inaccessible).

By taking this perspective and combining it with Simon's insight that complex systems are typically organized into nested layers of abstractions, we can now show how applying POLA to each level can recursively reduce the attack surface of a system. While it is well-recognized that the active entities in an access matrix can be either people or processes, the precise relationship between them is rarely recognized in any systematic way. We show how the same nesting of levels of abstraction, used to organize system functionality, can be used to organize the authority needed to provide that functionality.

We now take a tour through four major levels of composition of an example system:

1. among the people within an organization
2. among the applications launched by a person from their desktop
3. among the modules within an application
4. among individual language-level "objects"

Within this structure, we show how to practice POLA painlessly at each level, and how these separate practices compose to reduce the overall attack surface multiplicatively.

Some common themes will emerge in different guises at each level:

- the relatively static nesting of subsystems
- the dynamic subcontracting networks within each subsystem
- the co-existence of legacy and non-legacy components
- the limits placed on POLA by the "TCB" issue, explained below, and by legacy code.

3.1   Human-Granularity POLA in an Organization

When an organization is small, when there's little at stake, or when all of an organization's employees are perfectly non-corruptible and non-confusable, the internal distribution of excess authority creates few vulnerabilities. Otherwise, organizations practice separation of responsibilities, need to know, and POLA to limit their exposure.

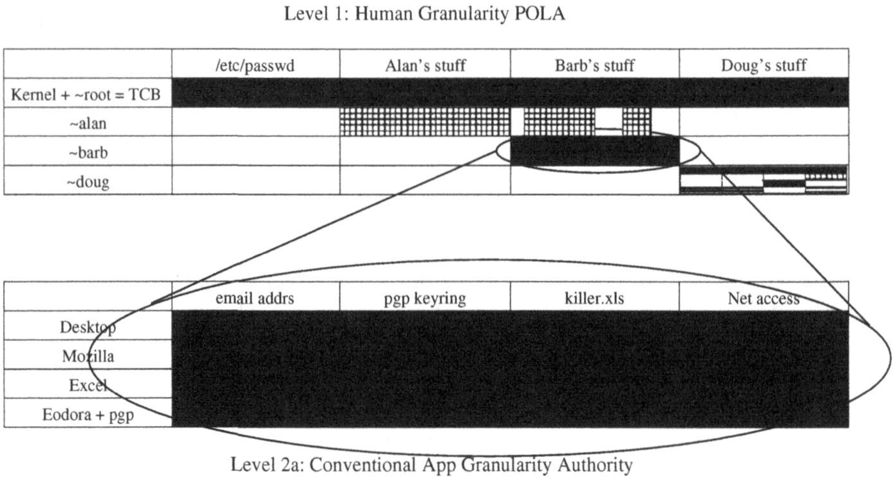

Level 1: Human Granularity POLA

	/etc/passwd	Alan's stuff	Barb's stuff	Doug's stuff
Kernel + ~root = TCB				
~alan				
~barb				
~doug				

	email addrs	pgp keyring	killer.xls	Net access
Desktop				
Mozilla				
Excel				
Eodora + pgp				

Level 2a: Conventional App Granularity Authority

Fig. 2. Barb's situation

The figure labeled "Level 1" (in Figure 2) uses the access matrix to visualize how conventional operating systems support POLA within a human organization. Alan (the "~alan" account) is given authority to access all of Alan's stuff, and likewise with Barb and Doug. In addition, because Barb and Alan are collaborating, Barb gives Alan authority to access some of her stuff. The organization should give Alan those authorities needed for him to carry out his responsibilities. This can happen in both a hierarchical manner (an administrator determining which of the organization's assets are included in "Alan's stuff") and a decentralized manner (by Barb, when she needs to collaborate with Alan on something) [Abrams95]. If an attacker confuses Alan into revealing his password, the assets the attacker can then abuse are limited to those entrusted to Alan. While better training or screening may reduce the likelihood of an attack succeeding, limits on available authority reduce the damage a successful attack can cause.

To the traditional access matrix visualization, we have added a row representing the TCB, and a column, labeled /etc/passwd, which stands for resources which are effectively part of the TCB. Historically, "TCB" stands for "Trusted Computing Base", but is actually about vulnerability rather than trust. To avoid the confusion caused by the traditional terminology, we here define TCB as that part of a system that everything in *that* system is necessarily vulnerable to. In a traditional timesharing context, or in a conventional centrally-administered system of accounts within a company, the TCB includes the operating system kernel, the administrator accounts, and the administrators. The TCB provides the mechanisms used to limit the authority of the other players, so all the authority it manages is vulnerable to the corruption or confusion of the TCB itself. While much can be done to reduce the likelihood of an exploitable flaw in the TCB – primarily by making it smaller and cleaner – ultimately any centralized system will continue to have this Achilles heel of potential full vulnerability. (Decentralized systems can escape this centralized vulnerability, and distributed languages like E and Oz should support the patterns needed to do so. But this issue is beyond the scope of this paper.)

3.2   Application-Granularity POLA on the Desktop

With the exception of the TCB problem, organizations have wrestled with these issues since long before computers. Operating System support for access control evolved largely in order to provide support for the resulting organizational practices [Moffett88]. Unfortunately, conventional support for these practices was based on a simplifying assumption that left us exposed to viruses, worms, Trojan horses, and the litany of problems that, now, regularly infest our networks. The simplifying assumption? When Barb runs a program to accomplish some goal, such as killer.xls, an Excel spreadsheet, conventional systems assume the program is a perfectly faithful extension of Barb's intent. But Barb didn't write Excel or killer.xls.

Zooming in on Level 1 brings us to Level 2a (Figure 2), showing the conventional distribution of authority among the programs Barb runs; they are all given all of Barb's authority. If Excel is corruptible or confusable – if it contains a bug allowing an attacker to subvert its logic for the attacker's purposes – then anything Excel may do, the attacker can do. The attacker can abuse all of Barb's authority – sending itself to her friends and deleting her files – even if her operating system, her administrator, and Barb herself are all operating flawlessly. Since all the assets entrusted to Barb are exposed to exploitable flaws in any program she runs, all her programs are in her TCB. If Barb enables macros, even her documents, like killer.xls, would be in her TCB as well. How can Barb reduce her exposure to the programs she runs?

Good organizational principles apply at many scales of organization. If the limited distribution of authority we saw in Level 1 is a good idea, can we adopt it at this level as well?

Level 2b (Figure 3) is at the same "scale" as Level 2a, but depicts Doug's situation rather than Barb's. Like Barb, Doug launches various applications interactively from his desktop. Unlike Barb, let's say Doug runs his desktop and these apps in such a way as to reduce his exposure to their misbehavior. One possibility would be that Doug runs a non-conventional OS that supports finer-grained POLA [Dennis66, Hardy85, Shapiro99]. In this paper, we explore a surprising alternative – the use of language-based security mechanisms, like those provided by E [Miller03] and proposed for Oz by the paper on Oz-E in this volume [Spiessens-VanRoy05]. We will explain how Doug uses CapDesk and Polaris to reduce his exposure while still running on a conventional OS. But first, it behooves us to be clear about the limits of this approach. (In our story, we combine the functionality of CapDesk and Polaris, though they are not yet actually integrated. Integrating CapDesk's protection with that provided by an appropriate secure OS would yield yet further reductions in exposure, but these are beyond the scope of this paper.)

CapDesk [Stiegler02] is a capability-secure distributed desktop written in E, for running *caplets* – applications written in E to be run under CapDesk.

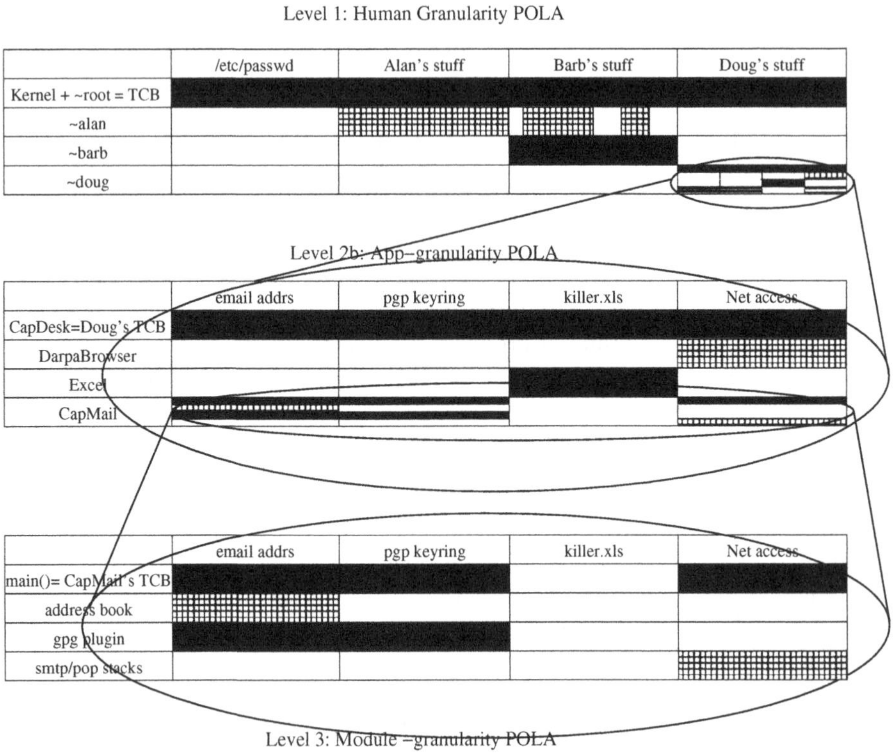

Level 1: Human Granularity POLA

	/etc/passwd	Alan's stuff	Barb's stuff	Doug's stuff
Kernel + ~root = TCB				
~alan				
~barb				
~doug				

Level 2b: App–granularity POLA

	email addrs	pgp keyring	killer.xls	Net access
CapDesk=Doug's TCB				
DarpaBrowser				
Excel				
CapMail				

	email addrs	pgp keyring	killer.xls	Net access
main()= CapMail's TCB				
address book				
gpg plugin				
smtp/pop stacks				

Level 3: Module –granularity POLA

Fig. 3. Doug's situation

CapDesk is the program Doug uses to subdivide his authority among these apps. To do this job, CapDesk's least authority is all of Doug's authority. Doug launches CapDesk as a conventional application in his account, thereby granting it all of his authority.

Doug is no less exposed to a flaw in CapDesk than Barb is to a flaw in each app she runs. CapDesk is part of Doug's TCB; but the programs launched by CapDesk are not. Doug is also no less exposed to an action taken by Barb, or one of her apps, than he was before. If the base OS does not protect his interests from actions taken in other accounts, then the whole system is in his TCB. Without a base OS that provides foundational protection, no significant reduction of exposure by other means is possible. So let us assume that the base OS *does* at least provide effective per-account protection. For any legacy programs that Doug installs or runs in the conventional manner – outside the CapDesk framework – Doug is no less exposed than he was before. All such programs remain in his TCB. If "~doug" is corrupted by this route, again, CapDesk's protections are for naught.

However, if the integrity of "~doug" survives these threats, Doug can protect the assets entrusted to him from the programs he runs by using CapDesk + Polaris to grant them least authority. This granting must be done in a usable fashion – unusable security won't be used, and security which isn't used doesn't protect anyone. As with cat, the key to usable POLA is to bundle authority with designation [Yee02, Yee04]. To use Excel to edit killer.xls, Doug must somehow designate this file as the one he wishes to edit. This may happen by double clicking on the file, by selecting it in an open file dialog box, or by drag-and-drop. (Drag-and-drop is supported by CapDesk, but not yet by Polaris.) The least authority Excel needs includes the authority to edit this one file, but typically not any other interesting authorities. Polaris [Stiegler04] runs each legacy app in a separate account, created by Polaris for this purpose, which initially has almost no authority. Under Polaris, Doug's act of designation dynamically grants Excel the authority to edit this one file. Polaris users regularly run with macros enabled, since they no longer live in fear of their documents.

3.3   Module-Granularity POLA Within a Caplet

Were we to zoom into Doug's legacy Excel box, we'd find that there is no further reduction of authority within Excel. All the authority granted to Excel as a whole is accessible to all the modules of which Excel is built, and to the macros in the spreadsheets it runs. Should the math library's sqrt function wish to overwrite killer.xls, nothing will prevent it. At this next smaller scale (the third level) we'd find the same full-authority picture previously depicted as Level 2a.

Caplets running under CapDesk do better. The DarpaBrowser is a web browser caplet, able to use a potentially malicious plug-in as a renderer. Although this is an actual example, the DarpaBrowser is "actual" only as a proof of concept whose security properties have been reviewed [Wagner02] – not yet as a practical browser. We will instead zoom in to the hypothetical email client caplet, CapMail. All the points we make about CapMail are also true for the DarpaBrowser, but the email client makes a better expository example. Of the programs regularly run by normal users – as opposed to system administrators or programmers – the email client is the worst case we've identified. Its least authority includes a dangerous combination of authorities. Doug would grant some of these authorities – like access to an smtp server – by static configuration, rather than dynamically during each use.

When Doug decides to grant CapMail these authorities, he's deciding to rely on the authors of CapMail not to abuse them. However, the authors of CapMail didn't write every line of code in CapMail – they reused various reusable libraries written by others. CapMail should not grant its crypto library the authority needed to read your address book and send itself to your friends.

Zooming in on the bottom row of Level 2b brings us to Level 3. A caplet has a startup module that's the moral equivalent of the C or Java programmer's "main()" function. CapDesk grants to this startup module all the authority it grants to CapMail as a whole. If CapMail is written well, this startup module should do essentially nothing but import the top level modules constituting the bulk of CapMail's logic, and grant each that portion of CapMail's authority that it needs during initialization. This startup module is CapMail's TCB – its

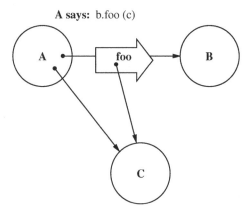

Fig. 4. Level 4: Object Granularity POLA

logic brings about this further subdivision of initial authority, so all the assets entrusted to CapMail as a whole are vulnerable to this one module.

When a CapMail user launches an executable caplet attachment, CapMail should ask CapDesk to launch it, in which case it would only be given the authority the user grants by explicit actions. CapMail users would no longer need to fear executable attachments. (The DarpaBrowser already demonstrates equivalent functionality for downloaded caplets.)

3.4   Object-Granularity POLA

At Level 3, we again see the co-existence of boxes representing legacy and non-legacy. For legacy modules, we've been using a methodology we call "taming" to give us some confidence, under some circumstances, that a module doesn't exceed its proper authority [Miller02]. Again, for these legacy boxes, we can achieve no further reduction of exposure within the box. Zooming in on a legacy box would again give a full authority picture like that previously depicted as Level 2a, but at the fourth level. Zooming in on a non-legacy box takes us instead to a picture of POLA at Level 4 (Figure 4). This is our finest scale application of these principles – at the granularity of individual programming language objects. These are the indivisible particles, if you will, from whose logic our levels 2 and 3 were built.

By "object", we do not wish to imply a class-based system, or built-in support for inheritance. We are most comfortable with the terms and concepts of object-oriented programming, but the logic explained below applies equally well to lambda calculus with local side effects [Morris73, Rees96], Actors [Hewitt77], concurrent logic/constraint programming [Miller87], and the Pi calculus. Oz's semantics already embodies this logic. (The following explanation skips some details; see [Miller03] for a precise statement of the object-capability model.)

Let's examine all the ways in which object B can come to know about, i.e., hold a reference to, object C.

1. *By Introduction.* If B and C already exist, and B does not already know about C, then the only way B can come to know about C is if there exists an object A that
   - already knows about C
   - already knows about B
   - decides to share with B her knowledge of C.

   In object terms, if A has variables in her scope, b and c, that hold references to B and C, then A may send a message to B containing a copy of her reference to C as an argument: "b.foo(c)". Unlike the cp example, and like the cat example, A does not communicate the string "c" to B. B does not know or care what name A's code uses to refer to C.

2. *By Parenthood.* If B already exists and C does not, then, if B creates C, at that moment B is the only object that knows about C (has a reference to C). From there, other objects can come to know about C only by inductive application of these steps. Parenthood may occur by normal object instantiation, such as calling a constructor or evaluating a lambda expression, or by import, which we return to below.

3. *By Endowment.* If C already exists and B does not, then, if there exists an object A that already knows about C, A can create B such that B is born already endowed with knowledge of C. B might be instantiated by lambda evaluation, in which case a variable "c" which is free within B might be bound to C within B's creation context, as supplied by A. Or A might instantiate B by calling a constructor, passing C as an argument. If A creates module B by importing data describing B's behavior (in Oz, a functor file), then A's importing context must explicitly provide bindings for all the free variables in this functor file, where these values must already be accessible to A. The imported B module must not be able to magically come into existence with authorities not granted by its importer. (The underlying logic of the Oz module manager seems ideally designed to support this, though various details need to be fixed.)

4. *By Initial Conditions.* For purposes of analysis, there's always a first instant of time. B might already know about C when our universe of discourse came into existence.

By these rules, only connectivity begets connectivity – new knows-about relationships can only be brought about from existing knows-about relationships. Two disjoint subgraphs can never become connected, which is why garbage collection can be transparent. More interestingly, if two subgraphs are almost disjoint, they can only interact or become further connected according to the decisions of those objects that bridge these two subgraphs.

An object can affect the world outside itself by sending messages on references it holds. An object can be affected by the world outside itself by receiving messages from objects that hold a reference to it. If objects have no possibility of causal access by other means, such as global variables, then an object's permissions are the references it holds. The object reference graph becomes the access graph. Together with designational integrity (also known as the y-property [Close03]), and support for defensive correctness, explained in the paper on Oz-E in this volume, these *are* the rules of object-capability security [Spiessens-VanRoy05].

But knowing the rules of chess is distinct from knowing how to play chess. The practice of using these rules well to write secure code is known as capability discipline. As we should expect, capability discipline is mostly just an extreme form of good modular software engineering practice. Of the people who have learned capability discipline, several have independently noticed that they find themselves following capability discipline even when writing programs for which security is of no concern. We find that it consistently leads to more modular, more maintainable code.

Table 1. Security as extreme modularity

Good software engineering	Capability discipline
Responsibility driven design	Authority driven design
Omit needless coupling	Omit needless vulnerability
assert(..) preconditions	Validate inputs
Information hiding	Principle of Least Authority
Designation, need to know	Permission, need to do
Lexical naming	No global name spaces
Avoid global variables	Forbid mutable static state
Procedural, data, control, ⋯	⋯ and access abstractions
Patterns and frameworks	Patterns of safe cooperation
Say what you mean	Mean only what you say

This completes the reductionist portion of our tour. We have seen many issues reappear at each level of composition. Let's zoom back out and see what picture emerges.

3.5   Nested TCBs Follow the Spawning Tree

The nesting of subsystems within each other corresponds to a spawning tree. The TCB of each system creates the initial population of subsystems within it, and endows each with their initial portion of the authority granted to this system as a whole. The organization decides what Alan's responsibilities are, and its administrators configure Alan's initial authorities accordingly. Doug uses CapDesk to endow CapMail with access to his smtp server by static configuration. CapMail's main() grants this access to its imported smtp module. A lambda expression with a free variable "c" evaluates to a closure whose binding for "c" is provided by its creation context. The spawning tree has the hierarchic structure that Herbert Simon explains as common to many kinds of complex systems [Simon62]. Mostly static approaches to POLA, such as policy files, may succeed at mirroring this structure.

3.6   Subcontracting Forms Dynamic Networks of Authority

Among already instantiated components, we see a network of subcontracting relationships whose topology dynamically changes as components make requests of each other. Barb finds she needs to collaborate with Alan; or Doug selects killer.xls in an open file dialog box; or object A passes a reference to object C as an argument in a message to object B. In all these cases, by following capability discipline, the least authority the subcontractor needs to perform a request can often be painlessly conveyed along with the designations such requests must already carry. The least adjustments needed to the topology of the access graph are often identical to the adjustments made anyway to the reference graph.

3.7   Legacy Limits POLA, But Can Be Managed Incrementally

Among the subsystems within each system, we must engineer for a peaceful co-existence of legacy and non-legacy components. Only such co-existence enables non-legacy systems to be adopted incrementally. For legacy components, POLA can and indeed must be practiced separately. For example, Polaris restricts the authority available to killer.xls without modifying the spreadsheet, Excel, or WindowsXP. However, we can only impose POLA on the legacy component – we cannot enable the component to further practice POLA with the portion of its authority it grants to others, or to sub-components of itself. Following initial adoption, as we replace individual legacy components, we incrementally increase our safety.

3.8   Nested POLA Multiplicatively Reduces Attack Surface

The cross-hatching within the non-legacy boxes we did not zoom into – such as the "~alan" row – represents our abstract claim that exposure was further reduced by practicing POLA within these boxes. The claim can now be explained by the fine structure shown in the non-legacy boxes we did zoom into – such as the "~doug" box. Whatever fraction of the attack surface we removed at each level by practicing POLA; these effects compose to create a multiplicative reduction in our overall exposure. Secure languages used according to capability discipline can extend POLA to a much finer grain than is normally sought. By spanning a large enough range of scales, the remaining attack surface resembles the area of a fractal shape which has been recursively hollowed out. Although we do not yet know how to quantify these issues, we hope any future quantitative analysis of what is practically achievable will take this structure into account.

4   Conclusions

To build useful and usable systems, software engineers build sparse-but-capable dynamic structures of knowledge. The systems most successful at supporting these structures – such as object, lambda, and concurrent logic languages – exhibit a curious similarity in their logic of designation. Patterns of abstraction and modularity divide knowledge, and then use these designators to compose divided knowledge to useful effect. Software engineering discipline judges these design patterns partially by their support for the principle of information hiding – by the sparseness of the knowledge structures they build from these designators.

To build useful, usable, and safe general purpose systems, we must leverage these impressive successes to provide correspondingly sparse-but-capable dynamic structures of authority. Only authority structures aligned with these knowledge structures can both provide the authority needed for use while narrowly limiting the excess of authority available for abuse. To structure authority in this way, we need "merely" make a natural change to our foundations, and a corresponding natural change to our software engineering discipline.

Capability discipline judges design patterns as well by their support for the principle of least authority – by the sparseness of the authority structures they build from these permissions. Not only is this change needed for safety, it also increases the modularity needed to provide ever greater functionality.

An object-capability language can extend this structuring of authority down to finer granularities, and therefore across more scales, than seem practical by other means. The paper on Oz-E in this volume explores how Oz can become such a language [Spiessens-VanRoy05]. In this paper we have presented a proof-of-concept system – consisting of *E*, CapDesk, and Polaris – that explains an integrated approach for using such foundations to build general purpose systems that are simultaneously safer, more functional, more modular, and more usable than is normally thought possible.

Acknowledgements

For various comments and suggestions, we thank Per Brand, Scott Doerrie, Jack High, Alan Karp, Christian Scheideler, Swaroop Sridhar, Fred Spiessens, Terry Stanley, and Marc Stiegler. We thank Norm Hardy for first bringing to our attention the intimate relationship between knowledge and authority in computation.

References

[Abrams95]	Marshall Abrams and David Bailey. "Abstraction and Refinement of Layered Security Policy." In Marshall D. Abrams, Sushil Jajodia, and Harold J. Podell, eds. Information Security: An Integrated Collection of Essays. IEEE Computer Society Press. Los Alamitos, CA 1995: 126-136.
[Bishop79]	Matt Bishop and Lawrence Snyder. "The Transfer of Information and Authority in a Protection System." Proc. 7th ACM Symposium on Operating Systems Principles (Operating Systems Review **13**(4)), 1979, pp. 45–54.
[Close03]	Tyler Close "What Does the 'y' Refer to", 2003. http://www.waterken.com/dev/YURL/Definition/
[Dennis66]	J.B. Dennis, E.C. Van Horn. "Programming Semantics for Multiprogrammed Computations", Communications of the ACM, 9(3):143-155, March 1966.

[Dijkstra74]   Edsger W. Dijkstra, "On the role of scientific thought", EWD 447, 1974, appearing in E.W.Dijkstra, Selected Writings on Computing: A Personal Perspective, Springer Verlag, 1982.

[Graham72]   Graham, G.S., and Denning, P.J. Protection-principles and practice. Proc. AFIPS 1972 SJCC, Vol. 40, AFIPS Press, Montvale, N.J., pp. 417-429.

[Hardy85]   N. Hardy. "The KeyKOS Architecture" ACM Operating Systems Review, September 1985, p. 8–25.
http://www.agorics.com/Library/KeyKos/architecture.html

[Hayek45]   Friedrich A. Hayek "Use of Knowledge in Society" American Economic Review, XXXV, No. 4; September, 1945, 519-30.
http://www.virtualschool.edu/mon/Economics/
HayekUseOfKnowledge.html

[Hayek64]   Friedrich A. Hayek "The Theory of Complex Phenomena", 1964, in Bunge, editor, The Critical Approach to Science and Philosophy.

[Hewitt77]   Carl Hewitt, Henry Baker, "Actors and Continuous Functionals" , MIT-LCS-TR-194, 1977. Locality Laws online at
http://www.erights.org/history/actors.html

[Howard03]   Michael Howard, Jon Pincus, Jeannette M. Wing. "Measuring Relative Attack Surfaces" Proceedings of the Workshop on Advanced Developments in Software and Systems Security, 2003.

[Lampson74]   Butler W. Lampson. "Protection" ACM Operating Systems Review. 8:1, Jan. 1974.

[Miller87]   M. S. Miller, D. G. Bobrow, E. D. Tribble, J. Levy, "Logical Secrets" Concurrent Prolog: Collected Papers, E. Shapiro (ed.), MIT Press, Cambridge, MA, 1987.

[Miller02]   Mark S. Miller, "A Theory of Taming", 2002.
http://www.erights.org/elib/legacy/taming.html

[Miller03]   Mark S. Miller, Jonathan S. Shapiro, "Paradigm Regained: Abstraction mechanisms for access control" , Proceedings of ASIAN'03, Springer Verlag, 2003. Complete version online at
http://www.erights.org/talks/asian03/index.html

[Moffett88]   Jonathan D. Moffett and Morris S. Sloman, "The Source of Authority for Commercial Access Control" IEEE Computer, February 1988.

[Morris73]   J. H. Morris. "Protection in Programming Languages" CACM 16(1) p. 15–21, 1973.
http://www.erights.org/history/morris73.pdf

[Parnas72]   David L. Parnas. "On the Criteria To Be Used in Decomposing a System into Modules." Communications of the ACM, Vol. 15, No. 12, December 1972: pp. 1053–1058.

[Rees96]   J. Rees, A Security Kernel Based on the Lambda-Calculus. MIT AI Memo No. 1564. MIT, Cambridge, MA, 1996.
http://mumble.net/jar/pubs/secureos/

[Saltzer75]   J. H. Saltzer, M. D. Schroeder, "The Protection of Information in Computer Systems" Proceedings of the IEEE 63(9), September 1975, p. 1278–1308.

[Schneider03]   Fred B. Schneider. "Least Privilege and More." IEEE Security & Privacy, September/October, 2003: 55-59.

[Simon62]   Herbert S. Simon, "The Architecture of Complexity: Hierarchic
                    Systems" Proceedings of the American Philosophical Society,
                    106:467-482, 1962
[Shapiro99]   J. S. Shapiro, J. M. Smith, D. J. Farber. "EROS: A Fast Ca-
                    pability System" Proceedings of the 17th ACM Symposium on
                    Operating Systems Principles, December 1999, p. 170–185.
[Spiessens-VanRoy05] Fred Spiessens and Peter Van Roy, "The Oz-E Project: De-
                    sign Guidelines for a Secure Multiparadigm Programming Lan-
                    guage", Lecture Notes in Artificial Intelligence, Vol. 3389,
                    Springer Verlag, 2005.
[Stiegler02]   M. Stiegler, M. Miller. "A Capability Based Client: The
                    DarpaBrowser", 2002.
                    http://www.combex.com/papers/darpa-report/index.html
[Stiegler04]   Marc Stiegler, Alan H. Karp, Ka-Ping Yee , Mark Miller, "Po-
                    laris: Virus Safe Computing for Windows XP", HP Tech Re-
                    port, in preparation.
[Tulloh02]   Bill Tulloh, Mark S. Miller. "Institutions as Abstraction Bound-
                    aries", To appear in Economics, Philosophy, & Information
                    Technology: The Intellectual Contributions of Don Lavoie,
                    George Mason University, Fairfax, VA. 2002.
                    http://www.erights.org/talks/categories/
[Wagner02]   David Wagner, Dean Tribble, "A Security Analysis of the
                    Combex DarpaBrowser Architecture", 2002.
                    http://www.combex.com/papers/darpa-review/index.html
[Wirfs-Brock02]   Rebecca Wirfs-Brock and Alan McKean. Object Design: Roles,
                    Responsibilities, and Collaborations. Addison-Wesley, 2002.
[Yee02]   Ka-Ping Yee, "User Interaction Design for Secure Systems",
                    In Proceedings of the International Conference on Information
                    and Communications Security, 2002. Complete version online
                    at http://zesty.ca/pubs/csd-02-1184.ps
[Yee04]   Ka-Ping Yee, "Aligning Usability and Security", In IEEE Se-
                    curity & Privacy Magazine, Sep 2004.

The Oz-E Project: Design Guidelines for a Secure Multiparadigm Programming Language

Fred Spiessens and Peter Van Roy

Université catholique de Louvain,
Louvain-la-Neuve, Belgium
{fsp, pvr}@info.ucl.ac.be

Abstract. The design and implementation of a capability secure multi-paradigm language should be guided from its conception by proven principles of secure language design. In this position paper we present the Oz-E project, aimed at building an Oz-like secure language, named in tribute of E [MMF00] and its designers and users who contributed greatly to the ideas presented here.

We synthesize the principles for secure language design from the experiences with the capability-secure languages E and the W7-kernel for Scheme 48 [Ree96]. These principles will be used as primary guidelines during the project. We propose a layered structure for Oz-E and discuss some important security concerns, without aiming for completeness at this early stage.

1 Introduction

The Oz language was designed to satisfy strong properties, such as full compositionality, lexical scoping, simple formal semantics, network transparent distribution, and so forth. Security, in the sense of protection against malicious agents, was not a design goal for Oz. In this paper, we give a road map for making a secure version of Oz, which we call Oz-E. Our approach is not to add security to Oz, but to remove insecurity. We start with a small subset of Oz that is known to be secure. We add functionality to this subset while keeping security. The ultimate goal is to reach a language that is at least as expressive as Oz and is secure both as a language and in terms of its implementation. It should be straightforward to write programs in Oz-E that are secure against many realistic threat models.

Structure of the Paper

This paper is structured into five parts:

- Section 2 summarizes the basic principles of language-based security, to set the stage for the rest.
- Section 3 discusses a possible structure for Oz-E and a migration path to get there.

P. Van Roy (Ed.): MOZ 2004, LNCS 3389, pp. 21–40, 2005.

- Section 4 discusses some concerns that will influence the design of Oz-E.
- Section 5 gives some practical scenarios with fragments of pseudocode.
- Section 6 summarizes the paper and the work that remains to be done.

Readers unfamiliar with the terminology of capabilities (authority, permission, etc.) are advised to have a look at the glossary at the end of the paper.

2   Basic Principles of Language-Based Security

We distinguish between three kinds of principles: mandatory, pragmatic, and additional. All principles serve a common goal: to support the development of programs that use untrusted modules and entities to provide (part of) their functionality, while minimizing their vulnerability to incorrectness and malicious intents of these entities.

To avoid excess authority the Principle of Least Authority (POLA) – explained in another paper in this book [MTS05] – has to be applied with scrutiny and supported by the language. POLA is not just about minimizing and fine-graining the authority that is directly provided to untrusted entities, but also about avoiding the abuse – by adversaries or incorrect allies – of authority provided to relied-upon entities.

The latter form of abuse is known in the literature as the *luring attack* or the *confused deputy* [Har89]. A deputy is an entity that gets authority from its clients to perform a task. A confused deputy is a deputy that cannot tell the difference between its own authority and the authority it is supposed to get from its clients.

Figure 1 (left) shows what can go wrong with Access Control Lists (ACL's). The client wants the deputy to write its results to the file "`file#123`". Assume the deputy has the authority to write to this file. Should the deputy write to the file? It may be that the client is abusing the deputy to write somewhere that the client itself should not be allowed to write. There is no simple way to solve this problem with ACL's.

Figure 1 (right) shows how capabilities solve the problem. Instead of providing a mere designation, the client now provides a capability that bundles the

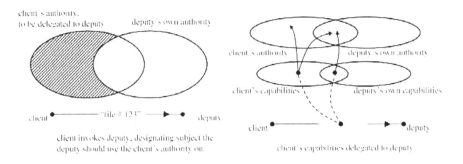

Fig. 1. ACL's vs. Capabilities

designation with the authority to write the file. The deputy can use this capability without second thoughts, because the client can no longer trick the deputy into writing into a place it should not.

2.1 Mandatory Principles

This section explains the principles that form the *minimum necessary* conditions to *enable* secure programming, following the object-capability approach [MS03].

No Ambient Authority. All authority is to be carried by capabilities: unforgeable entities that combine designation with permissions. To enable the individual entities to control the propagation of authority, the language has to cut off every other way of getting authority. All entities come to live with no default authority, and capabilities can only be acquired in the following ways:

- By endowment and parenthood (as defined in Sect. 7).
- By introduction: an entity can initiate an exchange of capabilities with another entity, by exerting a permission of a capability that designates the other entity (Sect. 7).

The language thus has to make sure that no authority can be acquired in any other way, whether via globally or dynamically scoped variables, or via memory probing and forging. This means that the language has to be *purely lexically scoped* and *completely memory safe*.

No Authority Generation. The availability of two capabilities can result in more authority than the simple sum of both authorities. This phenomenon is called "authority amplification".

Except for the purpose of authentication – which will be handled in section 2.2 – authority amplification is very dangerous and should be avoided when

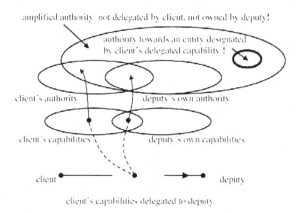

Fig. 2. Authority amplification can confuse deputies

possible. It is as if "ambient authority" becomes available to an entity, thereby turning the entity into a confused deputy, because the extra authority is not provided by the client nor by the deputy.

Figure 2 shows what can happen. The client passes a capability to the deputy. This capability designates an entity. Authority amplification will increase the authority that the deputy has over this entity. This is shown by the small bold oval. In that way, designation and authority have effectively become separated again, just like with ACL's, and the same problems arise.

Since the language will represent capabilities as data abstractions (e.g. objects, procedures, abstract data types (ADT's)) it must make sure that these abstractions can handle delegation of authority appropriately. Unbundled abstractions (ADT's), that provide operations separately from values, can lead very easily to the creation of deputies that are confused by authority amplification.

To minimize the opportunities for deputies to be confused by authority amplification, a secure language must provide all access to system resources as bundled data abstractions that *completely encapsulate* their internal state. Authority amplification is defendable only in cases where normal capabilities would not suffice.

2.2   Pragmatic Principles: Promoting Secure Programming

With the basic principles in place, all essential control of authority distribution and propagation becomes available to programmers, and they can now – in principle – start building entities that will perform reliably in collaboration with untrusted ones. However, it is not enough that Oz-E *enables* secure programming, it should also make secure programming *feasible in practice* and consequently *favor* secure programming (Sect. 7) as the default.

Defensive Correctness. The dominant pattern of secure programming, which the language must make practical, is that clients may rely on the correctness of servers, but that servers should not rely on the correctness of clients. In other words, a server (any "callee" in general) should always check its preconditions. A client (any "caller" in general) may rely on the server, if it has the means to authenticate the server. The usefulness of this pattern has emerged from experience with E and its predecessors.

In traditional correctness arguments, each entity gets to rely on all the other entities in the program. If any are incorrect, all bets are off. Such reasoning provides insufficient guarantees for secure programming. To expect programmers to actually check all preconditions, postconditions, and invariants is not a realistic approach either. *Defensive correctness* is when every entity explicitly checks its input arguments when invoked. This is a realistic and effective middle way.

We require the language to make it practical to write most abstractions painlessly to this standard. We require the libraries to be mostly populated by abstractions that live up to this standard, and that the remaining members of the library explicitly state that they fall short of this standard.

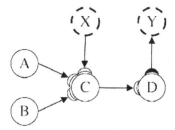

Fig. 3. Paths of vulnerability

Figure 3 shows an access graph. Dashed nodes are entities not relied upon in any way. White crescents indicate explicit checking of input arguments when invoked. A black crescent indicates explicitly checking all arguments when invoking. A and B are vulnerable to (rely upon) C and C is vulnerable to D, and since vulnerability is a transitive relation, A and B are also vulnerable to D. Because C checks its incoming arguments when invoked, it will protect itself and its clients from malicious arguments (e.g. provided by X). Paths of vulnerability are easy to follow and go one way only. Two clients vulnerable to the same server are not for that reason vulnerable to each other.

To support defensive correctness, Oz-E has to make it easy for the programmer to check incoming arguments. Guards, authentication primitives, and auditors, presented in the next sections, realize such support.

Guards. *E*'s *guards* [Sti00] form a soft typing system [CF91] that provides syntax support to make dynamic checking as easy as using static types. Guards are first class citizens and support arbitrary complex dynamic checking without cluttering the code with the actual tests. They can be user defined, and combined into more complex guards by logical operators.

Authentication. For an entity to defend its invariants in a mutually distrusting context, it can be important to know the origin of collaborating entities. The entity might want to authenticate a procedure before invoking it, and an argument before applying the procedure to it. Because capabilities unify designation and permission, and because the confused deputy problem can be naturally avoided, there is no need to authenticate the invoker.

We do not necessary want to know who wrote the code for that entity – since that knowledge is not very useful in general – but whether we want to rely upon the entity that loaded it and endowed it with initial authority. For example, if we rely upon bank B, we can authenticate an account-entity A by asking B if A is genuine, in other words if B recognizes A as one of the accounts B – or maybe an associated branch – created earlier.

Authentication by Invited Auditors. The above form of authentication is only useful to authenticate entities of which the alleged creator is a relied-upon third party. Moreover, this form of authentication cannot tell us anything further about the actual state of an entity at the time of authentication.

To reliably interact with entities of unknown origin, it must be possible to have them *inspected* by a relied-upon third party. Without breaking encapsulation – which would violate the principles in section 2.1 – that can be done as shown by E's *auditors* [YM00]. When an entity is created, a relied-upon third party *auditor* is *invited* by the creator, to inspect the entity's behavior and lexical scope. Later, when the auditor is asked to vouch for the relied-upon properties, it will reveal its conclusions, or if necessary re-inspect the state of the entity before answering yes or no. If inconclusive or uninvited, it will answer no.

Failing Safely. When an entity cannot guarantee its invariants in a certain condition, it should raise an exception. The default mechanism should not enclose any capabilities or potentially sensitive information with the exception that is raised. Part of this concern can be automated by the guards discussed earlier, who will throw an exception on behalf of the entity.

Preemptive Concurrency and Shared State. Preemptive concurrency enables an activation of an entity at some point in its progress to destroy the assumptions of another activation of the same entity at another point in its progress. This phenomenon is called *plan interference.*

Semaphores and locks give programmers control over the interaction between concurrently invoked behavior, but their use is error-prone and increases the overall complexity of a program. Good locking becomes a balancing exercise between the danger of race conditions and deadlocks. Preemptive concurrency with shared state makes defensive programming too hard because considering a single invocation of behavior is not enough to ensure preconditions and invariants.

For example, consider a simple "observer"-pattern [GHJV94]. With message-passing concurrency as explained in chapter 5 of [VH04] – all entities involved are *Active Objects*, subscription is done by providing a *Port*, and notification via a *Port.send* operation – all update notifications of an entity are guaranteed to arrive at all subscribers in the order of the update. With *threads* there is no guarantee whatsoever about the order of arrival and it becomes dauntingly hard to impose a proper order while at the same time avoiding deadlocks.

2.3   Additional Principles: Support for the Review Process

When the language is ready to provide all the necessary support for secure programming, one more important design concern remains. The programmers are now in the position to avoid security flaws while programming, but they also need to be able to quickly find any remaining vulnerabilities that might have got in. Oz-E must be designed to make security debugging easy. Its syntax should therefore allow programmers to quickly identify big parts in a program that *are* obviously safe, and concentrate on the remaining part.

A minimum set of tools to support debugging and analyzing the vulnerabilities is indispensable. These can range from support for syntax coloring to debuggers of distributed code and tools for security analysis. To this goal, we are currently researching formal models that allow us to analyze authority confinement amongst entities collaborating under mutual distrust [SMRS04]. A tool based on this model would allow us to investigate the limits of the usability of patterns of safe collaboration that emerged from experience (e.g. the Power-box [SM02] and the Caretaker[MS03]), and enable the discovery of new such patterns.

3   Proposed Structure of Oz-E

The Oz language has a three-layered design. We briefly introduce these layers here, and refer to chapter 2 and appendix D of [VH04] for a detailed explanation.

The lowest layer is a simple language, kernel Oz, that contains all the concepts of Oz in explicit form. The next layer, full Oz, adds linguistic abstractions to make the language practical for programmers.[1] The final layer, Mozart/Oz, adds libraries and their interfaces to the external environment that depends on the operating system functionality.

We realize that in an ideal world, the language and the operating system should be developed together. Pragmatically, we will provide as much of the oper-ating system functionality as possible inside the third layer of the language. Any remaining functionality – not fitting the language without a complete rewrite of the operating system – will be accessible through a general system interface.

The importance of the layered architecture for security is stressed by a flaw in the current Mozart system that was found by Mark Miller. The module *Time*, currently available in the second layer as ambient authority, provides access to the system clock and should therefore be transferred to layer three, the func-tionality of which can only be available via explicitly granted capabilities.

Read access to the system time can be used to read covert channels regard-less of the countermeasures (e.g. randomness in thread execution sequence and adding randomizing delays) the system could have taken to prevent this. Ad-versaries that are prevented from reading the system type might still be able to send out the secrets they can discover, but there are countermeasures that can make it arbitrary hard for them receive their instructions via covert channels.

We propose for Oz-E to keep as much of this layered structure as possible, while staying within the boundaries of the security requirements. We will start with very simple versions of these layers and grow them carefully into a full-featured language, maintaining the security properties throughout the process. The project will start by showing formally that the initial versions of kernel lan-guage and full language are secure. During the growth process, we will maintain at all times a formal semantics of the kernel language.

In the following three subsections, we present each of the three layers and we discuss some of the issues that need to be resolved for each layer. Of course, the early stage of the project does not allow us to attempt completeness in this respect.

---

[1] A *linguistic abstraction* is an abstraction with syntactic support. An *abstraction* is a way of organizing a data structure or a control flow such that the user is given a higher-level view and does not have to be concerned with its implementation.

3.1   Kernel Language

The kernel language should be complete enough so that there is no need to go lower, e.g., to a byte code level. As the kernel language is the lowest level seen by (normal) application developers and library designers, reasoning and program development will be simplified. Only the language designers themselves will go below that level. The implementation will guarantee that the kernel language satisfies its semantics despite malicious interference by programs written in it.

The initial kernel language will be as close as possible to the general kernel language of Oz, which has a complete and simple formal semantics as given in chapter 13 of [VH04]. This is the most complete formal semantics of Oz that exists currently. As far as we know, the relevant part of the Mozart system implements this semantics. It is straightforward to show that this kernel language satisfies basic security properties such as secure closures (encapsulation based on lexical scoping), absence of ambient authority, and unforgeable identity of kernel language entities.

In the rest of this subsection, we address two specific issues that are directly related to the kernel language, namely authentication and finalization. Authentication is an issue that is directly related to security. Finalization is an issue that is indirectly related to security: the current design has problems that would make building secure systems difficult.

We prefer the kernel language of Oz-E to be a subset of the full language. This results in semantic clarity, uniformity of syntax and simplicity, all important pedagogical assets when teaching Oz-E. Furthermore, the kernel language subset will allow us to experiment with language extensions while staying within the language.

Authentication via Token Equality. A basic requirement for building secure systems is authentication of authority-carrying entities. Entities that were created by relied-upon third parties should be recognizable with the help of the third party. This means that the entity needs an identity that is unforgeable and unspoofable, otherwise a creator could never be sure the entity is really the one it created earlier. Unforgeable means that it is impossible to create an identity out of thin air that matches with the identity of an existing entity. Unspoofable means that the authenticity check cannot be relayed (man in the middle attack).

The kernel language has to let us achieve these properties for its own authority-carrying entities and also for user-defined entities built using the kernel language. Both of these categories impose conditions on the kernel language semantics. Let us examine these conditions. In the following paragraphs we use the term "entity" to mean a language entity of a type that can carry authority (be a *capability*), as opposed to pure *data* (Sect. 7).

For kernel entities, authentication is achieved by the kernel language syntax and semantics. The kernel semantics ensures that each newly created entity has a new identity that does not exist elsewhere and that is unforgeable.

For user-defined entities, authentication has to be programmed. For example, say we have a user-defined entity called "object" that is implemented as a one-argument procedure. The object's identity should not be confused with the procedure's identity. This implies that the kernel language should have operations to build unforgeable and unspoofable identity into user-defined entities. One way to do this uses the concepts of chunk and name from the Oz kernel language. A *chunk* is a record with only one operation, field selection. A *name* is an unforgeable constant with an equality operation. With chunks and names, it is possible to build an operation that wraps an entity in a secure way, so that only the corresponding unwrap operation can extract the entity from the wrapped one [VH04]. This is similar to the sealer/unsealer pairs [Mor73] in the *E* language [Sti00].

Finalization. Finalization is the user-defined "clean-up" operation that is related to automatic memory management. When an entity is no longer reachable from an active part of the program, its memory can be reclaimed. Sometimes more than that has to be done to maintain the program invariants. For example, there might be a data structure whose value depends on the entity's existence (it counts the number of entities satisfying a particular property). Or the entity might hold a descriptor to an open file. Finalization handles cases such as these.

The current finalization in Oz does not guarantee that an entity that became unreachable is no longer used. The last operation performed on an entity before it becomes unreachable should truly be the last operation performed on the entity. To guarantee this, we propose to follow the "postmortem finalization" technique (executor of an estate). This was invented by Frank Jackson, Allan Schiffman, L. Peter Deutsch, and Dave Ungar.[2] When an entity becomes unreachable, the finalization algorithm invokes *another* entity, which plays the role of the executor of the first entity's estate. The executor will perform all the clean-up actions but has no reference to the original entity.

3.2   Full Language

The full language consists of linguistic abstractions built on top of the kernel language and (base) libraries written in the full language itself. Giving this linguistic support simply means that there is language syntax that is designed to support the abstraction. For example, a `for` loop can be given a concise syntax and implemented in terms of a `while` loop. We say that the `for` loop is a linguistic abstraction.

The full language has to be designed to support the writing of secure programs. This implies both building new abstractions for secure programming and verifying that the current language satisfies the properties of secure programming. The language should not provide ambient authority or leak potentially confidential information by default. For example, the current Mozart system has an exception handling mechanism that in some cases leaks too much information through the exceptions.

Modules and Functors. Like Oz, the full language will provide operations to create and manipulate software components. In Oz, these components are

---

[2] We searched for a publication to reference this work but found none.

values in the language called *functors*, which are defined through a linguistic abstraction. Functors are instantiated to become *modules*, which are executing entities. Modules are linked with other modules through a tool called the *module manager*. This linking operation gives authority to the instantiated module.

In Oz-E, the module manager has to be a tool for secure programming. For example, it should be easy to run an untrusted software component in an environment with limited authority, by linking it only to limited versions of running modules. Such modules can be constructed on the fly by the user's trusted shell or desktop program, to provide the right capabilities to host programs. This mechanism can also be used for coarse grained "sandboxing", e.g. to run a normal shell with a limited set of resources.

3.3 Environment Interaction

The security of Oz-E must be effective even though the environment is largely outside of the control of the Oz-E application developers and system developers. How can this be achieved? In the long term, we can hope that the environment will become more and more secure, similar to Oz-E itself. In the short term, we need libraries to provide controlled access to the operating system and to other applications.

Security of an application ultimately derives from the user of the application. An application is secure if it follows the user's wishes. The user should have the ability to express these wishes in a usable way through a graphical user interface. Recent work shows that this can be done [Yee02]. For example, selecting a file from a browser window gives a capability to the application: it both designates the file and gives authority to perform an operation (such as an edit) on the file. A prototype desktop environment, CapDesk, has been implemented using these ideas. CapDesk shows that both security and usability can be achieved on the desktop [SM02].

Oz has a high-level GUI tool called QTk. It combines the conciseness and manipulability of the declarative approach with the expressiveness of the procedural approach. QTk builds on the insecure module Tk and augments that functionality instead of restricting it. QTk has to be modified so that it satisfies the principles enunciated in [Yee02] and implemented in CapDesk.

4 Cross-Layer Concerns

The previous section presented a layered structure for the Oz-E language and system. In general however, security concerns cannot be limited to a single layer in such a structure. As explained by another paper in this book [MTS05], they are pervasive concerns. Some them will affect several layers. In this section we discuss three such concerns: pragmatic issues of how to make the system easy to program, execution on distributed systems, and the need for reflection and introspection.

4.1   Pragmatic Issues in Language Design

A secure language should not just make it *possible* to write secure programs, it must also make it *easy* and *natural*. Otherwise, one part of a program written with bad discipline will endanger the security of the whole program. The default way should always be the secure way. This is the security equivalent of fail-safe programming in fault-tolerant systems.

We propose to use this principle in the design of the Oz-E concurrency model. The two main concurrency models are message-passing concurrency (asynchronous messages sent to concurrent entities) and shared-state concurrency (concurrent entities sharing state through monitors). Experience shows that the default concurrency model should be message-passing concurrency. This is not a new idea; Carl Hewitt anticipated it long ago in the Actor model [Hew77, HBS73]. But now we have strong reasons for accepting it. For example, the Erlang language is used for building highly available systems [Arm03, AWWV96]. The *E* language is used for building secure distributed systems [MSC+01]. For fundamental reasons, both Erlang and *E* use message-passing concurrency. We therefore propose for Oz-E to have this default as well. One way to realize this is by the following semantic condition on the kernel language: *cells can only be used in one thread*. This simple semantic condition has as consequence that threads can communicate only through dataflow variables (declarative concurrency) and ports (message-passing concurrency).

4.2   Distributed Systems

The distribution model of Oz allows all language entities to be partitioned over a distributed system, while keeping the same semantics as if the entities were on different threads in a single system, at least when network or node failures are not taken into account. For every category of language entities (stateless, single-assignment, and stateful) a choice of distributed protocols is available that minimizes network communications and handles partial failure gracefully. Fault-tolerant abstractions can be built within the language, on top of this system.

We want to keep the Oz-E distribution system as close as possible to this model and put the same restrictions on communication with remote threads as with local threads (such restrictions were discussed in section 4.1).

We are in the process of replacing the current, monolithic implementation of distribution in Mozart by a modular implementation using the DSS (Distribution Subsystem) [KEB03]. The DSS is a language-independent library, developed primarily by Erik Klintskog, that provides a set of protocols for implementing network-transparent and network-aware distribution. We will briefly consider the opportunities offered by the DSS to add secure distribution to Oz-E.

Responsibility of the Language Runtime System. The division of labor between the DSS and the language system assigns the following responsibilities to the language runtime system:

1. Marshalling and unmarshalling of the language entities.
2. Differentiating between distributed and local entities.
3. Mapping of Oz-E entities and operations to their abstract DSS-specific types, which the DSS will distribute.
4. Choosing amongst the consistency protocols provided by the DSS, based on the abstract entity types, and adjustable for individual entities.

Secure marshalling should not break encapsulation, and every language entity should be allowed to specify and control its own distribution strategy and marshalling algorithm. E provides such marshalling support via "Miranda" methods that every object understands and that provide a safe default marshalling behavior which can be overridden. Oz-E could build a similar implementation for the language entities that can perform method dispatching (e.g. objects). For the other entities (e.g. zero-argument procedures), Oz-E could allow specialized marshalers to be invited into the lexical scope of an entity when it is created. Section 5.2 gives two examples of how invitation can be implemented in Oz-E. Alternatively, Oz-E's kernel language could use only object-style procedures that by default forward marshalling behavior to marshalers, and that can override this behavior.

Depending on these choices, marshalling might need support at the kernel language level. The other three responsibilities of the language system can be provided as part of an Oz-E system library.

Responsibility of the Distribution Subsystem. The DSS itself takes responsibility for:

1. Distributing abstract entities and abstract operations.
2. Providing consistency, using the consistency protocols that were chosen.
3. Properly encrypting all communication, making sure that external parties cannot get inside the connection.
4. Ensuring that it is unfeasibly hard to get (guess) access to an entity without having received a proper reference in the legal way.
5. Authenticating the distributed entities to ensure that no entity is able to pretend to be some other entity.

In [BKB04] the DSS is shown to have security requirements that are compatible with the requirements for safely distributing capabilities. Three attack scenarios have been investigated:

1. Outsider attacks. It should be impossible (infeasibly hard) for an attacker node that does not have legal access to any distributed entities, to access an entity at a remote site or to make such an entity unavailable for legal access.
2. Indirect attacks. It should be impossible for an attacker node that has legal access to a distributed entity but not the one being attacked, to perform this kind of intrusion or damage.
3. Insider attacks. It should be impossible for an attacker node that has legal access to a distributed entity, to render the entity unavailable for legal access.

This can only be guaranteed for protocols that do not distribute or relocate state such as protocols for asynchronous message sending or stationary objects (RPC), and only if the attacker node did not host the original entity, but only a remote reference to it.

Apart from the requirements of the second scenario, the current DSS implementation claims to follow all these requirements. DSS distribution protocols will be made robust to ensure that no DSS-node can be crashed – or forced to render entities unavailable for legal access – by using knowledge of the implementation. This is called "protocol robustification" and is still under development.

The fact that only asynchronous message sending and RPC-style protocols are protected from insider attacks is no objection for Oz-E. In section 4.1 such restriction was already put on the interaction between entities in different threads: normal threads on as single node will not be able to share cells.

4.3   Reflection and Introspection

To verify security properties at runtime, we propose to add the necessary primitive operations to the kernel language, so that it can be programmed in Oz-E itself. How much should a program be able to inspect itself, to verify security properties? The problem is that there is a tension between introspection and security. For example, a program might want to verify inside a lexically scoped closure. Done naively, this breaks the encapsulation that the closure provides. In general, introspection can break the encapsulation provided by lexical scoping.

To avoid breaking encapsulation the E language allows a user-defined entity to invite relied-upon third parties (auditors) to inspect an abstract syntax tree representation of itself, and report on properties that they find. Section 5.2 shows how this could work in Oz-E.

Safe Debugging. In a distributed environment, where collaborating entities spread over different sites have different interests, how can debugging be done? The principle is similar to safe introspection: entities are in control of what debugging information they provide, and the debugger is a third party that may or may not be "invited into the internals" of the entity.

Code Verification. Loaded code should not be able to bring about behavior which exceeds behavior that could be described within the kernel language. Since we plan to use the Oz VM to run Oz-E bytecode, and the Oz VM itself provides no such guarantee, we must verify all code before loading it. Such verification of byte code is a cumbersome and error-prone task. Oz-E should be restricted to load code from easily verifiable abstract syntax tree (AST) representations of kernel and full language statements instead of byte code.

5   Some Practical Scenarios

In this section we take a closer look at how some of these ideas could be implemented. We want to stress that the examples only present one of the many possible design alternatives and do not express any preferences or recommendations from the authors. They are only provided as a clarification to the principles and as a sample of the problems that Oz-E designers will need to solve.

5.1   At What Level Should We Implement Guards?

In section 2.2 we explained briefly the benefits of guards and how they are supported in E. Let us now show in pseudocode how expressions could be guarded in Oz-E and how a linguistic abstraction for guards could look like.

```
fun {EnumGuard L}
   if {Not {List.is L}}
   then raise notAList(enumGuard) end
   end
   for X in L do {Wait X} end
   proc {$ X}
      try
         if {Member X L}
         then skip
         else raise guardFailed(enumGuard) end
         end
      catch _ then
         raise guardFailed(enumGuard) end
      end
   end
end
Trilogic = {EnumGuard [true false undefined]}
{Trilogic (x == y)}   % will succeed
{Trilogic 23}         % will raise an exception
```

Fig. 4. A three valued logic type guard

The example in Figure 4 guards a three valued logic type consisting of **true**, **false**, or unknown. EnumGuard ensures that the set is provided as a list and that all its elements are bound. Then it creates a single parameter procedure that will do nothing if its argument is in the set, or raise an exception otherwise. A guard Trilogic is created from that, and tested in the two last lines. The first test will succeed, the second one will raise an exception.

What if we want to use this guard in a procedure declaration? Let's first assume we want to guard an input parameter, in this case x. Then:

```
proc {$ X:Trilogic ?Y} <S> end
```
can be translated into:
```
proc {$ X ?Y} {Trilogic X} <S> end
```
Guarding output parameters is more difficult. If Y is unbound then:
```
proc {P X ?Y:Trilogic} <S> end
```

```
proc {$ X ?Y}
   Y2
in
   thread
      try {Trilogic Y2} Y = Y2
      catch Ex
      then Y = {Value.failed Ex}
      end
   end
   <S>{Y->Y2}   %(1)
end
```

Fig. 5. Guarding output parameters

can be translated as shown in Figure 5. Note that in Figure 5 the expression marked (1) represents the statement <S> in which all free occurrences of the identifier Y are replaced by an identifier Y2 which does not occur in <S> (see chapter 13 of [VH04]).

These examples work for atomic values that are either input or output parameters, but they cannot simply be extended for guarding partial values, because the latter can be used for both input and output at the same time. Another problem is the relational programming style where all parameters can be input, output or both depending on how the procedure is used. This definitely calls for more research, possibly revealing the need for a new primitive to support guards.

5.2   A Mechanism for Invitation and Safe Introspection

Let's assume we have a new construct NewProc that takes an abstract syntax tree (AST) and an environment record mapping the free identifiers in the AST to variables and values, and returns a procedure. Instead of creating a procedure like this:

```
P1 = proc {$} skip end
```

we could now also create a procedure like this:

```
P1 = {NewProc ast(stmt:´skip´) env()}
```

To create an *audited* procedure, an auditor is invoked with an AST and an environment. The client of the procedure can call the auditor to inquire about the properties that it audits. Let's build an auditor to check declarative behavior. We first present one that keeps track of the declarative procedures it creates.

Figure 6 builds an auditor procedure that takes a message as argument. If the message matches createProc(...) it will investigate the AST and environment provided, and create a procedure by calling {NewProc ...} with the same arguments. If the investigation returned **true**, it will store the resulting procedure in a list of all the created procedures that succeeded the Investigate test. If the message matches approved(...) it will check this list.

Rees [Ree96] gives strong arguments against the approach of Figure 6, as it easily leads to problems with memory management, performance, and to seman-

```
declare
local
   AuditedProcedures =   {NewCell nil}
   fun {Investigate AST Env}
      ... % return boolean indicating whether
          % {NewProc AST Env} returns a declarative procedure
   end
   proc {MarkOK P}     % remember that P is declarative
      AuditedProcedures := P | @AuditedProcedures
   end
   fun {IsOK P}        % checks if P is marked declarative
     {Member P @AuditedProcedures}
   end
in
   proc {DeclarativeAuditor Msg}
         case Msg
         of createProc(Ast Env ?P) then
            if {Investigate Ast Env}
            then
               NewP = {NewProc Ast Env}
            in
               {MarkOK NewP}
               P = NewP
            else P = {NewProc Ast Env}
            end
         [] approved(P ?B) then
            B = {IsOK P}
         end
      end
   end
end

P1 = proc {$} skip end
P2 = {DeclarativeAuditor createProc(ast(stmt:´skip´) env())}
P1OK = {DeclarativeAuditor approved(P1 $)} % P1OK will be false
P2OK = {DeclarativeAuditor approved(P2 $)} % P2OK will be true
```

Fig. 6. Stateful auditor that investigates declarativity

tic obscurity. For this reason W7 – like E – has chosen to provide a primitive function to create sealer-unsealer pairs. Figure 7 provides an alternative approach that avoids these drawbacks.

The auditor built in Figure 7 is stateless, and lets MarkOK wrap the created procedure in some kind of recognizable entity that can be invoked as a normal procedure. An invokable *chunk* would do for that purpose, as it could have a secret field accessible by the *name* Secret known only to the auditor. For this to work, Oz-E's kernel language has to provide either invokable chunks or a primitive function to create sealer-unsealer functions.

```
declare
local
    Secret = {NewName}
    fun {Investigate AST Env}
        ... % return boolean indicating whether
            % {NewProc AST Env} returns a declarative procedure
    end
    fun {MarkOK P}
        WrappedP in
        ... % wrap P in some sort of invokable chunk WrappedP
        ... % WrappedP when invoked, will transparently invoke P
        WrappedP.Secret = ok
        WrappedP
    end
    fun {IsOK P}   % checks if P is marked declarative
        try P.Secret == ok catch _ then false end
    end
in
    proc {DeclarativeAuditor Msg}
          case Msg
          of createProc(Ast Env ?P) then
             if {Investigate Ast Env}
             then P = {MarkOK {NewProc Ast Env $}}
             else P = {NewProc Ast Env}
             end
          [] approved(P ?B) then
             B = {IsOK P}
          end
       end
    end
end
```

Fig. 7. Stateless auditor that investigates declarativity

Instead of providing the environment directly for the auditor to investigate, [Rei04] suggests a mechanism to manipulate the values in the environment before giving them to the auditor (e.g. by sealing) to make sure that they cannot be used for anything else than auditing.

Instead of inviting an auditor, one could invite a relied-upon third party that offers general introspection and reflection. It would have roughly the same code-frame as the auditor, but provide more detailed – and generally non-monotonic – information about the internal state and the code of the procedure.

6   Conclusions and Future Work

A long-term solution to the problems of computer security depends critically on the programming language. If the language is poorly designed, then assuring security becomes complicated. If the language is well-designed, for example, by thoroughly following the principle of least authority, then assuring security is much simplified. With such a language, problems that appear to be very difficult such as protection against computer viruses and the trade-off between security and usability become solvable [Sti].

A major goal of Oz language research is to design a language that is as expressive as possible, by combining programming concepts in a well-factored way. The current version of Oz covers many concepts, but it is not designed to be secure. This paper has given a rough outline of the work that has to be done to create Oz-E, a secure version of Oz that supports the principle of least authority and that makes it possible and practical to write secure programs. We have covered both language and implementation issues. We also explain what problems arise when a secure language lives in an insecure environment. Building Oz-E will be a major undertaking that will require the collaboration of many people. But the potential rewards are very great. We hope that this paper will be a starting point for people who want to participate in this vision.

7   Glossary

Data. A reference to an Oz-entity that has structural equality and consists only of atoms, numbers, and completely grounded records that contain only data.

Capability. An unforgeable reference that designates an entity of any type with token identity. A capability comes with a fixed set of permissions: the different kinds of interactions it supports.

Permission. A means for interacting with the entity designated by a capability. For example, a procedure comes with the permission to be applied to values.

Authority. Any directly or indirectly observable effect an entity can cause. The entity has to use a permission to achieve such an effect. Invoking a procedure for instance could result in the update of a file, or influence the state of an object that will eventually effect the screen.

Dynamic Authority and Revocation. While the permission to invoke a procedure cannot be revoked, the authority that is provided by such a permission can dynamically change and even reduce to zero. Authority depends on the behavior of the invoked entity, which is usually influenced by its state and by the arguments provided to it. Authority also depends on the behavior of the *invoker*, which can decide whether or not it will use the returned values, and to which extent. Authority is thus generated via collaboration during the exertion of a permission, and both collaborators – invoker and invoked entity – have certain means to dynamically influence the authority that is realized.

Endowment. When creating an entity, the creating entity can provide part of its authority to the created entity.

Parenthood. When creating an entity, the creating entity automatically gets the only initial capability to the created entity.

Secure Programming. Programming using components of which the reliability is unknown or uncertain, while still guaranteeing that a predefined level of vulnerability is not exceeded. Secure programming has to guarantee two conditions:

1. all relied-upon components are programmed reliably so that they
   (a) do not abuse their authority to inflict unacceptable damage, and
   (b) cannot be lured into doing so by their collaborators.
2. no authority that can be abused to inflict unacceptable damage can become available to not-relied-upon components.

Acknowledgments

This work was partially funded by the EVERGROW project in the sixth Framework Programme of the European Union under contract number 001935, and partly by the MILOS project of the Walloon Region of Belgium under convention 114856. We owe a great deal of our insights and ideas on Oz-E to the e-lang community. We thank Raphaël Collet, Boriss Mejias, Yves Jaradin and Kevin Glynn for their cooperation during the preparation of this paper. We especially want to thank Mark Miller for contributing ideas on capability-secure programming and defensive correctness, for pointing out some security flaws in the current Mozart implementation, and for reviewing this paper and suggesting corrections and reformulations. Any remaining errors and obscurities in the explanation are the sole responsibility of the authors.

References

[Arm03]   Joe Armstrong. *Making Reliable Distributed Systems in the Presence of Software Errors*. PhD thesis, Royal Institute of Technology (KTH), Stockholm, December 2003.

[AWWV96] Joe Armstrong, Mike Williams, Claes Wikström, and Robert Virding. *Concurrent Programming in Erlang*. Prentice-Hall, Englewood Cliffs, NJ, 1996.

[BKB04]   Zacharias El Banna, Erik Klintskog, and Per Brand. Report on security services in distribution subsystem. Technical Report PEPITO Project Deliverable D4.4 (EU contract IST-2001-33234), K.T.H., Stockholm, January 2004.

[CF91]   R. Cartwright and M. Fagan. Soft typing. In *Proceedings of the SIGPLAN '91 Conference on Programming Language Design and Implementation*, pages 278–292, 1991.

[GHJV94]   Erich Gamma, Richard Helm, Ralph Johnson, and John Vlissides. *Design Patterns: Elements of Reusable Object-Oriented Software*. Addison Wesley, Massachusetts, 1994.

[Har89]   Norm Hardy. The confused deputy. *ACM SIGOPS Oper. Syst. Rev*, 22(4):36–38, 1989.
             http://www.cap-lore.com/CapTheory/ConfusedDeputy.html.

[HBS73]   Carl Hewitt, Peter Bishop, and Richard Steiger. A universal modular AC-TOR formalism for artificial intelligence. In *3rd International Joint Conference on Artificial Intelligence (IJCAI)*, pages 235–245, August 1973.

[Hew77]   Carl Hewitt. Viewing control structures as patterns of passing messages. *Journal of Artificial Intelligence*, 8(3):323–364, June 1977.

[KEB03]   Erik Klintskog, Zacharias El Banna, and Per Brand. A generic middleware for intra-language transparent distribution. Technical Report T2003:01, Swedish Institute of Computer Science, June 2003.

[MMF00]   Mark S. Miller, Chip Morningstar, and Bill Frantz. Capability-based financial instruments. In *Proceedings of the 4th International Conference on Financial Cryptography*, pages 349–378. Springer Verlag, 2000.

[Mor73]   James H. Morris. Protection in programming languages. *Communications of the ACM*, 16(1):15–21, 1973.

[MS03]   Mark S. Miller and Jonathan Shapiro. Paradigm regained: Abstraction mechanisms for access control. In *8th Asian Computing Science Conference (ASIAN03)*, pages 224–242, December 2003.

[MSC+01]   Mark Miller, Marc Stiegler, Tyler Close, Bill Frantz, Ka-Ping Yee, Chip Morningstar, Jonathan Shapiro, Norm Hardy, E. Dean Tribble, Doug Barnes, Dan Bornstien, Bryce Wilcox-O'Hearn, Terry Stanley, Kevin Reid, and Darius Bacon. E: Open source distributed capabilities, 2001. Available at http://www.erights.org.

[MTS05]   Mark S. Miller, Bill Tulloh, and Jonathan S. Shapiro. The structure of authority: Why security is not a separable concern. In *Multiparadigm Programming in Mozart/Oz: Proceedings of MOZ 2004*, volume 3389 of *Lecture Notes in Artificial Intelligence*. Springer-Verlag, 2005.

[Ree96]   Jonathan A. Rees. A security kernel based on the lambda-calculus. Technical report, MIT, 1996.

[Rei04]   Kevin Reid. [e-lang] Proposal: Auditors without unshadowable names, August 2004. Mail posted at e-lang mailing list, available at http://www.eros-os.org/pipermail/e-lang/2004-August/010029.html.

[SM02]   Marc Stiegler and Mark S. Miller. A capability based client: The darpabrowser. Technical Report Focused Research Topic 5 / BAA-00-06-SNK, Combex, Inc., June 2002. Avalalbe at http://www.combex.com/papers/darpa-report/index.html.

[SMRS04]   Fred Spiessens, Mark Miller, Peter Van Roy, and Jonathan Shapiro. Authority Reduction in Protection Systems. Available at: http://www.info.ucl.ac.be/people/fsp/ARS.pdf, 2004.

[Sti]   Marc Stiegler. The SkyNet virus: Why it is unstoppable; how to stop it. Talk available at http://www.erights.org/talks/skynet/.

[Sti00]   Marc Stiegler. *The E Language in a Walnut*. 2000. Draft available at http://www.erights.org.

[VH04]   Peter Van Roy and Seif Haridi. *Concepts, Techniques, and Models of Computer Programming*. MIT Press, Cambridge, MA, 2004.

[Yee02]   Ka-Ping Yee. User interaction design for secure systems. In *4th International Conference on Information and Communications Security (ICICS 2002)*, 2002. UC Berkeley Technical Report CSD-02-1184.

[YM00]   Ka-Ping Yee and Mark S. Miller. Auditors: An extensible, dynamic code verification mechanism. Available at http://www.erights.org/elang/kernel/auditors/, 2000.

A Program Verification System Based on Oz

Isabelle Dony and Baudouin Le Charlier

Université catholique de Louvain
{dony, blc}@info.ucl.ac.be

Abstract. We present an imperative program verification system that exploits many powerful aspects of Oz. Our verification system supports an expressive assertion language for writing specifications and loop invariants. It is able to prove the correctness of elaborated imperative programs consisting of several subproblems that are checked independently. We illustrate the functionalities of our system on a few non trivial examples. Then, we explain that, using Oz constraint programming and other convenient programming mechanisms of Oz, the implementation of the system is straightforward. We also provide information about the efficiency of our implementation.

1   Introduction

The work we describe in this paper originates from pedagogical objectives, which were first presented in [12]. Our goal is to build a practical tool that can help students to deeply understand the classical programming methodology based on specifications, invariants, and decomposition into subproblems, advocated by Dijkstra, Gries, and Hoare to name only a few famous computer scientists. Such a tool should support an imperative programming language and a logical language to express specifications and invariants. It should be able not only to prove that a program is correct but also, and maybe more importantly, to provide interesting counter-examples to highlight and explain programming and reasoning errors. Moreover, in our view, the assertion language supported by such a system should be extremely expressive and convenient because, in a learning context, specifications and invariants must express their meaning as directly as possible. On the contrary, the programming language can be kept very simple because, as far as program correctness is concerned, programming reasoning principles are exactly the same for any kind of languages, be they simple as Pascal or complicated as Java.

It appears that constraint programming over finite domains is especially convenient to check the kind of verification conditions that are needed to express the correctness of imperative programs. However, to conveniently generate the constraint problems equivalent to a given verification condition, it is desirable to have at hand a powerful language that allows us to interleave constraints generation, constraints solving, and to specify a distribution strategy to overcome the incompleteness of the usual consistency techniques used by finite domain

P. Van Roy (Ed.): MOZ 2004, LNCS 3389, pp. 41–52, 2005.

constraint programming. We show in this paper that the Oz language [1, 15, 14] includes all programming mechanisms that are needed to reach our goals.

The rest of this paper is organised as follows: In Section 2, we illustrate the functionalities of our system on two significant examples. In Section 3, we summarize the basics of Oz constraint programming. In Section 4, we describe the Oz implementation of our verification system. Section 5 is devoted to the related work and Section 6 contains the conclusion and a discussion of possible future work.

2   What Our System Can Do

A Binary Search Algorithm. We first discuss a classical binary search algorithm, which is notoriously difficult to construct correctly without a good programming method. Figure 1 depicts the algorithm, together with its specification and loop invariant, exactly as it must be given to our system.[1] To construct this algorithm,

---

- Declarations:
    const n;
    var a: array[1..n] of integer; x: integer; (input)
    var b: boolean; (output)
    var g, d, m: integer; (auxiliary variables)
- Pre: a, x initialised, n is the array size,
    $(\forall\, i : 1 \leq i \leq n - 1 : a[i] \leq a[i+1])$
    Post: a, x unchanged & $b = (\exists\, i : 1 \leq i \leq n : a[i] = x)$
    Inv: $1 \leq g \leq d \leq n + 1$ && $(\forall\, i : 1 \leq i < g : a[i] < x)$ & $(\forall\, i : d \leq i \leq n : a[i] > x)$
    & $b \Rightarrow (\exists\, i : 1 \leq i \leq n : a[i] = x)$
- Init : g:= 1; d:= n+1; b := false
    Iter : m:= (g+d)div 2;
            if(a[m]<x) then g:= m+1;
            if(a[m]>x) then d:= m;
            if(a[m]=x) then b:= true
    B : g=d or b

Fig. 1. A binary search algorithm and its specification

---

we have first fixed the set of variables (Declarations). Then, we have formally specified the problem by means of a precondition (Pre) and a postcondition (Post). The precondition states that the array is sorted; the postcondition says that variable b is equal to true if and only if x occurs in array a. Next, we have choosen an invariant (Inv). Finally, we have derived the statements: the initialisation (Init), the iteration (Iter), the closing (Clot) and the halting condition (B) so that the following propositions are true:

---

[1] The actual concrete syntax of assertions is just a bit more "computer readable" in our system

- $\{Pre\}$ $Init$ $\{Inv\}$
- $\{Inv$ & $\neg B\}$ $Iter$ $\{Inv\}$
- $\{Inv$ & $B\}$ $Clot$ $\{Post\}$

Following [10], we write $\{P\}$ S $\{Q\}$ to mean that if the assertion P holds, it is guaranteed that, after executing S, the assertion Q also holds. However, to the contrary of [10], we require the termination of S and the absence of run-time errors. The purpose of our system is to prove these propositions when they are true and to give counter-examples when some of them are not correct.

Proving the Correctness of the Binary Search Algorithm. Using a AMD ahtlon XP 2800+, $2GHz$ CPU with $1GB$ RAM, our system is able to prove the correctess of this program in 15ms (for $n = 0$), 16ms ($n = 1$), 78ms ($n = 2$), 328ms ($n = 3$), 2.5s ($n = 4$), and 12.5s ($n = 5$). We do not have to fix the array size: We can choose a upper bound for n, instead. It takes 1m 33s to prove the correctness of the program for $n \leq 6$. With finite domain techniques, [2] it is not possible to prove the correctness of the program for an arbitrary value of n but we can reasonably argue that the program is most probably correct, since it is correct for small values of n.

Finding Errors in an Incorrect Binary Search Algorithm. Now, we keep the same specification and loop invariant, but we introduce an error in the algorithm: we replace the statement $d := m$ by the statement $d := m - 1$. Assuming $n = 3$, the system gives the following counter-examples in 297ms:

$\{Inv$ & $\neg B\}$ $Iter$ $\{Inv\}$,
precondition $: n = 3$ $a = [1\ 1\ 1]$ $x = 0$
before $: n = 3$ $a = [1\ 1\ 1]$ $x = 0$ $b = false$ $d = 2$ $g = 1$
after $: n = 3$ $a = [1\ 1\ 1]$ $x = 0$ $b = false$ $d = 0$ $g = 1$ $m = 1$
violated assertion $: g \leq d$

This counter-example shows that proposition $\{Inv$ & $\neg B\}$ $Iter$ $\{Inv\}$ is not true; the *precondition* part gives the corresponding input values; the *before* part displays a state satisfying the assertion Inv & $\neg B$ before an execution of the iteration; the *after* part provides the state obtained after executing the iteration. It can be observed that the assertion Inv is false in this state. Additionally, the system is able to exhibit the part of the assertion that is violated, i.e. $g \leq d$. If we resume the execution of the system, the following counter-example is obtained:

$\{Inv$ & $\neg B\}$ $Iter$ $\{Inv\}$,
precondition $: n = 3$ $a = [0\ 1\ 1]$ $x = 0$
before $: n = 3$ $a = [0\ 1\ 1]$ $x = 0$ $b = false$ $d = 3$ $g = 1$
after $: n = 3$ $a = [0\ 1\ 1]$ $x = 0$ $b = false$ $d = 1$ $g = 1$ $m = 2$
violated assertion $: (\forall\ i : d \leq i \leq n : a[i] > x)$

We can see that the violated part of the invariant is different in this second counter-example. However, since variable d is involved in both cases, we have a clue that the error lies in the statement $d := m - 1$.

---

[2] To be fair, let us also mention that we need restricting the domain of values of x and a to get those execution times. See Section 4.

Finding Reasoning Errors. We can also consider the scenario where there is a mistake in the invariant. If, for example, we write $(\forall i : 1 \leq i < g - 1 : a[i] < x)$ instead of $(\forall\ i : 1 \leq i < g : a[i] < x)$, the system shows the following counter-example in 422ms (for $n \leq 3$):

$\{Inv\ \&\ B\}\ Clot\ \{Post\}$,
precondition $: n = 1\ a = [0]\ x = 0$
before $: n = 1\ a = [0]\ x = 0\ b = false\ d = 2\ g = 2$
after $: n = 1\ a = [0]\ x = 0\ b = false\ d = 2\ g = 2\ m = 1$
violated assertion $: b = (\forall\ i : 1 \leq i \leq n : a[i] = x)$

Predicting Run-Time Errors. Let us finally assume that we use the condition $g = d + 1$ instead of $g = d$ in the halting condition of the algorithm. In this case, the system finds input values for which an *index out of bound* error occurs.

An Algorithm to Find the Next Permutation. We consider a second more complicated example, whose verification needs a decomposition into four subproblems. Given a permutation of the natural numbers $1, \ldots, n$, the problem is to write an algorithm that finds the next permutation according to the lexicographic ordering (denoted by $\preceq$). For example, the next permutation of $a_0 = [1\ 2\ 3\ 5\ 4]$ is $a = [1\ 2\ 4\ 3\ 5]$. Informally, this problem can be decomposed as follows: First (SP1), we compute the largest index i such that $a[i] < a[i + 1]$ (in our example, above, $i = 3$). Then (SP2), we determine j, which is the index of the smallest element on the right side of $a[i]$ that is bigger than $a[i]$ (in our example, $j = 5$). Next, we exchange $a[i]$ and $a[j]$ (a becomes $[1\ 2\ 4\ 5\ 3]$). Finally (SP3), we reverse the order of elements in the sub-array $a[i + 1..n]$ ($a = [1\ 2\ 4\ 3\ 5]$ is the next permutation). To construct the algorithm, we must formally specify the three sub-problems, construct them with a loop invariant, and prove their correctness, independently from each other and from the main problem. The formal specifications of the subproblem are given below.

SP1: Pre: a initialised
Post: unchanged(a) &
$((i = 0\ \&\ (\forall\ k : 1 \leq k \leq n - 1 : a[k] \geq a[k + 1]))$
$\lor\ ((0 < i < n)\ \&\&\ (\forall\ k : i + 1 \leq k \leq n - 1 : a[k] \geq a[k + 1])\ \&\ a[i] < a[i + 1]))$

SP2: Pre: a initialised & $1 \leq i < n$
$\&\&\ (\forall\ k : i + 1 \leq k \leq n - 1 : a[k] > a[k + 1])\ \&\ a[i] < a[i + 1]$
Post: unchanged(a) & unchanged(i) &&
$((j = n\ \&\&\ a[j] > a[i])\ \lor\ (i < j < n\ \&\&\ a[j + 1] \leq a[i]\ \&\ a[j] > a[i]))$

SP3: Pre: a initialised & $1 \leq i < n$
Post: inchanged(i) &&
unchanged$(1, i, a)^3$ & $(\forall\ k : i + 1 \leq k \leq n : a[k] = a_0[n - (k - (i + 1))])$

Writing correct formal specifications for the subproblems is the key issue to prove the correctness of the complete algorithm in a compositional way. This

---

^{3} The subarray $a[1..i]$ is unchanged.

- Decl: const n;
  var a: array [1..n] of integer; (input)
  var b: boolean; (output)
  var $i, j, temp$: integer; (auxiliary variable)
- Pre: a initialised , n is the array size,
  $(\forall k : 1 \leq k \leq n : (\# w : 1 \leq w \leq n : a[w] = k) = 1)$
  Post:
  $(b \Rightarrow (\text{permut}(a, a_0) \;\&\; a \succ a_0 \&\&(\forall c[1 \ldots n] : (\text{permut}(a_0, c) \;\&\; c \succ a_0) \Rightarrow c \succeq a)))$
  $\&(\neg b \Rightarrow (\text{unchanged}(a)\&\&(\forall c[1 \ldots n] : \neg\text{permut}(a, c) \;\lor\; c \preceq a)))$
- Instr: SP1;

```
        if (i>0)
        then SP2;
            temp:= a[j]; a[j]:=a[i]; a[i]:= temp;
            SP3;
            b:= true
        else
            b:= false
        end
```

Fig. 2. Finding the next permutation in lexicographical order

task is not always completely straightforward. For instance, let's have a look at the postcondition of subproblem SP2. It must express that $a[j]$ is the least element greater than $a[i]$, on its right. Since the precondition states that the sub-array $a[i+1..n]$ is decreasing and that $a[i] < a[i+1]$, it is sufficient to write that $a[j] > a[i]$ and $a[j+1] \leq a[i]$ if $j < n$, but the case $j = n$ needs a special treatment, since there is no element $a[n+1]$. In the postcondition, is necessary to use the conditional operator && to avoid evaluating undefined conditions.

We are now in position to provide the code of the main algorithm with its specification. They are given in Figure 2. Notice that the code does not involve an iteration. Hence no invariant is needed. One should also observe that the post-condition is very understandable because it uses powerful primitive predicates of our assertion language, such as $\succ$, $\succeq$, and permut; universal quantification over an array variable is also needed. The precondition states that every natural number from 1 to n occurs exactly once in the array. Proving the correctness of the main algorithm takes $15ms$ (for $n = 1$), $16ms$ ($n = 2$), $187ms$ ($n = 3$), $3.9s$ ($n = 4$), $2m16s$ ($n = 5$). Assuming $n \leq 5$, proving the correctness of the subproblems takes $27s$ for SP1, $672ms$ for SP2 and $46ms$ for SP3. Let us now assume that we try to prove the correctness of the main algorithm with an inadequate (i.e., to weak) specification of a subproblem. So we forget the constraint $a[j] > a[i]$ in the postcondition of SP2. For $n = 5$, we get the following counter-example for the main algorithm.

precondition   : $n = 5$ $a = [4\ 5\ 3\ 2\ 1]$
postcondition   : $n = 5$ $a = [3\ 1\ 2\ 4\ 5]$ $b = true$ $i = 1$ $j = 3$ $temp = 3$
violated assertion : $a \succ a_0$

On the other hand, if we forget the special case $(j = n$ && $a[j] > a[i])$ in the postcondition of SP2, we get a run-time error prediction in the verification of the main algorithm. However, this error, which was actually made by one of the authors when she first solved this problem, can be detected if we analyse the subproblem itself: If we attempt to construct the algorithm according to this wrong specification, we have get an out of bound error prediction; if we check a correct algorithm with respect to the wrong specification, we get counter-examples for { *Inv* & *B* } *Clot* { *Post* }.

To conclude on this second example, we emphasize that proving the correctness of such an algorithm by hand is far from a trivial task. Notice also that there is no need to arbitrary reduce the domains of the input variables, here; so the proof is actually complete (for small values of n).

3   Overview of Oz Constraint Programming

The Oz language allows constraint programming over finite domains. In this section, we provide an overview of the Oz constraint programming model, a complete description of which can be found in [14].

Constraints. Oz constraint programming uses two kinds of constraints. *Basic constraints* are in the form $x \in D$ where x is a variable and D is a finite subset of the natural numbers, called the *domain* of x. *Non-basic constraints* express relations between variables; a simple example is $x + y \leq z$.

Constraint Solving. Operationally, computation takes place in a computation space. A *computation space* consists of a constraint store and a set of propagators. The *constraint store* implements a conjunction of basic constraints, which can be dynamically refined by the propagators. A *propagator* is a concurrent computational agent that imposes a non basic constraint by narrowing the domains of the variables involved in the constraint. Let us assume, for instance, that the constraint store s consists of two basic constraints $x \in \{1, \ldots, 6\}$, and $y \in \{1, \ldots, 6\}$. Moreover, let us suppose that the propagator pa_1 imposes the constraint $x + 3 = y$. The basic constraints are refined into $x \in \{1, 2, 3\}$ and $y \in \{4, 5, 6\}$ because other values of the domains are not compatible with the constraint $x + 3 = y$. Propagators communicate through the constraint store by shared variables. Consider again our example and let us add an other propagator pa_2, that imposes the constraint $y - 2 \times x > 1$. Once pa_1 has refined the basic constraints to $x \in \{1, 2, 3\}$ and $y \in \{4, 5, 6\}$, the second propagator ensures that $x \in \{1, 2\}$. Now, pa_1 can propagate again giving $y \in \{4, 5\}$, then pa_2 establishes $x = 1$, and, finally, pa_1 computes $y = 4$. At this moment, the computation space encapsulating s, pa_1 and pa_2 becomes *stable* (i.e., no further constraint propagation is possible). Moreover, one says that this computation space has *succeeded*, which means that the variable assignement $x = 1$ and $y = 4$ is a *solution* to the initial constraint problem. A computation space can also be *failed* if a propagator detects that its associated constraint is inconsistent with a basic constraint.

Variable Distribution. Constraint propagation is not a complete solution method: It may happen that a set of constraint has a unique solution and that constraint propagation does not find it. Similarly, constraint propagation may be unable to detect that no solution exists. Consider, for instance, the same problem where propagator pa_2 is replaced by propagator pa'_2, which imposes $y - x * x > 1$. After propagation, the computation space gets stable with the following store: $x \in \{1, 2, 3\}$ and $y \in \{4, 5, 6\}$. In such a situation, the computation space is said *distributable*, which means that it can be divided into two disjoint computation spaces by splitting the domain of a variable. To do so, we make two copies of the original computation space and we add a propagator that imposes $x = 1$ to the first copy and a propagator that imposes $x \neq 1$ to the second one. Propagators may then wake up in both spaces. The choice of the variable to be distributed and the choice of the value given to this variable is called a *distribution strategy*. The efficiency of constraint solving may heavily depend on the distribution strategy.

4   Checking Verification Conditions with Oz

To check the correctness of an imperative program with respect to a specification, we use verification conditions. A *verification condition* is a formula that is logically equivalent to propositions of the form $\{P\}S\{Q\}$, where P and Q are assertions and S is a program fragment. In our approach, verification formulas belongs to an interpreted logic that includes natural numbers, simple variables and arrays, a set of predefined functions and predicates, and quantifiers. Quantified variables are only allowed to range over a (dynamically defined) finite set of values as, for instance, in the formula $(\forall\, i : 1 \leq i < g : a[i] < x)$. Quantification on array variables is allowed, for instance, in the formula $(\forall\, c[1 \ldots n] :$ $(\mathrm{permut}(a_0, c)\ \&\ c \succ a_0) \Rightarrow c \succeq a)$. Providing a complete definition of our interpreted logic is outside the scope of this paper. We focus instead on the method we use to transform verification conditions into Oz constraint problems and to solve the constraint problems.

Generating the Constraints. A key choice of our method is to use reified constraints. *Reified constraints* are of the form $c \leftrightarrow b$ where c is a non basic constraint and b is a boolean $(0/1)$ variable. If $b = 1$, the reified constraint is equivalent to c. If $b = 0$, it is equivalent to $\neg b$. The main reason to use reified constraints is that any formula of our interpreted logic can be translated into a single conjunction of reified constraints, i.e., into a single constraint problem. For instance, consider a formula of the form $A \vee B$. It can be translated to the conjunction of reified constraints $(b = b_A \vee b_B)\ \&\ c_1\ \&\ \ldots\ \&\ c_n\ \&\ c'_1\ \&\ \ldots\ \&\ c'_{n'}$ where the c_i are the reified constraints translating A and b_A is the boolean variable associated to A (similarly for B). Without reified constraints, we should have to create different computation spaces for A and B, which is more complicated and less efficient. Another benefit of using reified constraints is that we maintain a different boolean variable for every subformula of the verification condition to check. The values of these boolean variables can be used to identify parts of the verification condition that are violated and, therefore, to provide interesting feedback to the user.

Let us show on an example how this method works in our system. We go back to our binary search example (see Figure 1) and we check part of the proposition $\{Inv \;\&\; \neg B\} \; Iter\{Inv\}$, namely the case where $a[m] > x$. Using the *strongest postcondition* approach (*sp*), introduced by Floyd in [9], we want to prove the following implication:

$$(\exists d_1 : d = m \;\&\; Inv_{d_1}^d \;\&\; g \neq d_1 \;\&\; \neg b \;\&\; m = (g+d_1)div\ 2 \;\&\; a[m] > x) \Rightarrow Inv$$

The notation $Inv_{d_1}^d$ means that we substitute the new variable d_1 to every free occurrence of the variable d in the formula Inv. Unfolding the formula $Inv_{d_1}^d$, the first part of the implication rewrites to the formula

$$
\begin{array}{llll}
& (\forall\ i : 1 \leq i \leq n-1 : a_0[i] \leq a_0[i+1])\ \& & & d = m \\
\& & a, x\ \text{unchanged}(\mathbf{1}) & \& & 1 \leq g \leq d_1 \leq n+1(\mathbf{2}) \\
\&\& & (\forall\ i : 1 \leq i < g : a[i] < x)(\mathbf{3}) & \& & (\forall\ i : d_1 \leq i \leq n : a[i] > x) \\
\& & b \Rightarrow (\exists\ i : 1 \leq i \leq n : a[i] = x) & \& & g \neq d_1\ \&\ b = false \\
\& & m = (g+d_1)\ div\ 2\ \&\ a[m] > x(\mathbf{4}) & &
\end{array}
$$

Subformulas (**1**) to (**4**) are translated to the following reified constraints.

$$
(1)\begin{cases} b1 = (x = x_0) \\ ba1 = (a[1] = a_0[1]) \\ ba2 = (a[2] = a_0[2]) \\ \dots \\ ban = (a[n] = a_0[n]) \\ b2 = (ba1\ \&\ ba2\ \&\ \dots\ \&\ ban) \end{cases}
\qquad
(3)\begin{cases} bb1 = (a[1] < x) \\ bb2 = (a[2] < x) \\ \dots \\ b6 = (bb1\ \&\ bb2\ \&\ \dots) \end{cases}
$$

$$
(2)\begin{cases} b3 = (1 \leq g) \\ b4 = (g \leq d_1) \\ b5 = (d_1 \leq n+1) \end{cases}
\qquad
(4)\begin{cases} z = g + d_1 \\ y = z\ div\ 2 \\ b7 = (m = y) \end{cases}
$$

In fact, the above description of the generated set of constraints is not totally accurate since the variables used by the imperative program and its companion assertions are different from the Oz variables that are used by the constraints. There is a one to one correspondence between the two sets of variables, however. Our implementation uses a dictionary to maintain the correspondence. The previous discussion also ignores a major difficulty in our method, which is that the number and the form of some constraints may depend on the value of one or several variables, such as g, d, and n in our example. To overcome this difficulty, we interleave constraint generation and constraint solving as explained later on.

Solving the Constraints. All verification conditions have the form $A \Rightarrow B$. Therefore, to check that a verification condition is valid, we first generate the reified constraints corresponding to A and B; then we impose that $b_A = 1$ and $b_B = 0$, where b_A and b_B are the boolean variables associated to A and B. This way, the

Oz constraint solving systems tries to find the solutions of a constraint problem equivalent to A & $\neg B$. If no solution exists, the verification condition is valid. Otherwise, counter-examples to the verification condition are found. In practice, constraint generation and constraint solving are interleaved as follows. Corresponding to each kind of formula in our assertion language, we have defined an Oz procedure which is responsible to generate the set of reified constraints corresponding to any such formula. For instance, Figure 3 depicts the procedure that translates assertions of the form $(\forall x : i \leq x \leq j : p(x))$. Notice that i and j may denote complex expressions with variables and $p(x)$, an arbitrary formula. A *precondition* to execute the procedure of Figure 3 is that the values of variables I and J are determined. This precondition can be ensured by adding WAIT statements for the actual parameters corresponding to I and J before any call to the procedure ForAll, as shown in Figure 4. However, adding those WAIT statements may result in a deadlock if variables $V1$ and $V2$ are never determined. To avoid such deadlocks we apply an appropriate distribution strategy:

```
proc {ForAll I J P Rs B}
      Dom = {List.number I J 1} (1)
in
      Rs = {Map Dom P}          (2)
      B = {FoldL Rs fun{$ X Y#_} {FD.conj X Y} end 1}   (3)
end
```

(1)Dom $= [I, I+1,...,J]$
(2)Rs $= [P\ I, P\ I+1, ...\ P\ J] = [B_I \# L_I, B_{i+1} \# L_{I+1}, ...B_I \# L_J]$
(3)B $= B_I$ & B_{I+1} & ...& B_J

Fig. 3. Generating propagators for $\forall x : i \leq x \leq j : p(x)$

```
proc{$ Bool}
    P= fun {$ K} Li Bo Mpl in
         {Dictionary.clone Mp Mpl}
         K = {Dictionary.put Mpl X}
         Bo = {{PropB P Mpl Li}}
         Bo#Li
       end
       V1 LV1 V2 LV2 L
in
       Liste = [[LV1 LV2]# L]
       {Eval A1 Mp LV1 V1}
       {Eval A2 Mp LV2 V2}
        thread {Wait V1} {Wait V2}
              Bool = {ForAll V1 V2 P L}
        end
end
```

Fig. 4. Translating the formula $(\forall\ x : a1 \leq x < a2 : p(x))$

In parallel to reified constraint generation, we incrementally build a partially instantiated data structure that defines a *priority* relation between Oz variables. Although every variable may eventually need being distributed, variables that must be determined to allow reified constraint generation must be distributed first. Thus, we introduce those variables first in the data structure. The data structure is read in parallel to its construction by the Oz procedure that implements distribution. This procedure first distributes the most prioritary variables and it may block when all variables are determined, until the data structure gets more instantiated. Figure 4 explains why the call to procedure `ForAll` will not be delayed forever: First the variable `Liste`, which is part of the partially data structure used for distribution, is further instantiated with two new variables `LV1` and `LV2`; then procedure `Eval` is executed to create two threads that will both evaluate `V1` and `V2` and instantiate `LV1` and `LV2` with the variables to be distributed in `A1` and `A2` (i.e., the Oz variables corresponding to the variables occurring in the expressions $a1$ and $a2$ of the assertion).

Limitations of Our System. Although we have not performed any formal complexity analysis of our system yet, it is quite obvious that its execution time is at least exponential in the size of the problem, most of the time. Nevertheless, we believe that its efficiency is sufficient for the pedagogical objectives we have in mind. In most cases, the correctness of an algorithm does not depend on the size of the problem. Moreover, we are often more interested in the discovery of counter-examples, which can be used to explain reasoning errors, than in correctness proofs. Obviously large input data are not needed to discover interesting counter-examples.

Nonetheless, the main weakness of our finite domain implementation is that, in many cases, we must restrict the domain size of input variables (mainly, arrays) to make the problem tractable. Such restrictions must be done carefully to avoid ruling out potential error cases. It should be desirable to elaborate a kind of theory of such "safe" restrictions.

5   Related Work

A lot of research has been done towards verifying the correctness of programs. A complete overview of this research is outside the scope of this paper. At the technical level, we briefly compare our work with three major approches: abstract interpretation, model-checking and (general) theorem-proving. At the methodological level, we relate it to formal software engineering approaches.

Abstract interpretation amounts to automatically compute a finite (abstract) description of an infinite set of program executions. To be efficient, program properties are approximated. For instance, P. Cousot and N. Halbwachs show how to infer properties of imperative programs using polyhedrons in [8]. The goal is not to provide complete formal correctness proofs but to infer specific properties that are useful for program optimisation or to ensure safety properties. Model-checking [3, 4, 7]applies to finite systems and is mainly used for the verification of concurrent systems. Temporal logics are used as specification languages. Once again, the goal is generally not to prove the full correctness of programs but some key properties such as mutual exclusion or reachability of certain states. Efficient implementations have been designed using BDDs and Sat-solvers. Altough our assertion language has been designed for different goals, it should be interesting to investigate its applicability to the verification of concurrent systems and to compare the efficiency of finite domain techniques with classical model-checking implementations. Theorem provers such as, for example, PVS [2] can be used to provide complete correctness proofs of imperative programs without restricting the size of the problem as we do. However, even for simple problems, using theorem provers requires a lot of "mathematical maturity", which makes them almost impossible to use in a pedagogical context. For instance, we are quite sure that proving the correctness of our next permutation example with PVS would be a major achievement.

At the methodological level, many researchers advocate formal methods to validate software construction. For instance, D. Jackson combines abstraction, model-checking, and executable specifications for imperative program verification (see [5, 6, 11]). Since the emphasis is on "real life" software, a complete verification of the system is hardly possible and only critic properties are checked. Our approach is different since we only consider small programs which we want to check in full details. Nevertheless, our approach has been adapted to the B specification language by Laka Moussa and Emmanuel Dieul (see [13]).

6   Conclusion and Future Work

We have presented a verification system that supports an expressive assertion language for writing specifications and loop invariants about programs written in a simple imperative language. We have shown on two significant examples that the system is able to prove the correctness of elaborated programs consisting of several subproblems that are checked independently of each other. The system is still better for finding errors in programs and/or inconsistencies in specifications and invariants; it is also much more efficient at this task since the discovery of a significant set of counter-examples generally requires to explore only a small part of the search space. The verification system is intended to be used in a teaching context, for educational goals (although it has been adapted by another researcher for software engineering applications).

In future work, we intend to make experiments with the system in the context of an advanced programming course, namely the course INGI2122 (*Méthodes de conception de programmes*), to study the benefit of such a tool for understanding both rigorous program construction methods and formal methods advantages and drawbacks. We also foresee to develop better distribution strategies to improve the system efficiency. Finally, we plan to compare our approach with relevant model-checking and theorem proving systems on a few classical examples in concurrent program verification.

Acknowledgements

The authors are indebted to the members of the Oz pool, in Louvain-la-Neuve, and particularly to Raphaël Collet for invaluable support and kindness.

References

1. The Mozart Programming System. http:www.mozart-oz.org.
2. The PVS specification and verification system. http://pvs.csl.sri.com.
3. T. Bal and S.K. Rajamani. Boolean programs: A model and process for software analysis. Technical Report 2000-14, Microsoft Research, 2000.
4. J.C. Corbett, M.B. Dwyer, J. Hatcliff, and Robby. A language framework for expressing checkable properties of dynamic software. In *Proc. of SPIN Model Checking and software Verifications*, volume 1885. LNCS.Springer, 2000.
5. Somesh Jha D. Jackson and Craig A.Damon. Isomorph-free model enumeration: a new method for checking relational specifications. *ACM Trans. on Programming Languages and Systems*, 20(2):302–343, March 1998.
6. C.A. Damon and D. Jackson. Efficient search as a means of executing specifications. In *Proc. TACAS 96*, March 1996.
7. O. Grumberg E.M. Clarke and D.E. Long. Model checking and abstraction. *ACM Transactions on Programming Langages and Systems*, 16(5):1512–1542, Sept 1994.
8. P.Cousot et N.Halbwachs. Automatic discovery of linear restraints among variables of a program. In *Proc. of the conference record of the Fifth annual ACM Symptium on Principles of Programming Languages*, pages 84–97, Tukson,Arizona, 1978. ACM Press.
9. R.W. Floyd. Assigning meanings to programs. In *Proc. of Symposia in Applied Mathematics*, volume 19, pages 19–32. Mathematical Society, 1967.
10. C.A.R Hoare. An axiomatic definition of semantics. *Communications of the ACM*, 12(10), 1969.
11. D. Jackson. Aspect: Detecting bugs with abstract dependences. *ACM Trans. on Software Engineering and Methodology*, 4(2):109–145, April 1995.
12. B. Le Charlier M. Derroite. Un système d'aide à l'enseignement d'une méthode de programmation. In *Actes du premier colloque francophone sur la didactique de l'informatique*, 1989.
13. Laka Moussa and Emmanuel Dieul. VICS, verification of an implementation conforming to its specification. http://vics.sourceforge.net.
14. Christian Schulte. Programming constraint services. Master's thesis, Saarbrucken, 2000.
15. Peter Van Roy and Seif Haridi. *Concepts, Techniques, and Models of Computer Programming*. The MIT Press, 2004.

Higher Order Programming for Unordered Minds

Juris Reinfelds

Klipsch School of Electrical & Computer Engineering,
New Mexico State University
juris@nmsu.edu

Abstract. In this paper we describe our experience with how Mozart-Oz facilitates the introduction of distributed computing to students of limited programming background and how the application of a few basic programming concepts can increase the students' comprehension of how distributed computations actually happen.

1 Introduction

In a graduate CS course in Spring 2003, there was a need to introduce distributed computing as quickly and concisely as possible. As it often happens in CS programs with students from all parts of the world, their background knowledge varied widely in scope and depth with hands-on lab-skills at a very low level.

Java with remote threads [1] or MPI [2] with C-programming was beyond the reach of most students. Instead we took advantage of the clear, concise and powerful semantics of Oz and Oz's natural inclusion of distributed computations. To illustrate how we fared, this paper will discuss the simple but canonical Compute Server/Client Problem of distributed computing.

First, in Spring 2003, we took the conventional approach as illustrated in the Mozart Documentation [3] and in Van Roy & Haridi [4]. The students quickly learned how to save and take tickets and where to put "their code" in the preparation of client's compute tasks. This enabled the students to complete the required homeworks, but their depth of understanding and interest in the power and possibilities of this new kind of programming remained low. Only one of 21 students of this course saw the power of the Mozart approach, learned more Oz and applied it to other projects in other courses. Section 2 describes this approach and defines our version of the Compute Server/Client Problem.

To improve the students' depth of comprehension, we set out to determine what programming concepts and mechanisms underlie the remarkable simplicity, directness and ease with which distributed computations can be initiated and controlled in Oz. In our opinion, the key to simple yet powerful distributed computing lies in the distributed, internet-wide value store of Oz. We developed a programmer's model of such value storage and management. This is discussed in Section 3.

P. Van Roy (Ed.): MOZ 2004, LNCS 3389, pp. 53–65, 2005.

Using our new approach, half the class of 18 students in Spring 2004 was sufficiently interested and able to use Mozart in their end of semester project although they had the freedom to choose any programming tools and methods and they had a wide range of project topics available to them. In Section 4 we augment the Compute Server/Client we introduce in Section 2 with an explanation of how it works in terms of the concepts that we define in Section 3.

In conclusion, we suggest that distributed computations would be facilitated even more if Mozart could provide an option to access a global value store as a network service by extending the existing mechanisms with which the runtime system of Oz accesses remote values.

2   A Simple Compute Server and Client

Let us define a simple compute-server and client by removing the unessential object orientation from the compute-server example that appears in Mozart documentation [3] volume "Distributed Computing", Section 3.2.4 as well as in VanRoy & Haridi [4] Chapter 11.

To further simplify the surprisingly concept-rich program, we have omitted exception message handling in the code that we give to the students. We ask them to insert exception handling into the given code in a homework assignment to expand and test the depth of their understanding of Oz programming.

2.1   The Server

The server uses an Oz-Port *(Port)* to collect incoming messages from one or more clients into a list *(PortList)*. The Port mechanism appends incoming messages at the end of the port list and maintains an unbound identifier at the end of this list. Processing of the list suspends when it reaches the unbound identifier until that identifier gets bound to a value which is the next incoming task.

The server expects incoming messages to refer to Oz-values that contain zero-arg-procedures and sets up a recursive *ForAll* loop that executes each zero-arg-proc from the head of the list until execution suspends on the unbound identifier at the end of the list. Here is the Oz program for our version of the server:

```
% Server waits for and processes compute tasks
% that are zero-arg-procedures.
proc {ComputeServer}
    PortList    % list of incoming tasks
    Port                % appends incoming tasks to PortList
    Q           % one-arg-proc for recursive loop
    TicketToPort        % offers remote access to Port
in
    Port = {NewPort PortList}
    TicketToPort = {Connection.offerUnlimited Port}
    {Pickle.save TicketToPort "/home/juris/filenameOfTicket"}
    proc {Q I} {I} end  % if incoming I's are zero-arg-procs
    {ForAll PortList Q}
end %ComputeServer
```

Here it is again. Expressed more concisely and parametrized for multiple server creation the server program looks simpler than it is:

```
proc {CompSrv FileName}
    PortList
    Port={NewPort PortList}
in
    {Pickle.save {Connection.offerUnlimited Port} FileName}
    {ForAll PortList proc {$ I} {I} end}
end %CompSrv
```

Students had no trouble with typing-in and executing this program to create one or more compute servers, yet understanding how the server works is another matter that we will take up in Section 4. At this stage students cannot understand open lists and external variables and have difficulties with the simplest modifications of the server program. For example, a simple modification to enable examination of the PortList while the server runs is beyond the grasp of most students because the idea that PortList could be an external variable in CompSrv needs to be introduced gently to students brought up on the string-of-pearls model [5] of side-effect avoidance in imperative programming.

2.2   The Ackermann Function

The Ackermann function is an example of a very simple code that defines nontrivial computations of any desired duration. In the days of early mainframes and compilers the Ackermann Number was used to measure the recursive capabilities of mainframe-op.sys.-compiler combinations [6]. The Ackermann Number is defined as the smallest value N for which Ack(3,N) crashes because some resource in the computer-operating system-compiler combination runs out. In the testing of our compute server we can choose suitable values of N to give a run time of a few minutes, so we can use an Oz-panel on each machine to observe the remote computations as they happen. Here is the code of the Ackermann function. The arguments are small non-negative integers.

```
fun {Ack M N}
    if M==0 then N+1
    elseif N==0 then {Ack (M-1) 1}
    else {Ack (M-1) {Ack M (N-1)} }
    end
end %Ack
```

2.3   The Client

The conventional explanation of the compute-client goes somewhat like this. Any Oz-invocation can become a client of our server if it has access to the file that stores the Oz-ticket to the server's Oz-port. To become a client an Oz-invocation has to *Pickle.load* the "pickled" ticket into the client's Oz invocation and then *Connection.take* the server's port-ticket to establish a connection to the server's port. The client can create a compute-task by taking a statement sequence in client's name-space and wrapping it into a zero argument procedure. Then the client uses the built-in *Send* procedure to send the zero-arg-proc to the server's port for processing. The Oz-runtime systems of client and server manage the network connections and transmissions between client and server in a program-transparent way.

Here is a statement by statement discussion of the client's Oz-code. The potential client becomes a client by establishing a connection to the server's Oz-port by executing

```
ServPort1 = {Connection.take {Pickle.load "filenameOfTicket"}}
```

Without a model of the global store students find it difficult to reason about the ticket mechanism. For example, is the connection made by transferring the remote value or its global store reference? Suppose that the client wants to calculate the value of Ack(3,18) remotely. In other words, the client wants to execute the following statement on the server:

```
M3N18 = {Ack 3 18}
```

The client constructs a zero argument procedure:

```
proc {ZeroArgProc}
   M3N18 = {Ack 3 18}
end %ZeroArgProc
```

sends it to the server for processing and displays the result in the Browser window at client:

```
{Send ServPort1 ZeroArgProc}
{Browse m3n18#M3N18}
```

and it works! The user is pleased but confused. Just how did all this happen? The client did not explicitly tell the server what *Ack* was. What if the server already has the identifier Ack bound to a different value? The calculation of Ack(3,18) makes millions of calls to the function Ack that is defined on the client but not on the server. Did our remote computation swamp the network?

A deeper understanding of the programming concepts and mechanisms that underlie our compute server is necessary to answer these questions. In the rest of the paper, we will explore one way to achieve more depth in minimal time even if students have a limited background in programming and mathematics.

3   Programming Concepts and Mechanisms on Which Compute Server Is Based

First we define several basic programming concepts especially where we differ from historically established traditional definitions. Then we define a programmer's model of a distributed, global value store which in our opinion is the key to a deeper understanding of why Oz achieves distributed computations so simply and naturally.

3.1   Definitions

Statement. An *Oz-statement* is a piece of information that defines one step in the transformation of input information toward a desired output. An Oz-program is a sequence of Oz statements.

Consequences of this definition: since a program is a sequence of statements, execution should start with the first statement of the program and proceed with the next statement until there are no more statements to execute. Since a statement defines one step, we should be able to compile and execute one statement at a time. Imposition of "main program" or function or method named "main()" is an unnecessary restriction on what the user may want to do.

Value. An *Oz-value* is *any piece of information* of a type that the Oz programming language can handle. The *type* of a value defines a set of properties that are common to all values of that type. In particular, a type defines which operators of a programming language can accept values of this type as arguments. Acceptable Oz-value types are int, char, procedure, function, class, object and others. The programmer is burdened with the least amount of semantic baggage if all values can be handled in the same way as much as possible.

Consequences of this definition: The historically established requirement for special handling of procedure and function-value introductions is an unnecessary restriction on the programmer. An introduction of integer 256 creates an Oz-value of type "int" and an Oz-value of type "function" is introduced by executing the Oz-declaration

```
fun {$ N} N*N*N end
```

which introduces a function that returns the cube of its argument. It should and does behave very much like an Oz-value that is an integer. We can form an expression with it where it is called with the argument 3 and the expression returns the value 283.

```
256 + {fun {$ N} N*N*N end  3}
```

Bowing to years of traditional practice, Oz also accepts proc/fun value creation combined with identifier binding as in

```
fun {Cube X} X*X*X end
```

Regardless of which form of introduction we choose, function introduction creates a value that is just another piece of information. Only when a function is executed, the function value is used to create an information transformation process that produces the desired result. With such an introduction of procedure and function values, higher order programming becomes the default without the need to explain to mathematically naive students what "higher order" is.

3.2   One Distributed Value Store for All Invocations of Oz

Here we will describe a programmer's model of a global value store that combines the design ideas of the declarative Oz-value store and the the design concepts of the Unix file system. We will use programming concepts that best allow a programmer to relate this model to program design and structure. Our aim is to provide a model that truthfully portrays the behavior and capabilities of the Mozart value store but that does not necessarily reflect every nuance of its implementation.

A key concept is that there is one universal, distributed value store. The runtime system of every Oz invocation maintains its piece of the universal value store of Oz. In other words, all invocations of Oz, past, present and future, maintain one distributed data base of Oz-values.

Each invocation of Oz maintains the Oz-values that were created in this invocation and which are still useful. An Oz *value is useful* if there is at least one valid Oz identifier in any Oz-invocation that references this value.

Traditional programming languages adhere to the implementation-inspired definition:

> *a variable is both a name that corresponds to the address of a memory location and a value at that memory location.*

In traditional programming languages we usually have a one to one correspondence between variable names and the values to which the names are bound (or as we say, assigned). To bind another name to a value that already has a name assigned to it, we use pointers or a similar mechanism. We teach ourselves to say that after the assignment X:=5 "X *is* five" and in doing so we attach a second meaning to X which already meant *a memory location containing int*. In the statement X:=X+1, we quietly overlook the de-referencing of one X, but not the other, hoping that the compiler will get it right.

Oz makes a clear separation between the local name space and scope of identifiers that programmers use in Oz-programs and global value store references that must uniquely distinguish between values from all Oz-invocations.

The binding statement of Oz supports variable-value binding as in traditional languages. It also supports variable-variable bindings so that both variables become bound to the same value. This removes the need for a pointer mechanism, but requires the introduction of a value-type "reference" and programmer-transparent de-referencing by the runtime system to explain the binding of additional identifiers to a value that is already bound to an identifier.

Oz supports the introduction and use of unbound variables. Our model accommodates unbound variables by introducing an additional value-type which we call *"no-value-yet"*. A store-item with type "no-value-yet" is created for every identifier at the moment this identifier is introduced. Similarly, whenever a value is introduced a store-item is created containing the value and its type. Store items are identified by globally unique reference tags. Binding statements link store-items of identifiers to store-items of values.

To remind us of the differences between Oz and traditional programming languages, we use the term "binding" instead of "assignment" and the terms "identifier" and "value" instead of "variable" which in conventional languages often denotes either the storage address allocated to that variable or the value that is stored there. In our model a global value store item has three components:

- a reference tag that is unique in all invocations of Oz;
- the type of this Oz-value;
- the bit-pattern that represents this Oz-value.

When a new identifier is introduced in the program, the compiler creates a global value store item with a new unique reference and with the type "no-value-yet". The compiler also updates its name table with an entry that relates the newly introduced identifier with its value store reference. The compiled byte-code of this and subsequent statements within the scope of this identifier will contain the globally unique reference to the value store item instead of the local identifier. In this way local name-space remains strictly local and unconcerned if same identifiers reference different values in other name spaces, while byte-code can be executed to give the same result in any context in any invocation of Oz.

Identifier introductions are executable statements in Oz, but the scopes of identifiers are known at compile-time from actual and implied **local ... in ... end** statements. Formal parameters of proc/funs are treated as belonging to a **local ... end** statement around the proc/fun body that includes the call of this proc/fun in the scope. This scope is somewhat unusual, but it turns the formal/actual parameter mechanism of a proc/fun call into a sequence of binding statements of formal parameters with their corresponding actual parameter expressions.

Internal **local ... in ... end** statements introduce identifiers that are scoped within the proc/fun's body. Other identifiers that appear in the procedure or function are called *"external variables"*. They must already have global store references and the compiler places their global store references into the Oz byte-code, so that the code can be executed in any context in any Oz-invocation with the same results.

Oz has no restrictions as to where procedures and functions may be introduced in a program or expression. In this sense the handling of procedure and function values is no different from the handling of integer and char values which are also compiled into their value store items when and where they appear in the program.

Store references may appear in store items as values with type "reference". Appropriate dereferencing is performed by the executing runtime system. One situation where a reference must appear as the value of a value store item is for an identifier that is bound to an Oz-cell. In the statement that creates a cell (a state variable that can change the value to which it refers) we have

local C **in** {NewCell 25 C} **... end**

First, the identifier C is introduced with the type "no-value-yet". The execution of the procedure NewCell *binds C to a cell*, which in terms of our model means that NewCell

- Creates a new store item containing int 25.
- Changes the type of store item of C from "no-value-yet" to "cell".
- Sets the value of C's store item to the reference to the newly created store item containing int 25.

In summary, the compiler compiles every identifier to a store reference, so that although we say that *"we send a compute task to Oz-port P"* when we execute the procedure call {Send P Task}, what actually gets transferred to the input queue of P is a reference to the store item represented by the identifier *Task*.

3.3   Global Value Store as a Network Service

The current implementation of the global value store works very well if all participating Oz-invocations stay up as long as needed. However, the handling of situations when a remote site has shut down making its global value store references unexpectedly invalid is extremely awkward. For a few references this can be remedied by pickling a ticket for each reference, so that on restart a new reference can be obtained more easily. For more connected distributed computations as well as for backup and data preservation it might be useful to provide at least a part of the global value store as a *network service* using currently well developed database and uninterruptable hardware technology that would provide backup and redundancy 24/7 with continuous availability and recovery of previous states of computation if so desired. On the surface, it seems that the cost of the extra network accesses would be well worth it, especially because the current remote value fetching mechanism is so effective and efficient. There is hope that relatively small extensions of the current mechanisms to provide such a network service might provide a substantial facilitation of distributed computations.

There is active Mozart research along these lines [7], but it is focused on management of fault-tolerance using ordinary machines as components. We believe that an uninterruptable global value store would be a valuable network service for Mozart users, especially when applying Mozart to cluster computing on medium to large clusters.

3.4   External Variables in Procedures and Functions

Here we summarize the concept of external variables of Oz. At the point of introduction of a procedure or function there may be previously introduced identifiers that are in scope. If these identifiers appear in the procedure that is being introduced, the compiler will compile their store references into the Oz-byte-code of the procedure. These identifiers and the values to which they refer are called "external variables" of the procedure. Whenever a procedure value is bound to an identifier, the lifetime (scope) of the procedure value and the lifetime of the value store items to which its external variables refer is extended by the lifetime of this identifier.

Our model creates the same semantics for declarative external variables as the more mathematical environments of VanRoy&Haridi [4] Section 2.4, but our model of the global value store includes Oz-cells and brings the external variable concept closer to the experience of programmers who have followed the traditional Algol-Pascal-C pearls-of-a-necklace of Dijkstra [5] style of program design and who have regarded any departure from strictly nested stack-implementable variable scopes such as the relatively modest *"own variables"* of Algol-60 [8] as unacceptable.

4   The Compute Server/Client in Terms of Our Value Store Model

Identifiers are introduced by explicit or implicit

local Identifiers ... **in** StatementSequence ... **end**

local-statements that determine the scope of each identifier. In our model the compiler associates each identifier with a unique global reference tag as it processes the left part of the local-statement. The compiler compiles global references and not local identifier names into byte code. At execution time the runtime system executes the byte code and creates a store item with the reference of this identifier and the type *no-value-yet*.

Values are introduced as text in the source code and byte code is compiled requesting the runtime system to create a store-item with a unique reference tag and appropriate type and value.

Binding statements bind store-items of identifiers to store-items of values by placing the reference of the value into the value part of the identifier's store item with type "reference". When execution requires actual values, but the store item of the identifier contains a value of type reference, the runtime-system dereferences values of type "reference" until a non-reference value is reached and performs dynamic type-checking to ensure that this value is compatible with the operator that requires it.

4.1   The Server

Let us discuss the global store and identifier scope aspects of the compute server.

proc {CompSrv FileName}

This is an abbreviation for a binding statement within some local-statement such as

```
local
    CompSrv
in ...
    CompSrv = proc {$ FileName}...end
    ...
end
```

where the formal parameter *FileName* has an implied **local** FileName **in** ... that includes the proc-call *and* the procedure body, so the identifier of this formal parameter, which appears in the procedure body, can be bound to its corresponding actual parameter value when the proc is executed. This removes the need for a special consideration of formal-actual parameter mechanisms. Continuing with the statements of the server:

```
proc {CompSrv FileName}
PortList Port in
```

There is an implied *local* before PortList that scopes the identifiers PortList and Port to the procedure body. Next:

```
Port = {NewPort PortList}
```

The identifier NewPort is external to this procedure. It does not appear as a formal parameter nor is it defined as a procedure-local identifier. If there is no lexically more recent local use of the identifier NewPort, the compiler compiles a call to the system function NewPort.

The identifier NewPort and its store reference were placed into the compiler's identifier table as this Oz-invocation started up. This applies to all system provided procedures and functions. Next,

```
{Pickle.save {Connection.offerUnlimited Port} "filename"}
```

A text-string, called ticket, which allows remote invocations of Oz to pick up the global store reference to the server's Oz-port, will be placed in a file in the current directory from which the server proc is executed. Next,

```
{ForAll PortList proc {$ I} {I} end}
```

The second argument of this call of the system-supplied procedure *ForAll* is a procedure value **proc** ... **end** that is introduced where it appears in the procedure-call. This procedure value (actual parameter) gets bound to the corresponding formal parameter of *ForAll*, so it can be used in the procedure body. It cannot be used anywhere else in the program because it is not bound to an identifier that is valid outside of the procedure body.

We also need to explain the Oz-Port mechanism and how ForAll works. Let us use source code statements to describe how the execution proceeds:

```
Port = {NewPort PortList}
```

There is very little information about how Oz-ports and Oz-runtime systems work. According to VanRoy&Haridi [4] p.719, an Oz-Port is a value that is a FIFO channel with an asynchronous Send-operation that allows many-to-one communications from multiple clients. NewPort needs an unbound identifier (we use PortList) as argument which NewPort binds to the list of incoming global value store references that clients will *Send* to this port. The type "port" value returned by the NewPort call gets bound to our unbound identifier *Port*. The port mechanism terminates the list *PortList* with an unbound identifier. The port mechanism ensures that each newly arrived Send-carried input extends the list with itself and a new unbound identifier. In this way, if we consume the list in the usual way from the head, we have a FIFO queue of incoming items in PortList.

```
{Pickle.save {Connection.offerUnlimited Port} 'filename'}
```

System function Connection.offerUnlimited returns an ASCII string version of the global store reference of the argument of the call. System procedure

Pickle.save writes the ASCII string value of its first argument into a file provided that the second argument is a valid file name on the platform on which this Oz-invocation runs. This is a convenient way to convey the global value store reference of the Oz-Port of the Compute Server to a number of potential clients in systems where NFS is used to share the same home directory over a cluster of computers.

```
{ForAll PortList proc {$ I} {I} end}
```

ForAll executes the second argument that should be a one-argument procedure value with each element of PortList as the argument. Since Oz expressions suspend execution if execution reaches a value of type "no-value-yet", ForAll waits at the end of the input list for the arrival of input items which it executes, in order of arrival, and then waits again. From the form of the procedure value in the ForAll call, we see that our server will execute incoming zero-argument procedure values. Any other incoming value will raise an exception which in this very simple version of the server will not get transmitted back to the client.

4.2   A Client

Assume that a potential client has introduced four identifiers

```
Ack M3N18 ServPort1 CompTask
```

and Ack is bound to the Ackermann function that we discussed in a previous section. To become a client of our compute server, we have to pick up the global value store reference to the server's Oz-Port that the server pickled into the file with the name "filename." Assuming this filename is valid where this invocation of Oz is executed, the client executes the binding statement

```
ServPort1 = {Connection.take {Pickle.load 'filename'}}
```

Pickle.load returns the ASCII string version of the value store reference of the Oz-Port of the server. *Connection.take* converts the ASCII string version to an actual value store reference that gets bound to ServPort1, so that after this statement completes the value store item of ServPort1 on the client contains the value store reference to the Oz-Port of the server with the value-type "reference." Whenever the client program needs the actual port-value, as in a Send call, the runtime system of the client will recognize that the reference is remote and in collaboration with the runtime system of the server will obtain access to the actual port-value. The Oz-Port value at the server is now bound to two identifiers Port and ServPort1, which are in separate namespaces on separate invocations of Oz.

Client creates a zero-arg procedure that defines a computation task. The identifiers M3N18 and Ack are external variables in the zero-arg procedure. The identifiers Ack and M3N18 are local to the client, but their global value store references ref(M3N18) and ref(Ack) are compiled into the zero-arg-procedure value that is sent to the server.

```
CompTask = proc {$} M3N18 = {Ack 3 18} end
{Send ServPort1 CompTask}
```

The system procedure *Send* arranges help from the runtime systems of the client and the server to use the network connection between these runtime systems that was established when the ticket to the server's Port was taken. "Send" transfers the value store reference of CompTask from client to server-port Port. The server-port appends this reference to the end of its input list. Although we like to say: *"We send a compute task to the server"*, only the global value store reference ref(CompTask) gets attached to the end of the server's ProcList. If and when the execution of some expression on the server (as in the ForAll call) requires the value itself, the server's runtime system will use the remote reference to get to its Oz-value. The Send procedure terminates when the network transfer of the reference is completed.

In our server, the incoming reference creates a value store element of type "reference" that becomes a list element in the input list and does not have its own identifier in the identifier table of the server.

The ForAll procedure fetches the remote value from the client and executes it as a zero argument procedure. If the remote value is not a zero arg proc, an exception is raised and our very simple server crashes. Programming of crash avoidance is a good exercise for the students.

During the execution of the remote ref(CompTask), the runtime system of the server encounters two more remote references for M3N18 and Ack. If the runtime system of Oz is implemented efficiently, the server copies the value of Ack from the client calls it locally millions of times. The server determines that the value of M3N18 is of type "no-value-yet" and binds it to a type "int" value that is the result of the computation. The client can now see the result of the remote computation because it is bound to the client's local identifier M3N18.

5   Conclusions

Our model of the global store helps Oz programmers to untangle and visualize the way in which computations take place when values are referenced from several different name spaces by identifiers with non-nested, non-overlapping scopes. The negative history of Algol-60's modest break with stack-friendly scopes with "own variables" [8], [9] shows that scopes that are not cleanly nested and therefore stack-implementable are a hard nut for imperative programmers and compiler writers. It is wonderful that Oz has cracked this nut so cleanly, elegantly, and effectively.

It is interesting to observe that the design of our model is similar to the design of the UNIX file system with

- value <> i-node,
- identifier <>file-name or link-name
- identifier-table <>directory.

Cluster computing and well connected distributed computations in general would benefit greatly if the existing remote value handling mechanisms of Oz could be extended to provide the global value store as a 24/7 network service with backups, crash-proof redundancy and optional restoration of previous states of computation.

Acknowledgements

The author is grateful to the students of CS5340 at UTEP in Spring 2003 and Spring 2004 for their patience, understanding and willingness to try new ideas while our global value store model was under development. The author is grateful to Denys Duchier for the rescue of our Mozart system in early 2003 when the Emacs-based API refused to run because SUSE Linux 8.1 had not loaded a font that no one needed, but nevertheless Emacs decided to check for its existence before it allowed the Oz-menu to be created although Oz did not need this font either. The author is grateful to the authors of the Mozart-Oz system, especially to Peter Van Roy for many discussions on the deeper aspects of the Kernel Language and Oz design.

References

1. Oaks, Scott,& Wong, Henry, *Java Threads*, Second Ed. O'Reilly (1999).
2. Pacheco, Peter S., *Parallel Programming with MPI*, Morgan Kaufmann Publishers Inc. (1997).
3. Mozart-Oz: web site and home-page: http://www.mozart-oz.org (2004).
4. Van Roy, Peter., Haridi, Seif, *Concepts, Techniques, and Models of Computer Programming*, MIT Press (2004).
5. Dijkstra, Edsger W., *A Necklace of Pearls*, p.59, Section 14, Structured Programming, Academic Press (1972).
6. Sundblad, Yngve, *The Ackermann Function, a Theoretical, Computational and Formula Manipulative Study*, BIT, Vol. 11, p. 107-119 (1971).
7. Al-Metwally, Mostafa, Alouini, Ilies, *Fault Tolerant Global Store Module*, http://www.mozart-oz.org/mogul/doc/metwally/globalstore (2001).
8. Naur, Peter, Editor: *Report on the Algorithmic Language Algol 60*, CACM, Vol. 3, #5, p. 299-314, (1960).
9. Wirth, Niklaus, *Computing Science Education: The Road Not Taken*, SIGCSE Bulletin 34(3), 1-3., (2002)

Compiling Formal Specifications to Oz Programs

Tim Wahls

Dickinson College, P.O. Box 1773, Carlisle, PA 17013, USA
wahlst@dickinson.edu

Abstract. Although formal methods have the potential to greatly enhance software development, they have not been widely used in industry
(particularly in the United States). We have developed a system for executing specifications by compiling them to Oz programs. Executability
is a great aid in developing specifications, and also increases the usefulness of specifications by allowing them to serve as prototypes and test
oracles. In this work, we describe how we have used the Oz language
both as a translation target and in implementing a library of procedures
used by the generated programs. Oz is ideal for our purposes, as it has
allowed us to easily use declarative, concurrent constraint and graphical
user interface programming together within a single framework.

1 Introduction

Formal specifications of software system functionality have a number of important advantages over specifications expressed in English, such as conciseness, the
ability to serve as a basis for proofs of program correctness or of other important system properties, and freedom from ambiguity and implementation bias.
A large number of formal specification notations have thus been developed, including VDM [1, 2], Z [3, 4], B [5, 6], JML [7], and SPECS-C++ [8, 9].

However, formal specifications have not been widely adopted in industry, particularly in the United States. The perception is that the cost of using formal
methods does not justify the benefits. The use of formal methods is difficult
to justify to clients and managers who typically do not understand the notation. Hence, there is a need for tools and techniques that make specifications
accessible to nontechnical users, and that reduce the cost of developing formal
specifications.

One way to approach these problems is through the use of executable formal
specifications. The ability to execute and validate specifications eases their development, as specifiers can immediately check intuition about their specifications.
An executable specification can serve as a prototype of the final system, allowing
nontechnical users to interact with the specification and to provide feedback on
it. Clients and managers can also see the utility of an executable specification
as a test oracle. Unsurprisingly, many executable specification languages and
execution techniques have been developed [10, 11, 12, 13, 14, 15, 16, 17, 18].

P. Van Roy (Ed.): MOZ 2004, LNCS 3389, pp. 66–77, 2005.

We have developed a system for executing SPECS-C++ specifications [9] by compiling them to Oz [19, 20, 21] programs[1]. Our system requires no hand translation, no explicit identification of the range of possible values for variables in most cases, and also introduces almost no implementation bias into specifications. We have also developed a formal semantics [8] and a graphical user interface [22] for our system.

SPECS-C++ is similar to other model-based specification languages such as VDM and Z in that operations are specified using first order pre- and postconditions written over a fixed set of model types. These types include C++ primitive types, as well as tuples, sets, sequences, multisets, functions and maps. SPECS-C++ is designed for specifying the interfaces of C++ classes, and so operation signatures are given as C++ member function prototypes. The model types in SPECS-C++ include references so that interface specifications can handle aliasing and object containment.

Figure 1 presents the specification of a C++ template class Table, which allows references to values of any type to be stored and indexed by integer keys. This type would most naturally be modeled as a function from integers to value references, but we have modeled it as a sequence of tuples in order to better demonstrate the kinds of specifications that can be executed. In fact, the specification becomes much easier to execute if a function is used, as there is then no need to use quantifiers and the sortKeys operation becomes nonsensical.

The domains section of the specification defines types for later use, while the data members section gives the abstract data members used to model instances of the class. The constraints section specifies any invariants that all instances of the class must satisfy. Here, the invariant is that for any two tuples at different indices within the sequence, the key values must be different (i.e. the sequence of tuples properly represents a function)[2]. The abstract functions section defines "specification only" functions that are not part of the interface of the class, but are useful for specification purposes. The abstract functions presented here respectively check that the table values are sorted by key, and that a particular integer value is in the domain of the table.

The member function specifications (following public:) describe the interface of the class that is available to client code. Angle brackets are used as sequence constructors, and || is sequence concatenation. The modifies clause specifies which objects can change from the prestate (before the operation executes) to the poststate. The ^ is used to dereference an object in the prestate, while ' is used for the poststate value. The notation theTable^ (for example) is a shorthand for self^.theTable. Note that the postconditions of lookUp and sortKeys are highly implicit – they simply describe the return value (specified as result) or poststate resulting from the operation with no indication of how

---

[1] The system originally generated Agents Kernel Language (AKL) programs, and was later ported to Oz.

[2] SPECS-C++ specifications are intended for use as C++ header files, so quantifiers (for example) can not be written as $\forall$ and $\exists$.

```
template <class Value> class Table {
/* model
  domains
    tuple (int key, Value& val) ElemType;
    sequence of ElemType TableType;
  data members
    TableType theTable;

  constraints
    \forall int i [1 <= i <= length(theTable) =>
      \forall int j [1 <= j <= length(theTable) /\ i != j =>
        theTable[i].key != theTable[j].key]]
  abstract functions
    define sorted(TableType t) as bool such that
      result = tobool(\forall int i [ 1 <= i < length(t) =>
                              t[i].key <= t[i + 1].key]);
    define inDom(int key, TableType t) as bool such that
      result = tobool(\exists int i [1 <= i <= length(t)
                                  /\ t[i].key = key]);
*/

public:

Table();
/* modifies: self
   post: theTable' = <>
*/

void addEntry(int key, Value& val);
/* pre: ! inDom(key, theTable^)
   modifies: self
   post: theTable' = <(key, val)> || theTable^
*/

Value& lookUp(int key);
/* pre: inDom(key, theTable^)
   post: \exists ElemType e [e \in theTable^
                          /\ e.key = key
                          /\ result = e.val]
*/

void sortKeys();
/* modifies: self
   post: range(theTable^) = range(theTable') /\ sorted(theTable')
      /\ length(theTable^) = length(theTable')
*/

bool inDomain(int key);
/* post: result = inDom(key, theTable^)
*/

};
```

Fig. 1. The SPECS-C++ specification of class **Table**

this result is to be constructed. In particular, the postcondition of sortKeys simply specifies that the poststate value of the calling object is a sorted permutation of the prestate value. The postcondition of sortKeys is strong enough to uniquely determine the poststate, assuming that the prestate satisfies the invariant. The inDomain member function is provided so that client code can check the preconditions of addEntry and lookUp.

Our compiler translates SPECS-C++ specifications such as this one to Oz programs. The scanner for the compiler was generated using flex, and the parser using bison. The remaining components of the compiler are implemented in C++. All of the operations on the SPECS-C++ model types are implemented in a library of Oz procedures (as a functor), which are called from the generated programs. The library also includes the code for the graphical user interface (using the Oz embedding of Tk) and various utility procedures. Poststate values and variables bound by existential quantifiers are represented by fresh Oz variables, which are then constrained by the generated code. Additional information about the translation and the library is presented in the following section. A complete description of the translation is contained in [9], and a formal presentation of selected portions of the translation can be found in [8].

2   Compiling to Oz

In this section, we describe how we have used various features of Oz in implementing the specification execution system. We highlight features that have been particularly useful, or that we have used in potentially novel ways.

2.1   Threads

In a formal specification, conjuncts and disjuncts should be ordered in the most natural way for the specifier, or in a way that is intended to increase readability. Of course, the order has no effect on the meaning of the specification. However, in an Oz program, the order of statements in a procedure body and the order of choices in a **choice** or **dis** statement has a tremendous impact on performance and even on whether or not the program terminates. This issue is well known in the logic and constraint programming communities, where it is referred to as *literal ordering* [23, 24, 25]. Requiring the specifier to write specifications in a particular order is an unacceptable form of implementation bias, so the specification execution system must not rely on ordering properties of specifications.

Our primary approach to this problem has been to make liberal use of threads – the majority of the library procedures that implement SPECS-C++ operators are threaded. When called, these procedures block until their arguments are sufficiently defined to permit execution. This greatly decreases the sensitivity of the system to the order in which the specification is written – if a procedure is called "too early", it simply suspends and waits until enough of its arguments are available to permit execution. Oz's data-flow threads are ideal for this purpose, as no code is required for this synchronization. Additionally, Oz threads are sufficiently lightweight so that execution times remain reasonable, even for programs that create many hundreds of threads (as the programs generated by our system often do).

For example, the procedure implementing the `length` operation on sequences is threaded. The procedure takes two arguments (the sequence and the length) and unblocks when either becomes known. If the sequence becomes known, the procedure constrains the length. (If only some prefix of the sequence becomes known, the procedure finds the length of the prefix and resuspends.) If the length becomes known, the procedure constrains the sequence to contain that number of free variables. Those variables can then be constrained by other parts of the specification that refer to index positions within the sequence. Note that implementing the length procedure in this manner makes it a constraint propagator in the Oz sense.

It is advantageous to call such threaded library procedures as soon as they could possibly perform some propagation. Calling such an operation too early does no harm (it simply suspends), while calling it too late may drastically hurt performance if unnecessary search is done. Hence, the specification compiler does some explicit reordering to move up calls to threaded procedures. An alternative to using threading in this manner is to reorder (unthreaded) statements/literals based on data flow analysis (to ensure that a procedure can always execute at the time that it is called). That has been implemented within the Mercury project [25], but is considerably more complex than our approach.

2.2   Choice Points

In Oz, choice points are explicitly created (by the programmer) when search is needed, and are later explored via backtracking. This contrasts sharply with traditional logic programming languages such as Prolog in which any conditional is expressed by creating an implicit choice point. Several of the procedures in the library of the specification execution system create choice points by using **dis** statements, and disjunction in a specification is translated to a **choice** statement. The library procedures that create choice points correspond to SPECS-C++ operators that are frequently used in underdetermined or nondeterministic computations. For example, the procedure implementing sequence indexing is implemented using **dis** to allow all indices where a particular element occurs within a sequence to be found, or to allow a range of possibilities for where an element is to be inserted into a sequence (depending on the mode of use).

The reordering done by the specification compiler moves calls to library procedures that create choice points as late as possible in the generated programs. The idea is to delay search until variables are as constrained as possible, so that a search path that can not lead to success fails as soon as possible. This reordering, in conjunction with judicious selection as to which library procedures create choice points, seems to be effective in controlling the amount of search done by the generated programs, and in reducing the sensitivity of the system to the order in which the specification is written. We have tested the system extensively with specifications that were intentionally written to cause search (for example, the `sortKeys` member function specification of Figure 1, the specification of a maximum clique member function for a graph class, ...), and have systematically permuted the order of conjuncts, the order of disjuncts, the order of arguments where possible (i.e. to the = operator), and so on. In every case, the system could execute specifications over large enough inputs for reasonable testing purposes.

2.3   Computation Spaces

An Oz space is a complete encapsulation of a computation. A space consists of a constraint store and one or more threads that operate on the store. In Oz, the programmer can create and execute a space explicitly. Once the space becomes stable (can no longer execute), the programmer can query it to determine whether it succeeded, failed or suspended (contains at least one blocked thread), and the result of a succeeded space can be extracted. The idea of spaces in implicit in other languages – for example, backtracking search in Prolog can be thought of as creating one space for each of a set of rules with the same head, and then executing the space corresponding to the first rule. If that space fails, then it is discarded and the space for the second rule is executed (and so on). However, Oz is unique in that spaces can be explicitly created and manipulated by the programmer.

We have used explicit spaces in several ways in the specification execution system. In one (possibly novel) use, spaces are used to determine whether all threads resulting from a member function call have terminated. When a member function is called, a new space is created, and the Oz procedure representing that member function is executed within the space. If the space becomes stable and suspended, at least one thread blocked and could not be resumed. In this case, the system reports to the user that the specification did not contain sufficient information to permit execution. If spaces were not used in this manner, explicit synchronization would be necessary to determine if some threads remained blocked. This synchronization is not difficult in Oz (especially in programs written by an experienced human), but would have added some unnecessary complication to both the specification compiler and the library.

A nice property of spaces is that any binding of nonlocal variables is not visible outside of the space (and its child spaces). The specification execution system takes advantage of this property for executing assertions simply for their boolean value (rather than as constraints). For example, the antecedent of an implication is executed in a new space. If the space succeeds, the consequent is treated as a constraint. If the space fails, the consequent is ignored. If the space is stuck, the system reports that the specification is not executable. If the antecedent were just treated as a constraint (not executed in a new space), an explicit choice point would be required so that any variable bindings that resulted could be "backed out" in case the antecedent were false (i.e. treating $P \Rightarrow Q$ as $\neg P \vee Q$). We have experimented with both approaches and found creating a choice point for this purpose to be considerably less efficient in practice. Similarly, a negated assertion is executed within a new space and simply succeeds if the space fails and vice versa with no danger of determining nonlocal variables (that correspond to poststate values of the specification). This is quite similar to the behavior of the Oz **not** statement, but seems to be more general. We have found cases where this approach allows a specification to be executed, while using a **not** statement causes the thread to block.

Reification is another option for executing assertions for their value only, as the value of the assertion would then simply be the value of the boolean variable associated with it. However, this approach would require implementing reified versions of all of the SPECS-C++ predicates (operations that return boolean) and major changes to the structure of the generated programs. Additionally, it is not clear that this effort would lead to significant performance improvements.

2.4   The User Interface

The specification execution system can run specifications from the command line or via a graphical user interface (GUI). When running from the command line, the desired variable declarations and member function invocations are placed directly in the SPECS-C++ specification (.h) file. After the specification is compiled, running it will display the state resulting from the sequence of member function invocations, and the return value from the last member function invocation (if the return type of the member function is not **void**). The default is to display only the first solution, but all solutions can be generated by specifying appropriate arguments to the specification compiler.

The GUI can be used to declare variables (including those that instantiate template classes), to choose member functions to execute, to specify the actual arguments in a member function invocation, and to step through all post states that satisfy the member function specification. Figure 2 is a screen shot of the interface being used to execute the **Table** specification of Figure 1. The specification has been instantiated with **string** as the parameter type (note that strings are represented as sequences of characters), and after adding several entries, the **sortKeys** operation has been invoked.

SPECS-C++ references are displayed as arrows (i.e. pointers) in the interface using a canvas widget. This allows *aliasing* (multiple references to the same object) to be indicated by multiple arrows pointing to the same object [22]. Aliasing is a common source of errors and confusion in specifications (and programs!), so indicating aliases in this graphical fashion is extremely useful for developing specifications. In Figure 2, it is immediately apparent that each of the string objects s1 and s2 have been added to the table three times, and so that a great deal of aliasing is present. The interface allows allows the user to directly edit specification states, including adding and removing aliases using the mouse. New objects (targets of references) can also be added directly. If this functionality were not provided, building complex states for use in testing specifications would be much more tedious.

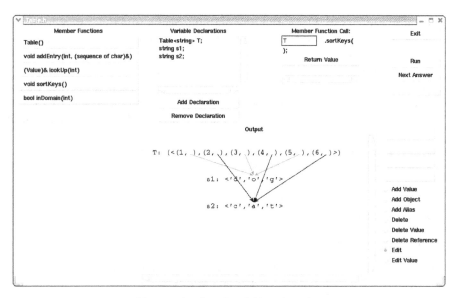

Fig. 2. The Graphical User Interface

2.5   Miscellaneous Features

Each specification is compiled to an Oz functor, and only the procedures implementing public member function specifications are exported. This enforces SPECS-C++ accessibility rules, as only these procedures are visible from client test code and the GUI.

An existentially quantified variable of type **int** is translated to an Oz finite domain variable if its domain is explicitly specified as a range of integers, i.e.:

```
\exists int x [1 <= x <= 10 /\ ...]
```

and the range is within the possible values of an Oz finite domain variable. As each such variable is found, it is added to a single instance of an Oz class. This instance is then used to *distribute* over all of these variables at at the same time (after all constraints have been seen). The distribution strategy used determines the order in which these variables are considered during search. In particular, the execution system uses the built-in first fail distribution strategy, which means that the variable with the smallest domain is considered first, then the variable with the next smallest domain and so on. This strategy often explores a much smaller search tree than a naive distribution strategy (simply considering the variables in order of appearance in the program) would. For the first fail strategy to be most effective, all finite domain variables should be distributed at the same time. Hence, it is convenient to collect all such finite domain variables within an instance of a class, as instances have state and can be updated. For similar reasons, several data structures used by the GUI are implemented as classes.

Currently, the execution system does not take advantage of *propagators* for finite domains. Propagators are operators or procedures that reduce the domains of finite domain variables without performing search, and thus often dramatically decrease running times. For example, if the domain of variable X is {3, 5, 7} and of variable Y is {1,2,3,4,5}, then the constraint X <: Y (using the propagator <: in place of a less than comparison) immediately reduces the domain of X to {3} and of Y to {4,5}. The search tree now has 2 leaves (rather than 15), and so can be explored much more quickly. The execution system does not use these propagators because they can only be used with finite domain variables and constants, and we have found it difficult to test whether or not a variable is a finite domain variable without introducing additional problems. However, this is an important area for future work.

3   Conclusion

3.1   Future Work

Currently, the execution system does not handle inheritance in general and inheritance of specifications in particular. Additionally, the system does not check invariants – they are parsed and typechecked, but never executed. We are currently working on a version of the system for the Java Modeling Language (JML) [7] that will address these deficiencies.

We are aware that the use of **dis** statements has fallen out of favor within some parts of the Oz community, and we are investigating how the **dis** statements used in our system could be replaced by **choice** or **or** statements, or (preferably) how choice points could be removed altogether. However, because we are executing programs generated from specifications, we frequently do not know and can not control the mode of use of library operations. For example, the sequence index operation is essentially implemented in the library as:

```
proc {Index S N V}
    dis N = 1 then
          S = V | _
      [] SR N1 in S = _ | SR
             {Greater N 1}
          then
             {Plus N1 1 N}
             {Index SR N1 V}
      end
  end
```

where Plus and Greater are threaded library procedures with the obvious functionality. If the index parameter N is known, this procedure creates no choice points, and so is much more efficient than a version using **choice**. If N is not known, this procedure can find all indices where the value V occurs in the sequence S, or can insert V at any index within S (via backtracking). The problem is how to achieve this combination of flexibility and efficiency without using **dis**.

We are currently attempting to reduce or eliminate the use of **dis** by taking advantage of the search that is implicit for finite domain variables. For example, the index operation can mimic the standard `FD.element` constraint propagator in a naive manner [3], i.e.:

```
proc {Index S N V}
   thread
      local L in
         {List.length S L}
         N::1#L
         {List.nth S N V}
      end
   end
end
```

providing that the variable N is then included in distribution. `FD.element` can not be used directly because the elements of the list are not finite domain variables. Preliminary performance results for this approach are encouraging, but considerable work remains to be done to extend it to all library procedures that currently use **dis**.

In general, we are interested in any technique that increases the range of specifications that can be executed, or that increases the efficiency of the generated Oz programs and library code (without introducing implementation bias into specifications, of course). Specific areas for further work include making more sophisticated use of finite domain variables, incorporating finite set constraints, eliminating explicit choice points whenever possible, and improving the constraint propagation done by the library procedures. We are also interested in testing the system on a wider range of practical specifications in order to determine what kinds of additional performance improvements would be most beneficial.

3.2   Summary

We have developed a system that allows many formal specifications to be executed directly. Our system can execute specifications that are written at a high level of abstraction, so that executability does not compromise other uses (documentation, proof, etc.) of specifications. The generated programs and library procedures take advantage of many features of Oz. Threads, constraint propagation, computation spaces and search are used heavily in finding post states that satisfy specifications. The graphical user interface capabilities of Oz are critical for enabling users to freely interact with specifications, and for displaying references and aliasing directly. We have found Oz to be nearly ideal as a translation target language for formal specifications.

References

1. Jones, C.B.: Systematic Software Development Using VDM. Second edn. International Series in Computer Science. Prentice Hall, Englewood Cliffs, N.J. (1990)

---

[3] Thanks to Christian Schulte for suggesting this idea at the conference.

 2. Fitzgerald, J.S., Larsen, P.G.: Modelling Systems: Practical Tools and Techniques in Software Development. Cambridge University Press (1998) ISBN 0521623480.
 3. Spivey, J.M.: An introduction to Z and formal specifications. Software Engineering Journal **4** (1989) 40 – 50
 4. Davies, J., Woodcock, J.C.P.: Using Z: Specification, Refinement and Proof. International Series in Computer Science. Prentice Hall (1996)
 5. Abrial, J.R.: The B-Book: Assigning Programs to Meanings. Cambridge University Press (1996) ISBN 0 521 49619 5.
 6. B-Core(UK) Ltd: B-Core website (2004) http://www.B-core.com/.
 7. Leavens, G.T., Leino, K.R.M., Poll, E., Ruby, C., Jacobs, B.: JML: notations and tools supporting detailed design in Java. In: OOPSLA 2000 Companion, Minneapolis, Minnesota, ACM (2000) 105–106
 8. Wahls, T., Leavens, G.T.: Formal semantics of an algorithm for translating model-based specifications to concurrent constraint programs. In: Proceedings of the 16th ACM Symposium on Applied Computing, Las Vega, Nevada (2001) 567 – 575
 9. Wahls, T., Leavens, G.T., Baker, A.L.: Executing formal specifications with concurrent constraint programming. The Automated Software Engineering Journal **7** (2000)
10. West, M.M., Eaglestone, B.M.: Software development: Two approaches to animation of Z specifications using Prolog. IEE/BCS Software Engineering Journal **7** (1992) 264–276
11. Fuchs, N.: Specifications are (preferably) executable. Software Engineering Journal **7** (1992) 323 – 334
12. Gray, J.G., Schach, S.R.: Constraint animation using an object-oriented declarative language. In: Proceedings of the 38th Annual ACM SE Conference, Clemson, SC (2000) 1 – 10
13. O'Neill, G.: Automatic translation of VDM specifications into Standard ML programs. The Computer Journal **35** (1992) 623–624
14. Elmstrøm, R., Larsen, P.G., Lassen, P.B.: The IFAD VDM-SL toolbox: A practical approach to formal specifications. ACM Sigplan Notices **29** (1994) 77 – 80
15. Fröhlich, B.: Program Generation Based on Implicit Definitions in a VDM-like Language. PhD thesis, Technical University of Graz (1998)
16. Jackson, D., Damon, C.: Semi-executable specifications. Technical Report CMU-CS-95-216, School of Computer Science, Carnegie Mellon University (1995)
17. Breuer, P.T., Bowen, J.P.: Towards correct executable semantics for Z. In Bowen, J.P., Hall, J.A., eds.: Z User Workshop, Cambridge 1994. Workshops in Computing, Springer-Verlag (1994)
18. Grieskamp, W.: A computation model for Z based on concurrent constraint resolution. In Bowen, J.P., Dunne, S., Galloway, A., King, S., eds.: ZB 2000: Formal Specification and Development in Z and B, First International Conference of Z and B Users. Volume 1878 of Lecture Notes in Computer Science., York, UK, Springer-Verlag (2000) 414 – 432
19. Mehl, M., Müller, T., Popov, K., Scheidhauer, R., Schulte, C.: DFKI Oz User's Manual. Programming Systems Lab, German Research Center for Artificial Intelligence (DFKI) and Universität des Saarlandes, Postfach 15 11 50, D-66041 Saarbrücken, Germany. (1998)
20. Mozart Consortium: Mozart Programming System website (2004) http://www.mozart-oz.org.
21. Van Roy, P., Haridi, S.: Concepts, Techniques and Models of Computer Programming. The MIT Press, Cambridge, Massachusetts (2004)

22. Wu, D., Cheng, Y., Wahls, T.: A graphical user interface for executing formal specifications. The Journal of Computing in Small Colleges **17** (2002) 79 – 86
23. Marriott, K., Stuckey, P.J.: Programming with Constraints: An Introduction. The MIT Press, Cambridge, Massachusetts (1998)
24. Struyf, J., Blockeel, H.: Query optimization in inductive logic programming by reordering literals. In Horváth, T., Yamamoto, A., eds.: Proceedings of the 13th International Conference on Inductive Logic Programming. Volume 2835 of Lecture Notes in Artificial Intelligence., Springer-Verlag (2003) 329 – 346
25. Overton, D., Somogyi, Z., Stuckey, P.J.: Constraint-based mode analysis of Mercury. In: Proceedings of the 4th ACM SIGPLAN International Conference on Principles and Practice of Declarative Programming, Pittsburgh, PA, USA, ACM Press (2002) 109 – 120

Deriving Acceptance Tests from Goal Requirements

Jean-François Molderez and Christophe Ponsard

CETIC Research Center, Charleroi (Belgium)
{jfm, cp}@cetic.be

Abstract. Acceptance testing is formal testing conducted to determine whether or not a system satisfies its acceptance criteria and to enable the customer to determine whether or not to accept the system. An Acceptance Test Generator has been built in Oz that receives as input the formalized goal-based requirements of a system-to-be. In this framework, we motivate our choice of the Oz programming language.

1 Introduction

Acceptance testing is formal testing conducted to determine whether or not a system satisfies its acceptance criteria and to enable the customer to determine whether or not to accept the system [1]. Acceptance tests are thus black-box tests or specification-based tests performed by a customer unaware of architecture and code aspects in contrast with code-based tests or white box tests which look inside the code. Software testing is labor intensive and there is a need to generate these tests automatically. Most tools generating specification-based tests use as main input an operational model and are based on model-checking (e.g. [4]). However, it can be advantageous to generate tests from the requirements themselves even in the absence of an actual operational model. This has at least two advantages : the designer can sooner validate the requirements and the tests produced can serve as plans for more detailed tests downstream the development cycle. In what follows, we describe an Acceptance Test Generator built with the Oz programming language and based on goal oriented requirements.

Goal oriented requirements engineering refers to the use of goals for requirements elicitation and elaboration. Goals are objectives to be achieved by the system under consideration. They refer to functional or non functional properties and range from high level concerns (e.g. safe transportation for a train control system[1]) to lower level ones(e.g. maintain door closed while moving).

In the KAOS methodology [2], the main elaboration process builds a *goal model*, i.e. a tree where ancestor nodes referring to abstract (strategic/system-wide) goals are successively refined into descendant nodes referring to more concrete (operational/local) goals. This refinement process can bear upon various

---

[1] As running example for this paper, we will use a simple railway system.

P. Van Roy (Ed.): MOZ 2004, LNCS 3389, pp. 78–88, 2005.

tactics known as refinement patterns [3] which help the designer in finding a correct set of children goals for a given goal. The refinement process goes on until the leaf goals or terminal goals become realizable [6]. A *realizable goal* is a goal whose satisfaction can be assigned as a responsibility to a software, hardware or human agent. If assigned to an agent in the system-to-be, it is a *requirement*. If assigned to an agent in the environment, it is an *assumption*. Besides requirements and assumptions, *domain properties* are properties in the environment that hold independently of the system-to-be.

By formalizing goals, requirements, assumptions and domain properties it becomes possible to check the validity of the refinements and to generate possible scenarii of use of the future system. These scenarii can be used to validate the goals and possibly to refine them further. Once the requirements become stable, these scenarii take the status of acceptance tests.

The concrete acceptance tests generated from the formal properties are finite sequences of states or traces where each state is a set of propositions holding in that state. These traces are representative logical models of the properties and are thus generated by satisfying them. The formal language used in KAOS is the Linear Temporal Logic, abbreviated LTL [7]. The standard models of LTL are infinite execution traces reflecting the behaviors of reactive and concurrent systems as being ideally always ready to respond to requests. However, in a testing context, the traces are finite and therefore we use a finite trace semantics of LTL [5] to generate the tests. The syntax and the finite trace semantics of LTL are described in section 2 where the choice of the semantics is further motivated.

In section 3, the derivation process is detailed on a simple railway unload system. This process relies on heuristics (1) to partition the set of possible histories, based on the metaknowledge captured in the goal model and (2) to stress the system with respect to the safety requirements. Both yield a set of constraints on the system history. The problem of producing a trace can thus be translated into a CSP problem and a constraint solver can be used to produce the actual acceptance tests. Section 4 describes our implementation and explains why the Oz programming language was chosen. Finally, in section 5, we summarize our approach and open further research directions.

2   Background on Linear Temporal Logic

In addition to the usual first order logic operators ($\wedge \vee \neg \rightarrow \leftrightarrow$), classical linear temporal logic (LTL) provides a number of temporal operators for the future: $\circ$ (next), $\square$ (always), $\diamond$ (eventually) and $\mathcal{U}$ (until)[7]. The dual past operators can also be defined but will not be considered here. The following shorthand notations will be used: $P \Rightarrow Q \equiv \square(P \rightarrow Q)$, $P \Leftrightarrow Q \equiv \square(P \leftrightarrow Q)$ and $@P \equiv \neg P \wedge \circ P$. The last one denotes a change of P's truth value from P from currently *false* to *true* in the next state; a similar notation is used in [4].

A standard LTL model is a function $t : \mathcal{N}^+ \rightarrow 2^{\mathcal{P}}$ for some set of atomic propositions $\mathcal{P}$, i.e. an infinite trace over the alphabet $2^{\mathcal{P}}$, which maps each time point (a natural number) into the set of propositions that hold at that point. However, in the context of a goal model, the traces are logical models of requirements and assumptions which are by definition realizable [6], i.e. properties that can be implemented as operations. A necessary condition for realizability of a property is that it must constrain the finite runs of its responsible agent. Therefore a finite trace semantics defining what it means for a finite trace to satisfy a LTL formula is adopted here.

In this finite trace semantics [5], each trace is regarded as an infinite stationary trace in which the last state is repeated infinitely. Assume two total functions on traces, $head : Trace \rightarrow State$ returning the head state of a trace and $length$ returning the length of a finite trace, and a partial function $tail : Trace \rightarrow Trace$ for taking the tail of a trace. That is, $head(e, t) = head(e) = e, tail(e, t) = t$, and $length(e) = 1$ and $length(e, t) = 1 + length(t)$.

The satisfaction relation $\models \subseteq Trace \times formula$ defines when a trace t satisfies a formula f, written $t \models f$, and is defined inductively over the structure of the formulae as follows, where A is any atomic proposition and X and Y are any formulae. In the case of state formulas that do not include temporal operators, the semantics is:

$$
\begin{aligned}
t &\models true & &\text{iff } true \\
t &\models false & &\text{iff } false \\
t &\models A & &\text{iff } A \in head(t) \\
t &\models X \wedge Y & &\text{iff } t \models X \text{ and } t \models Y \\
t &\models X \vee Y & &\text{iff } t \models X \text{ or } t \models Y
\end{aligned}
$$

In the case of formulas with temporal operators where the current state e is not terminal, the semantics is:

$$
\begin{aligned}
e, t &\models \circ X & &\text{iff } t \models X \\
e, t &\models @X & &\text{iff } e \models \neg X \text{ and } t \models X \\
e, t &\models \Diamond X & &\text{iff } e, t \models X \text{ or } t \models \Diamond X \\
e, t &\models \Box X & &\text{iff } e, t \models X \text{ and } t \models \Box X \\
e, t &\models X \, \mathcal{U} \, Y & &\text{iff } e, t \models Y \text{ or } e, t \models X \text{ and } t \models X \, \mathcal{U} \, Y
\end{aligned}
$$

In the case of formulas with temporal operators where the current state e ends the trace, the semantics is:

$$
\begin{aligned}
e &\models \circ X & &\text{iff } e \models X \\
e &\models @X & &\text{iff } false \\
e &\models \Diamond X & &\text{iff } e \models X \\
e &\models \Box X & &\text{iff } e \models X \\
e &\models X \, \mathcal{U} \, Y & &\text{iff } e \models Y
\end{aligned}
$$

The semantics of the $\circ$ operator reflects perhaps best the stationarity assumption of last states in finite traces. Finite trace LTL can behave quite differently from standard infinite trace LTL. There are formulas which are valid in the former but not in the later, for example: $\Diamond(\Box A \vee \Box \neg A)$ for any atomic proposition A.

3   Generation of Acceptance Tests

3.1   A Formal Requirements Model for a Train Docking System

In this section, we present a rather contrived example of a railway station managing four blocks on which trains can move to be unloaded: an *Accept* block on which the trains enter the station, a *Wait* block on which trains can wait until the *Unload* block becomes available and an *Out* block.

The object model in figure 1 shows that there is only one relation, the relation *On* between *Train* and *Block*. The *Accept* and *Wait* blocks have a signal *Ok* authorizing the trains to leave these blocks to proceed to the *Unload* block.

In the KAOS methodology, this model is derived from a full goal analysis in order to abstract only the relevant aspects of the problem. Those goals can be divided in two main categories:

- *progress goals*, stating a state that the system has to reach during its history. Figure 2 shows the refinement of the main progress goal for our system, ie. that all incoming train will eventually come out unloaded.
- *safety goals*, stating invariants which have to be maintained throughout the system history. Due to space limits, the goal analysis will not be shown here but notice that one of the cardinality constraints of the object model is related to such a goal ("there can be at most one train on a block"). Note also that the other cardinality ("a train cannot occupy 2 blocks") is a domain property.

In acceptance tests, the input-output relation between the system-to-be and its environment is considered. In our case, the system is composed of the *Station Manager* software agent while the environment is mainly composed of trains and their drivers.

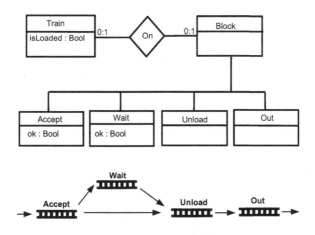

Fig. 1. Object Model

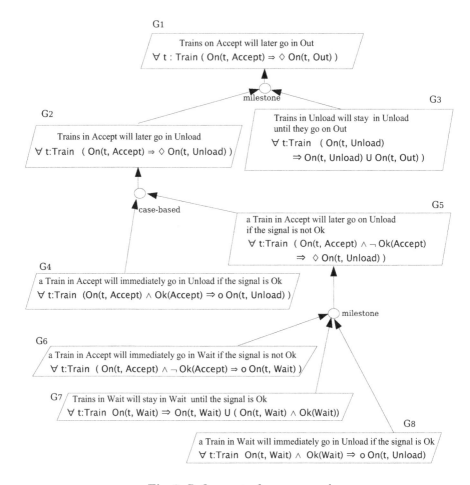

Fig. 2. Refinement of progress goal

In figure 2, the goal model obtained by refining the main progress goal G_1 stating that any train entering the station will eventually leave it, is shown. All leaf goals appear to be assumptions as the progress of a train is the responsibility of the train (driver), an agent in the environment.

In contrast, the *Station Manager* is mainly responsible of the following safety requirements:

- *Req$_1$*: It never happens that the two signals allow at the same time trains to proceed to the *Unload* block.

$$Ok(Accept) \Rightarrow \neg(\exists t : Train \quad On(t, Unload)) \land \neg(Ok(Wait))$$

- *Req$_2$*: When the *Unload* block is occupied, there is no signal allowing a train to proceed to the *Unload* block.

$$\forall t : Train \quad On(t, Unload) \Rightarrow (\neg Ok(Accept) \land \neg Ok(Wait))$$

We will also consider the following domain properties for capturing the spatial layout and making the temporal behavior more precise:

- Dom_1: A train on the blocks *Accept, Wait, Unload* is a train which is loaded.
  $$\forall t : Train \quad (On(t, Accept) \lor On(t, Unload) \lor On(t, Wait))$$
  $$\Leftrightarrow isLoaded(t)$$
- Dom_2: A train can only enter the station via the *Accept* block.
  $$\forall t : Train \quad @(\exists b : Block \quad On(t, b)) \Rightarrow \circ(On(t, Accept))$$
- Dom_3: Unloading a train takes at least two time steps.
  $$\forall t : Train \quad @On(t, Unload) \Rightarrow \circ(\circ On(t, Unload))$$

Those requirements together with the progress assumptions and domain properties ensure that there will never be two trains on the *Unload* block. No scheduling is performed and the responsibility of the occupation of the *Accept* and *Wait* blocks by only one train is left to the environment.

3.2   Generation of Acceptance Tests

The covering problem, how to define the relation between tests and the model from which to derive the tests, is a difficult one. One way to tackle this problem is to use heuristics bearing upon the rich KAOS ontology that includes concepts such as the refinement patterns, the responsibilities of agents, the obstacles and conflicts. These heuristics can be represented as rules extracting from the model additional properties used to select the best representative traces among all the possible behaviors of the system. These best representative are the acceptance tests and they will be generated by satisfying boolean constraints resulting from the translation of the assumptions, requirements, domain properties and additional properties. In what follows, two heuristics are detailed : the first one bears upon the case refinements in the goal tree while the second one aims at stressing the system as much as possible. For all these tests, we assume a same initial and final state where there are no trains on the blocks. A criterion to find a good representative is to minimize its cost. An important cost element of a trace is its length which will thus be minimized.

The complexity of the constraint satisfaction process is exponential in the length of the traces, in the size of the formula and in the cardinality of the product of the domains. This is an additional incentive to shorten the traces as much as possible as well as to minimize the number of instances involved in the acceptance tests.

Covering of the Case Refinements. The heuristics will first collect the subtrees in the goal tree that match the refinements by cases. A refinement by cases follows the common pattern in which a father goal $P \Rightarrow R$ is refined into cases $C_i \Rightarrow R$ where the C_i partition P. In the example on figure 2, the refinement of G_2 into G_4 and G_5 follow this pattern and the two cases are : $On(t, Accept) \land Ok(Accept)$ and $On(t, Accept) \land \neg Ok(Accept)$. These two conditions partition the set of all the admissible behaviors into two classes. Had there been additional refinements by cases in the subtrees of G_4 and G_5, these two classes would have been further partitioned.

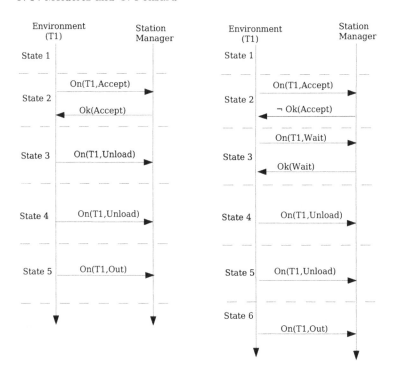

Fig. 3. Acceptance test derived from refinements by cases

Next, the heuristic creates, for each case, test specifications by adding the corresponding case conditions to the concerned formal properties. By concerned properties, we mean that only the properties present in the corresponding sub-tree of a case will be retained in the corresponding test specification. The case condition is the property that makes the test specification correspond to its class. In our example, the case conditions are:

$\Diamond(On(t_{\#1}, Accept) \wedge Ok(Accept)$ for G_4 and
$\Diamond(On(t_{\#1}, Accept) \wedge \neg Ok(Accept)$ for G_5
where $t_{\#1}$ is an instance of $Train$.

The initial and final state of the traces will also be included in these test specifications. In the example, the initial and the final state are a same state in which the substation is empty. As stated before, when trying to satisfy these specifications, the shortest traces where the final state is reached as soon as possible will be looked for. This is done by giving a preference to the presence of a final state in a trace of a predefined maximal length.

The two test specifications are then fed to the constraint satisfaction engine which outputs the two traces. Those are visually depicted in figure 3 using a *Message Sequence Chart* style. It mainly shows a sequence of states. Each state is specified as a (unordered) set of messages exchanged between the system and the environment, in a way or the other following who is monitoring/controlling

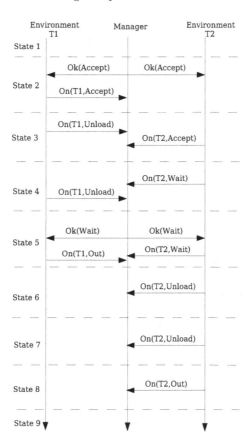

Fig. 4. Acceptance test stressing the system

that state information. Only messages carrying the state information delta with respect to the previous state are shown. The left trace shows a scenario where an incoming train is immediately accepted for unload, while the left trace shows a scenario where it as to go through the *Wait* block.

Stressing the System. With the two preceding acceptance tests, the basic logic of the system was covered. However, these tests are rather weak in the sense that they only cover the assumptions refined by cases. To validate the requirements that prevent two trains from being at the same time on the *Unload* block, we make two trains $t_{\#1}$ and $t_{\#2}$ enter the station by feeding the additional property:

$$\circ(@On(t_{\#1}, Accept)) \wedge \circ(\circ(@On(t_{\#2}, Accept)))$$

where $t_{\#1}$ and $t_{\#2}$ are two instances of $Train$.

Again, the two trains must leave the station as soon as possible. The resulting acceptance test of length 9 is shown on figure 4 and is an intertwined combination of the scenarii of figure 3: the first incoming train (T1, on the left lifeline) is immediately accepted but forces a second train (T2, on the right lifeline) to go through the *Wait* block until the *Unload* block becomes available. This kind of complex interaction is precisely the kind of tests wished for evaluating the system compliance to its requirements.

4   Implementation

As already mentioned, the very heart of the generation process is the translation of the formulas into boolean constraints that must be satisfied. Oz is a full fledged programming language that includes constraint programming facilities, ie. hard constraints expressing links (or relationships) among programmer defined entities can be stated and a constraint solver program ensures that these links are enforced. In our context, the entities are the components making up the states in the traces and the links relate these components. For example, a constraint could express that if a train is on the *Unload* block in this state, then in the next state, the same train must be on the *Out* block. Besides these hard constraints that must be enforced, weak constraints are optimization criteria for the constraint solver. In our context, the weak constraint is that the solver must look for a trace where the final state is reached as soon as possible. On figure 5, a data flow diagram shows the architecture of the acceptance test generator.

The test specification is a pickled record containing the object model, all the formal properties and the additional test data : number of instances, initial and final conditions, possible case conditions and predefined maximal length for the test. The formal properties are fed to the *LTL Formula Parser* while a *Knowl-*

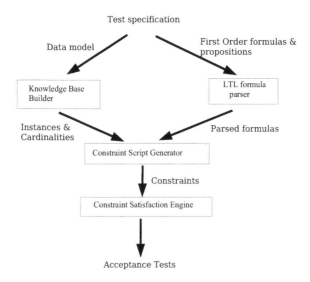

Fig. 5. Architecture of the acceptance tests generator

edge Base Builder processes the object model and outputs some dictionaries mainly used for instances bookkeeping purposes. The *Constraint Script Generator* is a set of functions that generate and tells the constraints to the *Constraint Satisfaction Engine*. There are two main functions : the first one tells the constraints obtained by recursively translating the parsed formula trees, following the rules of the LTL semantics (see Section2) and the second one tells the cardinality constraints. Finally, the *Constraint Satisfaction Engine* generates the shortest traces by branch and bound.

Alternatives to the Oz programming language are of course available to solve the same problem. But we experienced Oz as the best compromise for ease of programming and this, for three main reasons:

1. as already been mentioned, *Oz is a full fledged programming language with constraint programming facilities* and there is no need to implement a bridge between a mainstream language program on one side and a constraint solver on the other one.

2. another reason which makes us prefer Oz to other solutions like the use of a SAT solver or the precompilation of the formula into finite automata is the *ability to deal with weak constraints*. The ability to provide the constraint solver with search criteria to look for better solutions is essential in a testing framework since tests must be somewhere the best representatives among all the possible behaviors of a system. Every time there is a limit that may not be exceeded in a requirement, a weak constraint can be stated to produce an acceptance test corresponding to a behavior in which this limit is reached as often as possible. In a railway context, for example, the limit would be the distance expressed in number of blocks to maintain between successive trains and the acceptance test would exhibit a number of trains entering a station with a minimal distance between them.

3. a last reason is the *natural combination in Oz of higher order programming and constraint programming*. Consider a cardinality constraint stating that there may be between 0 and 10 trains on a block *Bl*. The following simple Oz code takes care of this:

    Again, this kind of constraints about integers would not so easily be handled with a SAT solver or a finite automaton.

5   Conclusion

Acceptance tests have been automatically generated from a formal model of the requirements. The generation algorithm receives as input a data and requirements model built with the KAOS methodology. Acceptance test specifications are then built by applying different heuristics. These specifications partition the set of all the possible behaviors by adding additional constraints to select the best representative traces. The formal properties and the additional constraints are then fed to a constraint solver engine which outputs the actual acceptance tests.

Starting from this, there are two directions to enhance the test generator. *Upstream*, a rule engine could be operated to apply the heuristics on the metaknowledge stored in the requirements model. For example, conflicts in requirements are often resolved by the introduction of boundary conditions. An additional heuristic could be designed to select these boundaries and generate test specifications. *Downstream*, if an operations model reflecting the transition relation among the states is available, the acceptance test specifications can be used as specifications of plans to generate more concrete tests which will show the explicit application of the operations.

The toy example presented in this paper is an excerpt from a larger railway signaling system including a level-crossing description. The model was built in the context of the replacement of a large number of level-crossings by the Belgian railway company. The initial specification is essentially an operational description leaving many critical goals implicit. Our plan is to validate our goal-coverage heuristics on this real-world case. The test generator will also be integrated in a larger requirements engineering toolbox, called FAUST, whose aim is to provide early quality assurance for critical systems [8]. An interesting feature will be the ability to animate the generated traces using a requirements animator providing domain-based visualizations [9].

Acknowledgement

This work is financially supported by the European Union (ERDF and ESF) and the Walloon Region (DGTRE). We also thank Andre Rifaut and Philippe Massonet for their helpful comments in writing this paper.

References

1. IEEE Std 610.12-1990, *IEEE standard glossary of software engineering terminology*, 1990.
2. A. Dardenne, A. van Lamsweerde, and Stephen Fickas, *Goal-directed requirements acquisition*, Science of Computer Programming **20** (1993), no. 1-2, 3–50.
3. R. Darimont and A. van Lamsweerde, *Formal refinement patterns for goal-driven requirements elaboration*, 4th ACM Symp. on the Foundations of Software Engineering, San Francisco, 1996.
4. A. Gargantini and C. Heitmeyer, *Using model checking to generate tests from requirements specifications*, ESEC/FSE 99 Toulouse (France), LNCS 1687, 1999.
5. K. Havelund and G. Rosu, *Rewriting-based techniques for runtime verification*, To appear in Journal of Automated Software Engineering. (2004).
6. E. Letier and A. van Lamsweerde, *Agent-based tactics for goal-oriented requirements elaboration*, 2002.
7. Z. Manna and A. Pnueli, *The reactive behavior of reactive and concurrent system*, Springer-Verlag, 1992.
8. The FAUST toolbox, http://faust.cetic.be, 2004.
9. H. Tran Van, A. van Lamsweerde, P. Massonet, and C. Ponsard, *Goal-oriented requirements animation*, 12th IEEE Int.Req.Eng.Conf., Kyoto, September 2004.

Using Mozart for Visualizing Agent-Based Simulations

Hala Mostafa and Reem Bahgat

Faculty of Computers and Information
Cairo University, Cairo, Egypt
{h.mostafa, r.bahgat}@fci-cu.edu.eg

Abstract. Scientists from various domains resort to agent-based simulation for a more thorough understanding of complex real-world systems. We developed the Agent Visualization System; a generic system that can be added to a simulation environment to enrich it with a variety of browsers allowing the modeler to gain insight into his simulation scenario. In this paper we discuss how the various features of the Oz language and the Mozart platform aided us in the development of our system. Of particular importance were dataflow variables, high-orderness, the support for distribution and concurrency, the flexibility offered by QTk which was crucial in generating browsers whose structure is only known at runtime, in addition to a miscellany of features that were conductive to our work. We also highlight some of the implementation difficulties we faced and explain the techniques we utilized in overcoming them.

1   Introduction

Domains as varied as biology and mechanical physics have resorted to Agent-Based Simulation (ABS) to capture the behavior of, and interaction between, entities in their respective systems. An agent can be thought of as a software component which not only encapsulates code and data as in object-oriented programming, but can also be pro-active, autonomous, adaptive and collaborative [14].

In ABS, a scenario of entities that interact with each other and with their environment is modeled as a multi-agent system, hence the name Multi-Agent-Based Simulation (MABS). A MABS usually involves agents of different types. Each type represents a class of entities in the real-world system and captures its relevant attributes and behaviors. Compared to simulation techniques which assume that all instances of a certain entity are alike, ABS has the advantage of being able to explicitly model the heterogeneity of real-world entities by allowing entities of the same type to differ in their attribute values and behaviors [13].

The increasing demand for MABS by scientists foreign to the field of computer science created a need for simulation environments that facilitate rapid development of MABSs. One of the main facilities that should be provided by such platforms is the ability to visualize the proceedings of a simulation scenario from different perspectives without requiring the modeler to delve into technicalities.

P. Van Roy (Ed.): MOZ 2004, LNCS 3389, pp. 89–102, 2005.
© Springer-Verlag Berlin Heidelberg 2005

Visualization

Information visualization (IV) is a research domain that aims at supporting discovery and analysis of data through visual exploration. Its principle is to map the attributes of an abstract data structure to visual attributes such as Cartesian position, color and size [2]. IV is one means of carrying out Exploratory Data Analysis which aims at the manipulation, summarization, and display of data to make them more comprehensible to human minds, thus uncovering interesting trends and relationships. Some IV tools rely on an *interface metaphor*; they allow the user to operate on data in the same way he operates on things in real life (e.g. the lens metaphor [11] where data is displayed differently when viewed through different lenses, and the rubber sheet metaphor [8] which allows the user to stretch parts of the display, thus revealing more details)

In this paper we illustrate how we used the Oz language, the Mozart development platform [7] and the QTk graphical package [5] to implement the Agent Visualization System (AVS); the first generic, distributed system specifically dedicated to the visualization of agent-based simulation scenarios [6]. The AVS is used as an add-on to a simulation environment to equip it with a rich set of visualization facilities offering a variety of textual and graphical browsers that allow the modeler to detect trends and relationships in the simulation scenario. Some techniques from IV were adapted and added to our system, while others were devised especially to be used in it. Regardless of their origin, all visualization techniques were thoroughly revised to make them generic enough to fit in our generic system.

The structure of the paper is as follows: Section 2 discusses some of the challenges faced in visualizing agents and the requirements fulfilled by our AVS. Section 3 describes the various browsers that make up the AVS while Section 4 outlines the high-level design of our system and its usage. Section 5 discusses some implementation issues and the various Mozart features that are involved in them. Some of the difficulties we faced are also mentioned, together with how they were overcome. We conclude and briefly discuss areas for future work in Section 6.

2   Agent Visualization Challenges and Requirements

The issue of visualization is of primary importance in ABS. The modeler needs to be presented with a view of the simulation that allows him to make and verify hypotheses regarding relationships between the various entities in it. However, the task of agent visualization poses major challenges, the most notable of which is that an agent's state is continuously changing, thus the data to be visualized is dynamic rather than static. At the same time, the responsiveness of the system is a key requirement, so those changes have to be visually reflected within an acceptable time limit. The volume of data to be visualized poses another challenge since a large number of agents is typically involved in a MABS, each of which has a set of attributes that the modeler may like to observe. Moreover, the nature of simulation data is usually not restricted to variable-value pairs with which traditional IV techniques are most effective. Rather, the simulation produces data concerning actions, events and communication between agents in addition to variable-value pairs describing agents states. A visualization system should therefore include means to visually represent this multitude of data types.

Our AVS attempts to handle these challenges. In addition, the following are some requirements that are fulfilled by our system: In order to be usable in a wide variety of MABSs, the AVS needs to be completely generic; it should not require any a priori information about the particulars of the simulation scenario being visualized (agent types, together with their attributes and attribute meta-data, should be known only at run time), nor should it make assumptions about the domain of the simulation. Another requirement concerns the flexibility of the AVS. The user should have full control over the way his agents are represented, whether textually or graphically. Moreover, the user should be able to specify which subset(s) of agents he wants to observe in any given browser by choosing agents by ID, type, or location, or by expressing interest in agents satisfying certain criteria. In order to abide by the famous IV mantra *"Overview first, zoom and filter, then details on demand"* [10], the AVS is required, at all times, to provide an overall view of the proceedings of the simulation scenario, as well as allow the user to obtain details about any part of it. In order to both promote collaboration and distribute the computational load, it is advantageous to have a distributed AVS where observers can launch browsers from remote sites just as easily as they would from a central site. Another requirement concerns how often the display of an AVS browser is refreshed. Depending on the rate at which interesting events happen in a simulation scenario, the modeler may choose to be shown every single step of the simulation. Alternatively, he may only be interested in every nth step. For any browser, the user should be able to set the value of n, with the ability to freeze a view and create static browsers which are only refreshed on demand. Finally, when running in real-time mode, the AVS can skip the visualization of some older time units in favor of newer ones. The modeler may then miss some important or rare events in the course of a simulation. The AVS should therefore be able to run in playback mode where the user can step through the simulation at leisure.

3   AVS Browsers

The AVS offers the following browsers which provide graphical and textual representations of the simulation scenario (for more details, please refer to [6]).

- **Lens browser**: in Magic Lens filters [11] the lens metaphor is used for filtration, as well as presenting alternative views, of the underlying data. Our adaptation of the lens filter allows the user to set the acceptance criteria for the lens, move it over the environment where his agents live, and only view through it those agents satisfying the criteria.
- **Labeling browser**: this browser uses *dynamic labels* illustrated in Ex-centric Labels [1] for agents in densely-populated areas where static labels would occlude neighboring agents. The user moves a labeling region over his area of interest and only the agents within this region are labeled (Fig-

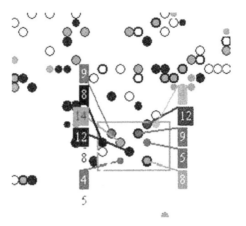

Fig. 1. Dynamic Labeling in a crowded area

ure 1). When the user moves the region, the set of labeled agents changes accordingly. Color is used to associate agents and their labels. We devised a placement algorithm to make sure that a label is as close as possible to its associated agent. In addition, the modeler can specify, for each agent type, the agent attribute whose value will be used to label agents of this type.

- **Aggregation browser**: when the region of interest is too large to be displayed in its entirety, the aggregate browser uses 1 cell to represent every N x N sub-region in the original simulation landscape, where N is specified by the user. All agents of a certain type in the sub-region appear as a single agent whose attributes are calculated from those of individual agents according to functions specified by the user (e.g. minimum, maximum, average). Choosing to expand a marquee-selected region creates a new browser showing the interesting region at normal size. The high degree of flexibility offered by Mozart made it possible to treat aggregate agents the same as normal ones; features like lens filters and dynamic labeling operate on a grid of agents, regardless of the nature of the agents inside the grid.

- **Dynamic Query (DQ) browser**: DQ is a way to dynamically and visually control the amount of data on display [4]. In a DQ display, the user executes a query on his dataset and watches the results of this query. This is done by associating with each data attribute an input control whose manipulation changes the chosen values for this attribute. The sub-queries formed by the controls are ANDed to form the overall query. In our DQ browser (Figure 2), the controls are automatically generated based on which attributes the user includes in the query (e.g. range slider controls for numeric attributes and radiobuttons for categorical ones). As the user manipulates these controls, the result pane instantly reflects the changes by showing agents that meet the current query and hiding all others.

- **Brushing-based browser**: the notion of brushing [9] is used in this browser to associate the sender of a message with its recipient(s). On clicking an agent's graphical representation, the same color is assigned to

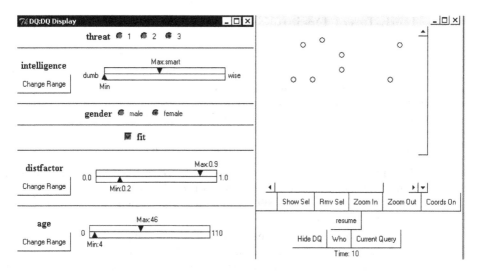

Fig. 2. A Dynamic Query browser with the controls on the left and result pane on the right

this agent and all the agents with whom he exchanged messages during the displayed time unit. A random color is assigned to the brushed entities. In order not to mislead the observer, the original colors of the agents are restored when brushing is no longer active, since color may encode an attribute value. The browser acts like a normal browser in all other respects and can be combined with any other feature.

- **Fading browser**: borrowing on ideas from Chat Circles [12], this browser makes it easier for the user to identify the most active participants in a conversation and observe the general pattern of communication. The color of an agent brightens every time he "speaks" and gradually fades during periods of silence. Optionally, a pop-up containing the message's label can appear next to an agent every time he sends a message.

- **Conversation sequence browser**: this browser focuses on conversations held among a group of agents. Inspired by Protocol Diagrams [3], we use a vertical line, called lifeline, for each agent, while messages are shown as labeled horizontal lines from sender to receiver. The user specifies the agents of interest and can later choose to add or delete a lifeline and change the message field used as a label. Clicking a message textually displays its details in a side browser.

- **Text browser**: the AVS allows the modeler to create text browsers that direct their output to either a file or a textual browser. This is convenient when the level of detail required by the user is high or when a persistent record is needed.

4   High-Level Design

In deciding whether the simulation system and the AVS should operate synchronously, we chose to allow them to go at their own paces, with the AVS operating on the most recent simulation data and discarding older data. The simulation should merely dump its output to files that the AVS can later process. These files also act as useful recordings of simulation runs, thus allowing the AVS to replay old runs.

The AVS therefore consists of the following four stages:

- **The readers** are notified by the mirror store to fetch data from files generated by the simulation system when the AVS is ready to process them.
- **The mirror store (MS)** uses input from the readers to construct a faithful replica of the simulation system at a certain point in time, thus acting as a local store for states/messages to avoid querying the simulation system every time a browser requires data. The MS also calculates values of *derived attributes* (as opposed to *raw attributes* which constitute the agent state as reported by the simulation system) using the calculation rules specified by the user (for example, the user can add the Boolean derived attribute isEligible that is true if the following conditions on raw attributes hold: (age == 18) and (gender == male)).
- **The dispatcher** is responsible for keeping track of the interests of the various browsers. In a large simulation, it would be unwise to forward data about every agent to every browser every time unit. Therefore, upon creation, a browser informs the dispatcher of its initial interests which are later used to decide which states/messages are sent to it and when. A browser can later modify its registered interests (e.g. when the user scrolls the display, the browser becomes interested in a different region of the simulation and thus updates its interests).
- **The browser** renders data received from the dispatcher depending on the graphical mapping specified for it (see next section). A browser can be *dynamic* or *static*. The MS pushes data to dynamic browsers on a regular basis whereas a static browser pulls data whenever the user explicitly asks for an updated view by pressing the refresh button.

AVS Usage

To use the AVS with a simulation system, the latter should periodically output the state of the simulation to a known location on the file system. It should also establish a socket connection with the AVS over which it sends a token at the end of every simulated time unit. When the AVS starts, it reads information about the simulation (environment dimensions, agent types, attributes, attribute types and legal values) from a simple text file. A GUI then asks the user to specify any derived attributes and the rules that will be used to calculate them from raw ones. To create a browser, the user provides a specification file containing the browser's type (e.g. text, aggregate), whether it is dynamic or static (and in the former case, the refresh rate), region of interest and criteria for displaying agents, together with any additional features (e.g. lens filter). In the case of graphical browsers, a GUI asks the user how each agent type will be represented graphically. All these specifications can be stored to a file for later use with other browsers.

5   Implementation Issues

5.1   QTk-Related Issues

The Graphical Mapping. For all graphical browsers except the Conversation Sequence browser, the user specifies how an agent's graphical representation is calculated from its state. This is done by specifying a *graphical mapping* from the values of the attributes making up an agent's state to the values of various graphical properties of the shape representing this agent (e.g. color can depend on attribute a1 through an if-statement, width can be calculated by dividing attribute a2 by 10 and height can be determined by the average of attributes a3 and a4).

The user specifies the mapping through a GUI that uses the Tree control developed by Donatien Grolaux at the Université Catholique de Louvain. Nodes at the first level of the tree are associated with graphical properties of the shape chosen to represent agents of the type in question (Figure 3). Our customized node inherits from Grolaux's TreeNode to extend it with an awareness of what kind of node this is (property, expression, if, then, end or elseif). Each of these kinds responds differently when clicked. For example, clicking a 'property' node results in a dialog box asking whether the value should be calculated using a constant, a mathematical expression involving constants and agent attribute names or an if-statement. If the user chooses an if-statement, a sub-tree of if-then-else/end/elseif nodes is attached to the 'property' node. On clicking an 'if' node, the user is asked to enter a Boolean expression. Clicking 'then' and 'else' nodes allows the user to either enter an expression, or choose to have a further level of if-statements, in which case a new sub-tree of if-then-else/end/elseif nodes is inserted.

The final form of the entire tree is parsed into a nested Oz record which, when it is time to draw an agent of the type in question, is evaluated by replacing attribute names with actual values of the agent's attributes and carrying out the operations specified by the sub-records. The result is a set of values used to set the various properties of the shape representing the agent.

Implementing Dynamic Queries. QTk's flexibility played an important role in the dynamic generation of input controls for the DQ browser. Because QTk allows the programmer to specify the window structure at run-time, it was possible to have the DQ browser consult the meta-data of the attributes forming the query and construct the DQ window accordingly (i.e. decide on the types of input controls based on the query attributes). However, we faced a certain difficulty: the controls for which DQ was most famous are missing in QTk. Range-sliders and alpha-sliders, used to manipulate numerical and ordered string attributes,

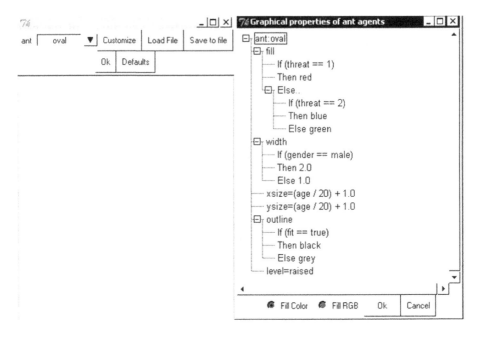

Fig. 3. The GUI for specifying the graphical mapping

respectively, are not part of QTk's repertoire. We therefore used QTk's canvas items to hand-craft a general slider control that can be used as a range-slider if initialized with a range of numbers, or an alpha-slider if initialized with an ordered list of strings.

We used the *callback* technique to allow the slider to call methods in the outside world when certain user actions take place. This was greatly facilitated by Mozart's high-orderness; the callback procedures can be passed as arguments to slider methods. These procedures are invoked when the user moves the maximum and minimum pointers, represented by two triangles that respond to the appropriate mouse events. The trough of the slider is a rectangle whose tag responds to mouse clicks by making the label and pointer jump to where the mouse is. The assembled whole was wrapped in a class to hide the numerous details while offering methods that are typically supported by slider controls (e.g. setting the range of the slider, the increment of the pointers and, in case of an alpha-slider, the list of ordered strings that acts as a value source).

Controls available in QTk were not used for DQ as-is. Each one was wrapped in a class that is aware of the attribute it manipulates, the values it can take, and the message that should be sent to the browser every time the user manipulates it. These messages, expressing sub-queries, are used by the browser to determine which agents will be added/removed to/from the result set. We therefore avoid re-processing the entire new query and only consider "delta"; the part of the query that changed as a result of the user's last action. We believe this greatly improved the performance of the DQ browser.

Wrapping QTk's Tags. QTk's canvas tags are very basic entities that allow simple manipulation (e.g. scaling, moving, deletion) but do not provide for more advanced manipulation (e.g. resizing, selection, dragging). To overcome this shortcoming, it was necessary to create bindings to associate certain events with certain actions to achieve the desired effects (e.g. bind the left-mouse-down event to an action that makes the width of the tag's outline thicker in order to give the effect of being selectable). We therefore implemented BaseTag which is a class that encapsulates QTk's tag and keeps track of things like tagID, scale and tag size in logical units. Also implemented are the mixin classes Resizeable, Dragable, Selectable and Marquee, each of which can be mixed with BaseTag to produce hybrid tags exhibiting a set of behaviors.

Callback functions were again extensively used. For example, in the lens and dynamic labeling browsers, the lens and labeling region are instantiated from a mixture of BaseTag, Resizeable and Dragable and initialized with callback functions that should be called in cases of resizing and dragging. The lens's callback function receives the new lens region as a parameter and uses it to apply the filter to agents in this region. The labeling region's callback function labels agents who have just gotten inside the region and removes the labels of those who have moved out of it. In the case of the aggregate browser, marquee selection uses a tag instantiated from BaseTag and Marquee whose callback function updates the value of an attribute called RegionToExpand.

5.2 Synchronization-Related Issues

Synchronizing Data Rendering. As mentioned earlier, the AVS fetches simulation data from files generated by the simulation system when it is ready to process them. To declare its readiness to receive a new batch of data, the mirror store needs to make sure that all browsers have finished rendering the previous batch. But the browsers render their data concurrently. Therefore, a browser needs a way of finding out whether it is the last one to finish rendering, in which case it should notify the mirror store so that the latter can fetch more data.

Dataflow variables markedly facilitated handling this issue. The following pseudocode shows what the dispatcher needs to do when it sends data to browsers:

```
proc {SendToAll BrowsersList Token}
   case BrowsersList of [Browser] then
      {SendTokens Browser Token finishToken}
   elseof Browser|OtherBrowsers then
      declare T to be a free variable
      {SendTokens Browser Token T}
      {SendToAll OtherBrowsers T}
   end
end
```

The initial call to SendToAll uses the value beginToken as Token. The following variant of the famous Test-and-Set technique forms part of any browser, with a Mozart lock to ensure its atomicity:

```
fun {TestAndSet T1 T2}
   start atomic section
      if T1 and T2 are both bound return true
      else
         T1 = T2
         return false
      end
   end atomic section
end
```

When a browser finishes rendering its data, it sends its 2 tokens to the TestAnd-Set function and notifies the mirror store if the function returns true. Therefore, as they proceed concurrently, browsers unify the two tokens passed to them. The last browser to finish will find that both tokens are bound, and can then notify the mirror store that all browsers are done.

The Readers-Writers Problem. Operations on the mirror store are divided into write operations (simulation data is fetched from files and written to the store) and read operations (extracting the interests of browsers). The store is in an inconsistent state while it is being written to because part of it reflects the state of the simulation system at a certain time, while another part reflects the state of an earlier time. The programmer is therefore faced with a readers-writers problem.

To synchronize the various readers and writers, a Semaphore class was implemented using dataflow variables and the built-in locking property of classes. Three semaphore instances are needed: a readers mutex, a writers mutex and a readers-writers semaphore. The scheme is as follows:

- The readers mutex is used to guarantee mutual exclusion during incrementing the counter in the following pseudocode (note that the first reader/writer waits on the readers-writers semaphore and the last one signals it):

```
NumberOfReaders := NumberOfReaders + 1
If NumberOfReaders == 1 then
   wait on the readers-writers semaphore
```

The same goes for these steps:

```
NumberOfReaders := NumberOfReaders - 1
If NumberOfReaders == 0 then
   signal the readers-writers semaphore
```

- The writers mutex is used in a similar fashion. The difference between the classical readers-writers problem and ours is that in our case, writers can work in parallel since they write to non-overlapping regions of the store.
- The readers-writers semaphore is used to make sure that when one or more writers are active, readers are blocked, and vise versa. It is waited on by the first reader or writer, and signaled when the last reader or writer finishes.

The Canvas Mutual Exclusion Problem. A graphical browser draws on a QTk canvas that is accessed by more than one method for rendering, clearing and destroying it. Without proper precautions, these methods can undesirably interfere with each other's actions. For example, if clearing takes place during rendering, only the part that was rendered will be cleared, while other parts continue to have graphical entities and yet will be considered clear. If the canvas is destroyed while it is being drawn to, attempts will be made to access a non-existent canvas resulting in an error. For these reasons, it is necessary to have a canvas lock shared by all concerned parties. Two dataflow variables are also needed; shouldClose indicates when the user wants to close the browser, and canClose indicates when the canvas can actually be closed.

The pseudocode for the three relevant methods in a graphical browser is as follows (the methods for clearing and rendering are written as one):

```
meth clear/Render
    free canClose
    obtain canvas lock
       for all items to clear/render
          if shouldClose then break
          clear/render item
       end
    release canvas lock
    bind canClose
end
meth RequestClose
    shouldClose = true
end
```

An additional method is needed to allow an outside entity to know whether it is ok to close a browser, thus destroying its canvas. The method is blocking; it waits until it is ok to close the browser then returns.

```
meth Closable
    wait on canClose
end
```

The combined use of dataflow variables, locks and the loop breaking mechanism (through the 'break' loop feature), all of which are provided by Mozart, allowed the development of this simple, yet effective synchronization solution.

5.3   Miscellaneous Issues

The Use of Mixin Classes. The classes implementing the various AVS browsers do not fit into a single inheritance hierarchy. Instead, a basic behavior is enhanced upon using inheritance, with possible add-ins in the form of *mixin classes* implementing features like the lens filter and DQ. This arrangement has a twofold advantage: adding a new feature is greatly simplified, since we only need to inherit from the appropriate class(es) and add methods realizing the new feature. In addition, combinations of classes can be created at run-time based on browser specifications. This precludes the need to have static classes for all possible combinations of browser types and features. Thus no matter how many new features we incorporate, it is left to the run-time combination of classes to add these features to the appropriate base browser types as desired.

Distribution Issues. As mentioned before, the dispatcher sends interesting data to the various browsers. To enhance uniformity, both local and remote browsers create ports for themselves and register these ports with the dispatcher. This has the advantage of making distribution transparent to the dispatcher, thus allowing it to send messages on the ports without worrying where the browsers actually reside.

One of the difficulties faced in allowing the dispatcher and browsers to reside on different sites is the problem of passing objects between sites. In the Mozart version we used (1.2.4), some of the commonly needed Mozart entities are sited, whereas the Abstract Data Types (ADTs) that we use to encapsulate states and messages depend on Mozart's Dictionary and Array which are both sited. To get over this problem, the ADTs were extended with a method that returns the object's contents in a simple unsited form (a record or a list). Those unsited entities are sent to the -possibly remote- browsers who can later reconstruct the original ADTs.

Improving Responsiveness. Throughout the AVS, various objects respond to various user actions. For example:

1. Scrolling results in data being pulled from the dispatcher (data is pulled lazily when a new region is revealed by scrolling or zooming out).
2. Moving a lens results in some agents being hidden (filtered out) and others being shown.
3. Manipulating DQ controls changes the number of agents on display.

Because the user can perform actions in rapid succession, we should consider whether it is necessary to respond to every single action. There are three alternatives matching the above three cases:

1. Queue the actions and process them in a First-Come-First-Served manner, but before processing an action, check whether it is still relevant and if not, disregard it. This is suitable in case 1 where the display should not scroll to a region that was already scrolled out of view by a subsequent scrolling action. Note though that in this case, new actions should not automatically overwrite older ones.
2. Process only the most recent action (new actions should overwrite older ones). This is suitable in case 2 where a user moving a lens filter very rapidly only cares about its effect on the final region it is placed on.
3. Process every single action in a First-Come-First-Served manner but do so asynchronously, i.e. the method call should not block until a particular action is responded to. This is suitable in case 3 where every change in the controls affects the agents in the result pane of the DQ browser.

Alternative 2 was realized using Mozart's attributes which are class members that allow destructive assignment. One such member stores the action to be processed, with new actions overwriting the value of the attribute, thereby discarding older actions. Alternatives 1 and 3 were realized using Mozart ports since they are, by definition, asynchronous channels on which messages appear in the order they were sent. The difference between 1 and 3 is that 1 blindly processes all the actions received by the port while 3 checks every action to see whether it is still relevant.

6   Conclusion and Future Work

In this paper, we illustrated the use of Mozart and Oz in developing the Agent Visualization System; the first generic, distributed system specifically dedicated to the visualization of agent-based simulation scenarios. The AVS provides several graphical and textual browsers that utilize a variety of Information Visualization techniques to offer a deeper insight into the simulation scenario being studied. Throughout the AVS, we made use of various features offered by Mozart including dataflow variables, threads, high-orderness, and many others. Mozart allowed us to use approaches from the object-oriented, functional, logic, concurrent and distributed paradigms in a smoothly-integrated way that would not have been possible with another development platform.

There are a number of useful extensions that can be made to the AVS. Currently, the fact that the Mirror Store is centralized makes it a bottleneck. The MS can be broken down by region, agents, or attributes. A central entity should keep track of which agents/regions/attributes are on which site. How the distributed fragments can be managed is a research topic. Another enhancement is to support landscapes that are not grid-like, possibly allowing the visualization of arbitrary-shaped landscapes, as well as nested landscapes where each cell is either a simple cell or a landscape.

Acknowledgements. The authors would like to thank Fredrik Holmgren of the Distributed Systems Lab at the Swedish Institute of Computer Science (SICS) for the numerous fruitful discussions with him during the design phase of the AVS. We would also like to thank Donatien Grolaux of the Université Catholique de Louvain for his patience with our technical questions regarding QTk.

References

1. Jean-Daniel Fekete, Catherine Plaisant: Excentric Labeling: Dynamic Neighborhood Labeling for Data Visualization, Conference on Human Factors in Computer Systems (CHI'99), ACM , New York, pp. 512-519, 1999.
2. Jean-Daniel Fekete, Catherine Plaisant: Interactive Information Visualization to the Million, Symposium on Information Visualization (InfoVis'02), Massachusetts, USA, October 2002.
3. Foundation For Intelligent Physical Agents: FIPA Interaction Protocol Library Specification. Document number DC00025F, 2000.

4. Jade Goldstein, Steven F. Roth: Using Aggregation and Dynamic Queries for Exploring Large Data Sets, Computer Human Interaction (CIH'94) Human Factors in Computing Systems, ACM, April 1994.

5. Donatien Grolaux, Peter Van Roy, Jean Vanderdonckt: QTk - A Mixed Declarative/Procedural Approach for Designing Executable User Interfaces, Engineering for Human-Computer Interaction (EHCI 2001), Canada, May 2001.

6. Hala Mostafa, Reem Bahgat: The Agent Visualization System: A Graphical and Textual Representation for Multi-Agent Systems. In Proceedings of the Second International Conference on Informatics and Systems (INFOS2004), Cairo, Egypt, 2004.

7. Mozart, http://www.mozart-oz.org.

8. Manojit Sarkar, Scott S. Snibbe, Oren J. Tversky, Steven P. Reiss: Stretching The Rubber Sheet: A Metaphor For Viewing Large Layouts on Small Screens. In Proceedings of the 6th Annual ACM Symposium on User Interface Software and Technology, 1993.

9. Chris North, Ben Shneiderman: Snap-together Visualization: Can users construct and operate coordinated views?, International Journal of Human Computer Studies, Elsevier Ltd., 2000.

10. Ben Shneiderman.: The Eyes Have It: A Task by Data Type Taxonomy for Information Visualization. In Proceedings of the IEEE Symposium on Visual Languages, pp. 336-343, September 1996.

11. Maureen C. Stone, Ken Fishkin, Eric A. Bier: The Movable Filter as a User Interface Tool, Computer Human Interaction (CHI'94) Human Factors in Computing Systems, ACM, April 1994.

12. Fernanda B. Viegas, Judith S. Donath: Chat Circles, Special Interest Group Computer Human Interaction Conference on Human Factors in Computing Systems: the CHI is the limit, Pittsburgh, Pennsylvania, United States, pp. 9-16, 1999.

13. Gerd Wagner, Florin Tulba: Agent-Oriented Modeling and Agent-Based Simulation, The 5th International Workshop on Agent-Oriented Information Systems (AOIS-2003), 2003.

14. M. Wooldridge: Intelligent Agents. In: Gerhard Weiss (Ed.). Multiagent Systems: A Modern Approach to Distributed Artificial Intelligence. The MIT Press, 1999.

Web Technologies for Mozart Applications

Mahmoud Rafea

The Central Laboratory for Agricultural Expert Systems, Egypt
mahmoud@claes.sci.eg

Abstract. In this paper we describe two architectures and a methodology for building Mozart applications using Web technologies and tools. The first architecture is for standalone applications and the second is for web applications. An implemented example is described.

1   Introduction

In the last decade, there were tremendous efforts to improve Web technologies [1]. Those efforts led to great advances that impact not only the quality of Web pages but also the development of application-user-interface (AUI) [2]. The discussion of those advances is out of the scope of this article. The concern of this article is to present an approach that enables Mozart programmers to develop AUI supported by Web technologies and tools. AUI is critical to the success of an application. AUI takes a lot of time and efforts in order to satisfy the end-users needs. While web applications are becoming more and more popular, the current Mozart implementation supports only Oz applets and Servlets. As a result, Mozart web applications cannot compete in the area of web application development, where efficient web tools that facilitate the development of elegant and highly functional interfaces exist. To overcome this, all what we need is to architect an integration approach and implement supporting code (components).

The work carried out, in this article, exploits the technologies provided by Microsoft Internet Explorer (IE) and the Internet Information server (IIS). The approach is still valid in other Internet Browsers (IB) and other web servers (WS), but different technologies may be used. The reusable code that supports this approach is designed and implemented as components that are available for free. Both Mozart and C++ are used to develop those components.

The next section describes the conceptual architecture or approach. In section 3, details about the application development methodology are presented. An implemented real example is briefly described in section 4.

2   Conceptual Approach

The main idea is that an application user-interface is a set of HTML web pages that incorporate script code. Consequently, an Internet Browser (IB) is used as an application-front-end. One can use available IBs. Interactions between

P. Van Roy (Ed.): MOZ 2004, LNCS 3389, pp. 103–112, 2005.

an application that is written in Mozart and its user-interface are achieved through remote procedural calls (RPCs). For instance, Mozart code can call JavaScript functions to either initialize or update the user-interface content, while JavaScript functions, which are activated through users actions, can call Mozart procedures (proc, fun, meth) to do processing using user-interface content as an input. The crucial issue is the implementation of RPCs.

The RPC implementation can be simple or complex. This depends on the requirements and specifications of the target application. In case of a stand alone application, which means that Mozart executable and IB will be running on the same machine, the implementation can be of a very simple type where RPCs are passed as messages over a socket connection (Fig. 1). The Mozart socket-support represents the server and enables one connection only. Once the user closes the application IB, the Mozart executable terminates.

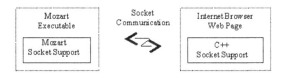

Fig. 1. Architecture of stand alone application

In case of a web application, a Mozart-executable will be running on a machine different from the machine running IB. Consequently, security issues complicate the communication, e.g., firewalls. To overcome these security problems, the application may interact with a Web Server (WS), possibly running on a different machine. The WS in turn communicates with the IB client. This necessitates the use of a web technology that can facilitate this scenario (Fig. 2). In the presented work, the web technology used is the Active Server Pages (ASP). Notice that if security issues are not important, the stand alone approach can be used after being modified to accept multiple connections and making it run as a server daemon. A similar approach has already been used before with Prolog applications, but using Java applets as a front end [3].

It should be remarked that the current Mozart implementation for the module Tk, in Microsoft Windows, is based on socket connection, too. Regardless of the details of user-interface particulars, the main differences are that the user-interface is not built in Mozart and interactions are indirect through another programming language. Whether this is better or worse, the current approach empowers Mozart programmers through using another very strong technology.

3 Implementation

The IB-socket-support and the WS-socket-support are both implemented as COM components so that they can be easily reused. Both components can be initialized to connect to a particular host-machine using a specified port number.

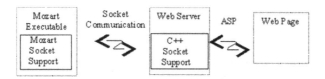

Fig. 2. Architecture of Web application

The need for two components arises because in case of a web application, the component which is running at the server side cannot execute directly a script in a web page while an IB is running at the client side.

The Mozart socket support is implemented as classes to exploit the reuse characteristic of object-oriented programming. The application class of both stand alone and web application inherits the same class. The difference is in how objects are initialized. In the next subsections, the Mozart socket support is described followed by descriptions of stand alone and web application implementations.

3.1   Mozart Socket Support

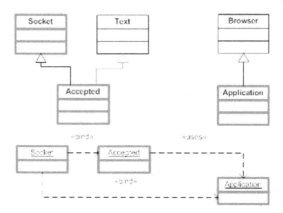

Fig. 3. Classes of Mozart socket-support component and the relation between their objects are represented using UML static structures

The purpose of this component is to collect code that will be used repeatedly in different applications. Mainly, this component performs the following tasks:

- Creates a socket stream
- Accepts clients connections
- Reads messages from different connections and passes them to an application class with the connection-parameter
- Sends messages
- Closes connections

There are two classes defined in this component: Accepted and Browser (Fig. 3). For each new connection an object of class Accepted is created. All information necessary for sending messages is stored in that object. The application developer needs to define another class that inherits from Browser. In this class, he needs to define a method named execute/3 because all received messages will be passed to this method with a reference to an Accepted object related to that message and a physical port number that he can use to keep a session history (Fig. 4). Notice that the procedure-call ComplaintAction/4 is part of the example that will be explained below.

```
class ApplClass from Browser
   meth execute(Accepted HostPort CmdArgs)
   Cmd = CmdArgs.1   Args = CmdArgs.2 in
       case Cmd
       of bye then {self close}
       [] complaint then
       {ComplaintAction HostPort self Args
Accepted}
       [] ... % rest of code here
       else
       {Exception.´raise´ error(cmd:Cmd arg:Args)}

   end
end
```

Fig. 4. An application class showing a fragment of execute/3 method

3.2   Standalone Application

In Microsoft Windows an application's main-HTML file can have the file-extension: 'hta' to load it in an IB-Window. We refer the reader to the Microsoft documentation to know how to customize an IB-Window according his/her needs [4]. This is only a professional tip, but it is not important for an application's functions. One can use any of the available web-development tools to create a professional look and feel of a user-interface. He/she can then writes the script code that is used to respond to user' actions. This may involve collection of data from this interface to be sent to Mozart code for processing.

In Fig. 5, two JavaScript functions that can be used in any application are demonstrated. The function initControl, which is intended to be generic, uses two variables: Host and Port. Those variables may be defined globally and assigned particular values. The default host defined in the COM component is the local host (127.0.0.1) and the default port is 4321. The best time to call this function is after the web page has been loaded. In Fig 3, we demonstrated how we call this function and how the COM object is declared. Notice that professional tools usually take care of defining COM objects.

```
<html>
<head>
<HTA:APPLICATION      See Microsoft documentation       />
<script LANGUAGE="JavaScript">;
  function initControl() {
    control.port = Port;
    control.host = Host;
    control.init(window.document);
  }

  function sendToOZ() {
      var cmd = arguments[0];
      var msg ="<M><"+cmd+">";
      for (var i=1; i<arguments.length; i++){
      msg += "<ARG>"+arguments[i]+"</ARG>"
      }

    msg +="</"+cmd+"></M>";
    control.sendToOz(msg);
  }
</script>
</head>
<body onload="initControl()">
<OBJECT id="control" data="data:application/x-oleobject;base64,0 =="
 classid="CLSID:43348D1A-84E3-4ABA-A165-37534CDAE6AE"></OBJECT>
</body>
</html>
```

Fig. 5. JavaScript functions that can be used in HTA file of any stand-alone application

3.3   Web Application

The second function   sendToOz takes a variable length of arguments and constructs an XML string to be sent to Mozart's executable part of the application. It assumes that the first argument is a Mozart procedure and the rest are arguments of that procedure.

The application Mozart code consists of the basic application method, the socket initialization code, and the application code. The basic application method is execute/3, (Fig. 4). This method can be used, as it is, in web applications. The socket initialization code is shown in the procedure Start (Fig. 6). The initialization of the object should provide the URI of the HTML file of the user-interface. It may also provide the port number. If it is not provided the default port (4321) is used. The method call isRunning/0 prevents the program from termination until the user closes the IB.

Generally, in web applications the main problems (difficulties) are:

- Security measures taken to prevent intrusion (e.g., firewalls) and hence socket connection will not be convenient
- Handling of multiple connections especially when the code is stateful.

```
proc {Start}
   W = {New ApplClass init(port:MyPort url:URI)} in
   {W isRunning}
end
```

Fig. 6. The basic methods of an application

The use of web technologies, as for instance ASP, JSP, and PHP can overcome the security problem through the use of WS to communicate with IB clients while the Mozart application communicates with the WS. In this article, the ASP approach will be described. In this approach, the sendTooZ function is modified so as to send RPC messages to the WS. Fig 7 shows those modifications.

Furthermore, a script file that is run by the WS is created so as to function as moderator (Fig. 8). Notice that the script file name (server.asp) is defined within the body of the sendTooZ function. So the role of this script file is the following:

1. accept RPC messages form IB clients
2. pass those messages to a Mozart application
3. receive messages from a Mozart application
4. pass those messages to IB clients to be executed

The next step is how to initialize the COM component, and how to ensure that a Mozart application is running and ready for connections. In the current approach, the "global.asa" file, which is part of ASP, is used to achieve these objectives. This file is a VBScript file that has a set of predefined subroutines. The programmer may fill one or more of those subroutines with appropriate code. In our case, the subroutine for Session_OnStart is used (Fig 9). Notice that the COM component initialization takes the Mozart executable's file name so that it may initiate its execution when necessary.

```
function sendToOZ() {
  var cmd = arguments[0];
  var msg ="<M><"+cmd+">";
  for (var i=1; i<arguments.length; i++){
    msg += "<ARG>"+arguments[i]+"</ARG>"
  }
  msg +="</"+cmd+"></M>";
  var nameStr="server.asp?msg="+msg;                    //(1)
  var OZxml=new ActiveXObject("Microsoft.XMLHTTP");
  OZxml.Open("POST", nameStr, false);
  OZxml.setRequestHeader("Content-Type","text/xml")
  OZxml.setRequestHeader("encoding", "windows-1256")
  OZxml.Send(null);
  window.execScript(OZxml.responseText);
}
```

Fig. 7. JavaScript function that can be used in web page of any web application

```
<script LANGUAGE="JavaScript" runat=server>;
  var control = Session("CONTROL");
  var Msg = Request.QueryString("msg");
  control.sendToOz(Msg);
  Response.Write(control.GetCode());
</script>
```

Fig. 8. Script of the file: server.asp

```
<script LANGUAGE=VBScript RUNAT=Server>
  sub Session_OnStart
    dim WebCon
    dim code
    set WebCon = Server.CreateObject("ASPUI.control")
    WebCon.port = 5555
    WebCon.host = "localhost"
    WebCon.init("c:\\sheep\\sheepWeb.exe")
    set Session("CONTROL") = WebCon
  end sub
</script>
```

Fig. 9. An example of global.asa file

```
proc {Start}
       W = {New ApplClass init(port:5555)} in
       {W webAccept}
end
```

Fig. 10. Web application initialization

The Mozart code related to initialization so that the application may accept multiple connections is shown in Fig. 10. The HTML file that represents the application user-interface is loaded as a web-page; hence it is omitted in the object initialization. The method webAccept/0 loops forever so that it may accept new connections.

4   Real Example Application

This example is a successful commercial product that is used by veterinary doctors and students. It is an expert system for the diagnosis and treatment of disorders affecting sheep and goats; hence its name is Caprine Clinical Expert System. The user-interfaces for standalone and web applications are shown in Fig. 11 and Fig 12, respectively. The only difference is that the IE menu, address combo box, and icons are hidden in the standalone application.

In Fig 12, all the disorders that affect the species: sheep, which are newly born, their sex is male, and the number of affected animals is sporadic, are

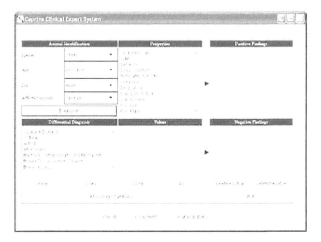

Fig. 11. User-interface of Caprine Clinical Expert System standalone-application

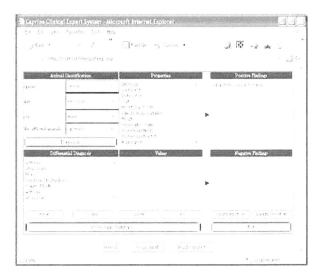

Fig. 12. User-interface of Caprine Clinical Expert System web-application

displayed in the Differential Diagnosis list (1stDD). The properties that can diagnose a condition are displayed in the Properties list (1stPr). Those two lists are filled in response to pushing the button Diagnose. In Fig 12, the state is displayed after applying further steps which are: 1) the selection of the property (*Abdomen wall*) and one of its characteristics (*distended*), 2) pushing the upper arrow to add this finding to the Positive Findings list with consequent update of 1stDD, and 1stPr.

The pushing of the button *'Diagnose'* calls the function complaint that is demonstrated in Fig 13 to show how the function sendToOz is called. In effect, the method `execute/3` (Fig 4) demonstrates how this call is handled in Mozart through calling the complementary procedure `ComplaintAction/4`. A fragment of this complementary procedure is shown in Fig 14 to demonstrate how a script function (Fig 15) is called from Mozart.

```
function complaint() {
   clear(lstDD);
   clear(lstPr);
   clear(lstPrVs);
   clear(lstPos);
   clear(lstNeg);
   sendToOZ("complaint",
            "Species",lstSpecies.options[lstSpecies.selectedIndex].text,
            "Age", lstAge.options[lstAge.selectedIndex].text,
            "Sex", lstSex.options[lstSex.selectedIndex].text,
            "No of affected animals",
            lstAffected.options[lstAffected.selectedIndex].text
            );
}
```

Fig. 13. JavaScript function executed in response to clicking the button '*Diagnosis*'

```
proc {ComplaintAction HP O Args Accepted} Ds Ps in
   ...
   {O sendToPage(Accepted ´fillList(lstDD,´#Ds#´);´)}
   {O sendToPage(Accepted ´fillList(lstPr,´#Ps#´);´)}
end
```

Fig. 14. Mozart code showing how a JavaScript function is called from Oz

```
function fillList() {
   var w = arguments[0];
   for (var i=1; i<arguments.length ; i++){
   var oOption = document.createElement("OPTION");
   oOption.text=arguments[i];
   w.options.add(oOption);                              }
```

Fig. 15. JavaScript function that is called from Oz in response to clicking the button 'Diagnosis'

5   Conclusion

In this paper, we have demonstrated how to develop Mozart applications using web technology for building their user-interfaces. Although a variant of this approach has been in conjunction with other languages, we have proved its feasibility and applicability for Mozart using a real example. In effect, we believe that the demonstrated approaches will empower Mozart programmers in developing their applications.

The feasibility and applicability of the proposed approaches need to be proved in different UNIX platforms. This will be the subject of future work.

References

1. Fraternali, P.: Tools and approaches for developing data-intensive web applications: A survey. ACM Computing Surveys **31** (1999)
2. Myers, B., Hollan, J., et al., I.C.: Strategic directions in human-computer interaction. ACM Computing Surveys **28** (1996)
3. ElBeltagy, S., Rafea, M., Rafea, A.: Practical development of internet prolog applications using a java front end. In: The 2nd International workshop on logic programming tools for Internet applications, in conjunction with ICLP97. (1997)
4. Microsoft: (Html applications) http://msdn.microsoft.com/library.

Overcoming the Multiplicity of Languages and Technologies for Web-Based Development Using a Multi-paradigm Approach*

Sameh El-Ansary[1], Donatien Grolaux[2], Peter Van Roy[2] and Mahmoud Rafea[1]

[1] Swedish Institute of Computer Science, Sweden
{`sameh, mahmoud`}`@sics.se`
[2] Université catholique de Louvain, Belgium
{`ned, pvr`}`@info.ucl.ac.be`

Abstract. In this paper, we present QHTML, a library for building Web-based applications in Oz. QHTML provides the Oz programmer with a basic set of abstractions through which creating Web-based interfaces becomes similar to traditional graphical toolkits. In the mean time, QHTML is an experiment investigating whether a single language can replace the numerous ad-hoc combined languages/technologies currently used for building Web-based interfaces. QHTML is realized thanks to the multi-paradigm features of the Oz programming language, which supports symbolic data structures, a functional programming style, an object-oriented style and concurrency via dataflow and lightweight threads.

1   Introduction

Building Web-based applications requires the mastering of a number of languages/technologies (e.g. HTML, CSS, CGI, ASP, PHP, XML, etc..). Such languages and technologies were created to address different aspects on a by-need evolutionary manner. The result is a plethora of tools that are fitted together in an ad hoc fashion. Such languages/technologies include and are not limited to the following:

- HTML [1] is the main language for describing a Web-based Graphical User Interface (GUI) and it is a declarative language.
- A scripting language such as Javascript [2] or VBscript [3] for implementing any client-side dynamic behavior. Such scripts are imperative and are usually inlined inside the HTML code using a special tag to fit the declarative and the imperative flavors together.

---

* This work was funded at UCL and SICS by the Information Society Technologies programme of the European Commission, Future and Emerging Technologies under IST-2001-33234 PEPITO.

P. Van Roy (Ed.): MOZ 2004, LNCS 3389, pp. 113–124, 2005.

- CGI Forms [4] provide a way to collect data from client-side. CGI Forms
  are neatly integrated in the syntax of HTML. However, server-side scripts
  written in ASP [5] or PHP [6] need to obtain the values entered by a user in
  the forms and repeatedly generate new pages to provide responses to client-
  side events. Server side-scripts in both ASP and PHP are also inlined with
  HTML using special tags.
- Cascading Style-Sheets (CSS) [7] are used for uniform and reusable format-
  ting. CSS syntax is declarative, however, yet another syntax that needs to
  be learned.
- XML [8] and XSL [8] and the family of related standards are used for - among
  other functions - separation of content and presentation. This, despite its
  elegance, adds another burden of learning a new technology to achieve the
  separation aspect.

This multiplicity of languages and tools has negative implications on Web-
based applications on the theoretical and practical levels. From a programming
languages point of view, Web technologies lack a comprehensive model that accounts for all the aspects needed for a Web-based application. From the practical
point of view, this multiplicity makes it harder to gain experience in Web development, as a developer needs to learn many technologies and languages and to
know how to combine them together to achieve desired functionalities.

2 The QHTML Approach

QHTML[1] provides an integrated model in the form of a set of abstractions to
make it possible for the developer to build a Web-based application in the same
way as any traditional application. In that model, the Web browser is perceived
as a toolkit with well-defined geometry management capabilities.

QHTML is built as a layer over existing Web technologies such as Dynamic
HTML (DHTML) [9] and the Document Object Model (DOM) [10].

QHTML is a module written in the multi-paradigm symbolic language Oz
[11] and it is developed using the Mozart system [12]. Oz has support for declarative, functional, logic, concurrent, object-oriented and constraint programming.
The diversity of paradigms in Oz has permitted the integration of many aspects
involved in authoring Web-based applications in one language. The declarative
paradigm in Oz is used to capture the declarative aspects such as interface description and style reuse. The functional and logic paradigms are used to provide
the imperative aspects of interactivity, namely event-handling and dynamism of
interface. The separation between the data and the presentation is enhanced by
the advantages of symbolic manipulation of data to achieve several presentations for the same data by using different mapping functions. Communication
between the client and the server is completely transparent to the application

---

[1] A working implementation of QHTML could be obtained from:
http://www.info.ucl.ac.be/people/ned/qhtml.

Fig. 1. A Basic Interface in QHTML

developer and is perceived as handling events in the graphical user interface. Abstractions for geometry management and more complete support for concurrency that accounts for threads is a consequence of having such an integrated model.

3   The QHTML Functionality

QHTML models the user interface as a structure of record values. An interface consists of a set of widgets, where each widget is specified by a record. Programming a complex interface then becomes a matter of doing computations on records. Since records are strongly supported by the Oz declarative pardigm, these calculations are efficient and easy to specify. This model is based on a similar model for higher abstraction for Tk [13] called QTK [14, 15], and it includes the following components: Windows, widgets, events, actions, handlers. In addition to those components, the model has support for enhanced semantics for geometry management, a more general concurrency support, and abstractions for context-sensitive interfaces.

3.1   Windows and Widgets

A window is a rectangular area of the screen that contains a set of widgets arranged hierarchically according to a particular layout. A widget is a GUI primitive that is represented visually on the screen and that contains an interaction protocol, which describes its interaction with a human user. An interaction protocol defines what information is displayed by the widget and what sequences of user commands and widget actions are acceptable. A widget is specified by a record, which gives its type and its initial state. The following is an example:

```
Descr=td(img(src:"mozart.gif")
        lr(
            button(value:"Hi")
            text(value:"Hello, please type here")))
Window={QHTML.build Descr}
{Window show}
```

In the above example, we have the `Descr` variable whose value is a record describing an interface where `img`, `lr` and `label` are widgets. The call `QHTML.build` creates a window containing that interface (figure 1) and the `show` method spawns the browser.

A stand-alone QHTML application uses the `show` method to spawn a browser process. A different method is used in case the interface is to be remotely loaded which is further discussed in section 4. The widgets `lr` and `td` are used to align other widgets in horizontal or vertical fashions respectively and are covered in section 3.4 about geometry management.

The importance of having interface descriptions represented by Oz records lies in preserving the declarativeness of the GUI. Declarativeness simplifies the mapping data to GUI. Such mapping can be accomplished by coupling technologies like XML and XSL. The contribution of QHTML is that the data, the GUI and the mapping between them is all provided in one programming language under the same model. Style uniformity and reuse are also supported in the QHTML model by the `look` abstraction without any additional particular syntax, e.g. the following code creates a `look` that makes a button red and a label green and then applies this `look` to a GUI description.

```
MyLook={QHTML.newLook}
{MyLook.set button(backgroundColor:red)}
{MyLook.set label(backgroundColor:green)}
Descr=td(look:MyLook
          label(value:"Hello world")
          label(value:"Amazing colors !")
          button(value:"Ok")
          button(value:"Ok also")))
```

3.2   Handlers

A handler is an object with which the program can control a widget. Each widget can have a corresponding handler. Consider the following example:

```
Descr=td(text(value:"Hello, please type here" handle:T))
Window={QHTML.build Descr}
{Window show}
. . .
X = {T get()}
. . .
{T set("A new text")}
```

By having the handle `T`, we were able to get and set the contents of the text widget after the whole interface has been displayed. Observe that the variable `X` is a server side variable while `T` is referring to a text widget which is in the client/browser side. Nevertheless, this fact is completely transparent to the author of the Web-based application so he/she should no longer care about that difference.

3.3   Events and Actions

An event is a well-defined discrete interaction made by the external world on the user interface. An event is defined by its type, the time at which it occurs, and possibly some additional information (such as the mouse coordinates). Events are not seen directly by the program, but only indirectly by means of actions. An event can trigger the invocation of an action. An action is a procedure that is invoked when a particular event occurs. Each widget has an associated list of actions. To illustrate actions, we can modify our simple example in the previous section as follows:

```
proc {Foo}
   X = {T get()}
end
Descr=td(text(value:"Hello, please type here" handle:T)
         button(value:"Hi" action:Foo))
```

Here we can see that we have exactly the same technique for handling events like HTML. Nevertheless, QHTML has the advantages of the integrated model because the actions, which are of an imperative nature, are written in the same language as the interface description, which is of a declarative nature. That was made possible by the functional paradigm in Oz where references to the action procedures are provided to the declarative description of the interface as values. The transparency property is also inherited from the model because when an author writes an action he/she does not differentiate whether this action is going to affect a server- or a client-side entity. This is a more intuitive and high-level way of performing interaction between the client and the server compared to the submission of a CGI form or the reloading of a certain PHP or ASP page. That transparency is a result of the integrated model implemented in one language.

3.4   Geometry Management

Current Web technologies lack a mature model for geometry management. It is the task of the HTML developer to figure out how to manipulate tables and frames to achieve a desired layout, which is a knowledge available only in the hands of experienced HTML programmers.

To cope with that, the integrated model also provides higher abstractions for geometry management. This is accomplished by having the top-down, left-right widgets: td and lr for controlling the placement of widgets and tdframe and lrframe for controlling relations between frames. That is in addition to a glue value that defines a constraint on the space taken by a widget and its response to resizing. The td and lr widgets are widget containers that pack widgets in a top-down and left-right orientation respectively. By default a widget takes only the space enough for it to be rendered and no more and is centered vertically and horizontally with respect to the containing widget/window. That layout could be further constrained by the glue feature that could be assigned the values n, s, e and w for north, south, east and west respectively or a combination of them. Gluing a side is asserting a constraint on that widget to let it always be tangent to its neighbor at that side and to occupy all the space available in the direction of that side. Gluing two opposite sides results in the widget taking all the space available in the direction of both these sides. This is illustrated by the following example:

```
td(glue:nswe
   button(value:"Button1")
   button(value:"Button2" glue:nse)
   button(value:"Button3" glue:w)
   button(value:"Button4" glue:we))
```

In figure 2, we see how the glue values affect the layout of the buttons. Button1 is not glued, so it is centered in the containing widget td. The gluing of Button2 and Button3 to east and west respectively made them take the available space in the direction of the respective sides. The result of gluing to opposite sides is exemplified in Button2 and Button4.

Fig. 2. Using Glue Values   **Fig. 3.** Response of gluing to resizing

Figure 3 illustrates the response of the widgets to resizing. We see that the constraints are maintained and that Button2 and Button4 grew when they found available space.

It is also possible to have a grid structure where all widgets are organized in lines or columns of the same size (figure 4). The lr (resp. td) widget supports the newline special code which makes the following contained widgets jump to a new line (resp. column) right below the previous widgets, keeping the same column structure (resp. line) with the widgets above them. The following code exemplifies the use of newline:

```
lr(button(text:"One" glue:we) button(text:"Two" glue:we)
   button(text:"Three" glue:we)    newline
   button(text:"Four" glue:we) button(text:"Five" glue:we)
   button(text:"Six" glue:we)    newline
   button(text:"Seven"  glue:we) button(text:"Height" glue:we)
   button(text:"Nine"  glue:we)    newline
   empty button(text:"Zero" glue:we) continue)
```

The empty special code leaves an empty space in a line (resp. column) and the continue special code spans a widget over several columns (resp. lines). The same logic is extended for arranging frames using the tdframe and lrframe widgets.

3.5   Concurrency

The concurrency support in dynamic HTML documents is limited to a main event loop that serializes the events happening in the browser window in addition

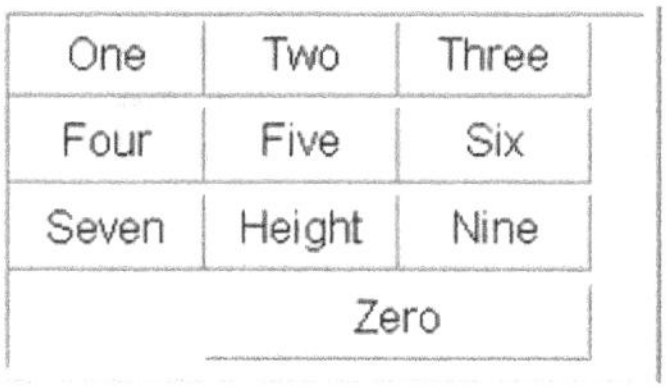

One	Two	Three
Four	Five	Six
Seven	Height	Nine
Zero		

Fig. 4. Using newline, empty and continue

to an ad-hoc way to have more concurrency by inserting new events in the event queue after a certain time delay namely using Javascript timers. As a consequence of the integrated model, we can offer a more general support for concurrency by providing threads. In the Oz abstract machine, concurrency is supported by the ability to have many light-weight threads in the same operating system process [16]. The following is an example of how to integrate a thread easily in a Web-based application.

```
Window = {QHTML.build td(text(handle:E))}
{Window show}
. . . %%Some manipulations
thread
    {Wait X}
    {E set(value:X)}
end
. . . %%rest of maninputlations
```

Where X is some dataflow variable. In that example, we have created a thread that blocked on X, i.e, it waits until X is bound to a certain value and then executes its manipulation on the handle E. Again, notice that, X could be bound as a result of some GUI event or as a result of any other action in the application.

3.6   Dynamic Window Subparts

Another high-level abstraction offered by the QHTML model is the placeholder widget that is particularly useful for context-sensitive GUIs. The contents of a place-holder can change dynamically during GUI execution. A placeholder widget defines a rectangular area in the window that can contain any other widget(s) at any time as long as the window exists.

One can declare at any level of the GUI description a placeholder by writing placeholder(handle:P) where P is a handle to the placeholder. Afterwards, the application can set the contents of that placeholder to contain an arbitrary interface description and with the ability to change those contents later. Placeholders are particularly useful for building context-sensitive GUIs because one could specify a window with subparts that are sensitive to the available visual resources and who change their contents accordingly, e.g. an application can do the following: {P set(label (text:"Hello") button(text:"World"))} is filling the placeholder with a label and a button after the detection of inadequate space, it

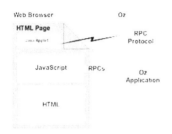

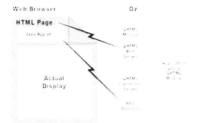

Fig. 5. Javascript-Oz RPC proto-col architecture

Fig. 6. Architecture of an application using QHTML

can change the contents of the placeholder to: `{P set(button(text:"World"))}` where the placeholder is filled with a button only.

4   QHTML Architecture

The first requirement for the implementation of QHTML is a means of communication between the Oz language and a Web browser. To achieve that, we developed a simple Remote Procedure Call (RPC) protocol between Javascript and Oz, which is an independent component that could be used separately.

4.1   Javascript-Oz RPC Protocol

As illustrated in figure 5, the protocol has two components, an Oz component and a Javascript component. The Javascript component is primarily a Javascript interface to a Java applet, which is providing the real implementation of the protocol on the browser side. The Oz component is a module that could be embedded in any Oz application.

The technique makes use of the tight integration between Java and Javascript on the client-side. The Java applet provides socket communication with an Oz application. Consequently, any client-side Javascript function can use the Java applet to make RPCs to Oz procedures. Similarly, server-side Oz code can make RPCs to Javascript functions.

QHTML is a module that an Oz application links to (figure 6). Its main role is to hide all the details of the interaction with the browser. The steps for delivering the GUI and achieving that goal are as follows:

1. The Oz application builds the GUI description using record structures. For example something like: `{Descr=label(value:"Hello World")}`.
2. The Oz application requests the creation of the described GUI by executing the following statement. `{Window={QHTML.build Descr}}`. Consequently, the QHTML module transparently executes two operations:
   (a) It creates a connection server, if it did not already exist, that waits for incoming connections. A connection represents an instance of the described GUI. `Window` is an object that maps to a particular connection in the connection server.

(b) It generates a page containing the RPC Java applet and an empty HTML display area, which we refer to by the connection page. Moreover, to facilitate the deployment of QHTML, a small HTTP server written in Oz was embedded inside the module in order to deliver the HTML connection page while its functionality is completely hidden from the application developer.

3. At that point, there are two ways to display the GUI: 1) A Web browser process is spawned locally by executing {Window show} where show is a method in the Window object. 2) A redirection page to the connection page is saved in a user-defined place by executing {Window save("<Publicly - Accessible - Dir>")}. In that way, it is accessible to other remote machines. In both cases, the connection page is generated with the right parameters to the Java applet depending on whether the browser is going to be spawned locally or will be used on a remote site.

4. Disregarding the Web browser spawning method, upon loading of the connection page, the Java applet runs and establishes a connection with the QHTML connection server. That connection becomes the communication link between the Web browser and the QHTML module and remains transparent to the Oz application.

5. Upon connection establishment, the QHTML module makes RPCs to generated Javascript functions that start to render the described interface using Dynamic HTML. After that GUI events can trigger server-side Oz code. Similarly, any events occurring on the Oz side can trigger GUI changes.

5   Conclusion

We have presented in this paper QHTML, a module for the Oz programming language that provides a model for symbolic authoring of Web-based applications through which the developer can treat the HTML document like a traditional graphical toolkit. QHTML makes use of: 1) The power of expression of the multi-paradigm language Oz. 2) An application architecture that realizes a transparent interaction mechanism between the Oz language and the Web browser.

The following table summarizes the aspects needed for the development of a Web-based application and enumerates the current languages/technologies that support those aspects in comparison with the Oz language constructs for supporting the same aspects in the QHTML approach.

In addition to the main advantage of the QHTML approach which is the integration of multiple aspects in one model implemented in a single language, two other features are realized:

1. A higher-level of abstraction for geometry management that simplifies the construction of complex layouts and that has support for context-sensitive interfaces.

2. A consequence of the integration of QHTML inside Oz is the ability to use threads which are the more intuitive and natural means of modeling concurrency. That is contrasted to the "hacky" incomplete way of using Javascript timers for supporting animation and similar tasks.

Table 1. Summary of QHTML approach

Aspect	Current Techs.	QHTML Model
GUI description	HTML	Oz records
Events/Actions	Client-side scripts	Oz procedures & concurrency
Client/server communication	CGI/PHP/ASP	Oz-Javascript RPCs
Uniform styling	CSS	Oz records operations
Content-layout	XML + XSL	Oz records operations

6   Related Work

We compare in this section our work to other approaches of authoring HTML-based GUIs through symbolic languages exemplified by Haskell [17] and Curry [18]:

1. Haskell, a purely functional language, has an HTML library [19] that aims at presenting Haskell data structures in HTML. For that, it encompasses some abstractions for building tables with constructs like "above", "below" and "beside". It also offers a mapping to all the HTML tags to make it easier for the Haskell programmer to generate HTML code. Thus, the Haskell HTML library is more of an interface rather than an abstraction layer in most of the parts except for the tables. There is no particular support for interaction other than by generating needed HTML tags.
2. Curry, a multi-paradigm language, provides an additional abstraction layer to HTML interfaces via its "High-Level Server Side Web Scripting" module [20]. In that module, syntactical details of HTML and passing of values with CGI are wrapped and abstracted as HTML forms. This leads to a high-level approach to server side programming that has the notions of event handlers, state variables and control of interaction. Despite of that, it does not account for any abstractions for better geometry management.

QHTML for Oz, shares with the libraries of Haskell and Curry the advantage of being able to symbolically transform data into user interface entities. QHTML shares the support for higher-level geometry management with the Haskell library but it has a more sophisticated model- based geometry abstractions that completely hide the notion of tables and is general for all interface elements. QHTML shares with the Curry library the support for interactivity and dynamism but without the administrative overhead for integrating programs with HTTP servers and with the ability to supply the user interface for Web sites or for stand-alone applications indifferently. Finally, QHTML has the advantage letting a developer treat the HTML document as a traditional graphical toolkit.

7   Limitations and Future Work

QHTML has some limitations and missing features where some of them constitute future work. Examples of those are the following:

1. In general, there is a performance penalty that is attributed to the fact that all events in the GUI are routed to the QHTML module first and are handled there, where communication is done over a stream connection between the Java applet at the browser side and the QHTML module at the server side. Nevertheless, The performance of a GUI constructed with QHTML is application-specific, in applications where the GUI contains many widgets, a QHTML implementation will perform better than a form-based implementation because changes will be done to individual widgets after an exchange of small messages with the server that is in contrast to reloading the whole page in a form-based approach.
2. QHTML has no support for vector graphics. The Scalable Vector Graphics (SVG) [21] recommendation is the most prominent candidate for integration within our model.
3. Due to the different implementations of standards in mainstream browsers, not all features could be provided in all browsers and some of them have to be implemented differently in different browsers. More work is planned to be done to achieve the same result on different Web browsers.

References

1. W3C: HTML 4.01 specification (1999) http://www.w3.org / TR / html4.
2. Netscape: Javascript documentation (2004) http://devedge.netscape.com.
3. Microsoft: VBScript documentation (2004) http:// msdn.microsoft.com/ library/ default.asp? url=/ library/ en-us/ script56/ html/ vbstutor.asp.
4. ncsa.uiuc.edu: The   common   gateway   interface   (2001)   http:// hoohoo.ncsa.uiuc.edu/ cgi/ overview.html.
5. Microsoft: Active server pages (2004) http:// msdn.microsoft.com/ library/ default.asp? url=/ nhp/ default.asp? contentid = 28000522.
6. PHP: PHP homepage (2004) http://www.php.net.
7. W3C: Cascading style sheet level2, CSS2 specification (1998) http:// www.w3.org/ TR/ REC-CSS2.
8. W3C: The extensible markup language (2001) http://www.w3c.org/XML.
9. Goodman, D.: Dynamic HTML: The Definitve Reference. O'Reilly & Assoicates (1998)
10. W3C: Document object model (DOM) level 3 core specification (2001) http:// www.w3.org/ TR/ 2001/ WD-DOM-Level-3-Core-20010913/.
11. Smolka, G.: The Oz programming model. In van Leeuwen, J., ed.: Computer Science Today. Lecture Notes in Computer Science, vol. 1000. Springer-Verlag, Berlin (1995) 324–343
12. Mozart Consortium: The Mozart Programming System homepage (2004) http://www.mozart-oz.org.
13. Ousterhout, J.: Tcl and the Tk Toolkit. Addison-Wesley (1994)
14. Grolaux, D., Van Roy, P.: QTk – an integrated model-based approach to designing executable user interfaces. In: 8. Lecture Notes in Computer Science, Glasgow, Scotland, Springer-Verlag (2001)
15. Grolaux, D., Van Roy, P., Vanderdonckt, J.: QTk – a mixed declarative/procedural approach for designing executable user interfaces. In: 8. Lecture Notes in Computer Science, Toronto, Canada, Springer-Verlag (2001)

16. Mehl, M.: The Oz Virtual Machine - Records, Transients, and Deep Guards. PhD thesis, Technische Fakultät der Universität des Saarlandes (1999)
17. Hudak, P.: The Haskell school of expression: learning functional programming through multimedia. Cambridge University Press (2000)
18. Hanus, M.: A unified computation model for functional and logic programming. In: Proc. 24st ACM Symposium on Principles of Programming Languages (POPL'97). (1997) 80–93
19. Gill, A.: The HTML library for haskell (1999) http:// www.cse.ogi.edu/ andy/ html/ intro.htm.
20. Hanus, M.: High-level server side Web scripting in curry. In: PADL'01. Volume 1990 of Lecture Notes in Computer Science. (2001) 76+
21. W3C: Scalable vector graphics (SVG) 1.0 specification (2001) http:// www.w3.org/ TR/ SVG.

P2PS: Peer-to-Peer Development Platform for Mozart[*]

Valentin Mesaros[1], Bruno Carton[2], and Peter Van Roy[1]

[1] CS Department, Université catholique de Louvain, Louvain-la-Neuve, Belgium
{valentin, pvr}@info.ucl.ac.be
[2] CETIC, Charleroi, Belgium
bruno.carton@cetic.be

Abstract. Recently, development of peer-to-peer (P2P) applications has been giving a paramount attention mostly due to their attractive features such as decentralization and self-organization. Providing the programmer with the "right" platform for developing such applications became a challenge. In this paper we describe the functionality of P2PS, a platform for developing P2P applications in Mozart. The P2PS platform provides the developer with a means for building and working with P2P overlay applications, offering different primitives and services such as group communication, efficient data location, and dealing with highly dynamic networks. P2PS implements Tango, an efficient algorithm for constructing structured P2P systems. It is delivered as a library and already made public, being used as underlying structure for different P2P applications.

1 Introduction

With the advent of popular peer-to-peer (P2P) applications and systems such as Gnutella (gnutella.wego.com) and Napster (www.napster.com), the development of P2P systems has become important and even a research topic. The main reasons for this "rush" is due to the practical and useful features and objectives of P2P computing, e.g., scalability, self-organization, decentralization. The very idea behind the peer-to-peer concept is the fact that the processes participating in a distributed computing can exchange information directly, without passing through a central point. Thus, they become *peers*. A peer can be client, server, and router at the same time. Generally speaking, peers have equal capabilities and eventually equal responsibility.

In this paper we present some of our ongoing work within the framework of extending Mozart/Oz (www.mozart-oz.org) to reflect new programming abstractions that use different distributed algorithms in order to offer P2P abilities. We describe the functionality of the P2PS [1] peer-to-peer development platform. The P2PS platform provides the developer with the ability of building and working with P2P overlay applications, offering him different P2P primitives and services such as group communication, efficient data lookup, and fault-resilience. Although independent of the underlying P2P technology,

---

[*] This work was funded at UCL by the Information Society Technologies programme of the European Commission, Future and Emerging Technologies under IST-2001-33234 PEPITO, and at CETIC by the Walloon Region (DGTRE) and the E.U. (ERDF and ESF).

P. Van Roy (Ed.): MOZ 2004, LNCS 3389, pp. 125–136, 2005.

P2PS currently only implements Tango [2]. Tango is a peer-to-peer algorithm that we developed to better structure relative exponential networks to increase their scalability. It extends and improves Chord [3], and thus it can be included into the category of structured P2P systems (see Section 2).

Mozart already provides the programmer with an advanced interface for developing distributed applications. However, the underlying distribution layer of Mozart is based on a client-server model which may lead to scalability problems with respect to the number of processes involved in the computation. There is ongoing work [4, 5] to reduce some of these problems. On the other hand, the P2PS development platform inherits all its functionality from the P2P algorithms. For example, it can provide full connectivity (though, multi-hop) between all nodes within the network, and this with a logarithmic number of physical connections per node. Moreover, the loosely coupled model together with the management of highly dynamic networks make of P2PS the right choice to develop P2P applications in Mozart.

Related to our work, there exists several research projects for P2P development platform. One is the Chord project (www.pdos.lcs.mit.edu/chord) written in C++ and based on the Chord algorithm. Another platform is FreePastry (freepastry.rice.edu) written in Java and based on the Pastry [7] algorithm. As P2PS, both platforms are based on a structured P2P system and aim to build scalable, robust distributed systems. They both offer a programming interface based on the "common API" [6]. P2PS provides rather a combination between layers tire 0 (i.e., key-based routing) and tire 1 (e.g., multicast and broadcast) of the "common API". P2PS as well as Chord project and FreePastry are in ongoing research and they all three are more or less similar with respect to the services they offer. One thing that differentiate them from one another is the programming language they are written in. Hence, we believe that, given the expressiveness of Mozart/Oz, P2PS represents an attractive choice for writing P2P applications with.

JXTA [8] and JXTAnthill [9] are two other development platforms for P2P applications. JXTA defines a set of basic protocols for a number of P2P services such as discovery, communication, and peer monitoring. JXTAnthill is written on top of JXTA and it implements algorithms rooted in complex adaptive systems, based on the behavior of ants. The difference between P2PS and these two platforms is mostly based on the P2P algorithms they each implement. While P2PS is based on algorithms offering strong data lookup guarantees, this is not the case for JXTA and JXTAnthill.

The remainder of this document is organized as follows. We continue by briefly recalling the principles of structured P2P systems. In Section 3 we present the main functionality provided by P2PS. In Section 4 we describe the internal architecture of P2PS. In Section 5 we show how to write a simple application for P2PS, and in Section 6 we describe a more realistic application that uses P2PS, and then conclude.

2   Structured P2P Systems

In this section we briefly recall the principles and notations of the structured P2P networks. Unlike unstructured P2P systems like Gnutella, whose overlay topology is ad-hoc, structured P2P systems organize their overlay by following well specified rules in order to improve overall efficiency. A key challenge in building P2P systems is providing means for efficient location of information distributed across a large number of processes (or nodes) of a highly dynamic network. We take the Chord algorithm as a case study since Chord is one of the first P2P algorithms based on the idea of Distributed Hash Table – DHT, and also because Chord and Tango have many commonalities.

There are three main characteristics of a P2P structured system. First is the fact that it is DHT-based, where key#value pairs are associated to nodes in the overlay network depending on the "distance" between the key *id* and the nodes' *id*s. (Hereinafter, we will use the term *node* to refer both to the node itself and to its identifier under the hash function, as the meaning will be clear from the context.). Both, nodes and keys, take values in the same identifier space. In the case of Chord, the identifier space is a virtual ring within which hashed node and data item key *identifiers* are spread by using a consistent hashing. Second is the fact that the overlay network is well defined in order to achieve logarithmic key lookup. With the advent of the DHT-based systems, the main procedure in the P2P systems, i.e., the key *lookup*, is provided with clear guarantees. For instance, while in Gnutella a flooding-based algorithm is used, leading to network resource waste, in Chord and Tango the lookup for a key will not take more than a certain maximum number of hops and messages, i.e., $O(logN)$, where N is the maximum number of nodes in the overlay. Third is the system's resilience to node failures and its ability to self-organize face to the network's dynamics. That is, when nodes join or leave the network, the nodes pointing to them will adapt their local routing tables in order to guarantee overall efficient lookup. Furthermore, since the system is totally decentralized, there is no risk for single points of failure to occur.

In Chord each node has a *predecessor* and a *successor*, representing references to the previous and respectively the subsequent node in the identifier space. A key is stored at the node succeeding the *id* of that key on the circular identifier space. Thus, the naive lookup procedure for a certain key reduces to looking for the first node whose *id* is greater than, or equal to, the *id* of that key along the identifier space, going clockwise. To speed up the lookup process, each node maintains supplementary references (called *fingers*) to some other nodes inside a *routing table*. Given an identifier space of size N, beside the references to its predecessor and successor, each node in the Chord system stores $logN$ fingers. Note that in structured P2P systems there is a tradeoff between the size of the routing table at each node and the maximum number of hops a request would take when looking for a key.

3   Functionality

In this section we present the main functionality provided by our P2P platform, called P2PS: *Peer-to-Peer System*. The main functionality of P2PS is offered via the class P2PS.p2pServices. The P2PS library provides the developer with the possibility of building and working with P2P overlay applications, offering different P2P primitives and services. P2PS is providing the distributed peer-to-peer applications with a means to organize themselves in large scale structured overlay networks as well as providing them with management and communication primitives whose costs evolve logarithmically with the system size. Although implementing the Tango algorithm, P2PS offers an API that can apply to any structured P2P system. Thus, the programmer does not have to worry about the underlying details. For more info on the API, the reader should refer to the P2PS tutorial [1].

The main functionality provided by the P2PS library can be summarized as follows: network management primitives such as create, join and leave a network, communication primitives such as one-to-one, broadcast and multicast, and monitoring primitives. With P2PS we intend to provide basic P2P primitives on top of which more specialized services will be built. Dictionary functionality such as looking for the responsible of a key is not provided as a basic primitive in P2PS. Instead, the main basic primitives are sending and receiving a message from one node to another. Nevertheless, dictionary operations can be immediately provided by using the communication primitives offered by the P2PS library. Furthermore, we have undergoing research to extend the functionality of P2PS.

3.1   Create a Network

This functionality provides the programmer with the possibility to create a P2P overlay network. It will create the first node of a network. What this actually means is the fact that an AccessPoint is created for this node. (For the description of the access point, see Section 4.1.) In order to create a network in P2PS, one will use the method createNet. This method can be featured with different overlay network and node parameters (e.g., the maximum number of nodes in the overlay, the *id* of this node), as well as with parameters related to the local access point (e.g., IP and port number). Then, after creating a peer node, its access point can be published, thus allowing other nodes to connect and join the overlay network. Furthermore, the node is provided with message and event input streams on which messages from other nodes and respectively different node and network events will eventually be accessible.

3.2   Join a Network

When joining an overlay network, a peer node *n* needs to have the knowledge of an AccessPoint of another peer node *p* already present in the respective overlay network. The underneath protocols will actually join *n* to the network via the node *p*. Note that node *p* serves only as an entry point to the network for node *n*. Generally, the position of a node within the system does not depend on the entry point it used to get into the network. The system will self-organize in order to guarantee overall efficiency (see Section 4.2 for details). In order to join a network in P2PS, one will use the method joinNet. This method can be featured with different node parameters (e.g., the *id* of this node), as well as with parameters related to the local access point (e.g., IP and port number). As any other node in the overlay network, a new joined node will be associated an access point. Furthermore, once inside the network, a node may receive messages from other nodes from the network, and node and network events on the associated message and respectively event input streams.

3.3   Leave a Network

Leaving an overlay network means implicitly disconnecting this node from all the other nodes it is connecting to in the overlay network. Although, generally, a P2P network tolerates node failures, it is expected that a node does a gracefully leave. Thus, underneath, a node will run a simple protocol to disconnect it from its neighbors. In order to leave a network in P2PS, one will use the method leaveNet. This will terminate the message and the event streams.

3.4   Message Sending and Receiving

P2PS provides end-to-end communication primitives. That is, sending messages from one peer node to another throughout the overlay network. Due to its organization, the system performs efficient key based routing. Thus, a message from a node s to a node d is routed throughout the overlay network according with the corresponding key lookup procedure, where d is considered a key. In P2PS the message sending and receiving are asynchronous. Nevertheless, the reliable send can be made synchronous. In the following we describe how to send messages by using different communication primitives. In all cases, receiving a message at a node implies reading the message input stream at that node. The messages addressed to a node will appear on its associated message stream.

One-to-One Communication. This primitive is to be used to send messages from one node to another one, throughout the overlay network. It is important to note that in P2PS one can choose to send a message either to the node responsible for the key with value d, or directly to the node whose *id* equals d. While in the former case the message will eventually always reach its destination (since there will always be a node responsible for any key), in the latter the destination may simply not be present. Both flavors of message delivery are useful in practice. On the other hand, one can choose between a best-effort send or a reliable send. In the case of a best-effort send, although generally the message will reach its destination, there are situations when the message may be lost, e.g., due to the overlay network dynamics. In the case of a reliable send the message will be delivered to the destination; otherwise, its loss will be signaled to the sender. To send one-to-one messages in P2PS, one will use the method send for best-effort send and the method rsend for reliable send.

One-to-Many Communication. Another communication primitive that P2PS provides is one-to-many, where simple and efficient broadcast and multicast is provided. Both protocols employed are based on an idea [10] that exploits the tree structure of a Chord-like system. In the case of the broadcast, the message is sent to all the nodes in the network. In the case of multicast, the message is sent to a given list of nodes, i.e., explicit multicast. As in the case of one-to-one primitive, in the case of multicast one can choose to send the message either to nodes' responsibles, or directly to the nodes whose *ids* equal those in the destination list.

Send to Successor. To increase its resilience, an application might decide to replicate the content stored at a node to some of the node's successors. The method sendToSucc can be used to send a message to a number of successors of a node (whoever they be).

3.5   Monitoring

In a dynamic network, as in P2P overlay networks, being aware of the status and the changes with respect to the peer node and the network might be very useful for the upperlying application. A good example is the application running on nodes with limited resources. Hence, in P2PS we decided to provide a set of events on the event input stream associated with the peer node. These events indicate changes on the connections with the node's neighbors. This way, for example, if the successor of a node has changed, the application may do replication on the new successor.

Another way of monitoring a node is offered by the method getStatistics. It provides a set of information – most of it in the form of counters – about the status of the node. For example, one can obtain information about the followings: the number of incoming and outgoing connections, the number of data and control messages sent by this node, the number of data and control messages forwarded by this node.

4   Architecture

The P2PS library is organized in three layers: COM, Core, and Services (see Figure 1). They correspond to P2P services provided to the application: structural operations in order to preserve overlay network properties, and message sending/receiving and channel establishment operations.

4.1   COM Layer

The COM layer is in charge with interfacing with the underlying physical network. Basically, COM provides the Core layer with communication functionality through a common API, regardless the underlying transport protocol employed. The functionality provided by COM is: access point creation, connection establishment, basic communication primitives, and fault detection.

Access Point Creation. We define an access point to be an addressable entry point of a node. It is the COM layer who defines the form and the meaning of an access point. Moreover, the representation of an AccessPoint will have a meaning only to the COM layer. It can, for example, be defined as an ipAddr/socketNr pair, but its definition can also be security-flavored. The access point creation primitive consists in creating an

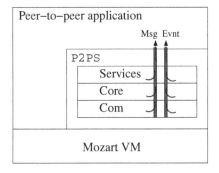

Fig. 1. The three-layer architecture of a P2PS node, and its interaction with the application and the transport module (here provided by the distributed layer of Mozart)

addressable entry point for a peer node. Then, a peer node can publish its access point, allowing remote connections to it, and thus providing an access point to the overlay network itself.

Connection Establishment. The connection establishment functionality offers the primitives connect and disconnect for point-to-point connecting to and respectively disconnecting from a node, given its AccessPoint.

Basic Communication Primitives. The basic communication primitives provided are send message and receive message. They are point-to-point primitives providing reliable transfer over connections established via an AccessPoint.

Fault Detection. The fault detection primitives provide a means for detecting two types of network anomalies relative to point-to-point connection, i.e., permanent faults and temporary faults. Given the high dynamics of a P2P network, this functionality is very important. For this end, P2PS uses indirectly the distribution functionality of Mozart.

4.2   Core Layer

An overlay network topology can be viewed as a graph composed of arcs and nodes. The Core layer provides high-level connectivity primitives between nodes, thus allowing to add and remove arcs to and respectively from a node. The Core layer, as its name indicates, is the central component of the P2PS library. It implements the Tango [2] algorithm. Its purpose is threefold: implement node join and leave mechanisms, route key based messages to their responsibles, and maintain the routing table and the successor list regardless the nodes joining and leaving, thus guaranteeing overlay efficiency.

Joining/Leaving a Network. Given an entry point to the system (i.e., AccessPoint), the join mechanism consists in finding the right place for the joining node within the overlay network (i.e., between its successor and predecessor), and establishing a communication channel with its neighbors. Obviously, the predecessor and successor of the joining node will be affected by the join operation and therefor they must update their references in order to reflect the network change. The particularity of the implemented distributed join is the fact that it is atomic. Indeed, once the joining node n has located its successor p, it asks p to insert it into the system. If a node receives an insertion request while inserting another node, it will delay the request until the current insertion has finished. Furthermore, a node can perform an insertion only after being itself correctly inserted into the overlay. The leave operation is much simpler and consists only in advertising its connected peers about the leave, and disconnecting from them.

Routing Messages. The message routing algorithm is based on the key lookup primitive of the P2P algorithm employed (i.e., Tango in the case of P2PS). It consists in handing the incoming message to the upper layer if it reached its destination (i.e., if the receiver peer is responsible of the message identifier) or forwarding the message to the closest peer entry of the routing table, according to the routing metric used.

Topology Maintenance. Another operation is overlay topology maintenance, or routing table maintenance. This procedure is run at each node and consists in maintaining connections to well defined neighbors in order to ensure certain global guarantees (e.g., a lookup for a key will not take more than a certain maximum number of hops). Instead of correcting the routing table by probing periodically the neighbors, the routing table of a node in P2PS is corrected when the peers are actually using the network (as described in [11]). While this economic way is well suited for maintaining the routing table, it is not for maintaining the successor list of a node. Since the reason to keep the successor list is to preserve the network coherence (i.e., when the successor of a peer has failed, the peer has to refer to the next peer in the successor list), a peer should be notified immediately about all modifications of the r next succeeding peers (r is the length of the successor list).

4.3   Services Layer

The Services layer is a kind of wrapper, building up the raw primitives offered by the Core layer; operations needed to implement peer-to-peer applications. These operations can fit into three categories. First is the overlay network management which comprises system initialization, create connection access, and system join and leave operations. Second are the communication primitives at the overlay network level which comprise one-to-one message send, and message broadcast and multicast operations. Third are the monitoring primitives.

The application can interact with the Services layer by invoking the corresponding methods directly as well as by simply reading information on the two available input streams: message and event associated with each peer node. The message and event streams are a way of asynchronously obtaining information about the received messages and respectively the node and network events.

5   An Example Using P2PS

Here is a simple example of a P2P application composed of three peers that uses the P2PS library. The system is composed of three nodes node1, node2, and node3, where node2 and node3 join the system through node1 and respectively node2. In this example node3 sends an one-to-many message to node1 and node2, and an one-to-one message to the responsible of key 42. For more clarity, we purposely omitted the exception handling. The code runs directly in the OPI – Oz Programming Interface.

The first node of a P2P system is always "special". Actually, it represents a system by itself. When creating a network (i.e., the first node) one can specify the network parameters. In our example, we decided to work with the default network values provided by the system. Nevertheless, we specify parameters for the node and its access point. That is, we indicate we want nodeId=1 and that it should work on port number 3001. Than, we run a loop over the message stream and displays the messages it receives. The following is the code implementing node1.

```
declare /* node 1 */
[P2PS] = {Module.link ['x-ozlib://cetic_ucl/p2ps/P2PS.ozf']}

% Create the first node (with id 1) in the P2PS network.
```

```
OP2PS = {New P2PS.p2pServices
         createNet(nodeConfig: nodeConfig(nodeId:1)
                   apConfig:   apConfig(pn:3001))}
```

```
% Get the message stream and display each message received.
for M in {OP2PS getMsgStrm($)} do {Show M} end
```

Then, we create `node2` with `nodeId` 16. This node joins the system via `node1`, specifying its remote `AccessPoint` as the IP address and port number. Further on, it runs a loop to wait and displays the messages sent to this node. The following is the code implementing `node2`.

```
declare /* node 2 */
[P2PS] = {Module.link ['x-ozlib://cetic_ucl/p2ps/P2PS.ozf']}
```

```
% Build an access point representation for the node to join to.
RAP = {P2PS.address2ap "127.0.0.1" 3001}
```

```
% Create a node with id 16 and join the network, using RAP.
OP2PS = {New P2PS.p2pServices
         joinNet(remoteAP:   RAP
                 nodeConfig: nodeConfig(nodeId:16)
                 apConfig:   apConfig(pn:3002))}
```

```
for M in {OP2PS getMsgStrm($)} do {Show M} end
```

Finally, we create `node3` without specifying its `nodeId`; the node will be provided with a random *id*. This node chooses to join the system via `node2`, specifying its address and port number. Note that it could have chosen to join via any other node within the network. Further on, it sends an one-to-one message to the responsible of key 42 (which can actually end up to any of `node1` or `node3`), and a multicast message to `node1` and `node2`. The following is the code implementing `node3`.

```
declare /* node 3 */
[P2PS] = {Module.link ['x-ozlib://cetic_ucl/p2ps/P2PS.ozf']}
```

```
RAP = {P2PS.address2ap "127.0.0.1" 3002}
```

```
OP2PS = {New P2PS.p2pServices joinNet(remoteAP: RAP)}
```

```
{OP2PS send(dst:42 msg:anOzValue toResp:true)}
{OP2PS multicast(dst:[1 16] msg:hello)}
```

6   An Application Using P2PS

There are different applications that have been developed with P2PS. Some examples (http://renoir.info.ucl.ac.be/twiki/bin/view/INGI/Peer2PeerSystem) are PostIt, P2P-Matisse, and Community-Panel. In this section we describe the Community-Panel.

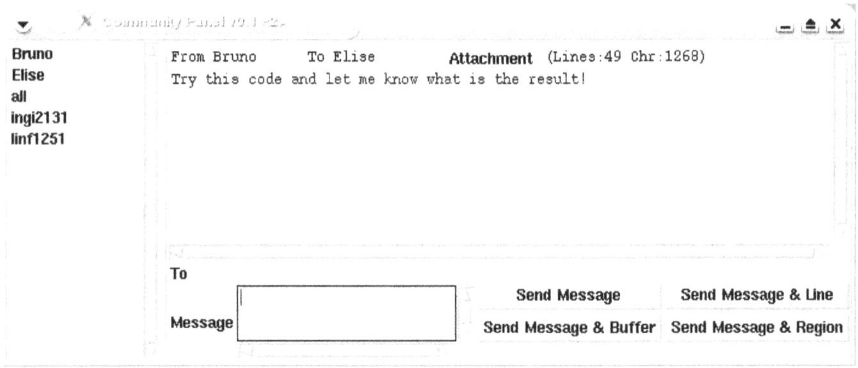

Fig. 2. The Community-Panel GUI

Software development is rarely a solo task. The development process of a software, starting from the conceptual design to the code implementation, is the concern of a team involving a lot of people not necessarily located at the same place. Despite of its benefits, collaboration is time consuming. Indeed, some studies reveal that the efforts dedicated to collaboration among developers leave less than half of the workday to do any real coding. Collaborative tools can help to increase the part of the day to do any real coding while still supporting a high level of collaboration. Since from the individual developer's perspective the IDE (Integrated Development Environment) is where coding take place, why not including collaborative code edition capabilities alongside the editor, compiler and debugger?

The Community-Panel, coming with the peer-to-peer facilities provided by the P2PS library, is a first step toward a collaborative IDE. Its main objective is to gather Oz developers concerned with a common problem in one community, and provide the community with tools for real-time collaborative edition.

The targeted functionalities of the Community-Panel are threefold. First, the application provides users with community membership information. This information can be partial or complete, regarding the size of the community and scalability issues, but can be extended at the user's request. Second, the application facilitates the communication between developers by supporting chat-like and instant messaging facilities.This allows to meet appropriated community or person according to the user matter, by involving social connections via the friends management tools. Finally, the Community-Panel provides a developing framework for exchanging code in text/binary format but also language entity. For instance, one can imagine to develop an application by adopting a component based architecture where the Community-Panel plays the role of real-time component connector.

From Figure 2 one can see that the GUI is composed of 3 areas: the membership, the received messages, and the submit. The membership area displays all the available groups and the connected users. The received messages area displays all the messages received during the session. The submit area is composed of a text box allowing to write a message and to attach some Oz-code. Once the user received a message with an attachment, she can retrieve the corresponding Oz-code by clicking on « Attachment

» in the received messages area. The retrieved Oz-code will be inserted in the current buffer of the OPI, just after the cursor's position.

The friends management tools and the language entity sharing are not yet supported but this does not prevent the usage of the Community-Panel. We have developed the core functionalities allowing a first experimentation on collaborative IDE.

7   Conclusion

This document presents part of our ongoing work within the framework of extending Mozart/Oz with new programming abstractions to offer P2P abilities. Throughout the document we described P2PS, a P2P development platform for Mozart. We focused on its functionality and on its architecture as well as on how to write simple applications. The P2PS library is developed in Mozart/Oz and it implements Tango, a DHT-based algorithm. From its functionality, one can see that P2PS is simple to use and very practical to construct and work with large scale distributed applications; thus taking advantage of the provided P2P services and primitives. Furthermore, given the expressiveness of Mozart/Oz, we believe that P2PS is an attractive choice for developers.

The feedback – since one year now from its first release – we have been receiving from different developers using P2PS allow us to continuously improve its API and functionality. The P2PS library is available to be (and it is already) used for developing P2P applications as well as to be extended with more specialized services. More encouraging, P2PS will be used as a distributed communication environment in further research projects at UCL and CETIC.

P2PS is the first Mozart/Oz development platform offering primitives for building P2P applications. It is delivered as a software package containing the source code together with an API documentation and an example-based user tutorial. Last fall we made the public release of P2PS on MOGUL (www.mozart-oz.org/mogul); the official archive of Mozart libraries. Since then, P2PS has become known to researchers in the domain of overlay networks and P2P systems, and its web site is daily visited.

References

1. Carton, B., Mesaros, V.: P2PS: Peer-to-Peer System Library. http://www.mozart-oz.org/mogul/info/cetic_ucl/p2ps.html (2003)
2. Carton, B., Mesaros, V.: Improving the Scalability of Logarithmic-Degree DHT-based Peer-to-Peer Networks. Euro-Par – International Conference on Parallel Processing (2004)
3. Stoica, I., Morris, R., Karger, D., Kaashoek, F., Balakrishnan, H.: Chord: A Scalable Peer-to-Peer Lookup Service for Internet Applications. ACM SIGCOMM – Special Interest Group on Data Communication (2001)
4. Klintskog, E., Mesaros, V., El-Banna, Z., Brand, P., Haridi, S.: A Peer-to-Peer Approach to Enhance Middleware Connectivity. OPODIS – International Conference On Principles Of DIstributed Systems (2003)
5. Klintskog, E., Brand, P.: Extended Distribution Subsystem. D4.6 PEPITO deliverable http://www.sics.se/pepito (2004)
6. Dabek, F., Zhao, B., Druschel, P., Kubiatowicz, J., Stoica, I.: Towards a Common API for Structured Peer-to-Peer Overlays. IPTPS – International Workshop on Peer-to-Peer Systems (2003)

7. Rowstron, A., Druschel, P.: Pastry: Scalable, Decentralized Object Location, and Routing for Large-Scale Peer-to-Peer Systems. IFIP/ACM Middleware – International Conference on Distributed Systems Platforms (2001)
8. Traersat, B., Abdelaziz, M., Pouyoul, E.: Project JXTA: a Loosely-Consistent DHT Rendezvous Walker. White Paper, Sun Microsystems, Inc. (2003)
9. Russo, F.: JXTAnthill. Master Thesis. Department of Computer Science, Bologna, Italy (2002)
10. El-Ansary, S., Onana, L., Brand, P., Haridi, S.: Efficient Broadcast in Structured P2P Networks. IPTPS – International Workshop on Peer-to-Peer Systems (2003)
11. Onana, L., El-Ansary, S., Brand, P., Haridi, S.: DKS: A Family of Low Communication, Scalable and Fault-Tolerant Infrastructures for P2P Applications. IEEE CCGRID – International Symposium on Cluster Computing and the Grid (2003)

Thread-Based Mobility in Oz*

Dragan Havelka[1,2], Christian Schulte[1], Per Brand[2], and Seif Haridi[1,2]

[1] IMIT, KTH - Royal Institute of Technology
Electrum 229, SE-16440 Kista, Sweden
phone(+46 8 633 1609)
{dragan, schulte}@imit.kth.se
[2] SICS - Swedish Institute of Computer Science
Box 1263, SE-16429 Kista, Sweden
{perbrand,seif}@sics.se

Abstract. Strong mobility enables migration of entire computations combining code, data, and execution state (such as stack and program counter) between sites of computation. This is in contrast to weak mobility where migration is confined to just code and data. Strong mobility is essential for many applications where reconstruction of execution states is either difficult or even impossible: load balancing, reduction of network latency and traffic, and resource-related migration, just to name a few. This paper presents a model, programming abstractions, implementation, and evaluation of thread-based strong mobility. The model extends and takes advantage of a distributed programming model based on automatic synchronization through dataflow variables. It comes as a natural extension of dataflow computing which carefully separates issues concerning distribution and mobility. The programming abstractions capture various migration scenarios which differ in how the source and destination site relate to the site initiating migration. The implementation is based on replicating concurrent lightweight threads between sites controlled by migration managers.

1 Introduction

In this paper we present a model and an implementation of strong mobility based on distributed dataflow computing. We identify a set of essential primitives and abstractions (`Go`, `Pull`, and `Push`) for explicit thread migration. Common programming patterns for mobile applications are presented. The paper describes how migration of thread-based execution states is implemented.

While the prototypical argument for strong mobility is load balancing, it is vital for a broad range of applications: mobile agent platforms, network traffic reduction, fault tolerance, etc. Strong mobility allows the migration of code, data, and execution state (stack and program counter), as opposed to weak

---

* This work was partially funded at KTH by the European project PEPITO IST-2001-33234.

P. Van Roy (Ed.): MOZ 2004, LNCS 3389, pp. 137–148, 2005.

migration which only requires migration of code and data [1]. The advantage strong mobility offers over weak mobility is that migration can take place at any time. Another important advantage is the fact that execution continues at the next statement (the statement which follows the migration call). In the case of weak migration the transferred code is accompanied by some initialization data which is used together with *a restart procedure*.

The migration model described here is compatible with systems where computation is organized into multiple concurrent lightweight threads and distribution is supported. Distribution includes both distribution of data and code (such as procedures, classes, and objects).

This paper makes the general contribution of a model, programming abstractions, and an implementation architecture for thread-based strong mobility for a distributed dataflow language. In detail, the contributions are as follows:

Thread-based Mobility. The paper contributes a model for strong mobility based on threads and distribution based on dataflow synchronization. The model is an extension of a well-established model for distributed programming in Mozart/Oz. The model insists on the fact that mobility is under explicit control of the programmer.

Programming Abstractions and Application Scenarios. Based on thread-based mobility, this paper contributes programming abstractions (Go, Push, and Pull) which capture common programming idioms in the construction of mobile applications. It is shown how the abstractions can be used in prototypical application scenarios.

Implementation Architecture. All programming abstractions are implemented on top of a primitive for thread mobility. The paper identifies thread replication together with migration managers as basic building blocks for an architecture to implement thread-based mobility. The implementation is currently under testing and will be incorporated into the official Mozart system.

Plan of the paper. The next section introduces the migration model. Section 3 introduces migration abstractions by presenting several application scenarios. The following section presents a migration primitive as foundation for the migration abstractions. An implementation of the model is sketched in Section 5. An evaluation is presented in Section 6 followed by discussion of related work. Section 8 summarizes our results.

2   Thread Migration Model

In this paper we assume that programs execute concurrently by running typically many lightweight threads, where one thread is executed at time. Threads synchronize automatically by using dataflow variables (also known as logic variables). Dataflow variables serve as place-holders for not yet known values. Threads are assumed to be first-class language entities in that they can be passed as arguments to procedures, stored in data structures, and so on.

A thread is a stack of statements. It executes by trying to execute its topmost statement. A thread automatically suspends if its topmost statement suspends due to insufficient information available on its dataflow variables. Thread resumption again is automatic: providing the value for a variable automatically and fairly resumes all threads suspending on this variable. For more details on our model of computation we refer the reader to [2].

We also assume that execution can be distributed across several sites of computation: both data structures as well as code (in form of procedures, objects and their attached classes) are distributed. A language entity has the same language semantics whether it is used on only one site or on several sites (network-transparency). If used on several sites, the language entity is implemented using a distributed protocol. This gives the language entity a particular distributed semantics in terms of network messages. For more details on our model of distribution, we refer the reader to [3, 4, 5, 6].

Migration. Thread migration is based on *thread replication* by creating an exact copy (a clone) of the original thread at the destination site and destroying the original thread at the source site.

When a thread migrates all data referred to by the thread's statements is migrated as well. This does not apply to resources. A *resource* is a data structure where its use is restricted to one site (such as standard output, standard error, GUI). In this paper we restrict ourselves to strong mobility and assume that resources are ubiquitous and dynamically rebound when threads are migrated. We are aware that this is a severe restriction. Work on a generic model for dynamic resource rebinding is under progress. The current model is based on combination of transparent rebinding of standard libraries and the explicit rebinding of other resources handled by the application programmer.

A thread executes at a location which we refer to here as *site*, for example a virtual machine run by an operating system process. Migration is always performed between *source* site and *destination* site. Thread migration implies migration of the computation state consisting of a stack of statements. A statement is a closure defined by a program counter that points to the next instruction and an environment needed for executing the instruction.

Thread migration can be initiated from any site including the source and the destination sites. On the source site thread migration can be initiated by the thread itself or by some other thread.

3   Programming Patterns

The migration abstractions and their common areas of application are identified in this section. The code fragments used are presented in Oz [7, 3]. To help the reader, {P Arg} calls the procedure P with the argument Arg. thread <s> end creates a new thread which executes the statement <s>. By X in a new dataflow variable X is introduced.

Self Migration. The abstraction Go is useful for proactive mobile agents (that is, agents which initiate their migration in anticipation of future problems, requirements, or changes).

Consider as an example: a mobile agent MA moves between sites and collects as well as offers information:

1. MA collects information about computing resources such as: processor power, amount of available memory, available software components and libraries, and available external hardware resources.
2. MA offers information collected on already visited sites to the local agents (that is, the agents that are located on the visiting site).
3. MA gets a list of neighbor sites and chooses one of them for migration.
4. MA performs migration.
5. MA repeats the outlined execution.

A code example for MA is as follows:

```
proc {Collector Info ThisSite}
    ListOfNeigh NextSite SiteInfo UpdatedInfo
in
    SiteInfo = {CollectInfo}
    {OfferInfo Info}
    UpdatedInfo = {UdateInfo Info ThisSite SiteInfo}
    ListOfNeigh = {GetNeigh}
    NextSite = {ChooseNext ListOfNeigh}
    /* Here comes the migration      */
    {Go NextSite}
    /* Executes on site ''NextSite'' */
    /* after migration has finished  */
    {Collector UpdatedInfo NextSite}
end
```

MA is started by spawning a thread which calls `Collector` appropriately:
`thread` {Collector StartInfo CurrentSite} `end`.

Please note that the `Go` abstraction has one argument representing the destination site.

Execution Attractor. The abstraction `Pull` is used to move execution from the *source site* to the *destination site*, and is invoked from the destination site. It is useful for several reasons: traffic reduction, network latency avoidance, and other resource-related issues.

An example of use in the case of traffic reduction can be implemented in the following way. A procedure `TrafficController` takes a list of remote threads and checks for each thread if it is worth moving. The decision is made based on specified criteria (for example, measuring amount of network-traffic produced by the thread). A matching code example is presented below:

```
proc {TrafficController RemoteThreads}
    for T in RemoteThreads do
        if {WorthMoving T} then
            {Pull T}
        end
    end
end
```

Please note that the `Pull` abstraction has one argument representing the thread to be pulled to the current site. Note that this is in contrast to `Go` which takes a site as single argument.

Execution Mediator. The abstraction `Push` is used to *mediate execution* between sites. An example of use is dynamic load balancing. For example: A *distributed scheduler (DS)* has access to a list of thread queues with one queue per involved site. The goal is to optimize performance by moving threads from heavily loaded sites to less loaded sites. The corresponding code example is presented below:

```
proc {LoadBalance SiteList}
   HighestLoadSite LowestLoadSite
   LoadList Thr
in
   LoadList = {GetLoads SiteList}
   HighestLoadSite = {Max LoadList}
   LowestLoadSite  = {Min LoadList}
   Thr = {ChooseThread HighestLoadSite}
   {Push Thr LowestLoadSite}
end
```

Please note that the `Push` abstraction takes two arguments, the thread to be migrated and the destination site. It can be invoked from any site including the source and destination site.

4   Migration Primitives

The abstractions discussed earlier use thread replication as follows: after the replica has been created, the *original* thread is destroyed.

Each site runs a *migration manager* which controls migration of threads. Thread migration is performed by sending messages between migration managers. The information needed to migrate a thread T is located at the source site of T and the replication process starts there.

In the following MM_s refers to the migration manager of the source site, whereas MM_d refers to the migration manager at the destination site.

Source Site. The thread T is suspended, its execution state is collected, serialized, and sent to the destination site. The migration manager MM_s waits until an acknowledgment on thread reception issued by the migration manager MM_d is received. The acknowledgment confirms the existence of two copies of T, the original thread at the source site and the replicated thread at the destination site. Then, the original is terminated and MM_d is informed that the replica can resume.

Destination Site. When the serialized thread is received by MM_d, it rebuilds the thread T_r from the network representation by unmarshaling. After rebuilding, an acknowledgment message is sent to MM_s. Then MM_d waits on a con-

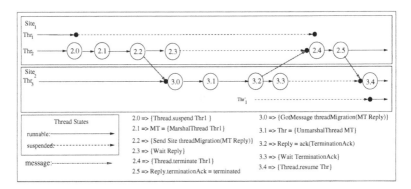

Fig. 1. Execution of $\{ThreadReplicate\ Thr_1\ Site_2\}$

firmation that the *original thread* has been terminated. When termination of T is confirmed, T_r is *resumed*.

MM_s and MM_d synchronize twice during thread migration. The first synchronization is on the *replica-thread creation* and the second synchronization is on the *original-thread termination*. Figure 1 shows the interaction and the synchronization between migration managers.

Migration and Thread States. A thread can be either *runnable*, *running*, *suspended*, or *terminated*. Thread migration can be requested on a thread regardless of its state. The thread state after migration remains the same.

Running. A running thread cannot be migrated directly. There is only one running thread at each site. Thus, a thread which wants to migrate itself delegates migration to another thread. The thread to be migrated is stopped first, and another thread (the thread executing the migration manager) performs the actual migration.

Runnable. A runnable thread waits to be scheduled for execution. The migration manager suspends the thread and performs migration. The original thread at the source site is terminated. The replicated thread at the destination site is created as suspended and is then resumed.

Suspended. This case is slightly more involved and exploits invariants on dataflow synchronization. In a language with dataflow variables, a thread suspends if its topmost statement cannot execute due to yet unbound dataflow variables.

The thread is replicated and during replication all *variables* on the thread stack are discovered and distributed. The original thread is terminated and the replicated thread is resumed. When the replicated thread is scheduled to run at the destination site, it will try to execute the same statement that caused suspension at the *source* site. Thus, the thread rediscovers its suspensions on its own. This allows to maintain suspension on dataflow variables locally (that is, suspension information is not distributed across the net). This property is a direct consequence of using dataflow variables for distributed computing [5].

Terminated. A terminated thread has no stack and can not become runnable again. Thus, its migration is not useful and the thread requesting migration is properly informed.

4.1 Programming the Abstractions

With the help of migration managers and thread replication as discussed above, the abstractions introduced in Section 3 can be programmed easily.

```
proc {Push Thr Site}              %'THS' is the home site
   THS S                          % of the thread to be
in                                % migrated. 'GetSite'
   THS = {GetSite Thr}            % returns the current
   {Send THS migrate(Thr Site S)} % site of the thread. 'S'
   {Wait S}                       % is a synchronization
end                               % variable.

proc {Go RemoteSite}              % The thread to be migrated
   Sync Thr                       % 'Thr' spawns a new thread
in                                % which performs migration.
   Thr = {Thread.this}            % 'Thr' blocks on the Sync
   thread                         % variable used to synchronize
      {Push Thr RemoteSite}       % on migration. 'Go' returns
      Sync = done                 % when the migration
   end                            % process is finished.
   {Wait Sync}
end

proc {Pull Thr}                   % 'MyThr' is the thread in
   MySite MyThr                   %  which Pull executes.
in                                % 'MySite' is the destination
   MyThr = {Thread.this}          %  site.
   MySite = {GetSite MyThr}
   {Push Thr MySite}
end
```

Failures. Extensive mechanisms for fault tolerance are not yet implemented, but we plan to adapt the model developed for the Mozart programming system.

5 Implementation

In this section we describe how strong mobility is implemented as an extension to the Mozart programming system [8].

Our implementation is based on the Mozart implementation of Oz [9]. Language entities can be transparently distributed between different sites (implemented by operating system processes). Distribution of stateless data entities is achieved by copying (replication). Consistency of distributed stateful entities is implemented by distribution protocols [4, 5].

The replication primitive is based on marshaling and unmarshaling of threads by extending the system. Marshaling a thread amounts to marshaling a stack of statements where each statement consists of a program counter for code to be executed and an environment of local variables.

The threads are extended with globally unique names which is the standard procedure in the Mozart system used for globalization of the stateful entities. The sites are made the first-class entities and are represented as Oz ports. Thus, the sites are input communication channels used by the migration managers.

One important design decision in Mozart to make marshaling simple is that only values are marshaled. To comply with that, program counters in stack entries are translated to a pair of procedure and relative offset of the PC from the start of the procedure. This construction ensures that only complete procedures are marshaled and also that absolute and site-specific addresses are translated into relative and hence site-independent values.

All values are first-class including procedures, objects and classes. A procedure accessed by a thread is transferred only once for each thread. Migration of another thread that has the same procedure reference leads to a second transfer of the same procedure. However all distributed stateful entities have globally unique identifiers which means that procedures (and other stateful entities) are represented at most once at each site.

6   Evaluation

The evaluation scenario used here is inspired by the paradigmatic mobile agent evaluation (see [10]). First, we compare the performance of the mobile agent model built on top of thread-based mobility with the client-server model. Then we compare the performance of two implementations of the mobile agent model: one is based on the Mozart implementation and the other is based on the NO-MADS [11] implementation.

The first test is performed on a single processor machine (Pentium 750 MHz, 384 MB RAM) running the Linux Gentoo 2.4.19-gentoo-r5 operating system. It is repeated 10 times and the standard deviation was smaller than 0.2 percent.

The second test is performed on a single processor machine (AMD Athlon XP 1700+, 512 MB RAM) running the Windows 2000 operating system (the NOMADS system is only available for the Windows platform). It is repeated 10 times and the standard deviation was smaller than 0.3 percent.

The task of the application is to collect a list of hotels with phone numbers in one town at a customer site S_c. Two database servers are consulted: The hotel database server H at the site S_H to obtain a list of available hotels in the specified town; the phone database server P at the site S_P to obtain a phone number of each hotel from the list, one at time.

6.1   Client-Server Versus Mobile Agent

Client-Server. The client at the customer site sends a hotel list request req_h to the H server. After the list has been received, the client sends one request req_p per hotel to the server P to obtain telephone numbers. The total time for

Table 1. Mobile Agent vs. Client-Server in the information collection

	Number of hotels				
	1	10	20	30	40
Client-Server (ms)	80	370	710	1040	1380
Mobile Agent (ms)	410	410	410	410	440

(a) On a WAN

	Number of hotels						
	10	20	30	40	50	100	200
Client-Server (ms)	3	6	10	13	17	35	82
Mobile Agent (ms)	6	7	7	8	9	12	24

(b) On a single computer

the task is equal to the time for req_h plus the time for $n * req_p$, where n is the number of hotels.

Mobile Agent. The mobile agent moves from the customer site S_c to the site S_H and requests a list of hotels locally. After the list has been received, the agent moves to the site S_P and queries the server P for telephone numbers. When all phone numbers are collected the agent moves back to the site S_c and returns the result.

Results. We assume that database operations have constant cost. We have performed two measurement:

– The customer is sited on a computer in Germany[1] and the servers are sited on computers in Sweden[2].
– The customer and the servers are sited on a single machine in three processes.

We vary the number of returned hotels and measure the total time in both solutions. Tables 2(a) and 2(b) summarize the results. We see that in the WAN case for small numbers of hotels the client-server is more efficient than the mobile agent. In all other cases the mobile agent is much more efficient and it scales.

The second test shows that the client-server performs better only if the number of hotels is less than 20. The test also shows that in the case of client-server the time increases linearly with the number of hotels, which is not the case with the mobile agent. In the case of the client-server, communication is performed between operating system processes. In the case of the mobile agent communication is performed between threads inside one operating system process.

The evaluation shows that the mobile agent model is not only well adjusted to the distributed applications that run over WAN, but for applications that run over cluster, grid, and LAN as well.

6.2   Mozart Versus NOMADS

In the second part of the evaluation two implementations of the mobile agent model are compared, our implementation in Mozart and the NOMADS system implemented in Java running on the virtual machine Aroma. The test is per-

---

[1] Universität des Saarlandes
[2] Swedish Institute of Computer Science, SICS

Table 2. Mobile Mozart vs. NOMADS in the Information Collection

	Number of hotels			
	10	20	30	40
Mozart (ms)	210	220	220	220
NOMADS (ms)	3609	4625	5656	6766

formed on a single machine. In the case of Mozart the same agent implementation is used as in the test described above.

The agent written in Java uses RMI for communication with H and sockets for communication with P. Sockets are used instead of RMI because the RMI implementation in Aroma does not work with mobile agents.

Table 2 shows that our implementation has much better performance and that it scales much better than the NOMADS system.

7   Related Work

Related work can be best classified with respect to the following main criteria: what is the unit of mobility for the approach; whether strong or weak mobility is supported; what is the connection to support for distributed programming; how is mobility implemented (or what is the underlying implementation architecture for mobility).

Which unit of mobility is chosen in a certain approach typically coincides with the preferred abstraction of structuring programs in a certain programming language. Current approaches choose either objects, agents, operating system processes, or active objects combining objects and threads. Prominent approaches are the following, where we highlight what decisions are made for the above mentioned criteria.

Emerald [12] has been the first system that offers *fine-grained* mobility. The unit of mobility are objects. Migration is provided by the *move()* statement. In Emerald, threads follow objects as an object moves.

JoCaml [13] is an implementation of the Join-Calculus, which is a reformulation of the π-calculus making places of interaction explicit. The programming model is based on *locations* and *channels*. Sites are toplevel locations and agents are nested locations. Threads are not first-class entities. The unit of mobility is a location. Migration is provided by the *go()* statement.

Obliq is an untyped object-oriented interpreted language with distributed lexical scope developed at DEC by Cardelli [14]. Obliq supports weak mobility. Thus, remote execution is provided and when remote execution is requested the code representing a procedure is sent and executed at the remote site. Remote execution is function-call based and suspends until execution returns.

ARA [15] is a multi-language system that provides strong mobility. A migration unit in ARA is an agent. Agents are managed by a language independent system core and interpreters for supported languages (C, C++, Tcl, Java). An ARA agent cannot share data with other agents and resource bindings are removed prior to migration.

D'Agents [16] is a multi-language system consisting of Agent Tcl [17], Agent Java, and Agent Scheme. The first two support strong mobility (Agent Java is based on the Sumatra system). The unit of migration in D'Agents is a process in the case of Agent Tcl. The system provides a migration abstraction *agent_jump*. A D'Agent server must be running at each cooperating site. When an agent calls *agent_jump*, the complete state of the agent is captured and marshaled to the target machine. The D'Agent server on the target machine on reception creates a new process running the Tcl interpreter.

Sumatra [18] is a Java-based system and implements strong mobility by extending JVM. The unit of mobility is a new abstraction primitive *object-group*. The system is based on JDK 1.02 VM which does not use native threads and is not longer supported.

JavaThreads [19] is a JVM extension. The portable thread state is provided by a type inference technique and thread serialization by combination of type inference and dynamic de-optimization techniques. Migration in JavaThreads depends on the deprecated *stop()* method in *Java.lang.Thread*. The unit of mobility is a thread. The migration is provided by the *go()* statement.

NOMADS [11] is a Java-based agent system. It uses a custom virtual machine, known as Aroma, with the ability to capture thread execution states. Java threads are mapped to native operating system threads. The unit of mobility is a thread. Migration is provided by the *go()* statement.

8   Conclusion

We have presented a model and an implementation of thread-based strong mobility in a distributed lightweight concurrent system based on dataflow variables. Important migration abstractions Go, Pull, and Push are identified. These abstractions provide programming support for explicit thread migration covering many aspects of migration found in mobile applications.

The paper describes an implementation architecture which rests on thread replication and mobility managers. The implementation extends the Mozart system and reuses systematically its support for transparent distribution. The evaluation provides evidence that mobile applications can be constructed easily using thread-based strong mobility. Moreover, the performance is sufficient to construct mobile applications which are more efficient and scalable than a corresponding client-server architecture.

References

1. Fuggetta, A., Picco, G.P., Vigna, G.: Understanding Code Mobility. IEEE Transactions on Software Engineering **24** (1998) 342–361
2. Smolka, G.: The Oz programming model. In van Leeuwen, J., ed.: Computer Science Today. Volume 1000 of Lecture Notes in Computer Science. Springer-Verlag, Berlin (1995) 324–343
3. Van Roy, P., Haridi, S.: Concepts, Techniques, and Models of Computer Programming. MIT Press (2004)

4. Van Roy, P., Haridi, S., Brand, P., Smolka, G., Mehl, M., Scheidhauer, R.: Mobile objects in Distributed Oz. ACM Transactions on Programming Languages and Systems **19** (1997) 804–851

5. Haridi, S., Van Roy, P., Brand, P., Mehl, M., Scheidhauer, R., Smolka, G.: Efficient logic variables for distributed computing. ACM Transactions on Programming Languages and Systems **21** (1999) 569–626

6. Haridi, S., Van Roy, P., Brand, P., Schulte, C.: Programming languages for distributed applications. New Generation Computing **16** (1998) 223–261

7. Haridi, S., Franzén, N.: Tutorial of Oz. The Mozart Consortium, `www.mozart-oz.org`. (1999)

8. Duchier, D., Kornstaedt, L., Müller, T., Schulte, C., Van Roy, P.: System Modules. The Mozart Consortium, `www.mozart-oz.org`. (1999)

9. Mozart Consortium: The Mozart programming system (1999) Available from `www.mozart-oz.org`.

10. Hagimont, D., Ismail, L.: A performance evaluation of the mobile agent paradigm. In: Proceedings of the 14th ACM SIGPLAN conference on Object-oriented programming, systems, languages, and applications, ACM Press (1999) 306–313

11. Suri, N., Bradshaw, J.M., Breedy, M.R., Groth, P.T., Hill, G.A., Jeffers, R.: Strong mobility and fine-grained resource control in nomads. In: The Second International Symposium on Agent Systems and Applications / Fourth International Symposium on Mobile Agents, Zürich, Switzerland, Springer-Verlag (2000)

12. Jul, E., Levy, H., Hutchinson, N., Black, A.: Fine-grained mobility in the Emerald system. ACM Transactions on Computer Systems **6** (1988) 109–133

13. Conchon, S., Fessant, F.L.: Jocaml: Mobile agents for Objective-Caml. In: First International Symposium on Agent Systems and Applications (ASA'99)/Third International Symposium on Mobile Agents (MA'99), Palm Springs, CA, USA (1999)

14. Cardelli, L.: Obliq: A language with distributed scope. Technical report, Digital Equipment Corporation Systems Research Center, 130 Lytton Avenue, Palo Alto, California 94301, USA (1994)

15. Peine, H., Stolpmann, T.: The architecture of the Ara platform for mobile agents. In Popescu-Zeletin, R., Rothermel, K., eds.: First International Workshop on Mobile Agents MA'97. Volume 1219 of Lecture Notes in Computer Science., Berlin, Germany, Springer Verlag (1997) 50–61

16. Gray, R.S., Kotz, D., Cybenko, G., Rus, D.: Mobile agents: Motivations and state-of-the-art systems. Technical Report TR2000-365, Dartmouth College, Hanover, NH (2000)

17. Gray, R.S.: Agent Tcl: A flexible and secure mobile-agent system. Dr. Dobbs Journal **22** (1997) 18–27

18. Acharya, A., Ranganathan, M., Saltz, J.: Dynamic linking for mobile programs. In: Mobile Object Systems: Towards the Programmable Internet. Springer-Verlag (1997) 245–262 Lecture Notes in Computer Science No. 1222.

19. Bouchenak, S., Hagimont, D.: Zero overhead java thread migration. Technical Report 0261, INRIA (2002)

A Fault Tolerant Abstraction for Transparent Distributed Programming*

Donatien Grolaux[1], Kevin Glynn[2], and Peter Van Roy[2]

[1] CETIC asbl, Rue Clément Ader 8,
B-6041 Charleroi, Belgium
dg@cetic.be
[2] Université catholique de Louvain,
Département d'Ingénierie Informatique,
B-1348 Louvain-la-Neuve, Belgium
{glynn, pvr}@info.ucl.ac.be

Abstract. This paper introduces a network fault model for distributed applications developed with the Mozart programming platform. First, it describes the fault model currently offered by Mozart, and the issues that make this model inconvenient for building fault-tolerant applications. Second, it introduces a novel fault model that addresses these issues. This model is based on a localization operation for distributed entities, and on an event-based mechanism to manage network faults. We claim that this model 1) is much better than the current one in all aspects, and 2) simplifies the development of fault-tolerant distributed applications by making the fault-tolerant aspect (largely) separate from the application logic. A prototype of this model has been developed on the existing Mozart platform. This prototype has been used on real applications to validate the aforementioned claims.

1 Introduction

With the Internet distributed applications have become commonplace, and software environments have adapted to offer adequate programming support. At first, TCP/IP offered a reliable communication channel between two processes on remote computers to exchange information in byte form. Then, different schemes were invented to further abstract from the network layer: remote procedure calls (or method invocations), message based and event driven communication mechanisms (examples are Java's Remote Method Invocation [1], Web Services, and Erlang [2]), peer to peer communication patterns (e.g., JXTA [3]), and the transparent distribution of language entities (e.g., Mozart [4]). Since the Internet is not a reliable environment where all components are constantly available, these

---
* The first author was funded at CETIC by the Walloon Region (DGTRE) and the E.U. (ERDF and ESF). The second author was funded by European project PEPITO IST-2001-33234.

approaches also provide mechanisms for dealing with network faults. This paper focuses on the Mozart system, an implementation of the Oz language, which provides transparent distribution of language entities. We assume the reader is familiar with the Oz language (tutorials are available from the Mozart web site [5], or an overview is provided in Chapter 1 of Van Roy and Haridi's text book [6]).

Section 2 introduces Mozart's distributed implementation of Oz. In Section 3 the current fault model of Mozart, which is based on the operations on language entities, is described and criticised. In Section 4 we propose a new approach based on the distributed entities, rather than the operations, and demonstrate its advantages. Finally, in Section 5 we conclude by describing a prototype version of this new model, a fault tolerant application written using it, and preliminary conclusions we can draw from this experience.

2   Transparent Distribution of Oz

The Mozart implementation of Oz offers distributed programming by attaching distributed protocols to the language entities [7]. In essence, a single Oz store is shared between the different inter-connected Oz processes. There is no explicit notion of communication channel between the processes at the language level. From the Mozart programmer's point of view, as long as there are no communication problems, there is no difference in operating on entities locally or remotely[1]. Similarly, a thread running in a remote process is equivalent to a local thread.

In practice, two or more processes have to share at least one common reference if they want to communicate. Once an entity is shared it can be used to introduce more shared entities. A typical example is a shared port: the output stream of the port stays local to the site that created the port and a reference to the port is shared with other processes. They can use the port reference to send information to the output stream of the port, and this information can include references to free variables, other ports, cells, locks, and so on. When exchanging a non-scalar reference a distributed protocol is transparently attached to the local entity (if not already done) to turn it into a global entity.

Of course, this mechanism requires a first reference to be exchanged between the different processes as a bootstrap mechanism. A built-in Mozart operation maps a local reference into a global identity, accessible by a unique, universal, human-readable name. Any process that knows this name can use it to create a reference to the original entity. The name can be transferred by any means, including voice call, email, web pages, and so on.

Figure 1 shows this mechanism being used to share variables between two Mozart processes. Process 1 exports a reference to the variable A as a text string. This string is given (by mail, phone, web interface, and so on) to process 2 which imports the variable as B. Now both sites have a shared virtual store. Process 2

---

[1] Assuming the entity does not refer to localised resources (local file system, keyboard or display, for example). We assume this to be the case in this paper.

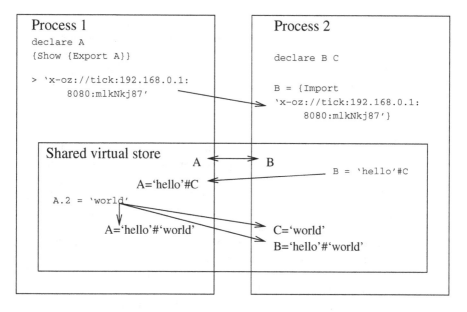

Fig. 1. Transparent Distribution in Oz

assigns a value to B containing a reference to C (B=`hello`#C); the shared virtual store reflects this assignation in Process 1 too. Now C is shared by both sites as they both have a reference to it. Process 1 indirectly assigns a value to C (A.2=`world`) and this is reflected back to Process 2.

3   Fault Tolerance Management

As already explained, a remote entity is equivalent to a local entity as long as the communication between the different processes is never interrupted. This condition is not respected on real networks like the Internet. To achieve fault tolerance at the application level the network problems must be made visible at the language level. This breaks the transparency of the distribution: an operation that cannot fail on a local entity can fail on a remote one because of network problems. Breaking the transparency is unfortunate, but unavoidable[2]. The goal of our proposal is to minimize the cost of adding fault management to real distributed applications.

3.1   Fault Tolerance Management in Mozart

First, we take a look at the current Mozart implementation and the mechanisms offered for managing network faults. There are two aspects involved:

---

[2] In the context of network transparency as provided by Oz. Other schemes use dedicated data structures and operations for remote entities where failure of communication is supported by the data type (for example, remote procedure calls).

1. The health of a distributed entity can be ok, permFail, or tempFail:
   - ok: operations on the entity are applied successfully for now.
   - permFail: the entity is in a permanent state of failure; no operation on the entity can succeed, ever. A permFail is definitive. permFails are detected only when the remote computer can certify the death of the process. This is usually only possible on local area networks when a process crashes; if the whole computer crashes, or no further communication is possible then the permFail cannot be detected.
   - tempFail: the entity is in a temporary state of failure. For now, the system cannot successfully apply operations on the entity but that may be possible in the future. A tempFail may turn into a permFail, may disappear, or may stay forever. Most network faults over the Internet produce a never-ending tempFail, instead of a permFail because of the lack of information about the remote site.

   An application can trigger a computation in a separate thread when an entity changes its state (these computations are called *watchers*)[3].

2. The behaviour of operations on distributed entities when there is a network fault. There are three possibilities:
   - Suspend the operation. This ensures that a distributed application that suffers from network problems does not do anything unwanted; instead all distributed operations block. In the case of a tempFail that eventually resolves itself the suspended operations are automatically resumed.
   - Raise an exception.
   - Replace the operation (message send, variable binding, and so on) by a user defined one. For example, a client could be configured to automatically switch to another server and retry the failed operation.

   An entity can be configured to have different behaviours for tempFail and permFail conditions. For example, operations may block during a tempFail and raise an exception during a permFail.

The idea behind this model is that Mozart programmers should first develop their applications centrally using threads to simulate the different processes. Once the application is locally complete and correct, the threads are taken away to become real processes on remote computers. At this stage, in the absence of network problems, the distributed application is already working correctly because of the network transparency. The designers of Mozart's distributed mechanisms assumed that fault tolerance could then be straightforwardly achieved by configuring each of the distributed entities to react correctly to failures.

In practice, this goal is almost impossible to achieve with Mozart's fault model for several reasons:

Network Transparency Conflicts with Modularity. With Mozart's current fault model entities change their semantics upon network problems. Depending

---

[3] Oddly this is not possible for the transition from tempFail to ok in the current Mozart implementation; so this mechanism cannot be used to trigger a computation when an entity is working again.

how the entity's fault management is configured, an operation on an entity might raise an exception, block, or execute an arbitrary piece of code, none of which it would ever do in the centralized case. This is a deep change of the entity's semantics that breaks the modularity of the language. A module is composed of a public interface and a private implementation; a module's user should only have to know the public interface. If a module is written for localized entities, it may not work in a distributed environment.

In practice, it is often necessary to understand the inner workings of code which we want to reuse for distributed entities and it is depressingly common that we must rewrite that code to make it fault-tolerant.

We demonstrate the difficulty of writing modular, transparent, fault-tolerant applications in the case study below.

Misleading Feedback from Asynchronous Operations. Probably the most heavily used communication scheme used by Mozart applications is to make remote procedure calls through an Oz port, using a free variable to hold the response from the other site. The fault detection provided by Mozart when sending a message to a Port is inadequate: the operation is intrinsically asynchronous but the fault detection mechanisms of Mozart are synchronous. Consequently, a Port.send operation might act as if it were successful when, in fact, the link is already down but not yet detected by Mozart. Similarly, a Port.send operation might fail when, in fact, the link is back up again but not yet detected by Mozart. As a general rule, the only way to be sure an asynchronous message was sent successfully is to have an acknowledgement protocol, i.e., to introduce some synchronization. Since the application must handle this anyway it is preferable that the Port.send operation should always succeed (as in Erlang), regardless of the current state of the network.

Lack of Control at the Application Level. Distributed applications can make good use of knowledge about the status of network connections. For example, to give feedback to the user, to allow the user to cancel a computation that is suspended due to a network problem, and so on. This is currently difficult to achieve.

Additionally, operations that are automatically retried by Mozart cannot be cancelled, they will be retried forever (until the whole process is killed). Unfortunately, it is not possible to completely avoid situations where that might happen.

This does not mean that it is impossible to write well-behaved, fault-tolerant Mozart applications. Several successful applications have been written using this model. However, in our experience, they circumvent the difficulties by hiding them in abstractions that offer a limited communication channel, and poor transparency, in exchange for nicer fault awareness and management. As a consequence, the transparency distribution of language entities is not directly used and it completely nullifies the benefits of transparent distribution in Mozart.

3.2   Case Study: A Simple Problem Requiring a Complex Solution

In this section we describe a simple distributed client server application. The server makes use of a procedure that was originally written for a centralized environment. Ideally, we would like to make the client-server application fault-tolerant without rewriting the given procedure, and without knowing how it is implemented. We show that this is not possible with Mozart's fault model.

For our case study we assume that we have a pair of Oz procedures, Add and GetValue. Add takes an integer as argument and adds it to the contents of an internal mutable cell shared only by Add and GetValue. A call to GetValue binds its argument to the current value of the shared cell.

If the argument to Add is an unbound variable then Add creates a thread to add the argument once it is bound. This thread only waits 3 seconds, if the variable is not bound in this time then it is bound to the atom ´ignored´ so that the caller can see that it was unsuccessful. In all cases, a call to Add returns without waiting or blocking.

It is simple to turn Add into a distributed server; we just create a port and call Add for all the entities received on the port's stream:

```
P={NewPort S}
thread {ForAll S Add} end
```

Here is a possible implementation of the Add and GetValue procedures:

```
local Counter={NewCell 0} in
   proc {Add V}
      if {IsDet V} then Old New in % do addition immediately
         {Exchange Counter Old New}
         New=Old+V
      else TimeOut in
         % run a thread to timeout the wait
         thread {Delay 3000} TimeOut=unit end
         % run a thread to wait for timeout or the value
         thread
            {WaitOr V TimeOut}
            % might have been already bound
            try V=ignored catch _ then skip end
            if V\=ignored then Old New in
               {Exchange Counter Old New}
               New=Old+V
            end
         end
      end
   end
   proc {GetValue V} V = @Counter end
end
```

If the entity sent to the server is already determined then it is immediately added to the internal Counter. If an unbound variable is sent then we create two threads and return. The first thread waits 3 seconds and binds the TimeOut variable. The second thread waits until either TimeOut or the variable are bound, then it binds V to ignored inside a **try** ... **catch** statement (if V was already bound then this statement has no effect, the unification error exception will be thrown away by the **try** .. **catch**). Finally, if V is not bound to ignored we add it to the internal counter. The additions to the counter are performed by Exchange which is atomic with respect to other threads attempting to update the counter.

In the absence of communication errors, this implementation is correct. Here are some possible calls from clients:

```
% Immediately adds 10 to the internal cell
{Port.send P 10}

% waits 2 seconds then adds 10 to the internal cell
local X in {Port.send P X} {Delay 2000} X=10 end

% waits 10 seconds, there will be a unification error
% as X will have been bound to 'ignored' already
local X in {Port.send P X} {Delay 10000} X=10 end
```

Now, consider making this application fault tolerant. Suppose a remote client sends a variable X to the server's port, as we have described previously we have a number of options:

We can make operations on X block. If the client has a tempFail or permFail condition then we might block in Add on the IsDet operation. In the case of a permFail we will block for ever, in the case of tempFail we may or may not eventually proceed. While Add is blocked the server is unable to service other clients. This is unacceptable, we would like the server to ignore this client and continue servicing other requests.

We can make operations on X raise an exception. The application may raise an exception when performing the V\=ignored test. This exception is not caught by the thread doing the test. In Oz, exceptions that are not caught by a thread terminate the whole application, so again this is unacceptable.

Finally, we can replace the operations on X. This mechanism replaces low-level, primitive operations on a distributed entity. For a variable the primitive operations are bind, wait, and isDet. For our application the only sensible replacement action would be to throw an exception, which we have already discussed. But even if we could modify this mechanism to give more control over the operations replaced, we can easily get problems. Suppose, for tempFail we replace the binding V=ignored with a **skip** operation. If the tempFail then immediately disappears we will block forever when testing if V\=ignored because V will be unbound!

In summary, it is impossible to make Add fully fault-tolerant without modifying it. Further, it is often necessary to understand the implementation of code in order to make it successfully tolerant to network failures.

The issues raised by this Add example (and more!) appear often when building real, distributed, fault-tolerant applications. In practice Mozart's current fault model is often difficult, and sometimes impossible, to use successfully.

4   A New Approach to Fault Tolerance Management

We have observed that fault management implies a change in the semantics of shared entities. The existing model spreads this semantic change to every operation on the entities in a very drastic way: temporary or infinite suspension of threads; exceptions where none was possible before; a completely new definition of the operation. To write an application that automatically recovers from network faults these semantic changes spread like a plague: every single distributed operation has to be taken care of, and asynchronous operations require complex workarounds.

We propose a model that minimizes the semantic impact of network faults on shared entities. We consider that shared entities are local entities synchronized with compatible local entities in remote processes. Entities act as a single global entity when there are no network problems. If this synchronisation fails then the synchronisation is dropped and the entity becomes an unsynchronised local entity. It is also possible for an application to explicitly remove the synchronization from an entity with the same result. If it is not possible to determine if the synchronisation is currently working (for example, because of a `tempFail`) then operations on the synchronised entity are suspended until it is working again, it fails, or the synchronization is explicitly dropped. In essence, the operations on the entities always keep their local semantics: if possible, operations are applied globally, otherwise they are applied only locally. If it is not possible to determine between these two then they are suspended until this determination is achieved.

This approach removes the need to define replacement operations for distributed operations, but it is not enough to achieve fault-tolerance. Applications need awareness about the synchronisation state of an entity in order to manage failures. In our approach we associate a possibly infinite list of states with each entity. `DistStates={Watch X}` assigns to the variable `DistStates` the list of states of entity `X`. The possible states when there are no network problems are:

`'local'` : the entity is not synchronized with any other entity.
`shared` : the entity is synchronized with at least one other entity in a remote process.

Figure 2 demonstrates the progression of distribution states with an example. Reading clockwise from the top left hand corner, the variable `V` is created in process 1 which then shares it with process 2. Process 2 terminates, and `V` is now local to process 1 again. Another process, process 3, shares `V` with process 1. `V` is assigned the atom `foo`. As scalar values are copied and do not need to be shared any more (scalar values are invariant over time), `V` becomes local for both process 1 and process 2 and will stay local forever.

By observing the change between these two states, an application can guess if a communication with a remote site has succeeded or not (in the above example, process 2 terminated itself and `V` became local again). However, it is not very easy to manage faults based on only this information:

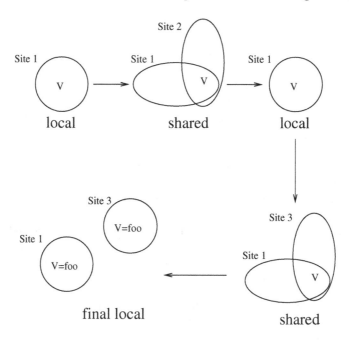

Fig. 2. Distribution States

1. The state stream is concurrent to the execution of the application; consequently, when an operation is applied on an entity that changes its state from shared to ´local´ it is not possible to know whether the operation was applied globally (the change occurred right after the operation) or only locally (the change occurred right before the operation).
2. It is important that the transparency property should go both ways: as well as turning a local application into a distributed one, we should also be able to turn a distributed application (or parts thereof) back into a local one. In particular, the modifications introduced to support fault tolerance in the distributed case should not break the application when it is run centralized. If the fault detection is based on the local/shared state then when run locally the application may think that the entity constantly has network problems.

Two more states are introduced to better manage network problems:

shared(suspend) : the entity is synchronized with at least one other entity in a remote process. However, due to a network problem, it cannot function globally for now. While this state lasts all operations on the entity block. When (if) the network problem disappears the blocked operations will be automatically resumed.

dirty: the entity used to be synchronized with at least one other entity in a remote process but a network problem, or an explicit operation, terminated that synchronization. Operations on the entity block while this state lasts.

Applications use the following operations to implement fault tolerance:

1. The `Break` operation takes an entity as parameter and puts it into the `dirty` state, whatever its original state. All remote synchronizations of the entity are dropped. By calling `Break` the application can force an entity from the `shared(suspend)` state.
2. The `Clean` operation takes an entity as parameter. If this entity is in the `dirty` state then it turns it into the ´local´ state, otherwise it does nothing. All operations that were blocked on the dirty entity resume on the local copy.
3. The `Watch` function returns the list of states of an entity, starting with its current state; new elements are added at each change of state. This list remains open as long as the current state can change; it is closed when the current state is final (as in Fig.2 above).
4. The `WaitCond` procedure blocks until the condition specified as parameter is fulfilled. The operation can specify complex conditions about the states of one or more entities. We do not provide further details here, but an example is shown below in the definition of `FaultTolerantAdd`.

Applications should be written to support the disconnection / unavailability of remote sites. This could happen at any time; threads working on entities shared with the remote site will block on them. Concurrently, watcher threads waiting (by using `WaitCond`) on the `shared(suspend)` and/or `dirty` state changes will be scheduled. If appropriate, the watcher thread can take whatever action is needed to cleanly separate the entity or application from the dead site. It can then resume the blocked operations by localizing the entities (using `Clean`). The work being done by threads on these broken entities is probably lost as they are now working on dummy local entities instead of the real globalized ones, but importantly they usually do not require to be adapted from their centralized version.

Fault detection via `shared(suspend)` and `dirty` does not break backward transparency (centralizing a previously distributed operation): in the local case these states never occur and the recovery actions are never triggered.

A fault tolerant version of `Add` in the case study (Section 3.2) would be:

```
proc {FaultTolerantAdd V}
   thread
      if {WaitCond ´or´(dirty(V) suspend(V) det(V))}\=det(V)
         then
         {Break V} {Clean V}
         try V=0 catch _ then skip end
      end
   end
   {Add V}
end
```

The server should call this procedure instead of `Add`. The additional thread waits for `V` to be bound, or to go into a network problem state. If it detects that `V` has a problem (`dirty` or `suspend`), then it breaks and cleans `V`, to make it 'local', and binds it to 0 so that this call to Add will not change the internal cell. The binding is done in a **try ... catch** in case the Add procedure has already bound V to ignored itself.

4.1 Properties of This New Model

1. It is possible to prevent distributed operations from suspending forever. Suspension is useful when one wants the system to retry the operation for some time. However, the retrying can be stopped using Break and Clean.

2. No semantic change to the entities. Contrary to the current Mozart model, a distributed entity cannot raise additional exceptions or execute arbitrary code compared to its local version. It can cause a suspension, but that suspension can be resumed externally. Consequently, in most situations, code written for local entities will also run unchanged for distributed ones. When a network failure occurs it is possible to complete running the code on a local version of the entity (to keep the current flow of the application) then take specific actions to recover from the failure. When this model is used efficiently the management of the failure can be achieved once per distributed entity, in a dedicated thread orthogonal to the rest of the application.

3. Asynchronous operations always succeed: detection of network problems is orthogonal to these operations. (Although they may block: asynchronous operations will be queued until sent or discarded, eventually an operation may block due to the unavailability of local resources such as buffers).

4. This model makes a trade-off. It simplifies applications by retaining local semantics for distributed entities, but possibly performs unnecessary computations on dummy entities. It is a fair trade-off for many cases where the rate of network faults is small or if the unnecessary computations are too small to be of any importance. If large, unnecessary computations may occur, it may be necessary to modify the application so that network fault detection can prematurely terminate the thread(s) of the computation.

5. The application has complete control over its communication channels. In particular, it may stop working with other sites at any time by breaking the distributed entities they are sharing.

6. This model is independent of the protocols used to synchronize distributed entities. In particular, if a protocol requires one or more particular communication links to run correctly this requirement does not appear directly at the application level. Instead, the distributed entity will switch from shared to shared(suspend) or dirty depending on the capacity of the underlying protocol to maintain its synchronization. If the protocols are changed then the application will not have to be adapted to reflect these changes.

7. The principle of a local entity synchronized with other local entities is independent of the type of entity being shared. As a result, this approach can be applied to any of Mozart's distributable entities, such as cells or locks. For example, in this model a cell shared among several sites can be broken then cleaned by any of the sharing sites. This site then has a local cell that contains the last locally known state of the distributed cell.

5   Conclusion and Future Work

A partial prototype version of this model, supporting ports and logic variables, has been implemented on top of Mozart's existing fault model. Due to restrictions in the current model it cannot directly use the usual Oz data types and operations because of the blocking requirement of the dirty state. Consequently, the prototype implements its own set of data types and associated operations.

This prototype was used to make a rather complex peer-to-peer algorithm fault tolerant. The algorithm was first written in a local setting, using threads to simulate nodes. It was extended to recover from the disappearance of any node in the network: this is the application-specific part which manages fault recovery. Then the node threads were turned into remote processes: this is straightforward thanks to the transparent distribution of Mozart. Finally, the algorithm was extended to add fault detection to the distributed entities. A watcher thread cleans faulty entities and tells the application to eject the corresponding node. This thread is a dozen lines of code, orthogonal to the remaining 5000 lines of code. The resulting application is fully fault-tolerant. This example validates the proposed approach, and shows it is possible to have a fault model that keeps both the modularity and transparency properties of distributed computing.

Due to space constraints this paper has omitted many details. A follow up paper will describe the implementation of the fault tolerant mechanisms for Mozart, we will address the problem of the identity of broken entities, and also we will describe how the different data types of Oz behave in case of faults.

We have described a novel fault tolerant abstraction for a language with transparent distribution and demonstrated that it solves fundamental problems that exist in Mozart's current fault tolerant abstraction.

References

1. Grosso, W.: Java RMI. O'Reilly (2001)
2. Armstrong, J., Virding, R., Wikström, C., Williams, M.: Chapter 6, Chapter 8. In: Concurrent Programming in Erlang. 2 edn. Prentice Hall (1996)
3. Flenner, R., Abbott, M., Boubez, T., Boubez, T., Cohen, F., Krishnan, N., Moffet, A., Ramamurti, R., Siddiqui, B., Sommers, F.: Java P2P Unleashed: With JXTA, Web Services, XML, Jini, JavaSpaces, and J2EE. Sams Publishing (2002)
4. Haridi, S., Van Roy, P., Smolka, G.: An overview of the design of Distributed Oz. In: Proceedings of the Second International Symposium on Parallel Symbolic Computation (PASCO '97), Maui, Hawaii, USA, ACM Press (1997) 176–187
5. The Mozart Consortium: Mozart documentation (2004) Available at http://www.mozart-oz.org/documentation/.
6. Van Roy, P., Haridi, S.: Chapter 1. In: Concepts, Techniques, and Models of Computer Programming. The MIT Press (2004)
7. Van Roy, P., Haridi, S., Brand, P.: Distributed programming in Mozart – a tutorial introduction (2004) Available at http://www.mozart-oz.org/documentation/.

The CURRENT Platform: Building Conversational Agents in Oz

Torbjörn Lager and Fredrik Kronlid

GU Dialogue Systems Laboratory,
Göteborg University, Department of Linguistics

Abstract. At the GU Dialogue Systems Lab in Göteborg we are embedding a conversational agent platform – the CURRENT platform – in the Oz programming language. CURRENT is based on a simple and intuitive characterization of conversational agents as interactive transducers, and on the fact that this characterization has a very direct implementation in Oz. Concurrency as offered by Oz allows our agents to 'perceive', 'think' and 'act' at the same time. Concurrency in combination with streams allow our agents to process input in an incremental manner, even when the original underlying algorithms are batch-oriented. Concurrency and streams in combination with ports allow us to specify the 'toplevel' transducer as a network of components – an interesting and highly modular architecture. We believe that software tools for specifying networks should have a strong visual aspect, and we have developed a 'visual programming language' and an IDE to support it. Also, we have found that if we specify the non-visual aspects of transducers and other components as class definitions that inherit the methods responsible for the interpretation of condition-action rules, regular expressions, grammars, dialogue management scripts, etc. from (abstract) classes provided by separate modules, we are able to hide most of the gory details involving threads, streams and ports from the agent developer.

1   Introduction

A *conversational software agent* is a program that is able to interact with a user, through typed text, spoken language and/or perhaps other modalities, and is capable of responding in an intelligent way to the user's requests. Building interesting and useful conversational agents is not an easy task as there are quite a few requirements that we want to impose on them. Since they are *agents* we expect them to interact with the environment, and perform (communicative) actions either on their own initiative (i.e. being proactive) or in response to (communicative) events which occur externally (i.e. being reactive). Since they are *conversational* agents we require of them the ability to process natural language – the ability to parse and to semantically and pragmatically interpret the user's (often fragmented or 'ill-formed') contributions as well as to generate sensible natural language responses in the course of a dialogue. Like with any

P. Van Roy (Ed.): MOZ 2004, LNCS 3389, pp. 161–174, 2005.

software we expect implementations to be modular and easily portable from one domain and/or task to another.

At the GU Dialogue Systems Lab in Göteborg we are embedding a conversational agent platform – the CURRENT platform – in the Oz programming language, taking advantage of what Oz has to offer in the form of streams, ports, lightweight concurrency and network-transparent distribution. We believe that this may provide new means for fulfilling some of the above requirements. Basically, the CURRENT platform comprises the following:

- An abstract characterization of what it means to be a conversational agent.
- A visual programming language allowing a developer to build a conversational agent by constructing a graphical representation of a network of NLP components on a canvas.
- An integrated development environment (IDE) supporting the development of collectives of conversational agents (where each 'project' corresponds to an agent).
- A number of ready-made NLP components such as lexica, taggers and parsers for a variety of languages, and dialogue managers for a variety of tasks.
- A number of libraries supporting the implementation of other such NLP components.
- A number of libraries providing support for 'other things', such as wrappers around databases, media players, http clients, etc.

We are interested not only in single agents in dialogue with single human users. We also intend to explore *multi-party dialogue*, where there may be three or more (human and/or artificial) agents engaged in dialogue (Kronlid, in preparation). In the simplest case, human agents are using simple chat clients to communicate with other agents in the community, but we also envision the use of multimodal chat tools, i.e. tools enhanced with speech recognition, speech synthesis and graphical input and output areas such as maps. From the beginning, CURRENT has been designed as an agent-based platform where different conversational agents/dialogue systems can be run in separate OS processes on different machines in a network, and may talk to each other over a server – an 'agent server'.

The present paper will concentrate on the development of single agents rather than whole communities, and the multi-party dialogue aspect of our work will not be dealt with at all.

2 Conversational Agents in CURRENT

2.1 An Abstract Characterization of Conversational Agents

From an abstract, theoretical point of view we think of a conversational agent as a kind of *transducer*.

> A conversational agent is an *interactive* transducer of one or more input streams of (representations of) communicative events into one or more output streams of (representations of) communicative events, accompanied by an evolving internal state.

By "interactive" we mean that the transducer is able to accept external input, as well as output (intermediate) responses, during the course of a transduction. Whereas ordinary transducers transform predetermined input strings into output strings, shutting out the world during the process of computation, interactive stream transducers are transducers of incrementally generated streams, which means that interaction with the external world – e.g. with a human agent – during computation is possible. The point is that a *whole* dialogue can and (we think) should be regarded as just *one* transduction, rather than one transduction per utterance or something like that. In fact, it makes sense to regard an agent's interaction with its environment throughout the agent's lifetime as just one transduction.[1]

2.2   The CURRENT Approach

Our characterization is abstract in the sense that it is meant to apply to all conversational agents – human as well as artificial – regardless of how they are implemented. The important thing from our point of view is that this abstraction has a very direct and straightforward implementation in a programming language such as Oz, where streams are provided as basic building blocks, where transducers working on streams are no harder to implement than transducers working on lists or strings, and where incrementality comes for free.

Our approach is *component based*. An agent consists of a network of components connected by *streams*. There are five kinds of components:

– A *source* turns real world communicative events into a stream of representations of communicative events, in the form of Oz records.
– A *transducer* reads records from exactly one input stream and writes records to exactly one output stream.
– A *splitter* reads records from exactly one input stream and writes records to two output streams.
– A *merger* reads records from two input streams and writes records to one output stream.
– A *sink* turns a stream of representations of communicative events into real world events.

Typically, sources correspond to input devices such a speech recognizers, text input widgets, clickable maps, etc., whereas sinks correspond to output devices such as speech synthesizers and text output widgets. The majority of natural language processing components are transducers. Here we find tokenizers, lexica, morphological analyzers, taggers, parsers, dialogue managers, etc. Exactly where and how splitters and mergers are going to fit in the scheme of things is more of an open research question at this stage of the project, but in section 4.4 we sketch a few ideas.

---

[1] Peter Wegner's work on "interaction machines" (Wegner [1997]) has provided some of the inspiration for this view. To our knowledge, however, we are the first to regard conversational agents/dialogue systems in this manner.

3   The CURRENT Integrated Development Environment

At the heart of the CURRENT development environment we have placed a *visual*
programming language for gluing different components together. A developer
selects components from a number of floating palettes – one palette for each kind
of component – and places them on a canvas. By connecting the output streams
of some components with the input streams of other components the developer
builds a *network* which implements the application. At any time, a component
may be double-clicked, which will bring up an Emacs window loaded with the Oz
source code associated with the component. The code may be edited and saved
back into the component again. Also, the visual appearance of components –
name, colour, icon, etc. – may be changed at any time. The canvas supports the
generation of postscript, so that pretty flow diagrams may be created for later
inclusion in documents.

A developer is able to run his application by selecting Start from the Run
menu or by clicking on the Start button placed in the lower left corner of the
main window. If Oz compilation errors are detected, the offending component

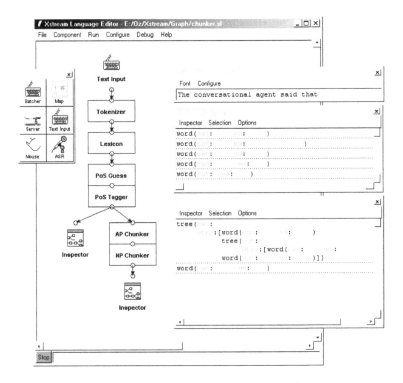

Fig. 1. Building and running an incremental part-of-speech tagger and chunker in
CURRENT. One inspector shows the output from part-of-speech tagging, the other the
chunker's output. Note the palette for source components in the upper left corner

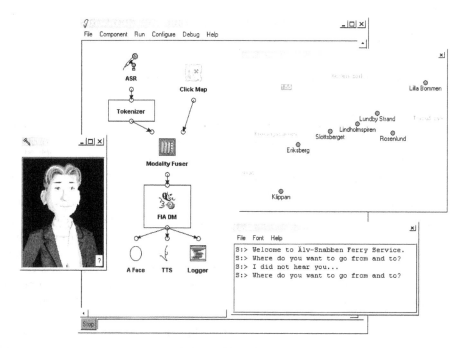

Fig. 2. Running a multimodal conversational agent in CURRENT. The speech recognizer (ASR), the text-to-speech module (TTS) and the animated face component are borrowed from the CSLU Toolkit (Sutton et al. [1998])

is marked with a thick red frame, and an error message dialogue is displayed. If compilation and initialization succeeds, some of the components, in particular the sources and the sinks, will display graphical widgets allowing textual, spoken or graphical input or output. Now, the developer is able to try his application out.[2]

As an aid for run time debugging, an edge blinks in red each time a record is placed on the corresponding stream, thus creating a 'running light' or 'electric current' effect indicating the flow through the network. The content of a stream may also be inspected by selecting from the right-click menu while the mouse pointer is placed over the corresponding edge. A modified version of the Oz Inspector is used for this purpose.

At any time, by selecting Add to Palette from the right-click menu, the developer may decide to copy a component from the canvas to the relevant palette. This is how the reuse of components is supported by the system.

We take the visual aspect of programming with a network of concurrent stream processors very seriously. Our design for a special purpose *visual programming language* embedded in Oz has been informed by (Lee & Webber [2003]). A lot of time and effort has gone into the implementation of a well-designed and

---

[2] An agent may also be run in a stand-alone mode, separately from the IDE.

robust user interface, and although still in alpha, we expect this tool to become widely used in the future, at least in our own projects.

4   CURRENT Components and Component Technologies

CURRENT components do not form a closed set. The platform is *extensible* in the sense that new components may always be added to it. In this section we will go into more detail about a few examples of components and component technologies available in the current version of CURRENT. Along the way, we try to say something about the underlying philosophy, and also a little about how Oz is used in the actual implementations.

On the Oz level, a CURRENT component corresponds to a *functor*. The functor exports a feature, either source, transducer, splitter, merger or sink, depending on what kind of component it is. The value of the feature is always a *class*, and (by inheritance) the class has features corresponding to the input and/or output stream(s) the component expects. For example, a class C corresponding to a transducer component has features in and out as well as a method run() that will initiate and run an object O of C in a separate thread, reading from O.in and writing to O.out.

We strive to *hide* the stream(s), the thread(s) and the implementation of a particular stream transduction strategy from the developer. Ideally, the only thing that should meet the eye of the developer double-clicking the graphical representation of (say) a transducer component is a description in linguistic or other high-level terms of the transduction between the input stream and the output stream.

4.1   Pattern Matching over Streams of Records

CURRENT supports an NLP paradigm which was pioneered with Appelt's ([1996]) CPSL (Common Pattern Specification Language) and which is used also on the well-known GATE platform (Cunningham et al. [2002]). The idea is based on condition-action rules where conditions are described in terms of patterns to match over some input and where actions involve building structured output. This method has been used mainly for batch-oriented information extraction purposes – for building keyword spotters, named-entity recognizers, phrase chunkers, etc. – but we believe that since a clever combination of threads and streams in Oz provides us with a general mechanism for turning what is usually done in batch into something incremental (cf. van Roy & Haridi [2004]), it has a role to play when building conversational agents and dialogue systems too.

We exemplify the use of the CURRENT pattern matching machinery by building a noun-phrase chunker which maps a stream of parts-of-speech tagged words represented by records of the form o(wd:<Word> cat:<Cat>) into a stream of parse trees represented by records of the form o(cat:<Cat> dtrs:<Subtree>).[3]

---

[3] The part-of-speech tags used here may be interpreted as follows: DT = determiner, NN = noun, JJ = adjective, and NNP = proper name.

This bottom-up, longest-match style of parsing is inspired by Abney ([1996]). Here is what meets the eye of a developer inspecting the source for this component:

```
functor
import
    TCS    at ´x-ozlib://current/control/TCS.ozf´
    Regexp at ´x-ozlib://current/interpreters/regexp/Regexp.ozf´
export
    transducer: NPchunker
define
    class NPchunker from TCS.chunkRule Regexp.match
        feat
            test: match(alt([con([opt(sym([cat#´DT´]))
                                  rep(sym([cat#´JJ´]) min:0)
                                  rep(sym([cat#´NN´]) min:1)])
                             rep(sym([cat#´NNP´]) min:1)]
                        label:np))
            todo: add(tree(cat:´NP´ dtrs:val(np)))
    end
end
```

The rule is implemented by a class **NPchunker** which inherits from two other classes. The class **TCS.chunkRule** implements a stream transduction control strategy based on a condition-action rule. A class inheriting from **TCS.chunkRule** is expected to provide values for two features **test** and **todo**, which specify the condition and the action of the rule, respectively. If the test applied to an initial part of the input stream succeeds, then the action (typically involving an update of the output stream) is performed, else the head of the input stream is placed in the output stream. In either case, the rule is then applied to the remaining part of the input stream in order to generate the rest of the content of the output stream.

The **NPchunker** class also inherits from the class **Regexp.match** which ensures that the rule will know exactly what to do with the value of the **test** feature, in this case treat it as (part of) a call to an interpreter of labelled regular expressions over the input stream of records. **Regexp.match** supports regular expression pattern matching, allowing operators for con(catenation), rep(etition), alt(ernation) and opt(ionality) to be used. Put in a more conventional notation, the above rule is looking for matches to [[(DT) JJ* NN+] | NNP].[4] Regular expressions matching has been enhanced with a labelling construct. If a subexpression is named by some label, whenever this subexpression matches some sequence of elements in a stream, that sequence, in the form of an Oz list, is assigned to the label. As a note of implementation, the regular expression interpreter has been implemented in roughly 150 lines of code using the Oz **choice** construct and the built-in search that Oz provides.

---

[4] We note that Abney argues that greedy (longest match) matching is the way to go here. This is what the **rep** operator does by default. The **rep** operator has a feature **mode** the value of which is either **greedy** or **lazy**. The default is **greedy**.

The value of the **todo** feature forms (part of) a call of a method **add()** that will update the output stream with a record representing a noun-phrase parse tree. The value assigned to the label in the **test** part of the rule is used to build the parse tree.

The module **TCS** gives access to a number of classes, implementing various stream transduction control strategies. Apart from **TCS.chunkRule** the module **TCS** also contains **TCS.caseRule** which allows a sequence of **test-todo** pairs to be tried in order, where the **todo** corresponding to the first succeeding **test** is performed, and **TCS.appeltRule** where the action corresponding to the longest-matching **test** is performed. We exemplify the former strategy with the "Hello World" of CURRENT – a simple Eliza style component:[5]

```
class Eliza from TCS.caseRule Regexp.match
    feat
        cases:[class $ from TCS.´case´
                  feat
                      test: match(con([sym(´I´)
                                       sym(nil label:x)
                                       sym(you)
                                       sym(´.´)]))
                      todo: add(´Why do you ´ # val(x) # ´ me? ´)
              end
              class $ from TCS.´case´
                  feat
                      test: match(sym(mother))
                      todo: add(´Tell me more about your family.´)
              end]
end
```

Sometimes, regular expression matching is not enough, and we would like to call on something more powerful, such as full, deep parsing (using e.g. phrase-structure grammars) and translation into logical forms. Parsing is easy, and thanks to the availability of first class functions in Oz, it is straightforward to do compositional logical semantics for natural language in a fairly orthodox style.

We give a simple example of a transducer able to process a stream containing sentences such as "John saw Mary" and translate them into their logical forms, like so:

```
´Indeed´|´John´|saw|´Mary´|and|´Mary´|saw|´John´|´.´|_<Fut>
```

is transduced into the stream

```
´Indeed´|saw(j m)|and|saw(m j)|´.´|_<Fut>
```

---

[5] In order to save space, functor declarations – imports, exports, etc. – are left out of the examples from here on.

Here is the code:

```
Grammar =
o(rules:[
           s  # [np vp] # fun {$ [NP VP]} {NP VP} end
           np # [pn]    # fun {$ [N]} N end
           vp # [tv np] # fun {$ [V NP]} {V NP} end
           ]
    lex:[
         'John' # pn # fun {$ P} {P j} end
         'Mary' # pn # fun {$ P} {P m} end
           saw  # tv # fun {$ W}
                              fun {$ X}
                                  {W fun{$ Y} saw(X Y) end}
                              end
                         end
         ]
  )

class MyParser from TCS.chunkRule Parser.parse
    feat
        test: parse(Grammar start:s label:sem)
        todo: add(val(sem))
end
```

Note that the semantics for "John" is represented by an Oz function corresponding to the lambda expression $\lambda P[P(j)]$, and for "saw" we have chosen a function corresponding to $\lambda W[\lambda x[W(\lambda y[saw(x, y)])]]$. Informed by this grammar, the parser inherited from **Parser.parse** takes care of parsing as well as the function applications and beta reduction steps necessary for putting together the logical forms corresponding to full sentences.

4.2   Tagging with Transformation Rules

CURRENT also supports the transformation-based tagging paradigm invented by Eric Brill ([1995]). In their CURRENT incarnation, the purpose of transformation rules is to replace some of the values of record features with other values, on the basis of values of features of records in the local input-stream context. Rules can be made to perform a variety of tasks such as part-of-speech disambiguation, noun phrase detection, word sense disambiguation and dialogue act recognition (Lager [2001]). Moreover, rule sequences may be induced from manually tagged corpora, using the transformation-based learning (TBL) method (Brill [1995]). In a component for part-of-speech tagging, we may find something like this:

```
class MyTagger from Core.tagger
    feat
        rules: [replace(pos `VB` `NN`) # [pos#`DT`#[~1]]
                replace(pos `IN` `RB`) # [wd#as#[0] wd#as#[2]]
                ...
                ]
end
```

The first rule means "replace value VB of the pos feature with NN if the value of the pos feature of the previous (-1) record has the value DT". The second rule is to be read "replace value IN of the pos feature with RB if the value of the wd feature of the current (0) record has the value 'as' and the wd feature of the record two steps behind has the value 'as'". Conditions may refer to different features in the input, conditions may look backward or forward, and complex conditions may be composed from simpler ones. Two or more rules may be connected into sequences – or composed – by placing them in a list, where the output of the rule at position i in the sequence forms the input to the rule at position $i + 1$.

The CURRENT platform comes with a component for part-of-speech tagging of English, consisting of 278 rules, and achieving an accuracy of 95-97% when evaluated on typical English language data. In this component, each rule is a stream transducer running in a separate thread, reading from the stream that the rule that is placed before it in the sequence is writing to, and writing to the stream that the rule after it is reading from. Thus, corresponding to the 278 rules we have 279 streams and 278 threads. This creates an overhead, but in the kind of applications that we are interested in, the speed is more than adequate, allowing us to part-of-speech tag around 10-25 words per second (which is faster than anyone can speak or write). The almost word-by-word incrementality that we achieve makes it worth it.

4.3   Dialogue Management in CURRENT

A dialogue manager is an important component in any conversational system, and we plan to experiment with several approaches in the future. At this time however, CURRENT supports only a simple dialogue management technology based on VoiceXML and the form-filling paradigm. VoiceXML is a W3C recommendation designed to be easy to use for simple interactions, and yet provide language features to support more complex ones, such as mixed initiative conversations (McGlashan [2004]). One motive for providing a component technology inspired by VoiceXML is to allow dialogue services written in VoiceXML to be straightforwardly translated into something that works on the CURRENT platform. Another motive is that the performance of a VoiceXML-based approach may serve as a baseline, to which the performances of future approaches may be compared.

Similar to a VoiceXML document, a CURRENT FIA-DM component consists of *forms* interpreted by an implicit form interpretation algorithm (FIA). A form defines an interaction that collects values for a set of *form items* such as *blocks* and *fields*.

The FIA has a main loop that repeatedly selects the first form item in the order of appearance which does not yet have a value. If a simple form contains only fields, the user will be prompted for each field in turn. A field may specify a regular expression or grammar that defines the allowable inputs for that field. If a form-level regular expression or grammar is present, it can be used to fill several fields from one utterance.

The example in Figure 3, adapted from an example in section 2.3.3 of the VoiceXML recommendation, shows a typical mixed-initiative form. A DM.initial item is visited when the user is initially being prompted for form-wide information, and has not yet entered into the directed mode where each field is visited individually. At this point the user may be able to fill more than one field (in our example both fromCity and toCity) using only one utterance.

```
class $ from DM.form
   feat
      id: getFromAndToCities
      test: match(con([opt(sym('from'))
                       sym(Station label:fromCity)
                       sym(to)
                       sym(Station label:toCity)]))
      items: [
             class $ from DM.block
                feat
                   todo: prompt('Welcome to the Driving Distance Service.')
                end
             class $ from DM.initial
                feat
                   name: bypassInit
                   todo: prompt('Where do you want to drive from and to?')
                meth nomatch()
                   if {self nomatchCount($)}==1 then
                      {self prompt('Please say something like "from Oslo to Kiel".')}
                   else
                      {self prompt('I\'m sorry, I still don\'t understand. '#
                                   'I\'ll ask you for info one piece at a time.')}
                      {self assign(name:bypassInit expr:true)}
                      {self reprompt()}
                   end
                end
             end
             class $ from DM.field
                feat
                   name: fromCity
                   todo: prompt('From which city are you leaving? ')
                   test: match(sym(nil label:fromCity))
                end
             class $ from DM.field
                feat
                   name: toCity
                   todo: prompt('Which city are you going to? ')
                   test: match(sym(nil label:toCity))
                end
             class $ from DM.trigger
                feat
                   trig: filled(namelist:[fromCity toCity])
                meth filled(From To)
                   Distance = {DistanceDB lookup(From.1 To.1 $)}
                in
                   {self prompt('From '#From.1#' to '#To.1#' is '#Distance#' km.')}
                   {self clear(namelist:[bypassInit fromCity toCity])}
                end
             end
             ]
end
```

Fig. 3. A CURRENT FIA-DM dialogue management example, inspired by the example in section 2.3.3 of the VoiceXML recommendation (McGlashan [2004])

The FIA is designed to trigger *events* at various points during processing. For example, the `noinput` event is generated when – after being prompted – no input is supplied by the user within a certain timeout period, and the `nomatch` event is generated when the input supplied does not match the current field's regular expression or grammar. Events (Oz method calls in the implementation) may be handled locally to the current field (like in the class inheriting from `DM.initial` in the example), but if no method is defined for it locally, it will be delegated to the form-level, and if not handled there either, a default handler provided by the FIA will eventually take care of it.

The assignment of values to fields may trigger *filled actions* – actions to be performed when some combination of field items are filled. In the example in Figure 3, the filling of the fields `fromCity` and `toCity` triggers a database lookup that provides the answer to the user's question.

Due to space limitations, the example in Figure 3 does not reflect the fact that in a FIA-DM component, as well as in a VoiceXML document, it is possible to have more than one form, and to define jumps between them in a state-machine manner, on the basis of actions or events being triggered.

4.4   Other Components

The previous sections have covered only a selection of the components and component technologies that are available in CURRENT. For the sake of completeness, let us mention a few others very briefly. *Lexica* are naturally treated as transducers from streams of wordforms into streams of records capturing lexical analyses of words. At this stage, an English lexicon with around 90,000 forms is available. Also, an *unknown-word guesser*, performing prefix and suffix analysis of wordforms not in the lexicon in order to guess their part-of-speech has been built, using a sequence of 56 machine-learned transformation rules. Abney-style chunkers for English adjective phrases and verb clusters has been constructed as well. These are all available for selection from palettes, and together they represent a significant resource for the analysis of English. Other NLP components under construction include components for language identification, stemming, morphological analysis, syntactic parsing, etc., but also more sophisticated components such as dialogue managers based on the information-state update approach (Larsson [2002]).

As we noted in Section 2.2, exactly where and how splitters and mergers of various kinds are going to fit in with the rest is an open research question at this stage of the project, and a very interesting one at that. Here are some tentative suggestions: Given a chain of transducers performing (say) part-of-speech tagging followed by (say) chunking, it may well be that we want to 'tap' the stream (by using a fair splitter) just after the part-of-speech tagger, in order to feed the stream, not only to the chunker, but also to other components having use for it. This is what is suggested in Figure 1. Furthermore, in multimodal settings, one needs to do so called 'modality fusion' and 'modality fission', and this suggests that variants of merging and splitting may be useful. This is hinted at in Figure 2. Finally, in NLP it is sometimes wise to process the same input using more than one method, and select the 'best' analysis afterwards. Splitting the input and using one component per method in parallel and then performing some sort of selective merge seems like a good approach that fits well into the CURRENT architecture. No doubt, other interesting ways of using splitting and merging may surface further down the road.

5 Summary and Conclusions

We have based the CURRENT platform for building conversational software agents on a simple and intuitive characterization of conversational agents as interactive transducers, and on the fact that this characterization has a very direct implementation in Oz. Concurrency as offered by Oz allows our agents to 'perceive', 'think' and 'act' at the same time. Concurrency in combination with streams allow our agents to process input in an incremental manner, even when the original underlying algorithms are batch-oriented. Concurrency and streams in combination with ports allow us to specify the 'toplevel' transducer as a network of components – an interesting and highly modular architecture. We believe that software tools for specifying networks should have a strong visual aspect, and we have developed a 'visual programming language' and an IDE to support it. Also, we have found that if we specify the non-visual aspects of transducers and other components as class definitions that inherit the methods responsible for the interpretation of condition-action rules, regular expressions, grammars, dialogue management scripts, etc. from (abstract) classes provided by separate modules, we are able to hide most of the gory details involving threads, streams and ports from the agent developer.

We have found that the expressiveness of Oz allows us to concentrate on semantics rather than on syntax. Indeed, we have resisted the temptation to design and implement special purpose notations for regular expressions and different kinds of rules, and have instead opted for an 'Oz syntax only' approach. It means that in order to become a serious CURRENT developer one has to learn Oz, but we think that this is easier and also more rewarding in the long run, than to learn a large number of different home-brewed notations – one for each component technology available on the platform.

We also believe that, as a consequence of our 'Oz syntax only' approach, CURRENT could develop into a useful teaching environment. Students would be able to learn the main ideas behind GATE's pattern matching language, transformation-based tagging, compositional-logical semantics and VoiceXML, on the same platform, and without having to learn four fundamentally different notations. We see this in analogy to how Oz is used in (van Roy & Haridi [2004]) to teach the concepts underlying Haskell, Erlang, Java and Prolog.

Acknowledgements

We thank the other members of the GU Dialogue Systems Laboratory – Robin Cooper, Stina Ericsson, David Hjelm and Staffan Larsson in particular – for interesting discussions and good cooperation.

References

Abney S (1996) Partial Parsing via Finite-State Cascades. In: Proceedings of the ESSLLI '96 Robust Parsing Workshop.

Appelt DE (1996) The Common Pattern Specification Language. Technical report, SRI International, Artificial Intelligence Center.

Brill E (1995) Transformation-Based Error-Driven Learning and Natural Language Processing: A Case Study in Part of Speech Tagging. Computational Linguistics 21, pp. 543-565.

Cunningham H, Maynard D, Bontcheva K and Tablan V (2002) GATE: A Framework and Graphical Development Environment for Robust NLP Tools and Applications. In: Proceedings of the 40th Anniversary Meeting of the Association for Computational Linguistics (ACL'02). Philadelphia.

Kronlid F (in preparation) Multi-Party Dialogue in Agent Communities. PhD thesis, Göteborg University.

Lager T (2001) Shallow Processing and Cautious Incrementality in a Dialogue System Front End: Two Steps Towards Robustness and Reactivity. In: Matousek V, Mautner P, Moucek R and Tauser K (Eds.) Proceedings of the Fourth International Conference on Text, Speech and Dialogue (TSD 2001). Springer-Verlag, Lecture Notes in Computer Science. VOL. 2166.

Larsson S (2002). Issue-based Dialogue Management. PhD thesis, Göteborg University.

Lee P and Webber J (2003). Taxonomy for visual parallel programming languages. School of Computing Science University of Newcastle upon Tyne. See also: http://www.cs.ncl.ac.uk/research/pubs/trs/papers/793.pdf

McGlashan S (Ed.) (2004) Voice Extensible Markup Language (VoiceXML) Version 2.0. W3C Recommendation 16 March 2004. Available at http://www.w3.org/TR/voicexml20/

van Roy P and Haridi S (2004) Concepts, Techniques, and Models of Computer Programming. MIT Press.

Sutton S, Cole R, de Villiers J, Schalkwyk J, Vermeulen P, Macon M, Yan Y, Kaiser E, Rundle B, Shobaki K, Hosom P, Kain A, Wouters J, Massaro M, and Cohen M (1998) Universal speech tools: the CSLU toolkit. In Proceedings of the International Conference on Spoken Language Processing (ICSLP), pages 3221-3224, Sydney, Australia.

Wegner P (1997) Why interaction is more powerful than algorithms. In: Communications of the ACM, v.40 n.5, p.80-91.

The Metagrammar Compiler:
An NLP Application
with a Multi-paradigm Architecture

Denys Duchier, Joseph Le Roux, and Yannick Parmentier

LORIA Campus Scientifique, BP 239,
F-54 506 Vandœuvre-lès-Nancy, France
{duchier, leroux, parmenti}@loria.fr

Abstract. The concept of metagrammar has been introduced to factorize information contained in a grammar. A metagrammar compiler can
then be used to compute an actual grammar from a metagrammar. In
this paper, we present a new metagrammar compiler based on 2 important concepts from logic programming, namely (1) the Warren's Abstract
Machine and (2) constraints on finite set.

1 Introduction

In order to develop realistic NLP applications and support advanced research in
computational linguistics, large scale grammars are needed. By the end of 90's,
several such grammars had been developed by hand; especially for English [1]
and French [2].

Unsurprisingly, wide-coverage grammars become increasingly hard to extend
and maintain as they grow in size and scope. There is often grammatical information which cannot be adequately modularized and factorized using the
facilities offered by standard grammar formalisms. As a consequence, grammar
rules become distressingly rife with structural redundancy and any modification
frequently needs to be repeated in many places; what should be a simple maintenance intervention turns into a chore which is both work intensive and error
prone.

For these reasons, and others, a new methodology for grammar development
has emerged that is based on the compilation of meta-descriptions. These meta-
descriptions should help express simply linguistically relevant intuitions, as well
as mitigate the redundancy issue through better means of factorizing the information present in the rules of the grammar.

In this paper, we present a system designed for generating a wide-coverage
Tree Adjoining Grammar (TAG) from such a meta-description (generally called
a metagrammar). Our proposal is especially novel in that it adopts a resolutely
multi-paradigmatic approach: it combines (1) an object-oriented specification
language for abstracting, structuring, and encapsulating fragments of grammatical information, (2) a logic programming backbone for expressing the combina-

P. Van Roy (Ed.): MOZ 2004, LNCS 3389, pp. 175–187, 2005.

tions and non-deterministic choices of the metagrammatical specification, (3) a constraint-based back-end to resolve underspecified combinations.

2   Tree Adjoining Grammars

In this section, we informally introduce the notion of a *tree adjoining grammar* (TAG).

A grammar is a formal device used to describe the syntax of natural (or artificial) languages. While details vary, at heart, a grammar consists in the stipulation of a finite number of building blocks and a finite number of operations to combine them together.

In the Chomskian tradition of context free grammars, the building blocks are *production rules* and the only operation is the expansion of a non-terminal by application of a matching production rule.

In TAG, the building blocks are tree fragments, and there are two operations to combine them called *substitution* and *adjunction*. Substitution plugs one tree fragment into a matching leaf, marked for substitution (i.e. marked with ↓) of another tree fragment:

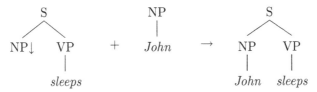

Adjunction splices in one tree fragment, from root to foot node (the latter marked with ∗), in place of a matching node in another tree fragment:

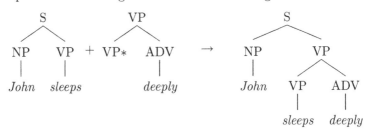

TAGs are used as a formalism designed for describing natural language syntax because of their linguistic properties [3]. A precise introduction to TAG is given in [4]. TAGs belong to the family of so-called *mildly context-sensitive* grammars as their generative capacity is larger than just the context free languages.

3   The Concept of Metagrammar

A TAG consists of a very large number (thousands) of tree fragment schemata. The reason for this large number of trees is that basically a TAG enumerates for each word all its possible *patterns* of use. Thus, not only can a verb be used in many ways (e.g. active vs. passive), but its arguments can also be realized in various ways such as direct object vs. clitic vs. extracted as illustrated in[1]:

- Jean mange *la pomme*
- Jean *la* mange
- la pomme *que* Jean mange

Thus, while a TAG will contain verbal tree fragments for these two constructions:

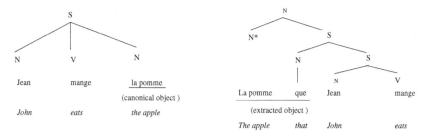

they actually both derive from the same linguistic intuitions about the possibilities for realizing a verb and its arguments. A formalism which only allows us to write tree fragments is insufficient to also express this higher-level view of how tree fragments actually arise simply from linguistic regularities governing how verbs and their arguments can be realized.

Adopting a more engineering-minded view, we arrive at a dual perspective on essentially the same issue: current large-scale TAG suffer from a high degree of structural redundancy as illustrated in:

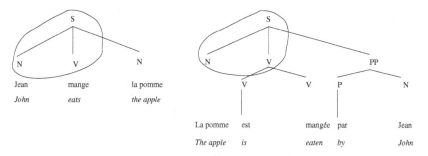

In order to ease development and maintenance, it would again be advantageous to be able to factorize such common chunks of grammatical information. Thus we have illustrated two important motivations for the factorization of grammatical information: (1) *structure sharing* to avoid redundancy [5], and (2) *alternative choices* to express diathesis such as active, passive. Attempts to address these issues lead to the notion of *metagrammar*, i.e. to formalisms which are able to *describe* grammars at a higher-level of abstraction and in more modular ways.

---

[1] In this paper, the tree schemas are inspired by [2] and are characterized by the absence of VP or NP nodes.

4   Existing Metagrammars and Compilers

The notion of metagrammar as a practical device of linguistic description (as opposed to merely increasingly expressive grammar formalisms) has a fairly short history, but is now rapidly gaining support in the linguistic community. In this section, we first review the seminal work of Candito [6], then the revised improvements of Gaiffe [7], finally leading to our own proposal[2].

4.1   A Framework Based on 3 Linguistic Dimensions

The first implementation of a metagrammar (MG) compiler was realized by Marie-Hélène Candito [6]. It laid down the bases of the MG concept which are:

- a MG is a modular and hierarchical representation of the trees of a TAG
- the hierarchy is based on linguistic principles

This compiler was used at the Université Paris 7 to automate the writing of the French TAG, was coded in Common LISP, and dealt with verbal trees.

Candito's MG methodology stipulates three dimensions, each containing hierarchically organized classes:

1. the first dimension provides the *initial subcategorization frame* (e.g. active transitive verb) which reflects the number of arguments of a verb and their positions.
2. the second dimension handles the *redistribution of syntactic functions*, i.e. the modifications of the function of the arguments defined in the 1st dimension (e.g. active becoming passive).
3. the third dimension expresses the different *realizations* for each syntactic function (canonical, cleft, etc).

Classes typically contain some topological information (e.g. tree descriptions [9]). The combination operation picks one class from the 1st dimension, one class from the 2nd dimension and n classes from the 3rd dimension, where n is the number of realized arguments of the verb. Figure 1 illustrates the idea of this 3-dimensional hierarchy and offers an example of a generated TAG tree. Candito's approach has the following drawbacks:

1. class evaluation is non monotonic, as some information can be erased during the compilation process, *e.g.* in agentless passive.
2. there is no clean separation between the knowledge encoded in the meta-description and the procedural knowledge encoded in the compiler. As a result (a) the compiler is hard to extend, and (b) you cannot define meta-descriptions with more than 3 dimensions.
3. the combination mechanism wildly attempts all possible class crossings. It is difficult to achieve enough control to avoid undesirable combinations.

---

[2] One should also consult Xia's work [8] to have a more complete view of the process of automatic generation of TAGs.

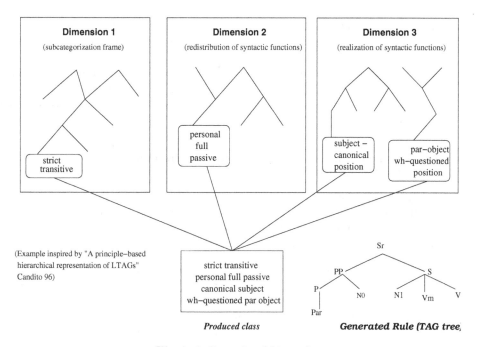

Fig. 1. 3-dimensional hierarchy

4.2   A Framework Based on the Concept of Needs and Resources

To address the issues identified with Candito's approach, Bertrand Gaiffe *et al.* at LORIA developed a new MG compiler [7], in Java, with the following properties:

- the process of class evaluation is monotonic;
- you may define an arbitrary number of dimensions instead of being limited to the strictly 3-dimensional approach of Candito.

In this implementation, a MG corresponds to several hierarchies of classes in multiple inheritance relation. The classes contain partial tree descriptions and/or node equations. The novelty is that classes can be annotated with *Needs* and *Resources*. For instance, the class for a transitive verb bears the annotation that it needs a subject and an object, while a class for a nominal construction would indicate that it supplies e.g. a subject. The combination process that produces the TAG grammar is entirely driven by the idea of matching needs and resources. However, there are still some drawbacks:

1. while the notion of needs and resources generalizes Candito's approach and allows to drive the combination process more accurately, it still exhibits the same practical drawback, namely that too many useless crossings must be explored. This problem, also present in Candito, comes from the lack of separation between the realization of *structure sharing* and the expression of *alternative choices*.

2. All node names have global scope (same as with Candito). In wide-coverage grammars, name management, and the discovery and handling of name conflicts become unrealistically difficult.
3. Since names have global scope, it is not possible to instantiate the same class more than once in a complex crossing because the names of the two instances would clash. This poses problems e.g. for constructions requiring two prepositional arguments.

4.3   A Framework Based on Nondeterminism and Underspecification

Our approach realizes a methodology developed jointly with Benoit Crabbé at LORIA and aimed at large TAG lexica [10]. Crabbé's essential insight is that instead of matching nodes very strictly by names, we can use some form of underspecification. The main requirements are:

1. There are no transformations, such as deletion, to compute a special form (*i.e.* passive, middle, extracted... for verbs) from the canonical form (basic active frame). Only alternative constructions are given. This is an important point (see [11]) since it makes our formalism monotonic and declarative.
2. Instead of being given names, nodes are assigned colors, which basically correspond again to a notion of needs and resources, that constrain how they can (or must) be matched.
3. Linguistically motivated global well-formedness principles can be stated that limit the admissibility of resulting combinations.

We depart from previous approaches on the following points:

1. The MG uses a logical language of conjunctions and disjunctions to express directly how abstractions are to be combined. With Candito, the mechanism is completely external to the MG. With Gaiffe, it is still implicit, but driven by needs and resources. Our method brings us consequent time savings during grammar generation.
2. The MG consists of classes arranged in a multiple inheritance hierarchy. Each class can introduce local identifiers, and their scope in the hierarchy can be managed with precision using import and export declarations. Renaming is supported.
3. We expressly wanted our MG to handle not only syntax, but also semantics. For this reason, our design is multi-dimensional, where each dimension is dedicated to a descriptive level of linguistic information. To our knowledge, ours is the first MG compiler to offer such a naturally integrated syntax/semantics interface.
4. Our design is not TAG-specific and can be instantiated differently to accommodate other formalisms. It is currently being adapted for Interaction Grammars [12].

Our tool is implemented in Mozart/Oz and has been used by linguists at LORIA to develop French wide-coverage grammars.

5   A New Metagrammatical Formalism

In this section, we first introduce the logical core of our formalism using the paradigm of *Extended Definite Clause Grammars* [13]. Then we introduce the object-oriented concrete level and show how it can be translated into this core.

5.1   Logical Core

Metagrammar as grammar of the lexicon. There is a well-known descriptive device which offers abstractions, alternations, and compositions, namely the traditional generative grammar expressed as production rules. In our MG application, the elements which we wish to combine are not words but e.g. tree descriptions, yet the idea is otherwise unchanged:

$$Clause \quad ::= \quad Name \rightarrow Goal \tag{1}$$

$$Goal \quad ::= \quad Description \mid Name \mid Goal \vee Goal \mid Goal \wedge Goal \tag{2}$$

We thus start with a logical language which can be understood as a *definite clause grammar* (DCG) where the terminals are tree *Description*s. We can already write abstractions such as:

$$TransitiveVerb \quad \rightarrow \quad Subject \wedge ActiveVerb \wedge Object$$
$$Subject \quad \rightarrow \quad CanonicalSubject \vee WhSubject$$

Tree description language. We adopt a tree *Description* language that is based on dominance constraints:

$$Description \ ::= \ x \rightarrow y \mid x \rightarrow^{*} y \mid x \prec y \mid x \prec^{+} y \mid x[f{:}E] \mid x(p{:}E) \tag{3}$$

x, y range over node variables, $\rightarrow$ represents immediate dominance, $\rightarrow^{*}$ its reflexive transitive closure, $\prec$ is immediate precedence, and $\prec^{+}$ its transitive closure. $x[f{:}E]$ constrains feature f on node x, while $x(p{:}E)$ specifies its property p, such as `color`.

Accumulations in several dimensions. When the meta-grammar terminals are syntactic tree fragments, we have a meta-grammar that can describe syntax, but we also want to support other descriptive levels such as semantics. Basically, we want to accumulate descriptive fragments on multiple levels.

This can be done simply by reaching for the formalism of *extended definite clause grammars* (EDCG) [13]: where a DCG has a single implicit accumulator, an EDCG can have multiple named accumulators, and the operation of accumulation can be defined arbitrarily for each one. In (2), we replace *Description* with:

$$Dimension \mathrel{+}= Description$$

which explicitly accumulates *Description* on level *Dimension*. In our application to TAG we currently use 3 accumulators: **syn** for syntax, **sem** for semantics, and **dyn** for an open feature structure accumulating primarily morpho-syntactic restrictions and other items of lexical information.

Managing the scope of identifiers. One of our goals is to support a concrete language with flexible scope management for identifiers. This can be achieved using explicit imports and exports. We can accommodate the notion of exports by extending the syntax of clauses:

$$Clause \quad ::= \quad \langle f_1{:}E_1, \ldots, f_n{:}E_n \rangle \Leftarrow Name \quad \rightarrow \quad Goal \qquad (4)$$

where $\langle f_1{:}E_1, \ldots, f_n{:}E_n \rangle$ represents a record of exports. Correspondingly, we extend the abstract syntax of a *Goal* to replace the invocation of an abstraction *Name* with one that will accommodate the notion of imports:

$$Var \Leftarrow Name \qquad (5)$$

To go with this extension, we assume that our expression language permits feature lookup using the dot operator, so that we can write $Var.f_k$, and that *Goals* can also be of the form $E_1 = E_2$ to permit equality constraints. Finally, we allow writing *Name* instead of $\_ \Leftarrow Name$ when the exports are not of interest.

5.2   Object-Oriented Concrete Syntax

A MG specification consists of (1) definitions of types, features and properties, (2) class definitions, (3) valuations. For lack of space, we omit concrete support for defining types, typed features attaching morpho-syntactic information with nodes, and properties annotating nodes with e.g. color or an indication of their nature (anchor, substitution node, foot-node...). We introduce the concrete syntax for class definitions by example, together with its translation into the logical core.

Class definitions. Classes may actually take parameters, but we omit this detail here. A class may introduce local identifiers, and export some of them, and has a body which is just a *Goal*. Here is an example on the left, and its translation into the logical core on the right:

```
class A
   define ?X ?Y
   export X
{ X=f(Y) }
```
$$\equiv \quad \langle X{:}X \rangle \Leftarrow A \quad \rightarrow \quad X = f(Y)$$

Inheritance is expressed with import declarations. Importing class A in the definition of class B is very much like instantiating (calling) it in B's body, except for scope management: when A is imported, all its identifiers are made available in B's scope and automatically added to B's exports.

```
class B { A }
class B import A
```
$$\equiv \quad \langle \rangle \Leftarrow B \quad \rightarrow \quad R \Leftarrow A$$
$$\equiv \quad R \Leftarrow B \quad \rightarrow \quad R \Leftarrow A$$

Our concrete language of course supports importing/exporting only selected identifiers, and renaming on import/export, but that is beyond the scope of this article. To get an intuitive understanding of how the concrete language is mapped to the core, let's look at the following example:

```
class C1              class C2              class C
declare ?X           declare ?Y           import C1 C2
export X             export Y             {
{                    {                      <syn>
  <syn>                <syn>                {X->Y}
  {node X[cat=s]}      {node Y[tense=past]}  }
}                    }
```

C1 (resp. C2) declares local identifier X (resp. Y) and exports it. Both of these classes accumulate some syntactic descriptions (a new node with some features). C imports both these classes and therefore can access X and Y as if they were locally defined, and adds the syntactic constraint that X immediately dominates Y. This code gets translated into the core as follows:

$$\langle \mathtt{X}{:}X \rangle \Leftarrow C_1 \quad \rightarrow \quad \begin{aligned} &\mathbf{syn} \mathrel{+}= \mathsf{node}(X) \\ &\wedge \mathbf{syn} \mathrel{+}= X[\mathsf{cat} = \mathsf{s}] \end{aligned}$$

$$\langle \mathtt{Y}{:}Y \rangle \Leftarrow C_2 \quad \rightarrow \quad \begin{aligned} &\mathbf{syn} \mathrel{+}= \mathsf{node}(Y) \\ &\wedge \mathbf{syn} \mathrel{+}= Y[\mathsf{tense} = \mathsf{past}] \end{aligned}$$

$$\langle \mathtt{X}{:}X, \mathtt{Y}{:}Y \rangle \Leftarrow C \quad \rightarrow \quad \begin{aligned} &E_1 \Leftarrow C_1 \ \wedge \ X = E_1.\mathtt{X} \\ &\wedge E_2 \Leftarrow C_2 \ \wedge \ Y = E_2.\mathtt{Y} \\ &\wedge \mathbf{syn} \mathrel{+}= X \rightarrow Y \end{aligned}$$

Valuations. While a grammar traditionally stipulates a start symbol, we have found it more convenient to let the grammar writer supply any number of statements of the form value E. For each one, all valuations of E, computed with our non-deterministic MG, are to be contributed to the lexicon.

6   Implementation of the Metagrammar Processor

The processor consists of 3 modules: a front-end to compile the object-oriented concrete syntax into the logical core, a virtual machine (VM) to execute core programs, and a solver to take the resulting accumulated trees descriptions and compute their minimal models, i.e. the TAG trees which they describe.

6.1   Compiler Front-End

The compilation process converts the MG object-oriented concrete syntax into our logic programming core, then compiles the latter into instructions for a VM inspired by the Warren Abstract Machine (WAM) [14].

Parsing was implemented using GUMP. The next step of compilation is to take care of scope management and resolve all identifiers. By examining and following import/export declarations, we compute for each class (1) all the identifiers in its scope, (2) its export record. This is sufficient to permit translation into the core.

We then compile the logical core into symbolic code (SCODE) for our VM. Every instruction is represented by a record and we have instructions for conjunction conj(_ _) and disjunction disj(_ _).

6.2   An Object-Oriented Virtual Machine

The VM implements a fairly standard logic programming kernel with chronological backtracking, but with some extensions. Contrary to the WAM which uses *structure copying*, our VM uses *structure sharing* where a term is represented by a pair of a pattern and an environment in which to interpret it. This technique enables us to save memory space, although pointer dereferencing can be time consuming. The VM is implemented as an object with methods for each instruction: in this manner it can directly execute SCODE. It maintains a stack of instructions (the success continuation), and a trail (the failure continuation) to undo bindings and explore alternatives.

The VM is meant to be extended with support for multiple accumulators. Each extension provides dedicated registers and specialized instructions for accumulating descriptions.

There are a number of reasons why it was more convenient to build our own VM rather than target an existing logic programming language. (1) this makes it easy to extend the VM with efficient support for non-standard data types such as open feature structures, properties, nodes and tree descriptions. (2) non-standard data types often require non-standard extensions of unification (e.g. the polarities of interaction grammars). (3) advanced constraint programming support is required to compute solutions of accumulated tree descriptions

When the VM has computed a complete derivation for a *valuation* statement, it takes a snapshot of its accumulators and sends it for further processing by the solver. It then backtracks to enumerate all possible derivations.

At the end of the execution we possibly have tree descriptions for each valuation of class. For TAG formalism trees are needed, thus we then have to find all the trees that are specifications of those descriptions. Because of the high complexity of this satisfiability problem, we chose a constraint-based approach to decrease the search space.

6.3   A Constraint-Based Tree Description Solver

In the last stage of processing, the snapshot $(D_1, \ldots, D_n)^3$ taken by the VM is then submitted to a solver module, where, for each dimension i, there is a specialized solver S_i for computing the solutions (models) $S_i(D_i)$ of the corresponding accumulated description D_i. The lexical entries contributed by the snapshot are then: $\{(M_1, \ldots, M_n) \mid M_i \in S_i(D_i) \text{ for } 1 \leq i \leq n\}$

In the case of semantics, the solver is trivial and basically just returns the description itself. However, for syntax, we use a dominance constraint solver based on the set constraint approach of [15] which we extended to implement Crabbé's semantics for the color annotation of nodes.

---

[3] assuming n dimensions.

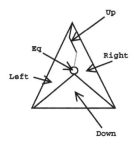

Fig. 2. node regions

When observed from a specific node x, the nodes of a solution tree (a model), and hence the variables which they interpret, are partitioned into 5 regions (see figure 2): the node denoted by x itself, all nodes below, all nodes above, all nodes to the left, and all nodes to the right.

The main idea is to introduce corresponding set variables Eq_x, Up_x, $Down_x$, $Left_x$, $Right_x$ to encode the sets of variables that are interpreted by nodes in the model which are respectively equal, above, below, left, and right of the node interpreting x. The interested reader should refer to [15] for the precise formalization.

Color constraints. An innovative aspect of Crabbé's approach is that nodes are decorated with colors (red, black, white) that constrains how they can be merged when computing models. The color combination rules are summarized in table 3: a red node cannot merge with any node, a black node can only merge with white nodes, and a white node must merge with a black node. Thus, in a valid model, we only have red and black nodes; in fact, exactly those which where already present in the input description.

Table 1. color merging table

	$\bullet_B$	$\bullet_R$	$\circ_W$	$\perp$
$\bullet_B$	$\perp$	$\perp$	$\bullet_B$	$\perp$
$\bullet_R$	$\perp$	$\perp$	$\perp$	$\perp$
$\circ_W$	$\bullet_B$	$\perp$	$\circ_W$	$\perp$
$\perp$	$\perp$	$\perp$	$\perp$	$\perp$

Intuitively, black nodes represent nodes that can be combined, red nodes are nodes that cannot, and white nodes those that must be combined. Thus, in valid models, all white nodes are absorbed by black nodes.

We extend the formalization of [15] with variables RB_x representing the unique red or black node that each x is identified with. We write V_B, V_R, and V_W for the sets of resp. black, red and white variables in the description. A red node cannot be merged with any other node (6), a black node can only be merged with white nodes (7), a white node must be merged with a black node (8):

$$x \in V_{\mathrm{R}} \quad \Rightarrow \quad RB_x = x \quad \wedge \quad Eq_x = \{x\} \tag{6}$$

$$x \in V_{\mathrm{B}} \quad \Rightarrow \quad RB_x = x \tag{7}$$

$$x \in V_{\mathrm{W}} \quad \Rightarrow \quad RB_x \in V_{\mathrm{B}} \tag{8}$$

Finally, two nodes are identified iff they are both identified with the same red or black node. Thus we must extend the clause of [15] for $x \neg= y$ as follows, where $\|$ denotes disjointness:

$$x \neg= y \quad \equiv \quad (Eq_x \| Eq_y \quad \wedge \quad RB_x \neq RB_y) \tag{9}$$

7   Conclusion

We motivated and presented a metagrammar formalism that embraces a multi-paradigm perspective, and we outlined its implementation in a Mozart-based tool. Our approach is innovative in that it combines an object-oriented management of linguistic abstraction, with a logic programming core to express and enumerate alternatives, and with constraint solving of dominance-based tree descriptions. That is why we chose Mozart/Oz: this multi-paradigm language provides parsing tools along with useful libraries for dealing with constraints.

Our new MG processor has already been used to develop a significant TAG for French, with over 3000 trees. And we are currently interfacing this tool with two parsers: the LORIA LTAG PARSER[4] version 2 [16] and the DyALog[5] system [17]. We are also extending it to support Interaction Grammars [12].

References

[1] XTAG-Research-Group: A lexicalized tree adjoining grammar for english. Technical Report IRCS-01-03, IRCS, University of Pennsylvania (2001) Available at http://www.cis.upenn.edu/~xtag/gramrelease.html.
[2] Abeillé, A., Candito, M., Kinyon, A.: Ftag: current status and parsing scheme. In: VEXTAL, Venice, Italy. (1999)
[3] Kroch, A., Joshi, A.: The linguistic relevance of tree adjoining grammars. Technical report, MS-CIS-85-16, University of Pennsylvania, Philadelphia (1985)
[4] Joshi, A., Schabes, Y.: Tree-adjoining grammars. In Rozenberg, G., Salomaa, A., eds.: Handbook of Formal Languages. Volume 3. Springer, Berlin, New York (1997) 69 – 124
[5] Vijay-Shanker, K., Schabes, Y.: Structure sharing in lexicalized tree adjoining grammars. In: Proceedings of the 16th International Conference on Computational Linguistics (COLING'92), Nantes, pp. 205 - 212. (1992)
[6] Candito, M.: Représentation modulaire et paramétrable de grammaires électroniques lexicalisées : application au français et à l'italien. PhD thesis, Université Paris 7 (1999)

---

[4] http://www.loria.fr/~azim/LLP2/help/fr/index.html
[5] ftp://ftp.inria.fr/INRIA/Projects/Atoll/Eric.Clergerie/DyALog/

[7] Gaiffe, B., Crabbé, B., Roussanaly, A.: A new metagrammar compiler. In: Proceedings of the 6th International Workshop on Tree Adjoining Grammars and Related Frameworks (TAG+6), Venice. (2002)

[8] Xia, F., Palmer, M., Vijay-Shanker, K.: Toward semi-automating grammar development. In: Proc. of the 5th Natural Language Processing Pacific Rim Symposium(NLPRS-99), Beijing, China. (1999)

[9] Rogers, J., Vijay-Shanker, K.: Reasoning with descriptions of trees. In: Proceedings of the 30th Annual Meeting of the Association for Computational Linguistics, pp. 72 - 80. (1992)

[10] Crabbé, B.: Lexical classes for structuring the lexicon of a tag. In: Proceedings of the Lorraine/Saarland workshop on Prospects and Advances in the Syntax/Semantics Interface. (2003)

[11] Crabbé, B.: Alternations, monotonicity and the lexicon : an application to factorising information in a tree adjoining grammar. In: Proceedings of the 15th ESSLLI, Vienne. (2003)

[12] Perrier, G.: Interaction grammars. In: Proceedings of the 18th International Conference on Computational Linguistics (COLING'2000), Saarbrucken, pp. 600 - 606. (2000)

[13] Van Roy, P.: Extended dcg notation: A tool for applicative programming in prolog. Technical report, Technical Report UCB/CSD 90/583, Computer Science Division, UC Berkeley (1990)

[14] Ait-Kaci, H.: Warren's abstract machine: A tutorial reconstruction. In Furukawa, K., ed.: Logic Programming: Proc. of the Eighth International Conference. MIT Press, Cambridge, MA (1991) 939

[15] Duchier, D.: Constraint programming for natural language processing (2000) Lecture Notes, ESSLLI 2000. Available at http://www.ps.uni-sb.de/Papers/abstracts/duchier-esslli2000.html.

[16] Crabbé, B., Gaiffe, B., Roussanaly, A.: Représentation et gestion du lexique d'une grammaire d'arbres adjoints (2004) Traitement Automatique des Langues, 43,3.

[17] Villemonte de la Clergerie, E.: Designing efficient parsers with DyALog (2004) Slides presented at GLINT, Universidade Nova de Lisboa.

The XDG Grammar Development Kit

Ralph Debusmann[1], Denys Duchier[2], and Joachim Niehren[3]

[1] Saarland University, Programming Systems Lab, Saarbrücken, Germany
[2] LORIA, Équipe Calligramme, Nancy, France
[3] INRIA Futurs, Mostrare Project, Lille, France

Abstract. Extensible Dependency Grammar (XDG) is a graph description language whose formulas can be solved by constraint programming. XDG is designed so as to yield a declarative approach to natural language processing, in particular to parsing and generation. In this paper, we present the XDG Development Kit (XDK), the first XDG-based grammar development system, which we have implemented in Mozart/Oz, thereby making full use of its multi-paradigmatic nature. The XDK supports an expressive lexicon specification language which which has not been published previously.

1 Introduction

Declarative grammar formalisms have a long tradition for modeling and processing natural language syntax and semantics [1, 2]. The idea is to specify linguistic knowledge in grammars independently from processing aspects, such that parsers, semantic constructions, or sentence generators can be created generically for all grammars of a given formalism.

The most prominent grammar formalisms support dialects of Lexical Functional Grammar (LFG) [1], Head-Driven Phrase Structure Grammar (HPSG) [3], Categorial Grammar [4, 5], Tree Adjoining Grammar (TAG) [6, 7], and Dependency Grammar (DG) [8, 9].

Grammar development systems are collections of tools that support the development of grammars in some formalism. They offer a concrete syntax for grammar specification, and contain parsers, generators, graphical output tools, debugging facilities, etc. The most powerful grammar development systems are the LKB system [10] for HPSG, the XTAG system [11] for TAG, and the Grammar Writer's Workbench [12] for LFG.

Parsers for grammars in LFG and HPSG rely on first-order unification for feature structures. Smolka raised the question [13] whether more advanced constraint technology could help to improve existing natural language processing methods. Duchier [14] proposed a first solution to this question. Motivated by Dependency Grammar, he proposed to axiomatize valid *dependency graphs* by finite set constraints, and reduced parsing to *finite set constraint programming*. Duchier and Debusmann [15] developed this approach further into a grammar formalism called Topological Dependency Grammar (TDG), which is particularly well suited for free word order, as in German, Czech, Latin, etc.

P. Van Roy (Ed.): MOZ 2004, LNCS 3389, pp. 188–199, 2005.

Recently, Debusmann et. al. [16] proposed a further generalization, Extensible Dependency Grammar (XDG). This is a general graph description language flexible enough to model multiple levels of linguistic structure, while still enjoying the same constraint-based parsing techniques [17]. In particular, XDG permits to extend TDG by a constraint-based, bi-directional syntax-semantics interface.

In this paper, we propose the first grammar development system for XDG, the XDG Grammar Development Kit (XDK). This includes a lexicon description language that has not been published previously. We have implemented the XDK in Mozart/Oz and published it in the MOGUL library [18]. The XDK provides a comprehensive suite of facilities for grammar development. It offers multiple concrete syntaxes for grammar specification: one XML-based for automatic grammar creation, and one more human-friendly for handcrafted grammars. Moreover, it provides a solver for parsing and generation, and various graphical output tools and debugging facilities. All of this is implemented in one coherent system, making use of the multi-paradigmatic nature of Mozart/Oz: We could use object-oriented programming for the GUI, functional programming for grammar compilation, and constraint programming for the solver.

2   Extensible Dependency Grammar

In XDG, we regard grammars as graph descriptions. This allows us to view parsing of natural language expressions and the generation of sentences as graph configuration problems which can be solved using constraint programming in Mozart/Oz.

2.1   Graphs

XDG describes finite labeled graphs, using the linguistic notion of Dependency Grammar [8, 9]. We show a typical *dependency graph* in Fig. 1 (left hand side). Each node corresponds one-to-one to a word in the sentence. The edges are labeled by grammatical relations such as subject, object and determiner. Here, "programmer" is the subject of "should", and "like" the verbal complement (vcomp). "every" is the determiner of "programmer", and "Mozart" is the object of "like".

An XDG analysis can be split up into an arbitrary number of dependency graphs, all sharing the same set of nodes, but having different edges. This is useful for the handling of word order [15], and for the representation of the semantics of natural language. We call each of the graphs a *dimension*. In Fig. 1 (right), we display an analysis of the same sentence on a second, semantic dimension. Here, "programmer" is simultaneously the agent of "should", and the agent of "like". "every" is the determiner of "programmer". "like" is the proposition of "should", and "Mozart" the patient of "like".

2.2   Graph Description Language

XDG describes the well-formedness conditions of an analysis by the interaction of *principles* and the *lexicon*. The principles stipulate restrictions on one or more

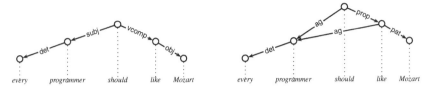

Fig. 1. Syntactic (left) and semantic (right) dependency graphs

of the dimensions, and are controlled by the feature structures assigned to the nodes from the lexicon. Here is a lexical entry for "like":

$$
\text{"like"} = \left[\begin{array}{l} syn : \left[\begin{array}{l} \text{in} : \{\text{vcomp?}\} \\ \text{out} : \{\text{obj!}\} \end{array} \right] \\ sem : \left[\begin{array}{l} \text{in} : \{\text{prop?}\} \\ \text{out} : \{\text{ag!, pat!}\} \end{array} \right] \end{array} \right]
$$

The entry is separated into a syntactic and a semantic part, and controls the *valency principle*, constraining the licensed incoming and outgoing edges of each node. In the syntax, "like" can have zero or one incoming edges labeled vcomp (in : {vcomp?}), and requires an object (out : {obj!}). In the semantics, it can have zero or one incoming edges labeled prop (in : {prop?}) and requires an agent and a patient (out : {ag!, pat!}).

XDG is "extensible" for two reasons: 1) the set of dimensions of graphs is arbitrary, and 2) the set of principles to describe the graphs is a subset of an extensible *principle library*. The principle library already contains the necessary principles to model the syntax and semantics for large fragments of German and English, and smaller fragments of Arabic, Czech and Dutch. We present a subset of the principle library below.

Tree principle. Dimension i must be a tree. In the example above, we use this principle on the syntactic dimension.

DAG principle. Dimension i must be a directed acyclic graph. We use this principle on the semantic dimension.

Valency principle. For each node on dimension i, the incoming edges must be licensed by the in specification, and the outgoing edges by the out specification.

Order principle. For each node v on dimension i, the order of the daughters depends on their edge labels. We use this principle to constrain the order of the words in a sentence. We can use it e.g. to require that subjects ("programmer") precede verbal complements ("like").

Linking principle. The linking principle allows us to specify how semantic arguments must be realized in the syntax. In our example, the lexical entry for "like" would contain the following feature specification:

$$\text{``like''} = \left[\, sem : \left[\, \text{link} : \left[\begin{array}{l} \text{ag} : \{\text{subj}\} \\ \text{pat} : \{\text{obj}\} \end{array} \right] \, \right] \, \right]$$

This stipulates that the agent of "like" must be realized by the subject, and the patient by the object.

3   Lexicon Specification

The XDG development kit offers a flexible method to define types of lexical entries, to build lexical abstractions, and to describe sets of lexical entries compactly using a descriptive device known as *metagrammar*. A metagrammar is processed to automatically generate all the entries of an XDG lexicon.

3.1   Lexicalization

Lexicalization is a widely accepted principle in computational linguistics that is indispensable in formal grammar approaches. Lexicalization means that linguistic information is mostly specified in the lexicon, given that information is often mostly specific to words.

The lexicon quickly becomes huge even for grammars with moderately ambitious coverage. They may contain thousands of words, each of which having multiple lexical entries, which are often large too. From the engineering perspective, it is important to provide facilities that allow to adequately modularize and factorize lexical information; otherwise, information needs to be duplicated and maintained in multiple places.

3.2   Ambiguity

XDG is very much a lexicalized grammar formalism. Most information is specified in the lexical entries for the words. The exceptions are some of the principles, which specify how words can interact, or how graphs in different dimensions are related.

We have already seen XDG lexical entries in the examples. Lexical entries are records of dimensions, and each dimension is itself a record representing linguistic information which pertains to the word. These items may have different types. We have already seen valency stipulations, specifying which labeled edges are permitted to enter or exit a node in a graph, and linking specifications, specifying how semantic arguments are to be realized in the syntax.

In a typical lexicon, there are a number of lexical entries for each word, e.g. if a word has different categories: "help" for instance can either be a noun or a verb. The problem is to describe such sets of lexical entries compactly, without representing the same information in different lexical entries twice. XDG provides lexical abstractions for this purpose.

3.3   Lexical Types

XDG supports a flexible system to define various types of lexical information. Each type consists of a set L and a partial function $\sqcap : L \times L \to L$, the *combination function* of L. Most typically, the operation $\sqcap$ defines the greatest lower bound with respect to the information amount represented by members of L.

The grammar writer starts by defining some domain types, for instance the type of edge labels in the syntactic dimension:

$$syn.label = \{\texttt{det}, \texttt{subj}, \texttt{obj}, \texttt{vcomp}\}$$

Domain types are always flat in that $a \sqcap a = a$ for all elements and $a \sqcap b$ is undefined for all $a \neq b$. Given a set of features $(f_i)_{i=1\ldots n}$ and a corresponding set of types $T_i = (L_i, \sqcap_i)_{i=1\ldots n}$, XDG allows you to define the record type $[f_1{:}T_1, \ldots, f_n{:}T_n]$ with values of the form:

$$[f_1{:}v_1, \ldots, f_n{:}v_n]$$

where $v_i \in L_i$, and where the composition operation is defined feature-wise by:

$$[f_1{:}v_1, \ldots, f_n{:}v_n] \sqcap [f_1{:}v_1', \ldots, f_n{:}v_n'] \quad = \quad [f_1{:}v_1 \sqcap_1 v_1', \ldots, f_n{:}v_n \sqcap_n v_n']$$

when $v_i \sqcap_i v_i'$ are all defined, and is undefined otherwise.

The grammar writer needs to define a type for valencies on the syntactic level. The XDG system provides a built-in constructor to define valencies over a given domain type of edge labels:

$$syn.valency = \texttt{valency}(syn.label)$$

This merely defines *syn.valency* to be the record type:

$$[\texttt{det}{:}mode, \ \texttt{subj}{:}mode, \ \texttt{obj}{:}mode, \ \texttt{vcomp}{:}mode]$$

where type *mode* consists of the values $\{0, ?, !, *\}$ — where 0 stands for no occurrence, ! for one unique and obligatory occurrence, ? for an optional occurrence, and $*$ for zero or more occurrences — and the following (commutative) combination operation:

$$0 \sqcap x = x \qquad * \sqcap ! = ! \qquad * \sqcap ? = ? \qquad ? \sqcap ! = !$$

Since *syn.valency* was declared with the **valency** constructor, the XDK supports the following more convenient notation:

$$\{\texttt{subj!}, \texttt{obj?}\} \quad \equiv \quad [\texttt{det}{:}0, \ \texttt{subj}{:}!, \ \texttt{obj}{:}?, \ \texttt{vcomp}{:}0]$$

In practice, record types serve for defining dimensions and lexical entries. A lexical entry is a record of named dimensions, and a dimension a record of lexical information about valency, agreement etc... The XDK also supports defining new types using Cartesian products, set type constructors, and other possibilities.

3.4   Lexical Meta Grammars

Once we have specified the type $(L, \sqcap)$ of lexical entries, we need to supply the set of values of this type that constitute the lexicon. For this purpose, we adapt a well-known descriptive device: generative grammar, consisting of a finite set of clauses with the following abstract syntax:

$$Clause \quad ::= \quad Name \rightarrow Goal$$
$$Goal \quad ::= \quad Goal \wedge Goal \mid Goal \vee Goal \mid Name \mid c$$

where each *Clause* defines a non-terminal *Name*, and where the terminals c range over elements of L, i.e. lexical entries Traditional context free grammars are similar. Name correspond to non-terminals and elements of $c \in L$ to terminals. Conjunction is usually written as juxtaposition, and disjunction as choice |. Here, we use grammars to describe sets of lexical entries. Compared to the traditional semantics, we replace words by lexical entries and word concatenation by the $\sqcap$ operator on lexical entries. We call such a device a *metagrammar* over $(L, \sqcap)$.

3.5   Example

In this section, we present a simple, idealized example of a metagrammar. First, we state that finite verbs can either be the head of the main clause or of a relative clause, i.e. either they have no incoming edges, or they can have incoming edge rel:

$$\text{finite} \quad \rightarrow \quad \text{root} \vee \text{rel}$$
$$\text{root} \quad \rightarrow \quad \big[\, syn : \big[\, \text{in} : \{\}\,\big]\,\big]$$
$$\text{rel} \quad \rightarrow \quad \big[\, syn : \big[\, \text{in} : \{\text{relcl?}\}\,\big]\,\big]$$

Then we state that verbs may be either intransitive, transitive or ditransitive:

$$\text{verb} \quad \rightarrow \quad \text{intr} \vee \text{tr} \vee \text{ditr}$$
$$\text{intr} \quad \rightarrow \quad \big[\, syn : \big[\, \text{out} : \{\text{subj!}\}\,\big]\,\big]$$
$$\text{tr} \quad \rightarrow \quad \text{intr} \wedge \big[\, syn : \big[\, \text{out} : \{\text{obj!}\}\,\big]\,\big]$$
$$\text{ditr} \quad \rightarrow \quad \text{tr} \wedge \big[\, syn : \big[\, \text{out} : \{\text{iobj!}\}\,\big]\,\big]$$

The notion of a finite verb can be stated as the composition of the previous two abstractions:

$$\text{finite.verb} \quad \rightarrow \quad \text{finite} \wedge \text{verb}$$

The generative process using finite.verb as start symbol produces the following six values which are alternative lexical entries for finite verbs:

$$(\text{root} \wedge \text{intr}) \quad (\text{root} \wedge \text{tr}) \quad (\text{root} \wedge \text{ditr}) \quad (\text{rel} \wedge \text{intr}) \quad (\text{rel} \wedge \text{tr}) \quad (\text{rel} \wedge \text{ditr})$$

For instance, the lexical entry for a ditransitive finite verb which is the head of a relative clause is:

$$\text{rel} \wedge \text{ditr} \quad \rightarrow \quad \left[\, syn : \begin{bmatrix} \text{in} : \{\text{relcl?}\} \\ \text{out} : \{\text{subj!}, \text{obj!}, \text{iobj!}\} \end{bmatrix} \,\right] \tag{1}$$

4   XDG Grammar Development Kit

The XDK is a complete grammar development kit for XDG. It defines concrete syntaxes for grammar specification, and various mechanisms for testing and debugging grammars, including a comprehensive graphical user interface. Additional non-interactive command-line tools can be used for automated grammar processing. Moreover, the XDK contains a solver for XDG, the extensible principle library, and an interface to external knowledge sources to (e.g. statistically) guide the search for solutions.

4.1   Concrete Syntax

The XDK defines three concrete syntaxes for grammar specification, each of which fulfills a different purpose. The User Language (UL) is an input language for manual grammar development. The XML language (XML) is based on XML, and is particularly well suited for automated grammar development (e.g. automatic grammar induction from corpora). The Intermediate Language (IL) is a record-based language tailored for Mozart/Oz and for further processing within the XDK, but is neither readable (as the UL), nor suited for automated processing outside Mozart/Oz (as the XML). The XDK offers functionality to convert the different languages into each other, e.g. to make XML grammars readable by converting them into the UL.

We illustrate how XDG grammars look like by a miniature example grammar using UL syntax. XDG grammars are split up into two main parts: 1) the header, and 2) the lexicon. The header includes type definitions (e.g. the set of edge labels or the type of a lexical entry), and specifies the principles used from the principle library. The lexicon is a metagrammatical lexicon specification. We display the header of the example grammar in Fig. 2, and the lexicon in Fig. 3.

The `usedim` keyword activates dimensions. In the example, it activates the `syn`, `sem` and `lex`[1]. In the `defdim` sections, we define the types pertaining to the respective dimensions of the grammar. `deftype` defines a type and binds it to a name, e.g. `syn.label` to {det subj obj vcomp}. These names can be dereferenced by their name. `defentrytype` defines the type of a lexical entry, and `deflabeltype` the type of edge labels. The `useprinciple` keyword indicates the use of a principle and `dims` binds dimension variables to actual dimensions. E.g. the linking principle `principle.linking` binds dimension variable D1 to `sem`, and D2 to `syn`. The `output` and `useoutput` keywords specify the output functors to visualize analyses.

The UL syntax of the lexicon specification is close to the abstract syntax presented before. `defclass` defines lexical classes (clauses). E.g. `defclass "det"` `Word` defines the lexical class named `det`, and with one argument Word. Lexical classes can be dereferenced by giving their name and the required arguments. E.g. `"det" {Word: "every"}` dereferences class `det` and binds its argument Word to `every`. `defentry` defines a set of lexical entries. Disjunction (∨) is written |.

---

[1] The `lex` dimension is not a real XDG dimension—it is used solely identify a word with each lexical entry.

```
usedim syn
usedim sem
usedim lex
%%
defdim syn {
  deftype                    {det subj obj vcomp}
  deftype                    {in: valency(          )
                              out: valency(          )}
  defentrytype
  deflabeltype
%%
  useprinciple                        { dims {D: syn} }
  useprinciple                        { dims {D: syn} }
  useprinciple                         { dims {D: syn} }
%%
  output
  useoutput
}
defdim sem {
  deftype                    {det ag pat prop}
  deftype                    {in: valency(          )
                              out: valency(          )
                              link: map(          iset(          ))}
  defentrytype
  deflabeltype
%%
  useprinciple                        { dims {D: sem} }
  useprinciple               { dims {D: sem} }
  useprinciple                         { dims {D: sem} }
  useprinciple                        { dims {D1: sem
                                             D2: syn} }
%%
  output
  useoutput
}
%%
defdim lex { defentrytype {word: string} }
```

Fig. 2. The header of the example grammar

4.2   Error Detection

The XDK offers various ways to detect errors, including a very fast static grammar type checker. This type checker is implemented for the IL, and hence also for the UL and the XML languages (since they are always compiled into the IL). The type checker also detects cycles in the definition of lexical classes.

4.3   Graphical Interfaces

The XDK comprises a comprehensive graphical user interface (GUI) for convenient access to all the functionality of the system. The GUI is most useful for debugging grammars, e.g. by switching off any of the principles to find out which constraints have ruled out desired analyses. The GUI visualizes the solver search tree using the *Oz Explorer* or optionally Guido Tack's new Explorer replacement *IOzSeF*, and can visualize partial and total analyses using functors from an extensible *output library* of output functors, including a graphical DAG display, a detailed display of the underlying analysis using the *Oz Inspector*, LATEX output

```
defclass       {                          defclass       Word {
  dim syn {in: {subj?} | in: {obj?}}        dim syn {in: {det?}}
  dim sem {in: {ag*} | in: {pat*}}}         dim sem {in: {det?}}
                                            dim lex {word: Word}}
defclass     Word {
                                          defclass         Word {
  dim syn {out: {det!}}                     dim syn {in: {vcomp?}
  dim sem {out: {det!}}                              out: {obj!}}
  dim lex {word: Word}}                      dim sem {in: {prop?}
                                                    out: {ag! pat!}
defclass     Word {                                link: {ag: {subj}
                                                          pat: {obj}}}
  dim lex {word: Word}}                      dim lex {word: Word}}
                                          %%
defclass         Word {                   defentry {       {Word:       } }
  dim syn {in: {}                         defentry {       {Word:           } }
          out: {subj! vcomp!}}            defentry {       {Word:       } }
  dim sem {in: {}                         defentry {       {Word:       } }
          out: {ag! prop!}               defentry {       {Word:     } }
          link: {ag: {subj}
                prop: {vcomp}}}
  dim lex {word: Word}}
```

Fig. 3. The lexicon of the example grammar

(as used to create Fig. 1), or an XML-based output for further processing. We depict the main GUI window and the Oz Explorer in Fig. 4, and an example XDG analysis as displayed by the DAG output functor in Fig. 5.

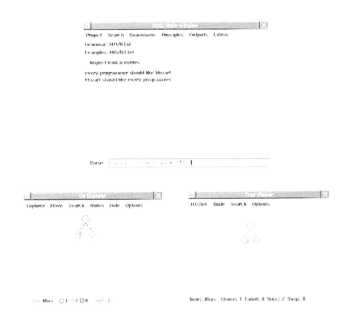

Fig. 4. The main window of the GUI (top), the Oz Explorer (bottom left), and IOzSeF (bottom right)

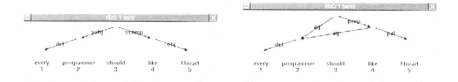

Fig. 5. The XDG analysis displayed by the DAG output functor

4.4   Solver

The XDK solver makes use of Denys Duchier's axiomatization of dependency parsing [14, 17], and turns it into a completely modular, extensible *principle library*. Principles are composed from sets of constraint functors: For instance the valency principle is composed from the *in constraint* and the *out constraint*, constraining resp. the incoming and outgoing edges of each node. The starting sequence of the constraints can be regulated by global *constraint priorities*. This can help gaining efficiency. New principles and new constraints can easily be added and integrated into the XDK, which makes it an ideal launchpad for new linguistic theories.

4.5   Preferences and Search

Following ideas by Thorsten Brants and Denys Duchier, Dienes et al. [19] introduce the idea to guide the search for solutions of the XDK solver by external knowledge sources called *Oracles*. Oracles interact with the XDK solver by sockets, and are based either on statistical information or heuristics. The XDK supports the use of Oracles using a standard architecture for Oracles developed by Marco Kuhlmann and others.

5   Mozart Implementation

In this section, we discuss selected aspects of our implementation of the XDK in Mozart/Oz.

5.1   Constraint Programming

Constraint programming is used to enumerate graph models of graph descriptions. The techniques used for XDG rely on ideas from TDG[17]. We illustrate them here in order to illustrate XDG's requirements on constraint programming.

Finite Set Constraints are used to model graph configuration problems. For example, the daughters of node w that can be reached by traversing an edge labeled obj are represented by the set variable $obj(w)$. A valency specification obj? can be enforced by posting the cardinality constraint $|obj(w)| \in \{0, 1\}$

Selection Constraints are used to efficiently handle ambiguity. Typically, a word w has multiple lexical entries $L_1, \ldots, L_n$. If we introduce a variable E_w to denote the lexical entry that is ultimately selected among them, and an integer variable I_w to denote it's position in that sequence, then we can relate these quantities by a selection constraint:

$$E_w = \langle L_1, \ldots, L_n \rangle [I_w]$$

with the declarative semantics that $E_w = L_{I_w}$. The basic selection constraints implemented for finite domains and finite sets can trivially be lifted to record types.

Deep Guards in Disjunctive Propagators. The construct or G_1 [] G_2 end is used to enforce complex mutually exclusive well-formedness conditions. For example that either (G_1) a certain tree edge exists and it satisfies some additional condition, or it does not exist (G_2). For every possible edge, there is a disjunctive propagator to monitor these alternatives concurrently.

5.2   Programming Environment

The XDK makes use of modules from the *MOzart Global User Library* (MOGUL), and applies *ozmake* for convenient compilation and deployment (again into MOGUL). The principle and output libraries are realized using dynamically linked *functors*.

The grammar compiler utilizes two parsers: 1) a flexible LR/LALR parser generator (fully written in Mozart by Denys Duchier) for parsing the UL, and 2) the fast XML parser by Denys Duchier from the Mozart Standard Library for parsing grammars written in XML. Per default, grammars are stored as pickles, but the XDK can also make use of Denys Duchier's interface to the *GNU GDBM database library*, with which very large grammars can be handled more efficiently.

The graphical user interface of the XDK is written using the Tcl/Tk interface of Mozart/Oz. Moreover, the XDK utilizes the Oz Explorer and optionally *IOzSeF* (by Guido Tack) to visualize the solver search tree, and the Oz Inspector to display XDG structures in more detail.

6   Conclusion

We have presented the XDG Development Kit (XDK), and described its lexicon specification language. The XDK includes a large number of grammar development tools fully implemented in Mozart/Oz, making use of its flexible multi-paradigmatic nature. No other programming system provides the required expressiveness to combine set constraints, selection constraints, and deep guards as used in the solver of the XDK. Furthermore, it was very easy to add a GUI, and support for multiple input languages, including an XML-based one, and much more.

A stable and thoroughly tested version of the XDK is freely available in the MOGUL library, including a comprehensive manual covering the entire system in quite some detail (more than 200 pages).

References

1. Bresnan, J., Kaplan, R.: Lexical-Functional Grammar: A Formal System for Grammatical Representation. In Bresnan, J., ed.: The Mental Representation of Grammatical Relations. The MIT Press, Cambridge/USA (1982) 173–281
2. Kay, M.: Functional Grammar. In C. Chiarello et al., ed.: Proceedings of the 5th Annual Meeting of the Berkeley Linguistics Society. (1979) 142–158
3. Pollard, C., Sag, I.A.: Head-Driven Phrase Structure Grammar. University of Chicago Press, Chicago/USA (1994)
4. Lambek, J.: The Mathematics of Sentence Structure. American Mathematical Monthly (1958) 154–170
5. Steedman, M.: The Syntactic Process. MIT Press (2000)
6. Joshi, A.K., Levy, L., Takahashi, M.: Tree Adjunct Grammars. Journal of Computer and System Sciences **10** (1975)
7. Joshi, A.K.: How much context-sensitivity is necessary for characterizing structural descriptions—Tree Adjoining Grammars. In Dowty, D., Karttunen, L., Zwicky, A., eds.: Natural Language Processing—Theoretical, Computational and Psychological Perspectives. Cambridge University Press, New York/USA (1985)
8. Tesnière, L.: Eléments de Syntaxe Structurale. Klincksiek, Paris/FRA (1959)
9. Mel'čuk, I.: Dependency Syntax: Theory and Practice. State Univ. Press of New York, Albany/USA (1988)
10. Copestake, A.: Implementing Typed Feature Structure Grammars. CSLI Publications (2002)
11. XTAG Research Group: A Lexicalized Tree Adjoining Grammar for English. Technical Report IRCS-01-03, IRCS, University of Pennsylvania (2001)
12. Kaplan, R.M., Maxwell, J.T.: LFG Grammar Writer's Workbench. Technical report, Xerox PARC (1996)
13. Smolka, G., Uszkoreit, H.: NEGRA Project of the Collaborative Research Centre (SFB) 378 (1996–2001) Saarland University/GER.
14. Duchier, D.: Axiomatizing Dependency Parsing Using Set Constraints. In: Proceedings of MOL6, Orlando/USA (1999)
15. Duchier, D., Debusmann, R.: Topological Dependency Trees: A Constraint-Based Account of Linear Precedence. In: Proceedings of ACL 2001, Toulouse/FRA (2001)
16. Debusmann, R., Duchier, D., Koller, A., Kuhlmann, M., Smolka, G., Thater, S.: A Relational Syntax-Semantics Interface Based on Dependency Grammar. In: Proceedings of COLING 2004, Geneva/SUI (2004)
17. Duchier, D.: Configuration of Labeled Trees under Lexicalized Constraints and Principles. Research on Language and Computation **1** (2003) 307–336
18. Duchier, D.: MOGUL: the MOzart Global User Library (2004) http://www.mozart-oz.org/mogul/.
19. Dienes, P., Koller, A., Kuhlmann, M.: Statistical A* Dependency Parsing. In: Prospects and Advances in the Syntax/Semantics Interface, Nancy/FRA (2003)

Solving CSP Including a Universal Quantification

Renaud De Landtsheer*

UCL, Département d'Ingéniérie Informatique, Belgium
rdl@info.ucl.ac.be

Abstract. This paper presents a method to solve constraint satisfaction problems including a universally quantified variable with finite domain. Similar problems appear in the field of bounded model checking. The presented method is built on top of the Mozart constraint programming platform. The main principle of the algorithm is to consider only representative values in the domain of the quantified variable. The presented algorithm is similar to a branch and bound search. Significant improvements have been achieved both in memory consumption and execution time compared to a naive approach.

1 Introduction

The minimal constraint satisfaction problem including a universal quantification (CSPU for short) with two variables is presented in (1) where X and Y are finite sets of integers and $P(x)$ and $Q(x, y)$ represent constraints on x and (x, y) respectively. They are expressions built with the connectives $\wedge, \vee, \neg, \rightarrow, +, *, =, <, \ldots$

$$(\exists x \in X) \begin{cases} P(x) \\ (\forall y \in Y)Q(x, y) \end{cases} \tag{1}$$

We want to solve this problem, i.e: find a value of x. An order of magnitude for the cardinality of Y is 10k.

This problem was encountered in the development of a bounded model checker prototype similar to [2]. The bounded model-checking problem was reduced to CSPU with many universally quantified variables and small domains. The paper focuses on CSPU with only two variables, but it can be extended to the general case.

---

* I want to thank Raphaël Collet for the many discussions on how to solve constraint satisfaction problem with universal quantification and also for the encouragement to build a dedicated search engine. I also want to thank Luis Quesada who suggested me the propagator for universally quantified expressions. This is the propagator presented as redundant propagator in this paper. The work reported herein was supported by the belgian FNRS (Fonds National de la Recherche Scientifique).

P. Van Roy (Ed.): MOZ 2004, LNCS 3389, pp. 200–210, 2005.
© Springer-Verlag Berlin Heidelberg 2005

Similar problems have already been approached. Non-linear real constraint systems with universally quantified variables have been approached in [1] by means of interval constraint solver. They have also been approached in the field of planning and resolved by regression techniques [4].

This approach achieves significant gains both in memory consumption and in execution speed compared to a naive approach. It turns out to be viable for simple cases, though it is still possible to build CSPU such that it will perform as bad as the naive approach.

The approach presented in this paper has been implemented in Oz, on top of the Mozart constraint satisfaction problem solver [6,5].

The paper is organized as follows: Section 2 presents a naive approach to solve the problem, discusses its deficiencies and introduces our approach, Section 3 presents some time and memory consumption measures of our approach compared to the naive one. Section 4 discusses some further improvements of our approach.

2   Solving the CSPU Problem

In this section, we first present a naive approach and then build on the deficiencies of this approach to elicit a better one.

2.1   A Naive Approach

The naive approach to solve CSPU consists in solving the expanded problem where y has been instantiated to each of the possible values in Y. The expanded problem is presented in (2) where $y_1, y_2, \dots$ are the values in Y [1].

$$(\exists x \in X) \begin{cases} P(x) \\ Q(x, y_1) \wedge Q(x, y_2) \wedge Q(x, y_3) \wedge \dots \end{cases} \tag{2}$$

This approach has many deficiencies:

- it is time consuming because a large number of $Q(x, y_i)$ must be generated by the expansion procedure, as the cardinality of Y is very large;
- it is time consuming because all the $Q(x, y_i)$ must be handled by the search procedure, i.e: cloned when the computation space is cloned by the search engine;
- it is memory consuming because all the $Q(x, y_i)$ must be stored in memory.

This algorithm aborts for simple problems because of excessive memory consumption. Recomputation makes it better, but still unusable.

---

[1] In this paper, the convention is that subscripted letters are values and non subscripted letters are variables. Moreover, x (resp y) denotes a variable whose domain is X (resp Y). For instance, y_1, y_2 and y_i are values in Y and x_1, x_2 and x_j are values in X.

2.2   Eliciting a Better Approach

The problems of the naive approach appear because the computation space is very heavy, because it contains too many propagators. Our objective is to make this computation space lighter in order to make it possible to perform search with it.

The basic observation is that not every $Q(x, y_i)$ is useful. Many of these $Q(x, y_i)$ are either redundant or not exploited by the search engine to find the *first* solution. This leads to the idea that we should make the problem lighter for the search engine in order to achieve better efficiency, by injecting only the useful $Q(x, y_i)$. In order to express this idea and to reason on it, we introduce here the concept of representative constraint.

A *representative* constraint is one such that some other constraints are redundant to it. A *good* representative constraint is one such that *many* constraints are redundant to it. The other constraints can be removed from the system without changing the result. We extend the notion of representative constraint to representative *value*. This concept is similar to the one used in black box software test case generation. [3]. The concept of representative value can be formalized in our context as follows: *A value y_i is a good representative if there are many $y_j \in Y$ such that for all $x_k \in X$: $Q(x_k, y_i) \rightarrow Q(x_k, y_j)$.*

The basic idea is to solve a simplified problem with only good representative $Q(x, y_i)$. However, we don't know which are the good representative $Q(x, y_i)$. The solution presented here consists in eliciting the representative constraint *during* the search. Our approach is then highly dependent on the existence of such representatives. We elaborate on this idea in the next two sections.

2.3   An Incremental Strengthening Approach

We first solve the simplified problem

$$(\exists x \in X)P(x)$$

If no solution is found to this simplified problem, no solution for the complete problem exists either. If a solution x_1 is found, we search a solution to the auxiliary problem

$$(\exists y \in Y)\neg Q(x_1, y)$$

Note that it is possible to do this because Q is an expression and $\neg$ is a connective of the expression language. It would be much more difficult to express this negation if Q was a script like the ones used by classical search engines of Mozart.

- If a solution y_1 is found to the auxiliary problem, then x_1 was not a good solution. We reinforce the initial simplified problem with $Q(x, y_1)$ and restart the algorithm. We make the assumption that y_1 is a good representative.
- If no solution is found to the auxiliary problem, then x_1 is a solution to the initial problem as

$$\neg\exists y\neg Q(x_1, y) \text{ is equivalent to } \forall y Q(x_1, y)$$

```
% This function returns a solution to the problem:
% (∃x ∈ X)(P(x) ∧ (∀y ∈ Y)Q(x,y)) Where X and Y are finite sets.
% It returns no_solution if no solution exists.
function Search_With_Universal_Quantification(P, X, Q, Y)
% Main search
Search for a solution to (∃x ∈ X)P(x)
if no solution is found then
   % There is no solution to (∃x ∈ X)P(x),
   % thus no solution to the original problem
   return no_solution
else if there is a solution x₁ then
   % Here, we know that P(x₁) but, we don't know if ∀yQ(x₁,y)
   % Auxiliary search
   Search for a solution to (∃y ∈ Y)¬Q(x₁,y)
   if no solution is found then
      % x₁ is a solution to the original problem,
      % as ¬∃y¬Q(x₁,y) ≡ ∀yQ(x₁,y)
      return x₁
   else if else there is a solution y₁ then
      % x₁ was not a solution to the original problem as ¬Q(x₁,y₁) holds.
      % Reinforce P(x) with Q(x,y₁) and solve the new problem.
      let R = (λx)(P(x) ∧ Q(x,y₁))
      return Search_With_Universal_Quantification(R, X, Q, Y)
   end if
end if
end function
```

Fig. 1. An incremental strengthening algorithm to solve CSPU

The initial constraint $P(x)$ is gradually strengthened with some $Q(x, y_i)$ until either the problem cannot be solved or a solution to the CSPU problem is found. We hope that the strengthened problem will be much lighter than the expanded CSPU problem of the naive approach. The search of the form $(\exists x \in X)P(x)$ is called the *main* search while the search of the form $(\exists y \in Y)\neg Q(x_1, y)$ is called the *auxiliary* search. A pseudo-code formulation of the algorithm is given in Fig. 1.

2.4   A Branch and Bound Approach

The main search of the algorithm presented in Fig. 1 is often performed on the same set of data, but with progressively strengthened constraints. During the execution of the algorithm, a main search will likely encounter failures that have been encountered by the previous main search. With a naive distribution for the main search, roughly, the engine will test if 0 is a solution, if not, it will test for 1, then 2 and so on. The next main search will progress similarly. We want to keep track of the last reached value for x by a main search, say x_1, so that the next main search can start at $x_1 + 1$ instead of 0.

In order to achieve that for all form of distribution, we have to transform our algorithm into a form of branch and bound. The auxiliary search is then initi-

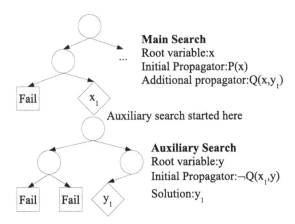

Fig. 2. Graphical representation of a snapshot of the search trees. The primary search finds a solution x_1 to its initial constraints $P(x)$. An auxiliary search is initiated and finds y_1, so that the constraint $Q(x, y_1)$ is added in the primary search and this search carries on

ated from within the main search. When the main search encounters a solution, an auxiliary search is initiated for the found x_1. If a solution to the auxiliary search is found, then the main search *carries on* with an additional propagator. This consumes more memory than the previous algorithm because there are sometimes two ongoing searches (the main and the auxiliary) stored together in memory. A graphical snapshot of the main and auxiliary search trees is given in Fig. 2. A pseudo-code formulation of the algorithm is annexed in Fig. 3.

We don't build our algorithm on top of the branch and bound search engine available in Mozart because it takes time to generate our additional propagators (the $Q(x, y_i)$). For this reason, we want to be sure that they will be generated only once, even if they are injected in many different spaces. This is not possible with the Mozart branch and bound search engine because it does not distinguish the additional constraint generation from its injection in a computation space.

2.5   A Redundant Constraint to Speed Up CSPU Solving

The main search tree of the algorithm presented in Fig. 3 is bigger than the one produced by the naive search because it initially lacks some propagators of the form $Q(x, y_i)$. In this section, we discuss a method do reduce the size of this search tree.

The Mozart programming system allows us to represent a propagator for universally quantified variables. This propagator can improve the primary search by pruning the exploration of a search subtree as soon as it detects that no solution in this subtree will enforce the universally quantified constraint. However, most of the time, this propagator cannot be used to solely represent the universally quantified constraint because it might be incomplete. We use it as a redundant propagator to improve the search.

```
% This function returns a solution to the problem:
% (∃x ∈ X)(P(x) ∧ (∀y ∈ Y)Q(x,y)) Where X and Y are finite sets.
% It returns no_solution if no solution exists.
function Search_With_Universal_Quantification(P, X, Q, Y)
let CurrentSpace = new space; root variable x, constraint P(x)
return Universal_Quantification_BB(CurrentSpace, [CurrentSpace], Q, Y)
end function


% This function solves the problem below with branch and bound search:
% (∃x ∈ X)(P(x) ∧ (∀y ∈ Y)Q(x,y)) Where X and Y are finite sets.
% The function returns the solution
% or no_solution if no solution exists.
% CurrentSpace is a space containing P(x)
% History is a stack of space clones used for backtracking.
function Universal_Quantification_BB(CurrentSpace, History, Q, Y)
if CurrentSpace is a successful space then
   let x₁ = Solution(CurrentSpace)
   % Auxiliary search
   Search for a solution to (∃y ∈ Y)¬Q(x₁,y)
   if no solution is found then
      % x₁ is a solution to the original problem,
      % as ¬∃y¬Q(x₁,y) ≡ ∀yQ(x₁,y)
      return x₁
   else if there is a solution y₁ then
      % x₁ was not a solution to the original problem,
      % as ¬Q(x₁,y₁) holds. Inject Q(x,y₁) in all the spaces of
      % the history and continue the search.
      for all space s in History do
         Inject constraint (λx)Q(x,y₁) in space s
      end for
      return no_solution
   end if
else if CurrentSpace is a failed space then
   return no_solution
else
   %CurrentSpace needs distribution.
   let Clone = a clone of Currentspace
   commit first possibility for CurrentSpace
   commit second possibility for Clone
   let FirstSearchResult =
       Universal_Quantification_BB(CurrentSpace, Clone|History, Q, Y)
   if FirstSearchResult == no_solution then
      return Universal_Quantification_BB(Clone, History, Q, Y)
   else
      return FirstSearchResult
   end if
end if
end function
```

Fig. 3. A branch and bound algorithm to solve CSPU

The principle of this propagator is based on the way Mozart handles the variables. At each node of the explored search tree, for each variable, the search procedure has a representation of the possible domain for the solution value of the variable. This domain is gradually reduced until either one possible value is left, the value of the variable is then determined or no possible value is left, leading to a failure in the search tree and a form of backtracking. Mozart propagators reduce the domain of variable in an eager way. As soon as a propagator can restrict a domain of a variable, this domain is updated to reflect this new knowledge. Note that propagators generally perform interval propagation. It means that they only focus on the upper and lower bound of the variables' domains.

The principle of this propagator is to insert a variable $\tilde{y}$ in the space that represents the universally quantified variable y. We also post the propagator $Q(x, \tilde{y})$. No distribution is performed on $\tilde{y}$. If the domain of $\tilde{y}$ is reduced, it means that some value in the previous domain of $\tilde{y}$ cannot enforce Q. We then have to watch the domain size of $\tilde{y}$ and ensure that any change of the domain of the $\tilde{y}$ variables results in a failure.

Practically, it is implemented by adding a thread to watch the size of the domain of $\tilde{y}$. This thread causes a failure as soon as it notices that the domain of $\tilde{y}$ has changed. The Oz code for such thread is given in Fig. 4. It uses the /?FD.watch.size *D1 +D2? function that returns true when the size of the domain of D1 becomes smaller than D2.

```
proc {ForAll X InitialDomainSize}
   thread
      if {FD.watch.size X InitialDomainSize} then
         fail
      end
   end
end
```

Fig. 4. A "propagator" that captures universal quantification

This propagator might be incomplete. For instance, let be the universally quantified variable $y \in [0..2]$ and the universally quantified constraint be $x \neq y$. If x is assigned the value 1 and the propagator for $\neq$ performs interval propagation, it will not be able to restrict the domain of the possible values of y. So that the currently explored search tree will not be pruned.

Also note that this method does not enable any kind of propagation on x. Propagation is provided by the representative constraints inserted by the branch and bound approach. This is another reason why this method should not be used alone. We use this propagator as a redundant propagator in the branch and bound approach presented in Section 2.4.

3   Efficiency Results

We present here some efficiency results. The benchmark problems (3,4,5) are presented below. In order to enrich the results, we use N as a parameter of the problems.

$$(\exists x \in [2..1000], y \in [2..1000] \begin{cases} x > 41 \\ x > 5y \\ (\forall z \in [0..N])x \neq yz \end{cases} \tag{3}$$

$$(\exists x \in [2..1000], y \in [2..1000] \begin{cases} x > 41 \\ x > 5y \\ (\forall a \in [0..N], b \in [0..N]) \\ \quad \neg(b < 10 \wedge x = ay + b) \end{cases} \tag{4}$$

$$(\exists x \in [2..1000], y \in [2..1000] \begin{cases} x > 41 \\ x > 5y \\ (\forall a \in [0..N], b \in [0..N]) \\ \quad \neg(1 \leq a < b \wedge 1 \leq b < x \wedge ax = by) \end{cases} \tag{5}$$

Timings and maximum memory of the naive and the branch and bound approaches to solve the three examples with various values for N are compared on Fig. 5 and 6. We measure the maximal memory and the time to find the first solution. These measures have been done on a Pentium4 1.7GHz with 768 Mb of RAM and no swap running Linux OS.

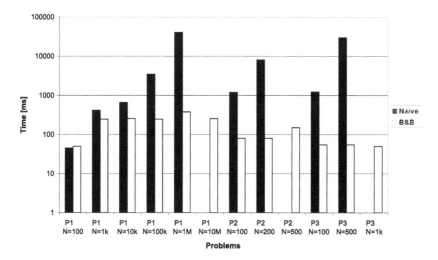

Fig. 5. Comparing the processing time of the naive approach and the branch and bound approach to find the first solution of various problems. This graphic reports the processing time in ms to find the first solution. Some measures of the naive algorithm are missing because the measure program aborts due to excessive memory consumption

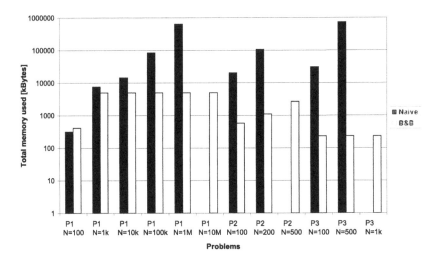

Fig. 6. Comparing the maximal memory use of the naive approach and the branch and bound approach to find the first solution of various problems. This graphic reports the maximal size of used memory in kB to find the first solution. Some measures of the naive algorithm are missing because the measure program aborts due to excessive memory consumption

The results clearly show an improvement from the naive approach. For each problem our approach is nearly insensitive to parameter N while the naive approach does not scale to large domain. The little variation between the first and the second measure is due to a change in the difficulty of the problem. Additional divisors of x are inserted when N increases from 100 to $1k$.

4   Further Improvements

In this section, we outline some weaknesses of our approach and some possible solutions.

4.1   Choosing the Good Representative

We don't have any indication that the $Q(x, y_1)$ are *good* representative for the universally quantified variable. For instance, for the problem (6) and for naive distributions for the main and auxiliary searches, the added $Q(x, y_i)$ will likely be: $Q(x, 0)$, $Q(x, 1)$, $Q(x, 2)$, $Q(x, 3)$ ... $Q(x, 10000)$. The best representative is actually the last inserted one.

$$(\exists x \in [0..1000]) \begin{cases} true \\ (\forall y \in [0..1000])x + 1 > y \end{cases} \tag{6}$$

A possible solution is to use randomized distribution for the auxiliary search. It will then find a y_1 somewhere in the range of the possible y, with a chance that it will be a good representative.

4.2   Simplifying the Additional Constraints

Recall that the primary objective of this approach is to make computation space lighter. It might be the case that the $Q(x,y)$ is of the form $R(x,y) \wedge S(x,y)$. It makes sense to consider this case because in this paper $Q(x,y)$ represents an expression with variables x and y. Suppose that R is very weak (few values of (x,y) are forbidden by R) and S is very strong (many values of (x,y) are forbidden by S). In this case, it might not make sense to insert the complete $Q(x,y_1)$ in the primary search. Rather, we would like to make it lighter, by injecting for instance only $S(x,y_1)$ if the R-part is useless.

A possible solution is to examine the y_1 delivered by the auxiliary search and inject $R(x,y_1)$ (resp. $S(x,y_1)$) only if $R(x_1,y_1)$ (resp. $S(x_1,y_1)$) does not hold. We can imagine going further, by resolving Q to a conjunctive normal form before starting the algorithm. This option should be carefully examined, as the conjunctive form of an expression is generally much bigger than its original form.

5   Conclusion

This paper presents an approach to solve constraint satisfaction problems including a universal quantification. The approach is built from the deficiencies of a naive approach that expands the universally quantified constraint before solving the resulting problem. The deficiencies are mostly due to the fact that the computation space contains a huge amount of propagators and cannot be handled efficiently. The approach exposed here mostly focuses on making the computation space lighter, so that search can be practically performed with it.

The approach is first introduced as a recursive algorithm performing a succession of search. For efficiency reasons, it is then transformed into a branch and bound search procedure. This algorithm was easily implemented on top of the Mozart constraint programming engine.

This algorithm is built on the hypothesis that it is possible to find good representative values in Y for the Q predicate of the CSPU defined in the introduction. A good representative value for y is a value y_i such that there are many $y_j \in Y$ such that for all $x_k \in X$: $Q(x_k, y_i) \rightarrow Q(x_k, y_j)$. If the CSPU does not meet this hypothesis, the algorithm will not be efficient.

This approach will produce a search tree at least as big as the one produced by the naive approach. All the improvement is in the size of the computation space. A method is proposed in section 2.5 to reduce the size of the search tree.

The resulting algorithm is compared for memory consumption and execution time to the naive approach on the basis of some benchmark. It turns out that interesting gains are achieved. However, it is possible to design CSPU's such that this method will perform very bad, as discussed in section 4.1.

This algorithm needs some improvements at least in the choice of the representatives. We make the assumption that the first value found by the auxiliary search is a good representative. Some solutions have been proposed in section 4.1, but we need a more reliable method than the proposed solution. This is an open issue.

It would also be interesting to examine how the Mozart branch and bound search engine could dissociate the additional constraint generation and its injection in a computation space, as discussed in section 2.4.

References

1. Frédéric Benhamou and Frédéric Goualard. Universally quantified interval constraints. In *Proceedings of the 6th International Conference on Principles and Practice of Constraint Programming*, pages 67–82. Springer-Verlag, 2000.
2. A. Biere, A. Cimatti, E. M. Clarke, M. Fujita, and Y. Zhu. Symbolic model checking using sat procedures instead of bdds. In *Proceedings of the 36th ACM/IEEE conference on Design automation*, pages 317 – 320, New Orleans, Louisiana, United States, 1999. ACM Press, New York, NY, USA.
3. Beizer Boris. *Black-box testing - Techniques for functional testing of software and systems*. John Wiley & Sons, 1995.
4. Golden K. and Frank J. Universal quantification in a constraint-based planner. In *AIPS 2002*, 2002.
5. Peter Van Roy and Seif Haridi. *Concepts, Techniques, and Models of Computer Programming*. MIT Press, March 2004. ISBN 0-262-22069-5.
6. Christian Schulte. *Programming Constraint Services*, volume 2302 of *Lecture Notes in Artificial Intelligence*. Springer-Verlag, Berlin, Germany, 2002.

Compositional Abstractions for Search Factories

Guido Tack and Didier Le Botlan

Programming Systems Lab, Saarland University, Germany
{tack, botlan}@ps.uni-sb.de

Abstract. Search is essential for constraint programming. Search engines typically combine several features like state restoration for backtracking, best solution search, parallelism, or visualization. In current implementations like Mozart, however, these search engines are monolithic and hard-wired to one exploration strategy, severely complicating the implementation of new exploration strategies and preventing their reuse.

This paper presents the design of a *search factory* for Mozart, a program that enables the user to freely combine several orthogonal aspects of search, resulting in a search engine tailored to the user's needs. The abstractions developed here support fully automatic recomputation with last alternative optimization. They present a clean interface, making the implementation of new exploration strategies simple. Conservative extensions of the abstractions are presented that support best solution search and parallel search as orthogonal modules. IOzSeF, the Interactive Oz Search Factory, implements these abstractions and is freely available for download.

1 Introduction

Constraint programming is at the heart of the Mozart programming system. Mozart provides a high-level language for describing the search problem in terms of propagators and distributors.

For programming exploration strategies, on the other hand, the situation is unsatisfactory: recomputation and exploration strategies are usually defined jointly, using low-level primitives. As a result, the implementor requires not only a deep understanding of the underlying abstractions but also carries the burden of implementing efficient recomputation strategies. This is a complex task: the book-keeping that is necessary for recomputation, especially when combined with other techniques like parallel search, last alternative optimization or branch & bound best solution search, is rather involved and a source of subtle bugs.

As an example, consider the Search module, the Explorer and parallel search (also called distributed search sometimes). All of these modules define independent search engines. Although most of the code for recomputation or search is similar, it is duplicated and therefore hard to maintain. Besides, if one wishes to implement a new exploration strategy, it is not possible to benefit from visualization for free, nor from parallelism.

P. Van Roy (Ed.): MOZ 2004, LNCS 3389, pp. 211–223, 2005.

Contribution. This paper presents the design of a search factory for Mozart.

The specific contributions of this paper are abstractions for the search tree that provide fully automatic, encapsulated recomputation and a clean interface for implementing exploration strategies. Recomputation is only efficient when combined with last alternative optimization. The paper shows how to make this automatic and orthogonal. As two more complex modules of a search factory, branch & bound search and parallel search are considered. The paper shows that they can be made orthogonal to exploration strategy, recomputation and last alternative optimization by conservative extensions to the base abstractions. The correctness of the resulting parallel search engine is discussed.

All these abstractions are modeled in the Mozart object system, using inheritance to combine them. The resulting system is called IOzSeF, the integrated Oz search factory. It is freely available and can be used as a replacement for the Mozart search libraries including the Explorer.

This work is based on and extends previous research on search in constraint programming [13, 2, 3]. Differences and similarities will be discussed in the paper, in particular in the related work section (Section 7).

Organization of This Paper. The next section gives a short overview of some of the main concepts used in this paper. Section 3 introduces space nodes, the abstraction that encapsulates recomputation, and gives details about their implementation. Section 4 builds the tree node layer on top; it provides a tree interface to search. In the same section, we show that these abstractions lead to a simple and concise way of formulating exploration strategies. Section 5 explains how to extend space and tree nodes to refine the search engine: we address branch & bound optimization, parallel search, and last alternative optimization. Section 6 discusses IOzSeF, the Mozart implementation of the search factory. The related work is summarized in Section 7. We conclude in Section 8.

2   Concepts

In Mozart/Oz, *computation spaces* are used to implement constraint propagation, branching (also called distribution) and search. A computation space is created by applying the system procedure `Space.new` to a unary procedure, the *search script*, which contains the problem specification. Propagation immediately starts. The space becomes *stable* as soon as no more propagation can occur. It is up to the *search engine* to react on the space's state, which may be one of `alternatives`,

Fig. 1. A search tree

`succeeded` or `failed`. Spaces with alternatives are *choice points*: the search engine *commits* to one of the alternatives (which triggers propagation again), choosing one of the possible branches.

A search engine thus traverses a tree: inner nodes represent choices, leaf nodes can be either failed or contain solutions. Such a tree is called a *search tree* and can be drawn as in Figure 1 (circles stand for choices, diamonds for solutions, squares for failures, and the triangle represents a yet unexplored subtree). Search engines must perform backtracking: once they reach a leaf node, they restore the state of the search engine to for example its parent node in order to explore the next branch. For state restoration, you can either memoize each node in the search tree, or have a method to reconstruct its state. In Mozart, memoization is called *cloning*, and the reconstruction of a state can be achieved by *recomputation*. The state of a node in the search tree can be reconstructed by redoing the choices on the path from the root node or any other ancestor node that has been cloned during search.

3   Abstracting Recomputation

In this section, we present the *space node* interface, an interface to computation spaces that abstracts from recomputation. From the outside, every space node looks as if it contained a computation space. Internally, space nodes perform recomputation automatically whenever it is needed.

We basically provide the same abstraction as the `Node` class introduced by Choi et al. [3]. We take a slightly different perspective though and split the interface into two parts: a space node deals with recomputation, but is not concerned with the interface for a search engine programmer. Search engines are built on top of the tree node interface, which is the topic of the next section.

At the implementation level, each space node contains two attributes for computation spaces:

– The first one possibly contains a *working space*, which represents its node's state (including propagators, distributors and constraint variables).

– The second one possibly contains a *copy*. Space nodes with a copy are used as a basis for recomputation.

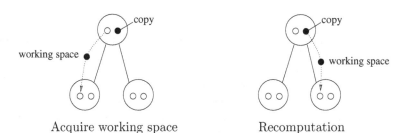

Acquire working space   Recomputation

In addition, as in the `Node` class in [3] again, space nodes are organized in a tree with parent links and store the number of the alternative they represent. The straightforward way of implementing such a tree in Mozart is reflected in the following interface:

```
class SpaceNode
    attr workingSpace              %% space or empty
    attr copy                      %% space or empty
    attr parent                    %% SpaceNode
    attr alternative               %% int

    meth constructRoot(Root)       %% space
    meth newChild(Alternative ?Child)   %% int, returns SpaceNode
    meth ask(?Status)              %% returns status
end
```

The constructor is straightforward. The newChild method takes an integer and creates a node representing that alternative, but with empty working space and copy. The ask method returns the status of a node's working space (whether it is failed, solved, or has alternatives for branching). What happens if the space node does not have a working space, for example because it has just been created? Space nodes obey the following protocol for creating and communicating computation spaces:

- If the parent has a working space, it will give it to its child.
- If the parent does not have a working space, recompute.

Recomputation. Given that there is a copy at least in the root of the search tree (which we will assume from now on), the basic recomputation mechanism can be implemented in Mozart in a straight-forward way:

```
meth recompute(?C)
    if @copy\=empty then {Space.clone @copy C}
    else
        {@parent recompute(C)}
        {Space.commit C @alternative}
    end
end
```

There are two obvious recomputation strategies:

- Full recomputation: let constructRoot place a copy in the root node.
- No recomputation: let recompute place a copy in every node.

These two make it very clear that recomputation is a means of trading space for time. Schulte [12] discusses recomputation in detail (including a comparison to trailing). Really efficient recomputation requires more sophisticated strategies that can be implemented by refining the recompute method:

- Fixed recomputation: place a copy in every n-th node (n is called *maximal recomputation distance* or *MRD*).
- Adaptive recomputation: place a copy on the middle of the path between the node that is to be recomputed and the ancestor it is recomputed from.

4   Abstracting the Search Tree

On top of the space node interface, the second abstraction layer is built, namely *tree nodes*. Space nodes make recomputation fully transparent: tree nodes need no knowledge of the underlying recomputation strategy.

In this section, we first elaborate tree nodes as a high-level interface to search trees. Then, we show how to use the tree node interface to implement exploration.

4.1   The Tree Node Interface

The tree node interface provides a simple interface to the search tree that abstracts from its dynamic construction.

Indeed, the full structure of the search tree can only be known by computing the status of each single node that indicates if it is a leaf or branching. However, we want to avoid the full construction of the tree prior to search because it is exactly the role of the search engine to explore the tree. As a consequence, it is necessary to build tree nodes lazily, that is, only once they are required by the search engine. To sum up, the tree node interface can be seen as a regular tree interface, although nodes of the tree are only built on demand.

Trees can be implemented in many different ways. In the following, we present an object-oriented interface to tree nodes; however, the same technique can be easily adapted to any other tree representation. Tree nodes are implemented following this interface:

```
class TreeNode from SpaceNode
   feat Children                   %% TreeNode tuple
   meth constructRoot(RootSpace)   %% space
   meth getChildren(?Children)     %% return TreeNode tuple
end
```

The constructor for the root node requires an initial computation space. Then, the exploration of the tree is performed using the method getChildren.

Implementation. As mentioned above, the main point is to create tree nodes lazily. We can use Mozart's by-need mechanism to achieve this: getChildren invokes ask to find out how many children to create, and then initializes children to a tuple of by-needs. The implementation is shown in Figure 4.1.

There are three levels of laziness in this design: The tuple of children is created only when getChildren is called, each child node is constructed by-need, and the underlying space node methods lazily copy and transfer their computation spaces.

4.2   Exploration Strategies

Implementing an exploration strategy is now as simple as traversing a tree. This makes the following code sample look like a text-book version of a depth-first tree traversal:

```
meth getChildren($)
   if {IsFree self.Children} then
      case {self ask($)} of alternatives(N) then
         self.Children = {MakeTuple c N}
      in
         {Record.forAllInd self.Children
          fun {$ I}
             {ByNeed fun {$} {self newChild(I $)} end}
          end}
      else self.Children=c
      end
   end
   self.Children
end
```

Fig. 2. Implementation of getChildren

```
proc {Explore Node}
   {Record.forAll {Node getChildren($)} Explore}
end
```

Incremental Search. It is possible to get more control over the search process, for example by defining a stateful search engine. Its interface consists of two methods initSearch and nextSolution. For parallel search (see Section 5.2), a more fine-grained control is necessary: we require only one exploration step, that is, explore only one node at each call.

Control. You may have noticed that search algorithms do not handle the case that a solution was found. We leave this task to a separate Control module that takes care of collecting solutions, setting up the root node and starting and stopping search. Some of the extensions presented in the following sections will also require global control, always realized as extensions to the Control module.

5   Extensions

The architecture we have so far can be extended in orthogonal ways to support some more advanced search techniques. The features we develop here in detail are *branch & bound search* for solving optimization problems, *parallel search* for distributing a search problem over several computers, and *last alternative optimization*, a technique that reduces the number of copies in the search tree. All extensions happen below the tree node interface, making them completely orthogonal to the implementation of exploration strategies.

5.1   Branch & Bound Optimization

A well-known mechanism for solving optimization problems is the *branch & bound* metaphor: each time a solution is found, every node that remains to be explored is constrained to yield a "better" solution (in terms of a given order). Branch & bound therefore maintains the invariant that every solution that is found is better than the previous one. As a direct consequence, the last solution is the globally best one. In practice, this optimization considerably reduces the size of the search tree by pruning whole subtrees that cannot give better solutions.

Implementation Model. Logically, every time a new solution is found, it is put in special nodes between all unexplored children and their parents. Each time a space is "pushed over" such a node (for example when a working space is given to a child, or during recomputation), the constraint that the space must be better is injected.

In Figure 3, the logical view of branch & bound is illustrated: assume the right child needs recomputation. It makes use of its mother's copy by cloning it, which gives a new computation space. Since a "best" constraint lies between these two nodes, the space must be constrained to yield a better solution (1) before being passed to the child (2). Still, this mechanism is transparent and does not appear in the space node or tree node interfaces: the special nodes are automatically inserted and traversed.

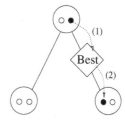

Fig. 3. Recomputation and B&B

Implementation. This scheme can be implemented by inheriting from the SpaceNode class and refining the ask and recompute methods to post the additional "best" constraints. The Control module maintains the current globally best solution. The newChild method of SpaceNode is refined so that it inserts a special node reflecting the current best solution when a child is created.

As this does not influence the tree node interface, optimization is completely orthogonal to search: all search engines can be used without any modification for solving optimization problems using branch & bound.

5.2   Parallel Search

In this section, we consider parallel search and show how it can easily fit within our layered abstractions. As a result, all exploration strategies designed over the tree node interface can be immediately used in a network-distributed setting.

Parallel search speeds up exploration of large constraint problems, by taking advantage of several networked computers that independently explore disjoint subtrees. This can be nicely implemented in Oz, as described by Schulte [13].

The main actors of the parallel search framework are a single *manager* and several *workers*. The former implements network distribution: it dispatches independent parts of the search problem to the workers and gathers solutions. In the case of branch & bound, the manager also propagates solutions in order to constrain each worker to yield a better solution.

The interface between the workers and the manager can be represented as follows (see Chapter 9 of [13] for a more detailed presentation of this interface):

Implementation. Implementing the parallel search framework amounts on the one hand, to setting up the network distribution layer, which makes use of the Mozart distribution library; on the other hand, to providing the actual code corresponding to the messages of the interface. We only focus on the messages that are not straightforward to implement.

The `explore` message carries along a path that describes the location of a tree node in the search tree. In order to reconstruct a node given its path, a straightforward extension to `SpaceNode` is needed, namely a method `fromPath` that builds a space node from a given path. Then, a search engine independent of the parallel search implementation can be used, starting at the given tree node. Still, each worker must be able to reply concurrently to a `share` message, that is, to provide the path of a subtree that remains to be explored. One way to do so is to use an incremental search engine, as described in Section 4.2, and to extend its interface with a method `getUnexploredPath` that (may) return a path to some unexplored node. In order to maximize the work being shared, it is usually wise to return the highest unexplored node in the tree, because it is likely to correspond to the largest unexplored subtree. The tree node and space node interfaces need to be enriched with a straightforward `getPath` method.

In the case of branch & bound search, solutions sent by the manager must be taken into account by the workers. This requires an interaction with the `Control` module to update the current best solution. As the tree node interface remains unchanged, branch & bound optimization is independent of the exploration strategy.

Since the parallel search only relies on the standard interface of tree nodes (up to the additional method `fromPath`), it is possible to freely use different implementations of tree nodes and space nodes. Thus, for instance, it is possible for some workers to display a graphical representation of the subtree being explored, and to dynamically choose the most suitable recomputation technique.

Discussion. In the following, we show that the network-distributed setting is correct in the sense that it yields the same solutions as a single search engine. The main difficulty arises from the fact that it is possible to use different exploration strategies on workers, as well as different recomputation techniques. We prove that this is not a problem, as long as some invariant is ensured.

Distributing search problems on networks mainly relies on paths, that is, an abstract representation of the location of a tree node in the search tree. Only two extra methods are needed: fromPath that builds a tree node given a path, and getPath that returns the path associated to a tree node. It is mandatory that paths have the same "meaning" across different workers. In order to formalize this statement, we give the following definition (at first, we do not consider branch & bound):

Definition 1. *Two computation spaces are* equipotent *if and only if they admit the same set of solutions. By extension, two tree nodes are equipotent if and only if their associated spaces are equipotent.*

Parallel search amounts to dispatching subparts of the problem to workers. Soundness (found solutions solve the problem) and completeness (no solution is discarded) follow from the invariant on paths, to be found next. The notation fromPath$_i$ means the method fromPath executed on worker w_i.

Invariant 1. *For every pair of workers w_1 and w_2,* fromPath$_2$ ∘ getPath$_1$, *considered as a binary relation, is a sub-relation of equipotence.*

In simpler words, the computation space at the origin (worker w_1) and the computation space reconstructed at the destination (worker w_2) are equipotent.

Notice that ensuring this invariant does not depend on the exploration strategy. As a consequence, all workers may use different exploration strategies.

In the case of branch & bound, it suffices to modify the definition of equipotence so that we only take into account the best *global* solution. Then, two computation spaces s_1 and s_2 are equipotent under a global solution g if and only if the best solution of $s_1 \cup \{g\}$ is as optimal as the best solution of $s_2 \cup \{g\}$. By lack of space, we omit the details.

5.3   Last Alternative Optimization

When all but one children of a node have been completely explored, and the node contains a copy, this can be handed down to the last child. This technique is known as *last alternative optimization* (LAO), and Schulte [13] presents a formal reasoning why it is important. To support it in an orthogonal, automatic way, we have to change the space node interface and the tree node implementation: space nodes need a special askLast method (analogous to createLastLeftChild and createLastRightChild in [3]) that acquires its parent's copy instead of working space – if available. Tree nodes internally maintain the number of *open children*, subtrees that have not been explored exhaustively yet. Thus getChildren can call either ask or askLast, depending on the parent's number of open children. This scheme makes LAO completely automatic, invisible to both search engines and recomputation strategies. It also fits seamlessly into our branch & bound setup, as pushing a copy over a special node during LAO of course constrains that copy.

We want to keep the invariant that the root node always stores a copy, so LAO must not be applied there.

Some search engines may require a different notion of last alternative, if they can say for sure that they will never visit a certain subtree again. This can be accomplished by a method `closeSubtree` in the `TreeNode` interface that simply sets the number of open children to 0. Note that even a badly designed search engine cannot break system invariants: With a copy in the root node, recomputation is always guaranteed to terminate, even if some LAO was done prematurely. An interesting extension might be a search engine that can speculatively close a subtree that it will most probably not return to.

6   IOzSeF – A Search Factory for Mozart

A complete implementation of the system described in this paper, the Integrated Oz Search Factory (IOzSeF), is available from the Mogul archive under the URL `mogul:/tack/iozsef`.

IOzSeF is a replacement for both the Explorer and the standard `Search` module. It currently features the following exploration strategies:

- Depth first search
- Breadth first search
- Iterative deepening [8]
- Limited Discrepancy search [5]
- A^* search [10]

The user can chose between no, fixed, adaptive, and full recomputation, last alternative optimization is always done automatically. Branch & bound optimization can be combined with all the other features. The graphical user interface is closely modeled after that of the Explorer; it basically offers the same functionality. A prototype implementation of parallel search supplies evidence that the design carries over to a parallel setting.

Visualization. Visualizing the search tree can be an important aid in modeling the problem. It helps to find sources of weak propagation and to match distribution heuristics and exploration strategy.

The space/tree node abstractions already provide a complete tree data structure. It can be refined further to contain all additional attributes necessary for computing a visual layout and displaying the tree. It is straightforward to reuse the Explorer's layout algorithm, which is an incremental version of Kennedy's tree drawing algorithm [7]. This yields a visualization module (similar to the one presented in [2]) that is truly independent of recomputation, branch & bound, and exploration strategy. We provide the tree visualization as an independent Mozart library, the `TkTreeWidget` (`mogul:/tack/TkTreeWidget`).

Implementation. The implementation makes heavy use of Mozart's object system, especially of dynamic inheritance: the interfaces are modeled as classes that are combined dynamically at run time. For example, the class `TreeNode` inherits either directly from `SpaceNode` or from `BNBNode`, a class derived from `SpaceNode` that provides the extensions necessary for branch & bound optimization.

Evaluation. IOzSeF is competitive with the explorer in terms of speed – for a number of standard examples, it performs sometimes better and never more than thirty percent worse. The overhead is due to the more complex data structures representing nodes, and the need for more method calls between the independent modules – the usual price that is paid for modularity. The implementation was not optimized towards efficiency but towards clean design and extensibility, so there is probably still quite some room for improvements.

The benefit of the principled design and orthogonality of the modules is that IOzSeF delivers correct results also when combining recomputation, branch & bound, and unorthodox exploration strategies (for example arbitrary manual exploration), whereas the Explorer is sometimes unpredictable.

7   Related Work

Schulte explains the need for a search factory in the *Future Work* section of his book "Programming Constraint Services" [13]. This book is the reference for computation spaces, recomputation, exploration strategies and parallel search. However, most of the algorithms presented there assume depth-first, left-to-right exploration, which we do not.

The Explorer [11], Mozart's graphical frontend to search, contains most of the features we present here, but in a monolithic, ad-hoc implementation. Besides, the combination of some features, especially branch & bound and recomputation, is not correct.

Chew et al. introduce STK [2], a SearchToolKit for Oz. Their design features several *dimensions*: memory policy, exploration, interaction, information, visualization, and optimization. They do not elaborate on how memory policy (recomputation) interacts with the other dimensions. Parallel search is not considered. However, their information dimension contains debugging functionality (like information on the choice a distributor made) that should be considered to be integrated into our setup.

Choi et al. [3] present an architecture for implementing state restoration policies in an orthogonal way. They also organize their fundamental data structures in a tree of nodes, making state restoration automatic and invisible to the user. Their version of last alternative optimization requires the search engine to collaborate, it is not automatic. The interactions of branch & bound and LAO with recomputation are only sketched. Choi et al. design their interface such that it supports novel state restoration policies (namely lazy copying, course-grained trailing and batch recomputation). We do not consider these extensions here, because Mozart does not provide for powerful enough primitives to implement them.

ILOG Solver [6] provides an object-oriented interface for programming exploration strategies. State restoration is realized through trailing. The exploration strategy is programmed only indirectly, by supplying a *node evaluator* and a *search selector* that specify which node and which branch to select, respectively (this is discussed in [9]). Although this also abstracts over state restoration, our interface is more intuitive to use. ILOG Solver does not allow to extend the underlying abstractions.

8   Conclusion and Outlook

Analyzing the main features provided by usual search libraries in constraint programming, we identify orthogonal concepts that are however interleaved in available implementations. Separating these key elements, we design a search factory for Mozart that is based on two abstractions: space nodes, encapsulating recomputation, and tree nodes, providing a clean interface for programming exploration strategies. Then, we show how to implement parallel search, branch & bound, and last alternative optimization by slightly extending the core abstractions. We notice that these extensions are mostly orthogonal and can be easily combined.

As a first example, a new implementation of an exploration strategy immediately benefits from recomputation and visualization, for free. As a second example, the workers used in parallel search may transparently use different exploration strategies, different recomputation techniques, and different visualization modules. Soundness and completeness of the search is preserved.

The search factory not only serves as a proof of concept, but can be used as a replacement for the Explorer and the engines found in the Search module.

In a prototype implementation, the search factory has been ported to the Alice programming language [1], using the Gecode constraint library (available at [4], some implementation details can be found in [14]). As a result, the design we develop here maps pretty well to a functional, statically typed, non-object-oriented language (Alice is based on SML). Besides, the tree node layer provides a very clean interface that integrates perfectly within a functional language. The stack of layers starting from the computation space paradigm to the tree node interface allows for a higher-order view of search in constraint programming that reconciles the incompatible natures of logic variables and functional abstractions. New features available in Gecode (like batch recomputation [3]) easily fit into our framework.

9   Future Work

Our future work goes in two directions: on the one hand, the Mozart-based implementation needs thorough testing and optimization for speed and memory requirements, and the parallel search engine should be fully incorporated. This will lead to a true alternative to Mozart's current search engines. On the other hand, the port to Alice/Gecode will be completed, to provide a full featured search environment on this platform. It may be interesting to build an extension similar to the "Information" dimension introduced by Chew et al. [2], which can provide important insight that is needed to debug constraint programs. Another opportunity for improvement consists in finding clear abstractions that describe precisely the chosen recomputation policy. In particular, it remains to design an interface that allows the programmer to easily specify hybrid recomputation strategies as suggested by Choi et al. [3].

Acknowledgements. We would like to thank Christian Schulte, who proposed this topic as a student's project to Guido Tack and supervised it. He and Thorsten Brunklaus made helpful comments on a draft version of this paper. Marco Kuhlmann helped in testing and debugging the implementation; he also provided the A^* exploration strategy. We also want to thank the anonymous referees for their constructive suggestions that helped improve the paper.

References

1. The Alice Project. http://www.ps.uni-sb.de/alice, 2004. Homepage at the Programming Systems Lab, Universität des Saarlandes, Saarbrücken, Germany.
2. Tee Yong Chew, Martin Henz, and Ka Boon Ng. A toolkit for constraint-based inference engines. In *Practical Aspects of Declarative Languages, Second International Workshop*, LNCS, Volume 1753, pages 185–199, Boston, MA, January 2000. Springer-Verlag.
3. Chiu Wo Choi, Martin Henz, and Ka Boon Ng. Components for state restoration in tree search. In *Proceedings of the Seventh International Conference on Principles and Practice of Constraint Programming*, LNCS, vol. 2239, Paphos, Cyprus, November 2001. Springer Verlag.
4. Gecode, the generic constraint development environment. http://www.gecode.org, 2004.
5. William D. Harvey and Matthew L. Ginsberg. Limited discrepancy search. In *Proceedings of the Fourteenth International Joint Conference on Artificial Intelligence (IJCAI-95); Vol. 1*, pages 607–615, Montréal, Québec, Canada, August 1995.
6. ILOG Inc., Mountain View, CA, USA. *ILOG Solver 5.0 reference Manual*, 2000.
7. A. J. Kennedy. Functional pearls: Drawing trees. *Journal of Functional Programming*, 6(3):527–534, May 1996.
8. Richard E. Korf. Iterative-deepening–an optimal admissible tree search. In Aravind Joshi, editor, *Proceedings of the 9th International Joint Conference on Artificial Intelligence*, pages 1034–1036, Los Angeles, CA, August 1985. Morgan Kaufmann.
9. Irvin J. Lustig and Jean-François Puget. Program does not equal program: Constraint programming and its relationship to mathematical programming. White paper, ILOG Inc., 1999. Available at http://www.ilog.com.
10. Stuart J. Russel and Peter Norvig. *Artificial Intelligence - A Modern Approach - Second Edition*. Prentice Hall, Englewood Cliffs, 2003.
11. Christian Schulte. Oz explorer: A visual constraint programming tool. In Lee Naish, editor, *Proceedings of the Fourteenth International Conference on Logic Programming*, pages 286–300, Leuven, Belgium, July 1997. The MIT Press.
12. Christian Schulte. Comparing trailing and copying for constraint programming. In Danny De Schreye, editor, *Proceedings of the Sixteenth International Conference on Logic Programming*, pages 275–289. The MIT Press, December 1999.
13. Christian Schulte. *Programming Constraint Services*, volume 2302 of *Lecture Notes in Artficial Intelligence*. Springer-Verlag, Berlin, Germany, 2002.
14. Christian Schulte and Peter J. Stuckey. Speeding up constraint propagation. In *Tenth International Conference on Principles and Practice of Constraint Programming*, LNCS, Toronto, Canada, September 2004. Springer-Verlag. To appear.

Implementing Semiring-Based Constraints Using Mozart⋆

Alberto Delgado, Carlos Alberto Olarte, Jorge Andrés Pérez,
and Camilo Rueda

Pontificia Universidad Javeriana - Cali
{albertod, japerezp}@puj.edu.co
{caolarte, crueda}@atlas.puj.edu.co

Abstract. Although Constraint Programming (CP) is considered a useful tool for tackling combinatorial problems, its lack of flexibility when dealing with uncertainties and preferences is still a matter for research. Several formal frameworks for soft constraints have been proposed within the CP community: all of them seem to be theoretically solid, but few practical implementations exist. In this paper we present an implementation for Mozart of one of these frameworks, which is based on a semiring structure. We explain how the soft constraints constructs were adapted to the propagation process that Mozart performs, and show how they can be transparently integrated with current Mozart hard propagators. Additionally, we show how over-constrained problems can be successfully relaxed and solved, and how preferences can be added to a problem, while keeping the formal model as a direct reference.

1   Introduction

Constraint Satisfaction Problems (CSP) have been studied for more than four decades. Real-life problems expressed as CSPs are in general closer to the application domain and thus simpler to understand than using other techniques. Despite its advantages, the CSP formalism still lacks flexibility when representing some situations, such as when dealing with preferences, uncertainties and similar notions. The need for relaxing problems such as constraints that do not always have to be satisfied, motivated the research on Soft Constraints Satisfaction Problems (SCSP) as an extension of the classical CSP. Several formal and practical works have been proposed in this direction. All of them allow users to find approximate solutions for a given problem, while considering all constraints in the problem at the same time. The quality or degree of usefulness for an approximate solution is given by an overall valuation. In this paper, we focus on the *Semiring-Based Constraints*, a formalism developed by Bistarelli et al [2, 7].

⋆ This work was partially supported by the Colombian Institute for Science and Technology Development (Colciencias) under the CRISOL project (Contract No. 298-2002).

P. Van Roy (Ed.): MOZ 2004, LNCS 3389, pp. 224–236, 2005.
© Springer-Verlag Berlin Heidelberg 2005

This formalism adds valuations to the problem solutions and provides a mechanism for choosing the best of them without implying the complete satisfaction of all the constraints in the problem.

Several implementations of the semiring-based constraints exist. To our knowledge, however, most of them are based on CLP (Constraint Logic Programming). These implementations include clp(FD,S) [9] which extends the clp(FD) solver with a new data type for handling semiring operations and the semiring extension for SICStus Prolog based on Constraint Handling Rules (CHR) [5]. In addition, there are other prototypes like [10] that propose interesting ideas that could be applied for implementing tuple evaluation, as well as [12], where an iterative algorithm is proposed in order to implement the abstraction scheme for semiring-based constraints proposed in [4].

We implemented semiring-based constraints by exploiting the extension mechanisms that Mozart provides, in particular the Constraint Propagation Interface (CPI) [11]. In this setting, the behavior of semiring-based constraints is implemented in propagators. The system allows Mozart programmers to naturally express soft and hard constraints in the same program. We believe this conservative approach is more practical for Mozart since the theoretical extension proposed in [7] would imply changing the formal model of the language.

We tested our implementation in some known problems. Such tests were useful to highlight some advantages of the implementation. They also provided a valuable experimental reference that can be generalized when dealing with over-constrained problems, or to handle both soft and hard constraints. We identified some strategic issues that should be considered when including soft constraints in existing CP applications. The main contribution of the paper is to show that semiring-based constraints can be efficiently included in Mozart by defining appropriate propagators.

This paper is structured as follows: in the next section, we introduce the semiring-based formalism for soft constraints. Then, our propagator implementation is described, demonstrating its use in section 4. In section 5, some directions in using soft constraints are discussed, and some of the factors that influence these directions are pointed out. Finally, we propose a set of concluding remarks and describe some ideas for future work.

2   Semiring-Based Constraint Satisfaction Problems

In this section we briefly summarize the main definitions and properties of the semiring framework for handling soft constraints. Further details can be found in [2].

2.1   Semirings and c-Semirings

A *semiring* is a tuple $\langle A, +, \times, \mathbf{0}, \mathbf{1} \rangle$ such that

- A is a set and $\mathbf{0}, \mathbf{1} \in A$
- $+$, the *additive operator* is closed, commutative and associative. Moreover, its unit element is $\mathbf{0}$.

- ×, the *multiplicative operator*, which is a closed, associative operation, such that **1** is its unit element and **0** is its absorbing element.
- × distributes over +.

A *c-semiring* (for constraint semiring) is a semiring with some additional properties: × is commutative, + is idempotent, and **1** is its absorbing element. The idempotency of + is needed in order to define a partial ordering $\leq_S$ over the set A, which serves to compare different elements of the semiring. Such partial order is defined as follows: $a \leq_S b$ iff $a + b = b$. Intuitively, given $a \leq_S b$, one can say that b is *better than* a. Moreover, for this order, it is possible to prove that + *and* × are monotonic, **0** is its minimum and **1** is its maximum, $\langle A, \leq_S \rangle$ is a complete lattice and, that for all $a, b \in A$, $a + b = lub(a, b)$.

2.2   Soft Constraint Systems and Problems

A *constraint system* is a tuple $CS = \langle S, D, V \rangle$, where S is a semiring, D is a finite set and V is an ordered set of variables. Given a constraint system $CS = \langle S, D, V \rangle$, where $S = (A, +, \times, 0, 1)$, a *constraint* over CS is a pair $\langle def, con \rangle$, where $con \subseteq V$ is called the *type* of the constraint, and $def : D^{k=|con|} \to A$ is called the *value* of the constraint. Therefore, a constraint specifies a set of variables (the ones in con), and assigns an element of the semiring to each tuple of values of these variables.

A *soft constraint problem (SCSP)* P over CS is a pair $P = \langle C, con \rangle$, where C is a set of constraints over CS and con is a subset of V.

2.3   Combination and Projection for Soft Constraints

Consider any tuple of values t and two sets of variables I and I', with $I' \subseteq I$. $t \downarrow_{I'}^{I}$, denotes the *tuple projection* for t w.r.t. the variables in I'. Let $c_1 = \langle def_1, con_1 \rangle$ and $c_2 = \langle def_2, con_2 \rangle$ be two constraints over CS. Then, its *combination* $c_1 \otimes c_2$, is the constraint $c' = \langle def', con' \rangle$, where $con' = con_1 \cup con_2$ and $def'(t) = def_1(t \downarrow_{con'}^{con_1}) \times def_2(t \downarrow_{con'}^{con_2})$. Informally, the combination of two constraints builds a new constraint which includes all the variables in both constraints. This new constraint associates a semiring value to each tuple of domain values for all variables. Such value is obtained by multiplying the elements associated by the two constraints to the appropriate subtuples.

Given the constraint $c = \langle def, con \rangle$ and a subset w of con, the *projection* of w over c, written $c \Downarrow_w$ is the constraint $\langle def^*, con^* \rangle$, where $con^* = w$ and $def^*(t^*) = \sum_{\{t | t \downarrow_w^{con} = t^*\}} def(t)$. Expressed in words, projection removes some variables by associating to each tuple over the remaining variables a semiring element. Such an element is obtained by summing the elements associated by the original constraint to all the extensions of this tuple over the removed variables.

Note the correspondence between the combination and the multiplicative operator as well as the one between the projection and the additive operator.

2.4   Solution of a SCSP

Given a constraint problem $P = \langle C, con \rangle$ over a constraint system CS, the solution of P is a constraint defined as $Sol(P) = (\bigotimes C) \Downarrow_{con}$ where $\bigotimes C$ is the obvious extension of $\times$ to a set of constraints C. In words, a solution represents the combination of all constraints in the problem; such a combination is projected over the variables of interest. Note that the solution for a problem is also a constraint.

Sometimes it is enough to know the best value associated with the tuples of a solution. This is called the *best level of consistency:* Given an SCSP $P = \langle C, con \rangle$, the best level of consistency for P is defined as $blevel(P) = (\bigotimes C) \Downarrow_{\emptyset}$. P is said to be consistent if $\mathbf{0} <_S blevel$. In the case where $blevel(P) = \alpha$, P is said to be α-consistent.

2.5   Instances of the Framework

C-semirings including the most known variants of CSPs are listed below:

- Classic CSP: $\langle \{false, true\}, \vee, \wedge, false, true \rangle$
- Fuzzy CSP: $\langle \{x \mid x \in [0,1]\}, max, min, 0, 1 \rangle$
- Probabilistic CSP: $\langle \{x \mid x \in [0,1]\}, max, \times, 0, 1 \rangle$
- Weighted CSP: $\langle \Re^+, min, +, +\infty, 0 \rangle$

In addition, it is possible to combine several c-semirings and obtain another: given n c-semirings $S_i = \langle A_i, +_i, \times_i, 0_i, 1_i \rangle$, for $i = 1 \ldots n$, let us define the structure $Comp(S_1, \ldots, S_n) = \langle \langle A_1, \ldots, A_n \rangle, +, \times, \langle 0_1, \ldots, 0_n \rangle, \langle 1_1, \ldots, 1_n \rangle \rangle$. Given $\langle a_1, \ldots, a_n \rangle$ and $\langle b_1, \ldots, b_n \rangle$ such that $a_i, b_i \in A_i$ for $i = 1, \ldots, n$. In this scheme, the semiring operations can be performed in the following way: $\langle a_1, \ldots, a_n \rangle + \langle b_1, \ldots, b_n \rangle = \langle a_1 +_1 b_1, \ldots, a_n +_n b_n \rangle$ and $\langle a_1, \ldots, a_n \rangle \times \langle b_1, \ldots, b_n \rangle = \langle a_1 \times_1 b_1, \ldots, a_n \times_n b_n \rangle$.

3   Implementing Semiring-Based Constraints

Frequently, applications using constraint programming need to express preferences, uncertainty and similar ideas in order to be more flexible and to support partially "inconsistent" inputs. Mozart programmers use the FD propagators to write procedures enforcing constraints modeling the real problem, but they have no elegant and formal mechanism to express softness or to deal with over-constrained inputs. Some language constructs like reified constraints [14] and disjunctions (*or*) can be used to fulfill these requirements. Nevertheless, solutions obtained in this way cannot be compared in a uniform way because some of them do not satisfy the same constraints.

Our propagator-based implementation aims at integrating the previously described c-semiring formalism into the efficient available propagator mechanisms in Mozart. This section describes our implementation of a c-semiring based constraint system using the Constraint Propagation Interface (CPI) [11] and points out some interesting advantages in using it.

3.1   Soft Propagators

Our first implementation of a c-semiring constraint system in Mozart was built using its functional and object-oriented features. Basically, we defined some structures representing most of the model concepts, implemented c-semiring operations like constraint combination and $Sol(P)$ over these, and finally built a search procedure based on arc-consistency algorithms. Using this implementation defining new constraints was easy, as the user only had to write the def function and then to combine this definition with the implemented semiring operations.

This implementation had serious performance problems because we had to implement our own version of some mechanisms like propagation queues and domain definitions, instead of using those provided by Mozart (CPI). Initially, we did not use CPI's facilities, because a relationship between semiring operations and propagators was not clear. For example, the constraint definition for the c-semiring formalism differs from the notion of propagation implemented in Mozart. Indeed, the c-semiring *constraint* definition only expresses a function (def) to evaluate tuples in the Cartesian product of the variable domains, while constraints in Mozart are enforced by means of propagators that narrow values of its associated variables.

Trying to unify both concepts, we decided to build some propagators dealing with the semiring valuation idea. These propagators should implement the propagation function (by overloading the propagate method from OZ_Propagator class) and a valuation method (def function). The propagate method must remove elements from the variable domain only when all the tuples with these values have a valuation less than the minimum level of preference accepted by the user.

3.2   Creating Soft Propagators

Soft propagators implement an efficient mechanism for handling softness in constraint applications, allowing transparent integration of soft constraints with current Oz propagators (hard constraints). In this approach, if the user wants to implement a new propagator, he/she must extend an abstract class, and deal with some low-level language implementation issues. Our idea for solving this drawback is to provide a wide set of soft propagators (much like in the FD system) to build most common applications, thus minimizing programming efforts. In the following, we first describe the basic class and procedures required to create new soft propagators. Later, we show the set of implemented soft propagators.

Semiring Class. This class implements the semiring structure and provides the following methods:

- **plus(a,b):** Computes $a + b$
- **times(a,b):** Computes $a \times b$

- **max():** Returns the max ring value (**1**)
- **min():** Returns the min ring value (**0**)
- **lt(a,b):** Tests $a <_s b$
- **decrease(u,dlevel):** Returns the ring value obtained from decreasing u times the ring value *dlevel* to the max value (**1**).

The first six functions are self explanatory. The last one allows writing propagators independently of the c-semiring selected by the user. For example, *decrease* $(2, 0.2)$ will return 0.6 $(1.0 - 2 * 0.2)$ when using the fuzzy semiring, and 0.4 $(0.0 + 2 * 0.2)$ when using the weighted semiring.

OZ_Soft_Propagator. This is the abstract class from which all soft propagators inherit. It inherits itself from OZ_Propagator, forcing the user to implement the propagate method as well as others like sClone and gCollect for memory management (see [11]). Additionally, this class provides the following methods:

- **setDegreeLevel:** changes the *Softness Degree* of the propagator, making it softer or harder (see section 3.3)
- **computeValuation:** Computes $def(t)$ when all propagator variables are singletons.
- **getRingValue:** Returns the overall semiring value, computed by applying the times operator over all the c-semirings values returned by all soft propagators.
- **propagate:** Filter function.

Before reaching the entailed state, all soft propagators must call their *ComputeValuation* method, allowing the abstract class to compute the overall semiring value. The filter function must be carefully written since it must be compatible with the valuation function. This implies that the propagator should only remove inconsistent values (i.e., $d_i \in dom(X)$ s.t. $def(t) <_s minLevel$ for all t with $t \downarrow_X = d_i$) and the valuation function should assign values corresponding to this selection (for all $t \in D^{|con|}$, $computeValuation \geq_s minLevel$). For non-idempotent times operators, an additional check is required: when a computation space reaches stability, the overall semiring value must be better than the minimal level of preference stated by the user ($\prod prop_i.ComputeValuation \geq_s minLevel$). Currently, this check is performed by the distributor using the procedure field in the generic distribution strategy specification.

Some Additional Functions. The user can invoke the following functions in Mozart:

- **{Soft.chooseRing R}:** Selects the semiring R. For example,

  ```
  {Soft.chooseRing fuzzy}
  ```

  chooses the *fuzzy* c-semiring.
- **{SetBLevel ML}:** Changes the minimal level of preference (*minLevel*) accepted by the user. For example, invoking

```
{Soft.chooseRing fuzzy}
{Soft.setBlevel 0.35}
```

makes the solver reject all solutions where the semiring value is less than 0.35. In general, all variable assignments with valuation $\alpha <_S minLevel$, will be considered as inconsistent.

- **{Soft.setSoftDegree Dl}:** This function defines the softness degree parameter with value Dl for all the propagators created after this statement. As the softness degree parameter is included in the state of a propagator, it is possible to define different degrees for each propagator in a program. The interaction of this parameter and the $minLevel$, makes propagators softer or harder as explained in the next section.
- **{GetValuation}:** Returns the overall semiring valuation when all propagators are entailed. This is computed by applying the $times$ semiring operator over the valuation of each soft propagator.

3.3   Current Soft Propagators

- **{Soft.lt X Y}:** Asserts the constraint $X < Y$. This propagator "allows" values for X equal to or greater than Y according to the softness degree. For example, if we impose the $Soft.lt$ propagator over two variables X and Y, set the softness degree to 0.4 and choose the $fuzzy$ semiring, the valuation criteria for all tuples $t_i = \langle x_i, y_i \rangle$ is :

$$def(t_i) = \begin{cases} 1.0 & \text{if } x_i < y_i \\ max(0.0, 1.0 - (0.4 * (1.0 + x_i - y_i))) & \text{otherwise} \end{cases}$$

Observe that a softness degree equal to **1** turns $Soft.lt$ into the classical $LessThan$ propagator. Furthermore, if the $minLevel$ parameter is fixed to 0.5, only tuples $\langle x_i, y_i \rangle$ where $x_i \leq y_i$ are accepted. This fact is used by the propagator to enforce bound consistency.

- **{Soft.distinct LVar}:** Asserts the $all\ different$ constraint over variables in $LVar$. In this case, according to the $Softness\ Degree$, the propagator allows that some values be equal in the list (or tuple) $LVar$. Consider the following fragment of code:

```
Sol = sol(var: Vars value:Val)
N=4 Vars = {FD.tuple sol N 1#N-1}
{Soft.chooseRing fuzzy}
{Soft.setBlevel 0.3} {Soft.setSoftDegree 0.4}
{Soft.distinct Vars}
{FD.distribute ff Vars}
Val = {Soft.getValuation}
```

Here, those solutions where two variables are pairwise equal, such as $\langle 1, 2, 3, 1 \rangle$, are allowed and evaluated to $0.6(1.0 - 0.4)$. Solutions where three or four variables are pairwise equal such as $\langle 1, 1, 1, 2 \rangle$ are rejected (its valuation is $0.2 = 1.0 - 0.4 - 0.4 \leq_s 0.3$).

- **{Soft.distance X Y RelOp Z:}** Asserts $|X - Y|$ *RelOp* Z constraint where *RelOp* stands for the basic relational operators. The softness (or hardness) of this constraint depends on the softness degree parameter.
- **{Soft.unaryPreference X RPref}:** Allows the user to express preferences over some values in the domain of X. For example, in

```
X::1#5
{Soft.chooseRing fuzzy}
{Soft.setBlevel 0.4}
{Soft.unaryPreference X val(1:0.3 3:0.7 5:0.4)}
```

the *UnaryPreference* propagators will remove $\{1\}$ in the first propagation step (since $0.3 <_s 0.4$), and the semiring value assigned by the propagator (*ComputeValuation* method) is 0.7 if $X = 3$, 0.4 if $X = 5$ and 1.0 (**max**) otherwise. This propagator is not affected by the softness degree parameter.
- **{Soft.nPreference LVar RPref}:** Like the previous one, but this function allows to express valuations for *n-ary* tuples. For example, in

```
[X Y]::1#4
{Soft.chooseRing fuzzy}
{Soft.setBlevel 0.4}
{Soft.nPreference [X Y] val('1-2':0.2 '3-2':0.6)}
```

Soft.nPreference will remove 1(resp. 2) from $dom(X)$ (resp. $dom(Y)$) iff the only value in $dom(Y)$ (resp. $dom(X)$) is 2 (resp. 1) respectively. If X is entailed to 3 and Y to 2, *computeValuation* will return 0.6 and 1.0 (**1**) otherwise.

Summing up, this implementation adopts the formal concepts of the semiring formalism with efficient propagation techniques in Mozart. We also provide some useful mechanisms for expressing soft statements in constraint applications, for example the softness degree for expressing accurate soft statements over constraints and the *minLevel* for filtering solutions obtained so far. Thus, we gain some interesting advantages: (1) Capability of mixing soft and hard (current Mozart FD propagators) constraints. In this case, we do not need to evaluate the hard constraint assuming a semiring value of **1** ; (2) ability to filter undesirable solutions w.r.t. a fixed parameter (*minLevel*) and (3) having criteria to compare different solutions.

4 Results

Although we have not tested the c-semiring based constraint implementation with real-life applications yet, we have run some small examples that show the level of expressiveness and offer some ideas about performance of our system. This section evaluates some examples, using an Intel Pentium IV CPU 1.80 GHz, 256 MB RAM computer running Mozart system 1.3 over Linux Gentoo Kernel 2.6.3.

4.1   An Over-Constrained Problem Example

We implemented a simple timetabling problem proposed in the Mozart tutorial [14]. The problem consists of allocating conferences with some precedence and disjoint constraints. The input for the solver is composed of:

- *nbParSessions*, an integer representing the maximum number of parallel sessions that can be assigned.
- *nbSessions*, the number of conference sessions to be assigned.
- A list of *before* tuples $\langle x, y \rangle$ asserting that conference x must take place before conference y
- A list of *disjoint* tuples $\langle x, [y_1, ..y_n] \rangle$ asserting that conference x must not be in parallel with conferences $y_1, y_2, ..., y_n$

The solution strategy proposed in [14] used the *FD.atMost* propagator to enforce the maximum number of parallel sessions (nbParSessions), $FD. <$ to enforce precedence constraints and $FD.'distinct'$ for disjoint constraints. When we added some new precedence constraints to the original data input, the problem became over-constrained. To solve this, we changed the *LessThan* ($FD. <:$) propagator by our *Soft.lt* propagator and obtained a solution to the new input data. Note that a slight change was necessary for solving the problem, keeping the same initial model.

This example is interesting because by making small and well located changes, we integrated soft and hard constraints in a consistent and efficient way. Additionally, it is possible to know when a solution is better than others by using the *plus* semiring operator (recall that a *is better than* b iff $a + b = a$).

4.2   Expressing Preferences

Many real life problems include expressing preferences such as "this color *is better than* that one" or "I prefer having more RAM than a faster processor". Implementing this kind of constraint is not easy using only hard propagators. For example, one could try implementing those preferences using $FD. <$, but usually not all user preferences can be satisfied at once. We can instead use soft propagators expressing preferences, compare, and choose a desirable solution according to its semiring value.

A formalism called CP-Network was proposed in [8] to reason with preference statements. For example, given two finite domain variables A and B, the preference statement $a_1 \succ a_2 \succ a_3$ expresses that the user prefers the assignment $A = a_1$ independently (regardless other assignments) over $A = a_2$ and $A = a_3$. We also have conditional preferences such as $b_1 : a_2 \succ a_1$ expressing that given an assignment of b_1 for B, the user prefers assigning a_2 rather than a_1 to A.

The user preferences can be represented by a *Conditional Preference Graph* $G = \langle V, A \rangle$ where V is the set of variables and $a_i = \langle X, Y \rangle \in A$ iff a preference of the form $x_i : y_1 \succ y_2 \succ ... \succ y_n$ is given. In [13] a solving strategy using the $S_{weighted}$ c-semiring was proposed. We implemented a CP-Network solver following those ideas.

The solver imposes the *UnaryPreference* propagator for each unconditional preference and imposes *nPreference* over each conditionally preference statement. For example, a customer trying to buy a car could give preferences such as:

$$White \succ Red \succ Black \succ Green \quad ; \quad Hydraulic \succ Mechanic$$

$$Chevrolet \succ Renault \succ Mazda \succ Fiat \succ Kia \quad ; \quad 1600cc^3 \succ 1300cc^3 \succ 2300cc^3$$

$$1300cc^3 : Mechanic \succ Hydraulic$$

$$Chevrolet : Red \succ White \succ Black \succ Green$$

In this case, we created variables related to each feature (Color, Transmission, Trademark, Capacity). Using the solver we obtained all ordered solutions (by $\leq_s$) in a few milliseconds (8ms). Observe that the trivial solution $\langle White, Hydraulic, Chevrolet, 1600cc^3 \rangle$ taking account only the unconditional preferences does not satisfy all the preferences (unsatisfiable using only hard constraints) but it is still a good solution.

4.3   Avoiding Reified Constraints

Reification is the usual means in Mozart for expressing soft statements or solving over-constrained problems. The reification of a constraint C w.r.t. a variable x is the constraint $(C \leftrightarrow x = 1) \wedge x \in 0\#1$ [14]. This new constraint is defined by the following propagation rules: if $x = 1$ (resp. $x = 0$) is entailed by the store then the reified propagator reduces to a propagator for C (resp. $\neg C$) and if the store entails C (resp. store in inconsistent with C) then the reified propagator tells $x = 1$ (resp. $x = 0$).

Using this approach, users can define satisfiability degrees (a_i) for each reified constraint and compute $Sat = \sum_{a_i \times x_i}$ by means of a propagator such as $FD.sumC$. Sat can be maximized (or minimized) using a suitable distribution strategy and its final value can be used to choose or reject solutions, giving some ideas about their "quality".

The following example shows that sometimes imposing soft constraints instead of reified constraints may be useful. In particular, the semiring structure offers well defined mechanisms for expressing softness over constraints involved in the problem and provides an operator for choosing solutions in a consistent way. Furthermore, we do not need to explicitly compute the valuation function because it is implicitly computed by the overall ring valuation.

The problem consists of aligning some people for a photo [14]. Some preferences about the distance between two persons are given. The original input in [14] turns the problem over-constrained. The solution proposed by the authors consists in adding reified constraints asserting $Sat.i = 1 \leftrightarrow |P.x - P.y| = 1$, meaning that $Sat.i$ is equal to 1 only if the i-th preference (x wants to be besides y) can be satisfied. Finally, the solver maximizes the satisfaction function $\sum Sat.i$ implementing a two-dimensional distribution strategy.

We rewrote the script using the soft version of the *distance* propagator instead of the reification mechanism. The soft propagator will allow distances not necessarily equal to 1, penalizing its valuation according to the softness degree parameter chosen for each propagator. The satisfiability (modeled as a distributed variable in the previous implementation) is now obtained via the overall semiring valuation (we do not require a two-dimensional distribution strategy). Furthermore, by stating preferences, we can fix the associated cost with a condition stating that two persons must be together when they cannot be.

5   Integrating Soft Constraints into Existing Applications

Once a soft constraints implementation is available, considering its use in real settings becomes a crucial issue centered around two basic factors:

- Modifications needed on existing constraint applications that wish to use soft constraints.
- Agreements regarding the obtained solutions by using a soft constraints implementation.

The first item is related with the cost of introducing soft constraints in an existing application. Although soft constraints allow a more faithful representation for constraint models, stating all or most of the constraints in a problem in terms of soft constraints is computationally harder, because soft propagators perform less pruning than hard ones. Consider any commercial application: the costs, in time and money, of changing the application are huge; the performance consequences of the soft constraints are also significant. For this reason, we consider that adding soft constraints in real settings depends on the identification of a specific set of constraints to be relaxed. Such a set must contain those constraints that reflect optional or variable features of the problem. Think of any application in operations research: constraints regarding the number of available resources can be relaxed, since some kind of arrangements are possible in real life. On the contrary, constraints stating mandatory conditions (such as the business rules), cannot be replaced by their soft counterpart, because of the serious consequences of such decisions for the final user. Moreover, this replacement (or relaxing) of constraints is related to the second item stated above: the agreement process derived from the approximate solutions obtained by using soft constraints.

By using soft constraints, the programmer must negotiate with the final user those solutions that are good enough with respect to the constraints of the problem, but does not hold for all of them. Moreover, as in the case described before, such approximate solutions will require additional effort on the part of the user. This implies that the programmer (and the final user) must be willing to deal with less than satisfactory solutions as a result of the software development process. We believe that either the process of convincing the user to accept an approximate solution and/or the effort of the user in arranging some conditions in its real setting, will be easier if the relaxed constraints are carefully chosen.

To make these arguments clear, remember the conference allocation example previously described. It is possible that the precedence constraints that were imposed by the **before** tuples (relaxed by using *Soft.lt*) were less important for the users of the application than the `disjoint` constraints. This implies that for such users, those solutions possibly not satisfying all the `before` constraints, but satisfying the rest of them, are acceptable approximations. Conversely, this also means that in that case, the `disjoint` constraints must always hold under any condition.

Summing up, using the soft constraints in existing applications can be very useful, but their inclusion must be carefully planned. Since our module for soft constraints in Mozart can be consistently used in conjunction with the efficient, existing hard mechanisms (the FD propagators), the main task of the programmer is to select and replace crucial constraints in the problem. This choice will influence the rest of the development process, since approximated solutions (obtained from a relaxed problem) can be more easily accepted by the final users of the application if the changes and/or trade-offs he/she has to make are reasonably manageable.

6   Conclusions

Our implementation offers a new alternative for dealing with over-constrained problems in Mozart. Such problems are often modeled using reified constraints and other constructs. The main drawback of such constructs is its lack of expressiveness. Since the number of satisfied constraints in a problem does not necessarily reflect its quality (or its usefulness), comparing several solutions for the same problem is not easy. On the contrary, our semiring-based implementation allows such comparison, because the resulting valuations are related to the entire solution.

Our implementation also allows the direct interaction between hard and soft constraints, in such a way that the hard constraints are not modeled using soft-based constructs (by using the c-semiring instance for Classical CSP), but taking advantage of the existent (often very efficient) hard constraints mechanisms. This feature allows us to consider that not all the constraints in a problem should be relaxed by soft constraints; it is important to choose a subset of the constraints carefully, and relaxing *just that subset*, avoiding poor valued solutions and/or efficiency overheads.

The semiring-based formalism has practical application for programs written in Mozart. Existing applications can take advantage of this approach, without changing the core of its model. Moreover, those applications that try to solve an over-constrained problem can benefit from this relaxation alternative, since they could obtain solutions that were previously rejected by a hard solver. We believe that these two issues – the modifications needed in existing applications and the solutions that can be obtained in over-constrained settings – are fundamental when considering the industrial and commercial application of soft constraints.

6.1   Future Work

We plan to increase the number of soft propagators available for finite domain constraints in Mozart. This will increase the number of applications that can introduce soft constraints in their models. We also plan to study a formal framework for proving properties of filter functions in propagators such as the one in [1, 6].

In order to include soft ideas in the distribution process, we consider that the labeling process in [3] could be a good starting point. Other approaches, like building a distributor that looks for those solutions that are better than a valuation threshold, or considering as alternatives for distribution the best valued variables could also be a subject of study in the near future.

Acknowledgements

We would like to thank the anonymous reviewers for their valuable comments for improving this paper. We are also grateful to Stefano Bistarelli for his comments about this work.

References

1. Krzysztof R. Apt. The rough guide to constraint propagation. In *Principles and Practice of Constraint Programming*, pages 1–23, 1999.
2. Stefano Bistarelli. *Semirings for Soft Constraint Solving and Programming*. Number 2962 in LNCS. Springer-Verlag, 2004.
3. Stefano Bistarelli, Philippe Codognet, Yan Georget, and Francesca Rossi. Labeling and partial local consistency for soft constraint programming. *Lecture Notes in Computer Science*, 1753, 2000.
4. Stefano Bistarelli, Philippe Codognet, and Francesca Rossi. Abstracting soft constraints: framework, properties, examples. *Artif. Intell.*, 139(2), 2002.
5. Stefano Bistarelli, Thom Frühwirth, Michael Marte, and Francesca Rossi. Soft constraint propagation and solving in constraint handling rules. In *Proc. of the Third Workshop on Rule-Based Constraint Reasoning and Programming*, 2001.
6. Stefano Bistarelli, Rosella Gennari, and Francesca Rossi. Constraint propagation for soft constraints: Generalization and termination conditions. In *Principles and Practice of Constraint Programming*, pages 83–97, 2000.
7. Stefano Bistarelli, Ugo Montanari, and Francesca Rossi. Soft concurrent constraint programming. In *European Symposium on Programming*, 2002.
8. Craig Boutilier, Ronen I. Brafman, Holger H. Hoos, and David Poole. Reasoning with ceteris paribus preference statements. In *Proc. 15th Conf. on Uncertainty in AI*, pages 71–80, 1999.
9. Yan Georget and Philippe Codognet. Compiling semiring-based constraints with clp(fd,s). In *Proceedings of CP'98*, 1998.
10. Jerome Kelleher and Barry O'Sullivan. Evaluation-based semiring metaconstraints. In *Proceedings of MICAI*, April 2004.
11. Tobias Muller. The Mozart Constraint Extensions Reference. Available electronically at www.mozart-oz.org, April 2004.
12. I. Pilan and F. Rossi. Abstracting soft constraints: some experimental results. In *Proc. ERCIM/Colognet workshop on CLP and constraint solving.*, June 2003.
13. F. Rossi, K. B. Venable, and T. Walsh. Cp-networks: semantics, complexity, approximations and extensions.
14. Christian Schulte and Gert Smolka. Finite Domain Constraint Programming in Oz - A Tutorial. Available electronically at www.mozart-oz.org, April 2004.

A Mozart Implementation of CP(BioNet)

Grégoire Dooms, Yves Deville, and Pierre Dupont

Computing Science and Engineering Department,
Université catholique de Louvain,
B-1348 Louvain-la-Neuve - Belgium
{dooms, yde, pdupont}@info.ucl.ac.be

Abstract. The analysis of biochemical networks consists in studying the interactions between biological entities cooperating in complex cellular processes. To facilitate the expression of analyses and their computation, we introduced CP(BioNet), a constraint programming framework for the analysis of biochemical networks. An Oz-Mozart prototype of CP(BioNet) is described. This prototype consists of the implementation of a new kind of domain variables, graph domain variables, and the implementation of constraint propagators for constraints over graph-domain variables. These new variables and constraints are implemented in Oz and they can then be used like other domain variables in the Oz-Mozart platform. An implementation of a path constraint propagator is described in depth and constrained path finding tests are analysed to assess the tractability of our approach. Finally, an alternative Oz-Mozart data-structure for the graph-domain variables is presented and compared to the first one.

Keywords: Mozart, Oz, Constraint Programming, Graph Domain Variables, Constrained Path Finding, Path Constraint.

1 Introduction

Biochemical networks are the networks describing the entities and interactions between entities in the cells. Some network models focus on some aspects of the cell [9, 2] while others [12, 1, 13] try to represent as much data as possible in a unified way.

Analyzing biochemical networks is an important issue to improve the understanding of the working of a cell. The analysis of such networks typically consists in answering (parameterized) queries such as:

- find the process(es) transforming A into B in less than X steps,
- find the genes whose expression is affected by entity A,
- find the compounds deriving from a given entity A in less than X steps,
- find the pathways including the list L of entity, ligand, reaction, etc..

Several projects (aMaze [1], KEGG [14], BioCyc [12], Um-BBD [6], Emp [7], PathDB [15], CSNDB [16]) provide a set of predefined queries as those listed

P. Van Roy (Ed.): MOZ 2004, LNCS 3389, pp. 237–250, 2005.
© Springer-Verlag Berlin Heidelberg 2005

above. Such queries cover several analyses thanks to the choice of their parameters (denoted in capitals in our examples). Available queries are however usually limited to simple ones which can be answered by the database management system or by simple ad-hoc routines.

More advanced queries are interesting from a biological viewpoint but they may require a significant design and programming effort while covering less generic analyses. Combining and/or extending analyses, as well as designing new analyses require lot of programming effort that cannot be reused for other analyses.

In [4,5], we proposed a constraint programming approach to biochemical network analysis. The goal is to be able to cover a broad range of analyses (including very computationally complex ones) by using a declarative query language and still be able to perform these analyses in reasonable time.

A first evaluation [4,5] of the CP(BioNet) framework consisted in implementing a prototype and testing it against a complex problem: constrained path finding. The implementation was done using Oz-Mozart. The results of this evaluation are:

- Different and complex analyses of biochemical networks can be done using CP(BioNet).
- Oz-Mozart is adequate to prototype a new computation domain with new variables and propagators.

During the implementation of CP(BioNet), we found Oz-Mozart possesses interesting qualities with respect to other constraint systems. First, it is free and open-source. Second, Oz-Mozart supports functional and procedural programming which can sometimes be more natural than rule-based programming for programming new domains and propagators. It supports several types of domain variables: finite domain variables (as a special case, boolean variables) and finite set variables. Finally, it's object-orientation and its higher-order approach of constraint propagation makes it easily extendable. Our new graph domain variable can then be seen as a new primitive domain variable for the programmer.

This paper focuses on the implementation of the prototype of CP(BioNet) over the Oz-Mozart system. This includes the implementation of a new kind of domain variables, graph domain variables (from now on denoted gd-variables) and of a few propagators for constraints over these gd-variables. All the implementation is done in the Oz language, no C++ extension is involved.

Section 2 describes the approach used in CP(BioNet) to express a biochemical analysis as a subgraph finding problem then as a constraint program over gd-variables. Section 3 describes the Oz data structure used for our first prototype of CP(BioNet), then some words will be said about another more efficient data-structure. Section 4 describes the implementation of a few propagators. Constraints available in the Mozart system were used whenever possible but a stateful propagator was necessary for the path constraint. Finally section 6 concludes with current and future work on this prototype.

2   CP(BioNet)

This section will briefly describe our biochemical networks modeling and our approach to their analysis. Then it will describe CP(BioNet), a new constraint programming computing domain for the analysis of biochemical networks. CP(BioNet) introduces graph domain variables and constraints over these variables.

2.1   Biochemical Networks Model

Biochemical networks are networks representing the working of the cell. We adopt the aMAZE [1, 13] model of these networks. This model integrates many aspects of the functioning of the cell in an integrated model. It consists of an object oriented model with relations to represent as many biological concepts as possible.

For the analysis of these networks, we model them as graphs whose nodes have attributes. The set of attributes attached to each node is determined according to the family of analyses under consideration. The simplest attributes are the three main classes present in the object-oriented aMAZE model: *entities*, *transforms* and *controls* (see Fig. 1). Entities are the physical small objects in the cell: molecules, proteins, compounds, genes, mRNA, etc.. Transforms link a set of entities to another set of entities: reactions, gene transcription, mRNA translation, protein assembly, etc.. Controls link an entity to either a transform or another control: catalysis, inhibition, regulation of gene expression, etc..

The described prototype uses undirected graphs but all the algorithms and data-structures have been extended and applied to directed graphs. We use undirected graphs in this paper for the sake of consistency and simplicity. Different types of arrow glyphs can be seen in Fig. 1. This is the classical representation of biochemical networks in the biological community. But as the type of an arrow is completely determined by the types of its end nodes, we use non-labelled arcs.

2.2   Analysis of Biochemical Networks

The size of biochemical networks became gigantic since a few years and these networks are no longer printable as a whole (even on huge posters) nor possible

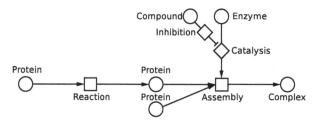

Fig. 1. A small biochemical network in the object-oriented model containing bioentities, transforms and controls

to store in a single head. They were then stored in computers using models such as the aMAZE model. This computer storage of biochemical data raised needs for specific data-mining tools. These tools are what the term "biochemical network analysis" stands for.

Biochemical networks analysis consists in answering user queries about, for instance, the organization and potential interactions between the components of the cell. We chose to model these queries as subgraph finding problems. The answer to a query is a graph extracted from the biochemical network under analysis. We think that kind of model covers a broad range of current and future queries about biochemical networks.

Queries like "Find the process transforming A into B in less than X steps", "Find all the paths expressed by a set of genes" or "Show how gene G is affected by entity E" are typical examples. They are translated into, respectively, "Find a path from A to B of length less than X, going only through entities and transforms", "Find the biggest subgraph containing no other gene than those given and respecting common biochemistry semantics rules (e.g. discard a reaction if its catalyst or one of its substrate is missing)", or "Find all the paths from any regulation node attached to the expression of gene G to node E".

2.3   CP(BioNet): Constraint Programming Model

To model and solve these subgraph extraction problems, we designed CP(BioNet). CP(BioNet) consists of graph domain variables and constraints over these variables.

Graph domain variables are variables which initial domain is the set of all subgraphs of a reference graph. This reference graph is the maximum element of their initial domain. In the present work, it is assumed that all gd-variables have the same initial domain, that is the same reference graph. Problems including the comparison of different graphs are not covered by this work.

The constraints over gd-variables currently defined and implemented are:

- The unary constraint $NodeInGraph(G, n)$ on the gd-variable G states that the node n (of the reference graph of G) must be present in graph G.
- The unary constraint $ArcInGraph(G, a)$ on the gd-variable G states that the arc a (of the reference graph of G) must be present in graph G.
- The unary constraint $EveryArc(G)$ on the gd-variable G states that if two nodes are in G and an arc joining these nodes belongs to the reference graph of G, then this arc must also belong to G.
- The binary constraint $SubGraph(P, G)$ on the gd-variables P and G states that P must be a subgraph of G (nodes and arcs of P must be in G too). P and G have the same reference graph.
- A constraint $Path(P, n_s, n_e, maxlength)$ states that the gd-variable P must be a path from node n_s to node n_e (both in the reference graph of P) of length at most $maxlength$.
- A constraint $ExistsPath(G, n_s, n_e, maxlength)$ on the gd-variable G, derived from the $Path$ constraint but weaker, states that there must exist a

path from n_s to n_e in G (and possibly other nodes and arcs). This is semantically equivalent to the introduction of a new gd-variable P and using the $SubGraph(P, G)$ and $Path(P, n_s, n_e, maxlength)$ constraints. However, such an expression would be far too inefficient.

- The unary constraint $Connected(G)$ states that a gd-variable G must be a connected graph. This is semantically equivalent to stating that the $ExistsPath$ constraint must be satisfied for any pair of nodes in G.

In $NodeInGraph$ and $ArcInGraph$, the parameters n and a must be determined. $NodeInGraph$ and $ArcInGraph$ are reified constraints, they can be used as boolean variables in conjunction with first order logic operators to build more complex constraints (i.e. with a disjunction). For $Path$ and $ExistsPath$, n_s and n_e must be determined and if $maxlength$ is a domain variable, the highest value of its domain is used.

3   The Data Structure Used for Graph Domain Variables

A gd-variable G can be implemented using boolean domain variables. A boolean variable per node in the reference graph states whether this node is present in the domain of the gd-variable. This vector of boolean variables is denoted $nodes(G)$. The presence of arcs in the domain of gd-variables is currently encoded with an adjacency matrix of boolean variables (see Fig. 2). If N denotes the number of nodes in the reference graph, every gd-variable is represented with $N^2 + N$ boolean variables (actually roughly half this number as the matrix is symmetric). This matrix is denoted $adjMat(G)$. Every graph domain variable has an associated constraint on its boolean domain variables to ensure that if an arc is present then both of its endpoint nodes must be present as well. Such a constraint can be implemented by a set of boolean constraints of the form

$$adjMat(G)_{ij} \Rightarrow nodes(G)_i \wedge nodes(G)_j$$

The gd-variable itself is implemented as a class. We chose to use a class for design matters (not because we need to encapsulate a state). A new gd-variable is created by instantiation of the class and by telling it its domain using an init method. Two init methods are available: one states the upper bound of the domain of the variable (the reference graph), the other one states that the variable is already determined and takes its reference graph and value as parameters. The constraints are available as methods of the gd-variable instance. The instance variables of the class are:

1. the domain graph
2. the adjacency matrix
3. the vector of node membership boolean variables

The adjacency matrix is implemented using a Tuple of Tuples of boolean variables (0#1). The node membership boolean variables are stored in a Tuple. That matrix is forced to be symmetrical by unifying symmetrical variables in the

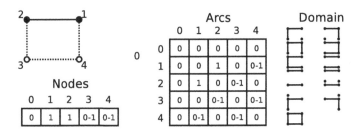

Fig. 2. Adjacency matrix implementation of a graph domain variable. The current domain of a variable, in the middle of the search process, is represented in this graph and coded in tables of boolean domain variables. A node or an arc is filled (nodes 1 and 2 and the arc joining them) when it is present in all graphs in the domain of the gd-variable. A light gray node or arc (node 0 and arc (0,4)) is never included in a graph of the domain. A dashed arc or unfilled node (all other nodes and arcs), may be present or absent in the graphs of the domain. All the graphs of the current domain of this gd-variable are displayed on the right

matrix. The built-in constraints for forcing that matrix and tuple of nodes to represent a graph are implemented using $N^2/2$ implication constraints (FD.impl).

In a second implementation, the adjacency matrix is replaced by an adjacency list: a Tuple of Records having a boolean variable only where the reference graph has an arc. This lead to an average twofold speedup relative to the test results showed in [4, 5] (these results are plotted in Section 5). A finite set implementation is currently being investigated.

4   Implementation of the Constraint Propagators

In this section, the adjacency matrix of the gd-variable G is denoted $adjMat(G)$, the vector of node membership boolean variables of G is denoted $nodes(G)$. To refer to a specific boolean variable, the matrix is subscripted twice and the vector once.

Most of the constraints listed above are very straightforward to implement using available constraints over boolean variables (or more generally finite domain variables):

- *NodeInGraph* and *ArcInGraph* are both reified. They just return the boolean variable under consideration.
- *EveryArc* simply posts an implication constraint for each arc ij in the reference graph:
$$nodes(G)_i \land nodes(G)_j \Rightarrow adjMat(G)_{ij}$$
- *SubGraph*(S, G) posts again a set of implications. For each node i in the reference graph:
$$nodes(S)_i \Rightarrow nodes(G)_i$$

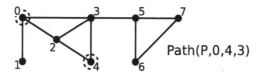

Fig. 3. The Path constraint. The graph domain variable must be a path from 0 to 4 and include at most 3 arcs (at most 2 additional nodes). Nodes 0 and 4 are outlined in the reference graph

For each arc ij in the reference graph:

$$adjMat(S)_{ij} \Rightarrow adjMat(G)_{ij}$$

The *Path*, *ExistsPath* and *Connected* constraints were partly implemented using a stateful propagator of our own. This section will focus on the *Path* constraint as the *ExistsPath* constraint is just slightly weaker and the *Connected* constraint propagator is part of the *Path* propagator.

4.1   The Path Propagator Implementation

The propagator of the constraint $Path(P, n_s, n_e, maxlength)$ is implemented in three parts. The first part uses integer domain propagators provided by the Oz-Mozart system. The second part is implemented using standard graph algorithms. The third part uses more advanced graph algorithms to further reduce the domain of the gd-variable.

1. P is constrained to contain only nodes of degree one or two. The start node n_s and end nodes n_e have a degree of one, the other nodes have a degree of two. By stating this simple constraint, P is forced to contain a path from n_s to n_e and possibly some cycles on nodes not in the path (in Fig. 3, a graph P consisting in a path from 0 to 4 and the cycle 5,6,7 is satisfying this first constraint). This first part of the propagator is implemented using the sum constraint on the rows of the adjacency matrix of the graph domain variable forcing the rows to contain exactly x (1 or 2) boolean variables with the value *true* (true is 1 while false is 0 in the sum):

$$\forall n \in \{n_s, n_e\} : \sum_j adjMat(P)_{n,j} = 1$$

$$\forall n \in nodes(P) \setminus \{n_s, n_e\} : \sum_j adjMat(P)_{n,j} = 2$$

These `FD.sum` constraints are posted when the path constraint is called on the gd-variable instance.

The cycles in other connected components are avoided by the second part of the propagator. It is also possible to constrain the number of nodes in the

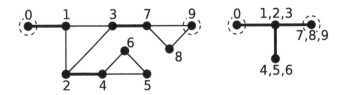

Fig. 4. *BridgeTree* on the right representing the 2-edge connected components and the bridges of the graph on the left. The bridge (2,4) and the 2-edge connected component 4,5,6 cannot be part of the path from 0 to 9 while both other bridges must be in that path

path using the *maxlength* information. A path of maximal length *maxlength* can contain at most *maxlength* + 1 nodes:

$$\sum_i nodes(P)_i \leq maxlength + 1$$

2. *P* is constrained to be a single connected component. This implies that *P* will only be the path from n_s to n_e as the cycles are in other connected components. A graph data structure *ConnGraph* is built. It is the supremum (with respect to graph inclusion) of all the graphs in the current domain of *P*. A node or an arc of the reference graph is not in *ConnGraph* if and only if its boolean variable in *P* is set to *false*. If this boolean variable is *true* or unknown (i.e. {*true,false*}) then the node/arc is in *ConnGraph*.

This *ConnGraph* is implemented with a class. This class holds the *ConnGraph* data structure (a Dictionary of Dictionaries of integers) and methods to operate on it. A *ConnGraph* instance is associated to a gd-variable and stores the maximum element of its domain. We use threads watching each boolean variable of the gd-variable to keep this instance up to date with the domain of the gd-variable. The job of each thread is to wait until a boolean variable is determined and if its value is false, update the *ConnGraph* accordingly.

Each time the boolean variable associated with an arc in the adjacency matrix is set to false, all the already included nodes of *P* (among those are n_s and n_e) could be checked to see if they are still in the same connected component. Two cases can arise:

– the constraint fails if they are not in the same connected component;
– otherwise, all nodes and arcs in other components can be eliminated from the domain of *P*.

A standard breadth-first depth-limited (*maxlength*) search in *ConnGraph* performs the connected component checking. During this search, all nodes in the same component as n_s are collected within a *maxlength* radius (if *maxlength* is an integer domain variable, the highest value of its domain is taken). As a by-product, the graph can be checked to see if it contains cycles. If there are no cycles, the connected component of *ConnGraph* starting from

n_s is a tree. In that case, the graph P can be forced to be the only available path from n_s to n_e in *ConnGraph*. This is implemented with a depth-first search from n_s to n_e in *ConnGraph*.

As we do not use an incremental algorithm [11] for the connected component checking, we avoid redoing this check for every arc deletion. Instead, this connected component checking is performed only when the computation space is stable (all other propagators have done their job). The stability check is not explicit: this stateful part of the propagator is automatically run by the generic distributor available in Mozart. The propagation procedure to be run by the distributor is returned by the path constraint method, the script passes this procedure to the distributor.

3. Parts 1 and 2 guarantee to find a solution whenever there is one. An additional routine improves the propagation by detecting as soon as possible that some arcs must or must not belong to the graph P.

A *bridge* in a connected component of a graph is an arc the removal of which breaks the connected component into two unconnected components. A connected component is said to be *2-edge connected* if it does not contain any bridge. A 2-edge connected component algorithm is used to find all bridges in *ConnGraph* [10, 8, 3]. It uses *BridgeTree*, an additional data structure representing a tree. The nodes of this tree correspond to the 2-edge components of *ConnGraph* and its arcs are the bridges of *ConnGraph*. Two nodes of *BridgeTree* are labeled $n1$ and $n2$, corresponding respectively to the 2-edge connected component of *ConnGraph* containing n_s and n_e (see Fig. 4).

In this *BridgeTree*, all arcs on the path from $n1$ to $n2$ must be in P and all other arcs (and the 2-edge connected components on the other end) cannot be present in P. This information is propagated by adding or removing these arcs and nodes from the domain of P.

The *BridgeTree* is just a theoretic definition. It is not built by the implementation. The selection of positive and negative bridges is implemented using the previously cited algorithm [10, 8, 3] which computes a DFS spanning tree of *ConnGraph* (stored as an adjacency list over the nodes of *ConnGraph*: Tuple of Dictionaries). The "Low" values (lowest node reachable from each node) are then computed in this tree which enables to find all bridges. A depth first search in the tree allows to find a path from n_s to n_e and all bridges on this path are the bridges to be included in the gd-variable while all others can be taken out of the domain.

A similar reasoning can be made about *cut-nodes* (nodes the removal of which breaks the connected component) and the same algorithm can take care of these nodes.

5   Experiments

Some experiments were conducted to assess the tractability of this framework for biochemical analyses. Constrained path finding tests were done using real biological data. This section will first describe the data used for these tests. Then the constrained path finding tests are described along with their results. One other test will show the impact of the data structure used for the gd-variable: an adjacency matrix and an adjacency list implementation are compared.

5.1   Data

Graphs of increasing size (50, 100, 200, and 500 nodes) have been extracted from a metabolic network consisting of 4492 chemical entities and 5281 reactions. This data comes from the KEGG project and concerns two organisms: *Escherichia Coli* and *Saccharomyces Cerevisiae*. Extraction of smaller graphs from this network was performed while preserving approximately the degree distribution in the original graph. More precisely, an extracted graph must be a single connected component. The average degree of its nodes is around 4 and the maximum degree is 18 percent of its number of nodes.

5.2   Tests and Results

Five tests were performed on the extracted graphs. They are path finding problems expressed in CP(BioNet) using the *Path* constraint. The *maxlength* parameter was set to the number of nodes in the graph (no constraint on the length of the extracted path).

1. Path finding between two random nodes in the graph (always a solution since the graph is connected).
2. Path finding between two random nodes in the graph, with the additional constraint of containing two randomly preselected intermediate nodes.
3. Path finding between two random unconnected nodes in a double graph (two separate connected components were created by cloning the extracted graph; no solution).
4. Path finding between two random nodes in the graph, with the additional constraint of containing from one up to five randomly preselected intermediate node(s).
5. Selection of a random path p of k nodes in the graph. Path finding between the first and last nodes of p, with the additional constraint of containing from one up to $k - 2$ intermediate nodes randomly preselected from p (always a solution).

The running time of every query was measured. For the first three tests, 1,000 queries were performed on each extracted graph. The fourth and fifth queries were performed on extracted graphs with 200 nodes. The fourth query was performed 1,000 times for every number of intermediate nodes. The fifth query was performed 1,000 times for every number of intermediate nodes and for values of k being 7, 10 and 15.

Figure 5 shows the average and standard deviation of the running time for these tests. Results from tests 2 and 4 are split in two groups: a curve for those where a solution was found and another for those for which no solution was found.

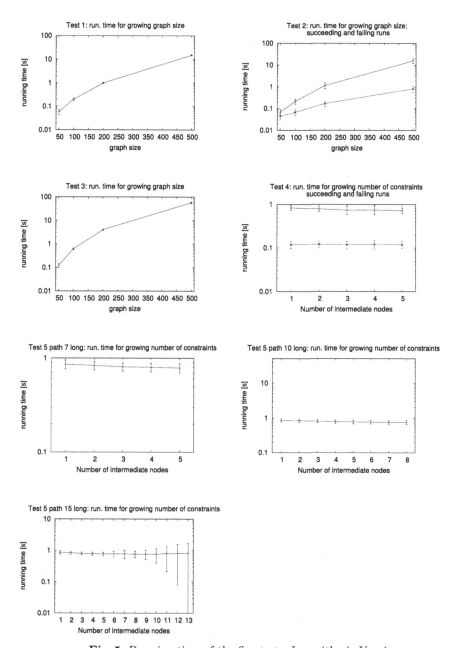

Fig. 5. Running time of the five tests. Logarithmic Y axis

5.3   Analysis

Tests 1 and 3 concern single path finding in a graph. This problem is not relevant alone for analyzing biochemical networks and dedicated algorithms are obviously

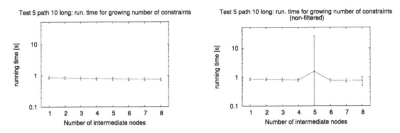

Fig. 6. Comparison of the results of test 5 path length of 10 when results are filtered (on the left) or not (on the right). The only difference lies in 2 runs (among the 8000 presented) for five intermediate nodes: one lasted 765 s and the other 18 s. The standard deviation is more affected by these rare results than the mean

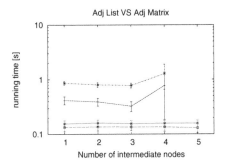

Fig. 7. Comparison of the adjacency matrix and adjacency list implementations of the graph-domain variable data-structure. The test is a test of random constrained path finding (test 4). The curves from top to bottom are "successful" queries with the matrix, with the list, then "failed" queries with matrix and with list

more efficient. These tests were done to analyze the path propagator on its own. For test 3, the reported size in the plots is the size of one component of the graph (the graph having twice that size). The plots for these tests show a sub-exponential curve and very low standard deviations. These tests illustrate the tractability of this propagator over increasing sizes of graphs.

Tests 2, 4, and 5 concern the constrained path finding problem. Two parameters were taken into account for this analysis: the size of the graph and the number of mandatory intermediate nodes. Test 2 shows the evolution of the running time of a query with 2 intermediate nodes versus the size of the graph. The plot shows two curves: one, for successful queries (the CSP solver found a path) and another, below, for failed queries (the CSP found no solution to this query). The results show that the curves are similar to the ones of the path propagator alone. The major difference is a larger standard deviation.

Tests 4 and 5 show the evolution of the running time on the graph of size 200 versus the number of mandatory intermediate nodes. Test 5 was performed to be able to show results of successful runs for high values of the number of intermediate nodes. When these nodes are chosen randomly in the graph (test 4), the odds of having a successful run are very low. The plots show that the average running time of these tests is nearly constant while the standard deviation has a slight tendency to grow.

A small fraction of the runs (from 0.08% up to 1%, depending on the tests) of the constrained path finding tests had running times several orders of magnitude worse than average. This somehow illustrates the NP-Hardness of these problems. Plots with and without these results are compared in Fig. 6. An additional test comparing an adjacency matrix (Tuple of Tuple) and an adjacency list (Tuple of Records) implementation of the gd-variable shows a near twofold speedup when using lists (see Fig. 7).

Our results show that the path constraint is tractable when used alone, although specialized algorithms are more efficient. When used along with other constraints (specifying a NP-Hard problem), the results show that the average running time is approximately the same (apart from rare diverging results) as the running time of the path constraint alone, independently of the number of additional constraints. Additional constraints on the type and attributes of the nodes of the biochemical network can thus be designed and used in our constrained path finding framework. This framework can then exploit the richness of the model of biochemical networks.

6   Conclusion

This paper showed how we used Oz-Mozart to implement a prototype of CP(BioNet), a new computing domain in constraint programming. A new type of variables, graph domain variables, was designed and implemented using the Oz language. New constraints were designed and implemented as well. Much time was saved by reusing domain variables and constraints available in the Mozart system modules (boolean variables, propositional logic constraints, sum of finite domain variables constraint). Another advantage of the Mozart system is the possibility to implement this prototype in C/C++ if necessary.

CP(BioNet) allows the bio-informatician user to specify complex and diverse analyses using a declarative language and should provide him/her with an answer in reasonable time. Constrained path finding tests were conducted to assess the tractability of this framework in the average case. We also showed that this framework is expressive enough to state complex analyses. We now intend to use it on real problems from bio-informaticians.

We intend to design and implement a specific distributor and an optimization search engine (using branch and bound). Current constraints will be improved (definition, mode of usage, propagator, etc.) and new constraints are also under investigation.

References

1. The aMAZE data-base project. http://www.amaze.ulb.ac.be/.
2. G.D. Bader, I. Donaldson, C. Wolting, B.F. Ouellette, T. Pawson, and C.W. Hogue. Bind the biomolecular interaction network database. *Nucleic Acids Research*, 29(1):242-5, 2001.
3. Joëlle Cohen.   Théorie des graphes et algorithmes.   Course notes. http://www.univ-paris12.fr/lacl/cohen/poly_gr.ps.
4. G. Dooms, Y. Deville, and P. Dupont. Constrained path finding in biochemical networks. In *Proceedings of JOBIM 2004*, pages JO–40, 2004.
5. G. Dooms, Y. Deville, and P. Dupont. Recherche de chemins contraints dans les réseaux biochimiques. In F. Mesnard, editor, *Programmation en logique avec contraintes, actes des JFPLC 2004*, pages 109–128. Hermes Science, 2004.
6. L.B.M. Ellis, B. Kyeng Hou, W. Kang, and L.P. Wackett. The university of minesota biocatalysis/biodegradation database : post-genomic data mining. *Nucleic Acids Research*, 31(1):262–265, 2002.
7. EMP   project.   Informations   about   EMP   can   be   found   at   : http://www.empproject.com/.
8. Michel Gondran and Michel Minoux. *Graphes et algorithmes*. Eyrolles, 1995. 3ème éd.
9. S. Goto, T. Nishioka, and M. Kanehisa. LIGAND: Chemical database for enzyme reactions. *Bioinformatics*, 14:591–599, 1998.
10. Jonathan Gross and Jay Yellen. *Graph Theory and its Applications*. CRC Press, 1999.
11. Jacob Holm, Kristian de Lichtenberg, and Mikkel Thorup. Poly-logarithmic deterministic fully-dynamic algorithms for connectivity, minimum spanning tree, 2-edge, and biconnectivity. *Journal ACM*, 48(4):723–760, 2001.
12. P.D. Karp, M. Riley, M. Saier, I.T. Paulsen, J. Collado-Vides, S.M. Paley, A. Pelligrini-Toole, C. Bonavides, and S. Gama-Castro. The EcoCyc database. *Nucleic Acids Research*, 30(1):56–8, 2002.
13. Chrisian Lemer, Erick Antezana, Fabian Couche, Frédéric Fays, Xavier Santolaria, Rekin's Janky, Yves Deville, Jean Richelle, and Shoshana J. Wodak. The aMAZE lightbench: a web interface to a relational database of cellular processes. *Nucleic Acids Research*, 32:D443–D448, 2004.
14. K. Minoru, G. Susumu, K. Shuichi, and N. Akihiro. The KEGG databases at GenomeNet. *Nucleic Acids Research*, 30(1):42–46, 2002.
15. Faye Schilkey. PathDB : a pathway database. http://www.ncgr.org/pathdb.
16. Takako Takai-Igarashi and Tsuguchika Kaminuma. A pathway finding system for the cell signaling networks database. *Silico Biology*, 1:129–146, 1999.

Playing the Minesweeper with Constraints

Raphaël Collet

Université catholique de Louvain,
B-1348 Louvain-la-Neuve, Belgium
raph@info.ucl.ac.be

Abstract. We present the design and implementation of a Minesweeper
game, augmented with a digital assistant. The assistant uses constraint
programming techniques to help the player, and is able to play the game
by itself. It predicts safe moves, and gives probabilistic information when
safe moves cannot be found.

1 Introduction

The Minesweeper game has been popular for several years now. Part of its pop-
ularity might come from its simplicity. A board represents a mine field, with
mines hidden under the squares. The game consists in finding the mines without
making them explode. You get new hints each time you uncover a non-mined
square. Though, the simplicity does not make the game easy. The Minesweeper
problem is hard: it has been proven NP-complete by Richard Kaye [1]. So simple
techniques are not enough to solve it.

In this paper we show how the problem of finding safe moves can be modeled
as a Constraint Satisfaction Problem (CSP). Techniques from the field of constraint programming can be used to program a digital assistant for a player. We
applied several of them in a real application, the Oz Minesweeper [2]. This relatively small program demonstrates the power of the programming language Oz.

Contribution. The paper describes a diverting application, that applies various
techniques from constraint programming to implement a digital assistant. The
contribution is mainly educational. We model a simple problem, and show the
key ideas underlying the application's implementation.

History. The Oz Minesweeper is born in spring 1998. It started as a student
work, in a course on constraint programming. The goal was to study a programming language called Oz, and give a presentation about it. To make the presentation attractive, I showed an example of a CSP in the "real world", namely the
Minesweeper game. I had hacked a small solver that was playing the game.

Later I rewrote it as a demonstration program, and gave it a graphical user
interface. A simple inference engine based on propagation was provided. It already impressed quite a lot of visitors. The next step was a solver, which was
basically making the inference engine complete. I wrote several implementations

P. Van Roy (Ed.): MOZ 2004, LNCS 3389, pp. 251–262, 2005.

of it, notably by hacking a special search engine. I eventually found a way to compute mine probabilities. I rewrote everything from scratch. The hacked special search engine went to the trash can.

The last step happened last year. I understood the issue of symmetries in the problem, and designed an improved solver that eliminates them. A better propagation-based inference engine was designed while implementing the solver. I reworked a bit the implementation, and integrated the inference engines in a proper way. I finally improved the user interface the week before submitting this paper.

Paper Organization. Section 2 recalls the rules of the game, and proposes a simple mathematical model for it. Section 3 investigates how constraint programming techniques can be applied in order to solve the problem with reasonable efficiency. Section 4 then gives an overview of the implementation of the Oz Minesweeper. Section 5 evaluates and quickly compares our work to other similar products.

2   The Game as a Constraint Satisfaction Problem

Let us recall the rules of the game. A mine field is given to the player as a rectangular board. Each square on the board may hide at most one mine. The total number of mines is known by the player. A move consists in uncovering a square. If the square holds a mine, the mine explodes and the game is over. Otherwise, a number in the square indicates how many mines are held in the surrounding squares, which are the adjacent squares in the eight directions north, north-east, east, south-east, south, south-west, west, and north-west. The goal of the game is to uncover all the squares that do not hold a mine.

	1	2	3	4	5	6	7	8	9	10
1					1					
2					2					
3	1	1	1		2					
4			1		1					
5			3	2	2					
6										
7										
8										
9										
10										

Fig. 1. An example of a board with 20 mines

Figure 1 shows an example of a board that contains 20 mines. We identify each square by its coordinates (*row*, *column*). The squares (1,1), (1,2), (1,3), (1,4), (2,1), (2,2), (2,3), (2,4), (3,4), and (4,4) have already been played, and have no mine in their respective surrounding squares. The squares (1,5), (3,1), (3,2), (3,3), (4,3), and (4,5) have been played, too, and are surrounded by one mined square each. The squares (2,5), (3,5), (5,4), and (5,5) each have two mines in their neighborhood, while the square (5,3) has three mines around it. In this example, the player might deduce from (3,3) that (4,2) is mined, and by (3,2) that (4,1) is a safe move.

Model. Finding safe moves on the board consists in solving the problem defined by those numbers in the squares. The unknown of the problem is the positions of the mines. We model this as a binary matrix that represents the mine field, with one entry per square. The value 1 means that the corresponding square is mined, while 0 means a safe square.

$$\begin{pmatrix} x_{11} & x_{12} & \cdots & x_{1n} \\ x_{21} & x_{22} & & x_{2n} \\ \vdots & & \ddots & \vdots \\ x_{m1} & x_{m2} & \cdots & x_{mn} \end{pmatrix}$$

By convention, x_{ij} always denotes the matrix entry corresponding to the square at position (i, j). The problem can be written as linear equations over the x_{ij}'s. In the example, we have 20 mines (first equation below), and the played squares are not mined (second equation below). The other equations are given by the numbers in the squares. The corresponding square coordinates are given on the left of each equation.

$$\sum_{i,j \in \{1,\ldots,10\}} x_{ij} = 20$$

$$x_{11} = x_{12} = x_{13} = \cdots = 0$$

$(1,1)$ $x_{12} + x_{21} + x_{22} = 0$
$(1,2)$ $x_{11} + x_{13} + x_{21} + x_{22} + x_{23} = 0$
$\cdots$
$(1,5)$ $x_{14} + x_{16} + x_{24} + x_{25} + x_{26} = 1$
$\cdots$
$(2,5)$ $x_{14} + x_{15} + x_{16} + x_{24} + x_{26} + x_{34} + x_{35} + x_{36} = 2$
$\cdots$

This binary model of the game defines a CSP, which we can solve to find hints for the player's next move. If we have all the solutions of the problem, we can look at what is common to all those solutions. For instance, if all solutions give $x_{41} = 0$, we know that the square at position $(4, 1)$ is a safe move.

But we even go further than this. Assuming that all those solutions have the same probability, we can compute the expected solution, i.e., the mean of all solutions. This gives us a probability for each square to be mined. In case no safe move can be found, the player might use this information to choose her next move.

3   Propagation, Search, and Probabilities

We now present specific information related to the implementation of the inference engines. Each of them provides a way to solve the CSP defined by the current state of the game. Sections 3.1 and 3.2 shows two implementation based on constraint propagation only. Sections 3.3 and 3.4 presents two solvers, and explains how their results are used to compute mine probabilities.

3.1   Simple Propagators

The simplest inference engine uses the binary model of the Minesweeper game, and posts the propagators that trivially implement the constraints of the model. We illustrate this with the example shown in Fig. 1. A quick sketch of the CSP is given at the end of Sect. 2. All those constraints can be implemented with the Oz propagator FD.sum, taking a list of FD variables with domain 0#1. For instance, the propagator for (2,5) is created by a statement like

```
{FD.sum [X14 X15 X16 X24 X26 X34 X35 X36] ´=:´ 2}
```

Let us examine the effect of those propagators. For the sake of simplicity, we assume that the "zero" constraints like (1,1) have been propagated, and we simplify the remaining constraints using the known values. The constraints are

$(1,5)$	$x_{16} + x_{26} = 1$		$(4,3)$	$x_{42} + x_{52} = 1$
$(2,5)$	$x_{16} + x_{26} + x_{36} = 2$		$(4,5)$	$x_{36} + x_{46} + x_{56} = 1$
$(3,1)$	$x_{41} + x_{42} = 1$		$(5,3)$	$x_{42} + x_{52} + x_{62} + x_{63} + x_{64} = 3$
$(3,2)$	$x_{41} + x_{42} = 1$		$(5,4)$	$x_{63} + x_{64} + x_{65} = 2$
$(3,3)$	$x_{42} = 1$		$(5,5)$	$x_{46} + x_{56} + x_{64} + x_{65} + x_{66} = 2$
$(3,5)$	$x_{26} + x_{36} + x_{46} = 2$			

The propagator for (3,3) immediately infers $x_{42} = 1$, which means that we have found the position of a mine. This information allows propagators (3,1) and (3,2) to infer $x_{41} = 0$, while the propagator (4,3) infers $x_{52} = 0$.

The remaining propagators cannot infer new constraints, and thus wait for more information to come. Still, more information can be deduced from those constraints. But the propagators that we have considered here cannot do it, because they share too few information with each other. For instance, propagators (1,5) and (2,5) could infer $x_{36} = 1$ if they were sharing $x_{16} + x_{26} = 1$ as a basic constraint. This insight leads us to an improvement in the propagation of the constraints.

3.2   The Set Propagators

We now show propagators that infer information about sets of squares, hence the name "set" propagators. We continue with the example shown in Fig. 1. Let us assume that the simple propagators have determined the variables as explained above. We consider the remaining constraints

$(1,5)$ $x_{16} + x_{26} = 1$

$(2,5)$ $x_{16} + x_{26} + x_{36} = 2$

$(3,5)$ $x_{26} + x_{36} + x_{46} = 2$

$(4,5)$ $x_{36} + x_{46} + x_{56} = 1$

$(5,3)$ $x_{42} + x_{52} + x_{62} + x_{63} + x_{64} = 3$

$(5,4)$ $x_{63} + x_{64} + x_{65} = 2$

$(5,5)$ $x_{46} + x_{56} + x_{64} + x_{65} + x_{66} = 2$

Remember that the weakness of the simple propagators was coming from their inability to share information about subterms like $x_{16} + x_{26}$. Consider for instance constraint $(2,5)$. The improved implementation of this constraint will actually create as many propagators as partitions of the set of indices $\{16, 26, 36\}$.

For each subset I of indices, we consider the "set" variable x_I defined by

$$x_I = \sum_{i \in I} x_i \qquad (0 \le x_I \le |I|).$$

The definition of x_I can be implemented by a simple propagator over finite integers. We can now express the constraint $(2,5)$ as follows. For each partition $P = \{I_1, \ldots, I_k\}$ of the indices, we create one propagator for the constraint

$$x_{I_1} + \cdots + x_{I_n} = 2,$$

which is logically equivalent to $(2,5)$. We thus have propagators for the following equations. Note that $(2,5)(a)$ has the same effect as the simple propagator for $(2,5)$.

$(2,5)(a)$ $x_{\{16\}} + x_{\{26\}} + x_{\{36\}} = 2$

$(2,5)(b)$ $x_{\{16\}} + x_{\{26,36\}} = 2$

$(2,5)(c)$ $x_{\{26\}} + x_{\{16,36\}} = 2$

$(2,5)(d)$ $x_{\{36\}} + x_{\{16,26\}} = 2$

$(2,5)(e)$ $x_{\{16,26,36\}} = 2$

Let us observe the effect of those propagators in the example. One of the propagators for $(1,5)$ infers $x_{\{16,26\}} = 1$, which makes $(2,5)(d)$ infer $x_{\{36\}} = 1$, giving $x_{36} = 1$. The simple propagator $(4,5)$ then infers $x_{46} = x_{56} = 0$. The propagation of $(3,5)$ and $(1,5)$ then gives $x_{26} = 1$ and $x_{16} = 0$.

3.3   A Binary Solver

As we said in Sect. 2, useful information can be deduced from the set of solutions of the Minesweeper problem. The issue is, there usually are *many* solutions. Consider the board in Fig. 2, which contains 20 mines. Four squares have been played. It defines the following CSP.

$$\sum_{i,j \in \{1,\ldots,10\}} x_{ij} = 20$$

$$x_{11} = x_{21} = x_{31} = x_{32} = 0$$

$(1,1)$ $x_{12} + x_{21} + x_{22} = 1$

$(2,1)$ $x_{11} + x_{12} + x_{22} + x_{31} + x_{32} = 1$

$(3,1)$ $x_{21} + x_{22} + x_{32} + x_{41} + x_{42} = 1$

$(3,2)$ $x_{21} + x_{22} + x_{23} + x_{31} + x_{33} + x_{41} + x_{42} + x_{43} = 3$

	1	2	3	4	5	6	7	8	9	10
1	1									
2	1									
3	1	3								
4										
5										
6										
7										
8										
9										
10										

Fig. 2. An example for search

Table 1. Solutions of the restricted binary problem

solution	s_1	s_2	s_3	s_4	s_5	s_6	s_7	s_8	s_9
x_{12}	0	0	0	1	1	1	1	1	1
x_{22}	1	1	1	0	0	0	0	0	0
x_{23}	0	1	1	0	1	1	0	1	1
x_{33}	1	0	1	1	0	1	1	0	1
x_{41}	0	0	0	0	0	0	1	1	1
x_{42}	0	0	0	1	1	1	0	0	0
x_{43}	1	1	0	1	1	0	1	1	0
class size	$\binom{89}{17}$	$\binom{89}{17}$	$\binom{89}{17}$	$\binom{89}{16}$	$\binom{89}{16}$	$\binom{89}{16}$	$\binom{89}{16}$	$\binom{89}{16}$	$\binom{89}{16}$

This problem has 3.333×10^{18} solutions. Computing all solutions is simply impossible, except for very small boards.

Though, that issue can be addressed. We simply restrict the problem to some of its variables. Each solution of the restricted problem defines a class of solutions of the full problem[1]. We consider the variables given by the squares neighboring the already played squares. In the example, this gives x_{12}, x_{22}, x_{23}, x_{33}, x_{41}, x_{42}, and x_{43}. The remaining unknowns can be determined by other simple means. The solutions of the restricted problem are given in Table 1. If we consider the solution s_1 in the table, there remains 89 unknowns, out of which 17 must be mined. The number of ways to choose 17 elements out of 89 is given by the binomial $N_1 = \binom{89}{17}$. This is the size of the class of solutions defined by s_1. The same argument applies for all classes.

---

[1] The word "class" is used with the meaning of "subset" here. The subset we consider is actually an equivalence class in the set of solutions.

The problem clearly has $N = N_1 + N_2 + \cdots + N_9 \simeq 3.333 \times 10^{18}$ solutions. Let X_{ij} denote how many solutions satisfy $x_{ij} = 1$. The probability that $x_{ij} = 1$ is simply given by X_{ij}/N. As a first example, take square $(1,2)$. As $x_{12} = 0$ in s_1, s_2, and s_3, we have $X_{12} = N_4 + N_5 + \cdots + N_9 \simeq 1.059 \times 10^{18}$. So the probability that $x_{12} = 1$ is $X_{12}/N \simeq 0.318$. Now take square $(6,9)$. In the class s_1, the number of solutions satisfying $x_{69} = 1$ is $\binom{88}{16} = \frac{17}{89}\binom{89}{17}$. Summing up those numbers for all classes of solutions, we have $X_{69} \simeq 6.247 \times 10^{17}$, which gives a mine probability of 0.187.

3.4   The Set Solver

The binary solver still computes too many solutions. In the example, one can see that the problem has *symmetries*. For instance, each permutation of the values of x_{23}, x_{33}, x_{43} in one solution leads to another solution. This symmetry comes from the fact that those three variables are constrained by $x_{23} + x_{33} + x_{43} = 2$ only.

The improved solver reformulates the CSP in terms of the set variables x_I in order to eliminate those symmetries. Taking all equations that define the binary problem, it computes a partition of the variable's indices. Every subset I in the partition is such that, for each equation $x_J = k$ in the problem, $I \cap J = I$ or $\emptyset$. The subsets are chosen to be *maximal*, so that symmetries are eliminated.

Let us reformulate the CSP of the example in Fig. 2, which gives

$$\sum_{I \in P} x_I = 20$$

$$x_{\{11\}} = x_{\{21\}} = x_{\{31\}} = x_{\{32\}} = 0$$

$$\begin{aligned}
(1,1) &\quad x_{\{12\}} + x_{\{21\}} + x_{\{22\}} = 1 \\
(2,1) &\quad x_{\{11\}} + x_{\{12\}} + x_{\{22\}} + x_{\{31\}} + x_{\{32\}} = 1 \\
(3,1) &\quad x_{\{21\}} + x_{\{22\}} + x_{\{32\}} + x_{\{41,42\}} = 1 \\
(3,2) &\quad x_{\{21\}} + x_{\{22\}} + x_{\{31\}} + x_{\{41,42\}} + x_{\{23,33,43\}} = 3
\end{aligned}$$

The indices have been partitioned into

$$P = \big\{\{11\}, \{12\}, \{21\}, \{22\}, \{31\}, \{32\}, \{41, 42\}, \{23, 33, 43\}, R\big\},$$

where R contains the remaining indices. This problem has two solutions, shown in Table 2. Each class of solutions is equivalent to the Cartesian product of the possible combinations for the set variables of the reformulated problem. Each valuation $x_I = k$ has $\binom{n}{k}$ solutions, where $n = |I|$. Therefore the size of each class is given by a product of binomials. The computation of the probabilities is similar to what the binary solver does. For instance, the probability that $x_{41} = 1$ is $\left(\frac{0}{2}N_1 + \frac{1}{2}N_2\right)/N \simeq 0.159$.

The efficiency is typically one order of magnitude faster compared to the binary solver. Let us illustrate this with an example. Figure 3 shows a snapshot of the application's window. The squares containing a mine have been marked with a black disk. The probabilities are drawn as filled rectangles in the squares. The more a rectangle is filled, the greated the mine probability. A precise value

Table 2. Solutions of the reformulated problem

solution	s_1	s_2
$x_{\{12\}}$	0	1
$x_{\{22\}}$	1	0
$x_{\{41,42\}}$	0	1
$x_{\{23,33,43\}}$	2	2
x_R	17	16
class size	N_1	N_2

$$N_1 = \binom{1}{0}\binom{1}{1}\binom{2}{0}\binom{3}{2}\binom{89}{17}$$

$$N_2 = \binom{1}{1}\binom{1}{0}\binom{2}{1}\binom{3}{2}\binom{89}{16}$$

$$N = N_1 + N_2$$

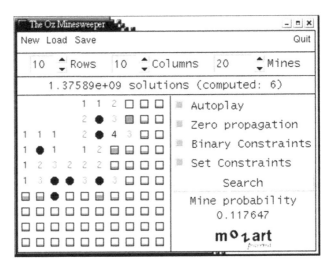

Fig. 3. A snapshot showing probabilistic information

of a probability is shown in the bottom right of the window when the player moves her mouse cursor over a given square. The set solver has computed 6 solutions to find the probabilities, while the binary solver would compute 246 solutions for the same problem!

4   Implementation

The general architecture of the Oz Minesweeper is depicted in Fig. 4. Boxes refer to concurrent agents (active objects), while "Symbolic field" and "Symbolic constraints" are simply shared data. Arrows from data to agents (resp. from agents to data) correspond to *ask* (resp. *tell*) operations. Arrows between agents represent messages or procedure calls. The removal of the components in the dashed box gives an implementation of the game without digital assistance.

4.1   The Core Components

The central point in the application is the *symbolic field*, which simply reflects the information known about the mine field. The symbolic field is a tuple whose elements correspond to the board squares. An element can be either safe(K) or mine(X). The value safe(K) means that the corresponding square is not mined, and K gives the number of mines in the surrounding squares. Note that K can be unbound, if the square is known to be safe, but has not been played yet. The value mine(X) means that the square is mined, and X is bound to exploded if the mine has exploded, i.e., the game is over.

The *user interface* updates the board by threads that synchronize on the symbolic field. For instance, if an entry in the symbolic field is safe(K) and K is unbound, the square is marked with a dash "-". This shows the user that this square is safe. As soon as K is determined, its value is shown in the square, which becomes inactive. When the user clicks on a square, the user interface calls the *game* agent to play that square. The game automatically tells the result in the symbolic field, which wakes up the thread that updates the square.

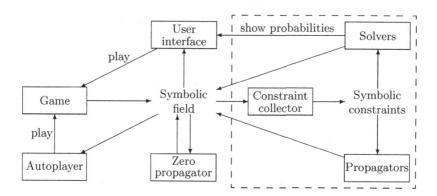

Fig. 4. Dataflow diagram of the Oz Minesweeper

4.2   The Zero Propagator and Autoplayer

The *zero propagator* simply asks and tells information in the symbolic field. If a square has no mines around it, which correspond to value safe(0) in the symbolic field, the surrounding squares are told to be safe. The code of the propagator is shown below. The symbolic field appears as the tuple SymField. The procedure WaitEnabled blocks until the user enables the propagator. The same mechanism is used by all inference engines, and allows to user to experiment with them. The call to function BoxI returns the coordinates of all the squares in a box around square I.

```
for I in 1..{Width SymField} do
   thread
      case SymField.I of safe(0) then
         {WaitEnabled}
         for J in {BoxI I 1} do SymField.J = safe(_) end
      else skip end
   end
end
```

The *autoplayer* works in a similar way. When enabled, it plays all the squares known to be safe in the symbolic field. So the user can let the various inference engines discover safe moves, and decide whether they should be played automatically.

4.3   The Constraint Inference Engines

The *constraint collector* incrementally builds the *symbolic constraints*, a list of the constraints that appear implicitly in the symbolic field. The inference engines using constraint programming simply read this list to get the constraints of the current problem. A constraint in the list has the form sum(Is K), where Is is a list of square coordinates, and K is a nonnegative integer. Its semantics is the equation $\sum_{i \in \text{Is}} x_i = K$. All the constraints in the Minesweeper problem can be written in this way.

Propagators. Both the simple and set propagators read the symbolic constraints and progressively post propagators as explained in Sect. 3. Those propagators are posted over binary constrained variables, that correspond to the x_{ij}'s in the model. Whenever such a variable is determined, the information is automatically told in the symbolic field with a statement like

```
thread
   SymField.I = if X.I==0 then safe(_) else mine(_) end
end
```

Recall that the set propagator for the equation $\sum_{i \in I} x_i = k$ reformulates it as $x_{I_1} + \cdots + x_{I_n} = k$, for every partition $\{I_1, \ldots, I_n\}$ of I. If I has 8 elements (the typical case in the Minesweeper), this gives 255 set variables, and 4140 equations! The implementation optimizes this simple scheme. First, the equation is simplified by subtracting the known x_i's. Second, the set variables are created lazily, and memoized for sharing between propagators. When a set variable x_I is created, a propagator is posted for $x_I = \sum_{i \in I} x_i$.

Solvers. A search with a solver is triggered by pushing a button in the user interface. The solver first takes the known part of the symbolic constraints list, and solves the problem given by those constraints. In the case of the set solver, it implies to first compute the optimal partition of the indices, to reformulate the constraints in terms of the set variables, and to solve the reformulated problem. If new safe moves or mine positions are found, they are told to the symbolic field. Otherwise, the mine probabilities are shown on the board.

5   Evaluation and Related Work

The Oz Minesweeper has been entirely written in Mozart [3], and is about 1000 lines of code. The digital assistant is capable to find all the safe moves in a given situation. The set propagator proved to be effective at this task, it usually finds most of them. The solver rarely finds new moves, and provides mine probabilities instead. It leaves the player with the toughest decision, involving a cost-benefit strategy. An interesting observation we have made is that the proportion of mined squares should be around 20% to make the game interesting. A proportion less than 20% makes the problem too easy, while more than 20% quickly makes the game unplayable.

We have not explored the problem of choosing a square to play when all you know is the mine probabilities. Playing the square with the lowest mine probability is a safe and conservative move. But we observed that such moves do not often bring much information to go further. It seems that taking a risk can be worth the candle. Our implementation is flexible enough to implement strategies on top of the existing solvers, which would provide a complete digital player.

We have found only one other application that solves the Minesweeper problem and computes the mine probabilities, called *Truffle-Swine Keeper* [4]. It seems efficient, but we have found the interaction with the solver not as practical as the Oz Minesweeper.

Other Techniques. Is constraint programming really a good choice for solving this problem? The Minesweeper problem is completely defined by linear equations. So one might think that integer programming could be a better choice. To my current understanding, integer programming can be applied successfully for some parts, but not all of them. We can use integer programming for checking a board square, for instance. Given a problem P and a variable x_{ij}, we check whether $P \wedge x_{ij} = 0$ is solvable. In case it is not, we can infer $x_{ij} = 1$ in our case. But I don't see how to use it for computing mine probabilities. The latter is a result about *all* solutions of a problem, while integer programming is oriented toward finding *one* solution.

6   Conclusion

We have designed and implemented a Minesweeper application with a digital assistant. The latter is based on a simple mathematical model of the Minesweeper game, and various techniques coming from the field of constraint programming. It proved to be effective, and is capable to infer every logical consequence of the problem to solve. It computes mine probabilities without computational burden.

The simplicity and efficiency of our application relies on the language Oz and the platform Mozart. The dataflow concurrency, symbolic data, and constraint system make the application's architecture modular and elegant.

References

1. Kaye, R.: Minesweeper is NP-complete. Mathematical Intelligencer (2000) See also
   `http://web.mat.bham.ac.uk/R.W.Kaye/minesw/ordmsw.htm` (08/26/2004).
2. Collet, R.: The Oz Minesweeper (2004) Program available at
   `http://www.info.ucl.ac.be/~raph/minesweeper/` (08/26/2004).
3. Mozart Consortium (DFKI, SICS, UCL, UdS): The Mozart programming system
   (Oz 3) (1999) Available at `http://www.mozart-oz.org`.
4. Kopp, H.: Truffle-Swine Keeper (2001) Program available at
   `http://people.freenet.de/hskopp/swinekeeper.html` (08/26/2004).

Using Constraint Programming for Reconfiguration of Electrical Power Distribution Networks*

Juan Francisco Díaz[2], Gustavo Gutierrez[1], Carlos Alberto Olarte[1], and Camilo Rueda[1]

[1] Pontificia Universidad Javeriana, Cali, Colombia
{ggutierrez, caolarte, crueda}@atlas.puj.edu.co
[2] Universidad del Valle, Cali, Colombia
jdiaz@univalle.edu.co

Abstract. The problem of reconfiguring power distribution systems to reduce power losses has been extensively studied because of its significant economic impact. A variety of approximation computational models have recently been proposed. We describe a constraint programming model for this problem, using the *Mozart* system. To handle real world reconfiguration systems we implemented and integrated into *Mozart* an efficient constraint propagation system for the real numbers. We show how the CP approach leads to a simpler model and allows more flexible control of reconfiguration parameters. We analyze the performance of our system in canonical distribution networks of up to 60 nodes. We describe how the adaptability of the *Mozart* search engine allows defining effective strategies for tackling a real distribution system reconfiguration of around 600 nodes.

1   Introduction

The purpose of an electric power distribution system is to deliver power to customers. The energy source in this system is a *power transformer* directly connected to a set of *feeders*. Each feeder acts as the energy supplier for a given section of the distribution system. Energy from the feeders reaches customers through a network of nodes linked by *branches* (transmission lines). Some of the branches have switches that can be opened (resp. close) to interrupt (resp. allow) the current flow.

The topology of lines interconnecting customers to feeders forms a mesh network in which *radiality* must be guaranteed (i.e. there cannot be a path connecting any two different feeders) while ensuring power delivery to all users (*Service Continuity*). Radial networks simplify overcurrent protections in the

---

* This work was partially supported by the Colombian Institute for Science and Technology Development (Colciencias) under the CRISOL project (Contract No.298-2002).

P. Van Roy (Ed.): MOZ 2004, LNCS 3389, pp. 263–276, 2005.

feeders. A power distribution network usually has to be reconfigured (i.e. the state of some switches changed) from time to time, for two reasons: 1) to restore power to customers following a fault, and 2) in order to minimize or reduce power losses induced by the resistance and current in branches. Although similarities exist between reconfiguration strategies in both cases we confine ourselves in this paper to reconfiguration to reduce power losses. When a network is reconfigured it is typically the case that some nodes that were previously connected by a path of branches to a given feeder, connect to a different feeder in the new configuration. For this reason the problem is sometimes referred to as *feeder reconfiguration*.

Customer power loads vary with time of day and day of the week. Each feeder serves a different mix of residential, commercial and industrial loads (i.e. amount of power requested), and each type of load has different time profiles. Consequently, the load pattern on each feeder varies constantly. To keep losses to a minimum in these changing situations, feeders must be reconfigured with a frequency that usually depends on the degree of automation available for switch control.

The power distribution system should in principle be operated with minimum losses, satisfying different types of constraints:

- All customers must be served (i.e. every node in the network should be connected to a feeder)
- Radial configuration must be maintained.
- Current in lines and transformers should fall within given capacity limits.
- Voltage drop limits should be obeyed.

For reasons including poor line maintenance, ill planned system growth policies or the presence of unauthorized connections, losses in power distribution systems are very high in developing countries([3]). Moreover, switch control is usually done manually which means that the number of switching operations performed in reconfiguration must be constrained. Finding (not necessarily optimal) distribution network configurations reducing losses and respecting switching constraints can thus have a significant economic impact.

Two main strategies have been previously used for power loss reduction by reconfiguration: 1) start with a feasible (i.e. radial) solution, select a tie switch (the ones linking two feeder circuits) to close (thus forming a loop) and then select a line switch to open to restore radiality ([4]), and 2) start with all tie switches closed (thus forming "weak" loops) and then opening selected switches one by one until radiality is restored ([14]). In both strategies computing losses of each trial configuration entails determining current values in the network by a process called *load flow* computation. Known values in this computation are essentially customer loads and resistance of network branches. Other electrical values have to be calculated. The process starts with an estimate of voltages and uses electrical laws to determine currents. These in turn serve to refine the initial guesses. The process iterates until computation of electrical parameters stabilizes.

We can thus identify two distinct processes in reconfiguration: selecting a switch to open or close (a combinatorial number of boolean possibilities) and performing load flow computation (calculations over the complex numbers). This constitutes a hybrid combinatorial optimization problem. Solutions proposed recently (simulated annealing [10], expert systems [16], tabu search [7]) usually employ approximation techniques to avoid generating (and performing load flow computation of) a combinatorial number of configurations, by focusing the search to a small subset of "promising" configurations.

In [5, 6] a system (called PLANET) performing power network reconfiguration is presented. This system, based on the constraint language CHIP, aims at finding an optimal maintenance schedule. Since maintenance involves isolating a section of the network, reconfiguration has to be performed to ensure that customers serviced through that section are kept energized (or to minimize those that are not, when full service is not possible). Load flow must also be done to compute fundamental electrical values of the reconfigured network so as to ensure operating constraints. *CRE2* , the application implementing the approach presented in this paper, differs from this system in two important ways. First, in its purpose, since *CRE2* does not address optimal maintenance scheduling, whereas PLANET does not address minimizing power losses. Second, in their technological choices: in *CRE2* all computations including load flow, are performed using constraint programming (CP) technology (a real intervals constraint system was developed for load flow). In PLANET, an electric library, written in C, is used for computing load flow and also for reconfiguring (using the heuristic approach in [14]).

The main contribution of this paper is to show that constraint programming can effectively be used both for load flow computation and for reconfiguration. Moreover, we show how the *interaction* of these two processes modeled in CP can be used to significantly prune the search tree. Implemented in *Mozart* ([15], www.mozart-oz.org), our model has been tested successfully in canonical reconfiguration problems of networks up to 60 nodes. To compute load flow we had to implement for *Mozart* a new efficient constraint propagation system over the real numbers, based on the interval arithmetic package in [9]. We used the modularity and extension facilities of *Mozart* to effectively couple these constraint propagators to the existing finite domain system and also to build into the labeling process strategies better suited to the reconfiguration problem. While our approach is arguably less efficient than some existing approximation schemes, we think that using CP provides definite advantages: 1) all electrical and operational power system constraints are always satisfied, 2) it provides a simpler computational model, directly related to fundamental electricity laws of the system, 3) it allows more flexible parameter control, such as a maximum number of switching operations and 4) leaves more room for the introduction of additional operational constraints or search control strategies.

Our research group is interested in studying the application of CP techniques, particularly the *Mozart* system, to real world problems. We are currently adapting this implementation to run a loss reduction reconfiguration of a power system network of around 600 nodes in the southern region of Colombia.

In section 3 we formally define the reconfiguration problem and describe a constraint model for solving it. In section 4, we analyze the results of running the implementation of this model in two canonical power distribution networks. Finally, sections 5 and 6 are dedicated to stating our considerations on the strong and weak points of using CP for this problem, and the line of work we plan to pursue.

2   XRI: A Constraints System Over Real Intervals

XRI is an implementation of a real intervals constraint system for *Mozart* . This implementation is an extension of the Real Interval module (RI) implemented by Tobias Müller ([12]) and distributed as a contribution with the *Mozart* sources. The XRI module provides constraint propagators for real intervals relations and a general customizable distribution procedure for real intervals domains.

In the following pages we describe the foundations of our module implementation (interval arithmetic, interval constraints and hull consistency) and its main features (real intervals domains, propagators and distribution).

2.1   Interval Arithmetic and Constraints

Interval arithmetic aims at bounding numeric errors that appear when making calculations with the classical representation of real numbers as floating-point numbers. A closed interval $[l, u]$, with $l, u \in \mathcal{R}$ can be regarded either as the set of real numbers $\{r \mid l \leq r \leq u\}$, or as an approximation of some real number laying within that set. Instead of using a single floating-point number to approximate a real number, interval arithmetic encloses the real number within a closed interval having (in general) floating-point bounds. Different intervals can thus approximate the same real number. When the width of the interval is sufficiently small (i.e. the approximation conforms to a desired precision), the interval is said to represent the real number.

Any function (arithmetical operation) f over the real numbers can be extended to a function F over intervals by

$$F(I) = \mathbf{outer}_I(\{r \mid \exists v. \, v \in I \wedge f(v) = r\}),$$

where $\mathbf{outer}_I(S)$ denotes an interval enclosing all values in the set S. It is in general desirable to have the *smallest* such interval.

Similarly, any relation over the real numbers can be extended to an interval relation. A Cartesian product of intervals, $B = I_1 \times ... \times I_n$ is called a *Box*. A relation $c(x_1, ..., x_n)$ over the reals (i.e. a set of tuples) is extended to a relation over intervals:

$$C(I_1, ..., I_n) = \mathbf{outer}_B(\{(r_1, ..., r_n) \mid r \in I_1, ..., r_n \in I_n \wedge c(r_1, ..., r_n)\},$$

where $\mathbf{outer}_B(S)$ is a box enclosing the set of tuples S.

A key issue in interval arithmetic is how to define **outer** so that tight intervals are obtained. For basic arithmetical functions this can be achieved by simple operations on the bounds of the intervals involved. For example,

$$[l_1, u_1] + [l_2, u_2] = [l_1 + l_2, u_1 + u_2],$$

$$[l_1, u_1] \times [l_2, u_2] = [min(l_1 \times l_2, l_1 \times u_2, u_1 \times l_2, u_1 \times u_2),$$

$$max(l_1 \times l_2, l_1 \times u_2, u_1 \times l_2, u_1 \times u_2)]$$

A problem is that these operations do not obey the usual algebraic properties (e.g. distributive laws). This means that equivalent arithmetic expressions do not lead to equivalence of their interval extension counterparts. The practical consequence of this fact is that the width of the interval computed by **outer** might depend on the form a particular expression takes (see [13] for a thorough discussion of these issues). Section 2.2 describes a way to avoid this problem in some particular cases.

In [9] an interval arithmetical system is presented, using function and relation extensions with the properties of correctness (operating on any values in the argument intervals always gives a value belonging to the result interval), totality (interval operations are defined on all intervals), closeness (interval operations return intervals), optimization (interval results are not wider than necessary) and efficiency. It is also shown how to implement basic arithmetic operators extensions over intervals (such as + and ×), on a computer meeting the IEEE754-Standard for floating-point arithmetic.

The term *interval constraint* denotes a constraint in which variables are associated to intervals. In our implementation this interval (the domain of the variable) represents in reality the *set* of all its subintervals. The *value* of a variable is thus always an interval (a sufficiently narrow one). XRI is an implementation of efficient techniques for solving sets of interval constraints, integrated as constraint propagators of *Mozart* .

Research in this area (see for example [2]) is devoted to finding correct and (near) optimal interval propagation techniques that can be efficiently implemented. These techniques are known as *narrowing algorithms* whereas propagators for constraints are called *constraint narrowing operators*. A constraint narrowing operator transforms the domains of those variables involved in it into tighter intervals such that:

- Result intervals are always included in the original ones (*contractance* property).
- All values in the original intervals verifying the associated constraint of the narrowing operator, belong to the result intervals (*soundness* or *correctness*).
- The subset interval relation is conserved by the transformation (*monotonicity*).

Well known examples of constraint narrowing operators are Hull and Box Consistency (see [2]) and $kB-$Consistency Operators (see [11]). The current version of XRI contains an efficient implementation of Hull consistency known as HC4 (see next section).

2.2   HC4

A major problem of interval arithmetic is the overestimation of results. As mentioned before, this might be a consequence of the form the arithmetical expression takes. For instance, extending the function $f(x) = x^2 - 2x + 1$ on the interval $x = [-1, 3]$ we get $F([-1, 3]) = [-4, 4]$. If the function is equivalently written $f(x) = (x-1)^2$, then we get $F([-1, 3]) = [0, 4]$. This is the so-called *data dependency problem*: interval operations work independently on each occurrence of a variable, i.e. they consider the above expression as $x_1^2 - 2x_2 + 1$ and then extend it with $x_1 = [-1, 3], x_2 = [-1, 3]$.

A related problem occurs when constraint propagators for arithmetical equations are defined over a fixed number of variables. For example, if a propagator for interval equations of the form $X + Y = Z$ expects three variables, then an interval equation like $X + Y + Z = W$ must be split into equations $T_1 = X + Y, T_2 = T_1 + Z, T_2 = W$ using two new "temporal" variables. Since interval values for these are not known, information on the fact that all variables in the original equation are related is lost. Moreover, the constraint system would have to launch three propagators instead of just one.

An efficient hull consistency algorithm called HC4 was proposed by Benhamou in [2]. Input to HC4 is a constraint in "user form" (i.e. without decomposing it in several equations). The algorithm efficiently computes an interval extension of the equation, narrowing intervals of the variables involved. In HC4 the input equation is represented as an attribute tree where the root node is a p-ary relation symbol and terms in the equation form subtrees rooted at nodes containing either a variable, a constant or an operation symbol.

Algorithm HC4 works in two phases called "forward evaluation" and "backward propagation". The forward phase is a tree traversal going from the leaves to the root, evaluating at each node the natural interval extension of that subterm of the constraint. The backward phase traverses the tree from the root to the leaves, projecting on each node the effects of interval narrowings already performed on its parent node. In the "backward propagation" phase" an interval may become empty. When this happens the constraint is inconsistent *w.r.t.* the initial domains.

In the XRI module, the user can define a precision for each variable. This value is used in propagators to control the minimum narrowing considered significant. If narrowing is less than that, HC4 does not change the intervals. Addition of this control is a consequence of a pathological behavior we observed in some problems: the algorithm may sometimes narrow an interval, say, by one floating point value, causing the HC4 propagator to be triggered again to narrow an additional float, and so on. In this case the rationale is to let other propagators narrow the intervals involved in a more significant way.

We implement HC4 as a *Mozart* propagator. It uses the *Mozart* propagator control, garbage collection and computation space cloning. This guarantees that it is triggered when the interval domain of any of its associated variables is changed by some other propagator (either basic or HC4). The user defines a HC4 propagator by a procedure call whose argument is the constraint written in prefix form. For example,

$$\{XRI.hc4\ eq(plus(square(X)Y1.0)\ plus(times(2.0\,X)W))\}$$

sets up a propagator for equation $x^2 + y + 1.0 = 2.0x + w$

Other than equality(eq), relational operators $< (lt),>(gt),\leq(leq)$ are supported by $XRI.hc4$, as well as several arithmetical and trigonometric functions.

2.3   XRI Variables and Propagators

As mentioned previously, the domain of a XRI variable is an interval with floating-point bounds, denoting the set of all its subintervals. Interval bounds are updated via the application of a set of hull-consistency based propagators.

A variable is *determined* when the width of the interval is less than a given precision. In XRI, precision can be defined globally or assigned locally to each variable. A failure occurs when the domain of a variable becomes empty, i.e when its interval lower bound is greater than the upper bound.

As is usual in constraints systems, computational agents (called *propagators*) in XRI work to enforce relations (constraints) among variables in the store. The XRI module offers two kinds of propagators: basic propagators enforcing basic arithmetic constraints, and the HC4 propagator described above.

Basic propagators implement interval extensions of basic arithmetic and trigonometric constraints. A constraint is asserted by a *Mozart* procedure call of the form {XRI.op X Y Z}, where suffix "op" is an appropriate operator. For example, {XRI.plus X Y Z} asserts constraint $X \oplus Y = Z$, where X, Y and Z are interval variables and $\oplus$ denotes interval addition. Constraint $Z = Y \ominus X$ can of course be asserted with the same propagator by invoking {XRI.plus X Z Y}).

Floating point operations performed by arithmetic constraints propagators comply with the IEEE754-standard. XRI also offers other propagators with floating point operations not covered by the IEEE754-standard, in particular for trigonometric and logarithmic constraints.

2.4   XRI Distribution

Distribution is the process used in most constraints systems to guarantee completeness. The XRI module provides a customizable distributor of interval variables similar to the one provided in the *Mozart* finite domains module. In the XRI distributor the user can specify the order in which variables are to be distributed, the order in which values should be tested (e.g. try first the lower half interval), and can also supply a procedure to be run when a computation space becomes stable (i.e. when no propagator is active). Well-known strategies are provided by default: *first-fail, naive* and *split-upper*. The first-fail strategy tells the distributor to select the variable having the smallest domain first and to test first the lower half of the interval. A naive strategy distributes the list of variables in the order they were originally supplied to the distributor, also checking first the lower half of the interval. The split-upper strategy tries the upper half of the interval first.

3   *CRE2* : A Power Distribution System Reconfigurator

CRE2 is an application written in *Mozart* for reconfiguring power distribution networks for power loss reduction. It includes two distinct interacting processes: load flow computation (finding values for electrical variables) using the XRI constraint system and reconfiguration (finding new network topologies) using the *Mozart* finite domain constraint system (FD).

As said before, an electric distribution network consists of a power transformer connected to a set of feeders, each supplying power to a subnetwork of nodes. Some of the nodes represent customer connected to the distribution system. These nodes have associated active (P) and reactive (Q) loads. Active loads are the amount of power (measured in watts) actually consumed by the user, whereas reactive power (measured in "volt-amperes-reactive", or *var*) is an abstract quantity used to describe the effects of a load which on the average neither supplies nor consumes power. It is known that reactive devices such as inductors and capacitors dissipate zero power, yet the fact that they drop voltage and draw current gives the deceptive impression that they actually do dissipate power. This "phantom power" is called reactive power. Power losses in a network are highly dependent on both P and Q.

Nodes (and feeders) are connected by branches. A resistance R and a reactance X is associated with each branch. In certain branches current flow (or lack thereof) along that branch is controlled by a switch.

The *load flow problem* consists of finding values for all electrical variables involved in the network, given values for P, Q, R and X. These variables include the current along each branch (I), the voltage in each node (V) and the output current (or *load current*) generated by the power consumed by each user denoted I_q. Active ($L_p = |I|^2 \times R$) and reactive ($L_q = |I|^2 \times X$) losses along each branch are then computed. Summing the latter for all branches gives the overall power loss of the system.

Values found must satisfy both the fundamental electrical laws described in section 3.1 and also the operational constraints listed in section 3.2.

3.1   Electrical Constraints

Values computed in the *load flow* process should obey: Ohm law equations (1) on each branch , Kirchoff laws on each node and two equations relating load current *w.r.t* P and Q. In the following equations, variable Z (impedance) is equal to $R + Xi$.

For each branch with a closed switch in the network, Ohm's law must hold:

$$\Delta V = Z \times I \tag{1}$$

Electrical equations such as 1 can be expressed either in rectangular form (real and imaginary parts) or in polar form (angles and magnitudes).

Constraints in polar form require trigonometric propagators whereas those in rectangular form need basic arithmetic propagators. Since the latter can be made stronger and more efficient than the former, *CRE2* uses the rectangular representation. Furthermore, magnitude and angle can easily be computed from the rectangular values.

Equation 1 can be decomposed into equations 2 and 3; figure 1 shows an *Mozart* procedure implementing those equations.

$$V_1.real - V_2.real = I.real \times R - I.img \times X \qquad (2)$$

$$V_1.img - V_2.img = I.real \times X + I.img \times R \qquad (3)$$

```
proc {LOhm InfBranches VarBranches VarNodes EstSw}
for I in 1..{Width InfBranches} do
        Id#N1#N2#R#X#CCR#Ss#Eso = InfBranches.I
        V1_real = VarNodes.vo_real.N1
        V1_img = VarNodes.vo_img.N1
        V2_real = VarNodes.vo_real.N2
        V2_img = VarNodes.vo_img.N2
        I_real = VarBranches.io_real.Id
        I_img = VarBranches.io_img.Id
in
        if Ss==0 orelse {Nth EstSw I} == 1 then
                {XRI.hc4 eq(sub(V1_real V2_real)
                   sub(times(I_real R) times(I_img X)))}
                {XRI.hc4 eq(sub(V1_img V2_img)
                   plus(times(I_real X) times(I_img R)))}
        end
end
end
```

Fig. 1. Ohm law procedure

For each node in the network Kirchoff Law asserts that:

$$\sum input\ branch\ current = \sum output\ branch\ current \qquad (4)$$

In radial systems the above equation can be simplified to:

$$input\ branch\ current = \sum output\ branch\ current + I_q \qquad (5)$$

where I_q can be computed by:

$$P = V.real \times Iq.real + V.img \times Iq.img \qquad (6)$$

$$Q = V.img \times Iq.real - V.real \times Iq.img \qquad (7)$$

3.2   Reconfiguration Procedure

The feeder reconfiguration problem can be modeled using finite domains to represent the state of each switch (0 for open, 1 for closed). The target configuration (network topology) must satisfy the following constraints:

- Radiality: The number of branches supplying current into a given node must be equal to one
- Service Continuity: current must flow to all nodes
- Maximum switching operations: limits the number of switches that can be changed
- Active losses reduction: active losses in the new topology must be less than in the original network.

We implemented an FD procedure enforcing *service continuity* using the $FD.sum$ propagator (each node has at least one incident closed branch). System radiality is enforced in the load flow procedure by computing the direction of current flow in the network and then verifying that each node has exactly one input current. Finally, the maximum switching operations constraint is implemented using a reified constraint computing the number k of switch changes and asserting a $FD.atMost$ propagator using k.

Our method uses a reconfiguration technique in which switch changes are guided by the goal of balancing power loads among the feeders. For each trial configuration the load flow procedure is invoked to compute its active losses. Configurations in which power losses are not less (by a given amount) than in the original one are rejected.

Operational Constraints. Most reconfiguration methods reported in the literature must verify their solutions against operational constraints. Since *CRE2* uses a CP model, operational constraints interact with the search procedure. Some operational constraints are expressed as HC4 equations and can be easily integrated to the load flow procedure itself. For example, we can easily impose operational limits over voltage in nodes and current in branches:

- Voltage limit in internal nodes:

$$1.0 - PvMNO \leq \sqrt{V_o.real^2 + V_o.img^2} \qquad (8)$$

  Asserting that voltage magnitude in each node cannot drop below an operational percentage ($PvMNO$).
- Limit of current in branches:

$$\sqrt{I_o.real^2 + I_o.img^2} \leq CCR \times (1.0 + PsCPR) \qquad (9)$$

  Asserting that the percentage of overcurrent in branches ($PsCPR$) cannot exceed the current limit of the conductor (CCR).

4   Results

This section describes the results obtained by running *CRE2* on two canonical problems we will refer to as Civanlar (16 nodes, [4]) and Baran (53 nodes, [1]). In both cases a reconfiguration minimizing active losses must be found.

All tests were done on an Intel Pentium 4 1.80 GHz computer with 256 of RAM, running Linux Gentoo 1.4 with kernel 2.6.20 and *Mozart* system 1.2.5.

The Civanlar system consists of 3 circuits (each one starting with a different feeder). Circuits have 5, 6, and 5 nodes, respectively (including the feeders). Each pair of circuits is connect each by a branch containing a switch (initially open).

A normalized active losses reduction (0.0054 **per unit**) of the initial configuration was found in 142ms using a precision of 10^{-5}.

Computing losses for all feasible reconfigurations achieving some reduction and performing at most four switching operations (see Table 1), took 8.30s. In Table 1, column "Proposed configurations" specify switches to open and/or close (only four out of seven possible reconfigurations are shown), and column "% gain" shows the reduction percentage *w.r.t* the initial active losses.

Table 1. Reconfiguration of Civanlar case

Active Losses [p.u]	% Gain	Proposed reconfigurations
0.0053	1.85	Open 4,7 and close 15,16
0.0054	0.00	The initial topology
0.0054	0.00	Open 7,13 and close 15,16
0.0049	9.25	Open 7,8 and close 14,15 (Best Configuration)

Table 2. Reconfiguration of Baran case

Active Losses [p.u]	% Gain	Proposed reconfigurations
0.0012	7.69	Open 47 and close 53
0.0011	15.38	Open 46 and close 53
0.0010	23.08	Open 32,35,46 and close 51,52,53

4.1   Baran Case

The Baran system consists of 5 circuits having 6,9, 6, 18 and 14 nodes, respectively. Active losses in the original network (0.0013 pu) were computed in 572ms. Not all reconfigurations were searched for, due to the huge size of the search tree. Some configurations reducing losses and performing at most four switching operations are summarized in table 2.

5   Conclusions

One of the main challenges we faced was to integrate into *Mozart* a robust, correct and efficient constraint system for real intervals. Although the XRI module is still being improved, we believe it does provide in its present state good functionality and reasonable performance.

As usual in CP, efficiency was strongly dependent on the constraint model used. We initially enforced all electric constraints both in polar and in rectangular form, trying to obtain better interval narrowing by constraint redundancy. We did not obtain the results we expected. We conclude that our propagators for trigonometric constraints are not yet efficient enough to handle real world applications. A redundant constraint that did cause a significant improvement was asserting that the number of closed switches in branches entering a node must be at least one. In this way, no configuration isolating nodes is generated.

We have shown that using CP is a real alternative for the problem of reducing power losses by network reconfiguration. Optimal configurations were found in reasonable time for two canonical problems. Moreover, other approaches aim at finding one (hopefully optimal) configuration. In some practical cases, a (not necessarily optimal) configuration reducing losses and satisfying some extra operational constraints (such as number of switch changes) might be a better option. Our CP model easily handles these cases. In addition, *CRE2* provides more flexibility, such as the ability to incorporate new load flow models or to add new operational constraints. It is also easy to integrate strategies that have been proved to be effective in some cases. For example, totally meshed networks have minimal losses. A good strategy is then starting with this type of network and opening selected switches one by one. This strategy is "free" in our CP model: the distribution strategy simply selects the upper value first per switch state (1= a closed switch) and constraints quickly prune non radial networks.

Although the computation time of *CRE2* on the canonical problems was greater than in other approaches, it has to be considered that our model actually solved a somewhat (more complex) different problem. We assumed every branch in the network had a switch. This, of course, greatly increases the size of the search tree. In real networks only a few number of switches exist. The reason we model the problem in this way is that, for the particular network we have in mind, we would also like to suggest the best places to *install* a given number of switches, an issue not considered in other approaches.

It is clear to us that handling bigger networks requires better distribution strategies than those currently implemented. We have tried some problem domain driven strategies, such as ensuring each time a switch has to be opened to choose the one that better *balances* loads in the resulting two circuits. For small problems, the potential gains of this strategy are countered by the time spent in computing subnetwork loads. We still lack enough evidence to claim that this improves performance significantly in large networks.

6   Future Work

We implemented in *CRE2* a network of around 600 nodes corresponding to six electric circuits of the power system for the city of Buenaventura in Colombia. We expect to have reconfiguration results in the short term.

We plan to pursue CP formulation of related problems in electrical engineering, such as the unit commitment problem and the service restoration problem ([8]).

Acknowledgments

We are greatly indebted to Gladys Caicedo and Carlos Lozano, from the GRALTA research group[1], for referring the reconfiguration problem to the authors and for many enlightening discussions. We are also grateful to James Ortiz, Janeth Rodríguez and Diana Torres for their patient debugging of the initial implementations. Finally, we would like to thank the anonymous reviewers for their valuable comments for improving this paper.

References

1. M.E. Baran and F.F: Wu. Network reconfiguration in distribution systems for loss reduction and load balancing. *IEEE Transactions on Power Delivery*, 4(2):1401–1407, April 1989.
2. F. Benhamou, Fréderic Goualard, and Laurent Granvilliers. Revising hull and box consistency. In *Proceedings of ICLP'99 - MIT Press*, pages 230–244, 1999.
3. G. Caicedo. Nueva propuesta en reconfiguracion de alimentadores utilizando programacion con restricciones, 2004. PhD thesis, Universidad del Valle, Cali, Colombia.
4. S. Civanlar, J.J. Grainger, H. Yin, and S.S. Lee. Distribution feeder reconfiguration for loss reduction. *IEEE Transactions on Power Delivery*, 3(3):1217–1223, July 1988.
5. T. Creemers, L. Ros, J. Riera, C. Ferrarons, J. Roca, and X. Corbella. Constraint-based maintenance scheduling on an electric power-distribution network. In *Third International Conference and Exhibition on Practical Applications of Prolog*, April 1995.
6. T. Creemers, L. Ros, J. Riera, C. Ferrarons, J. Roca, and X. Corbella. Programacin optima de tareas de mantenimiento y reconfiguracin sobre redes de media tensin. In *The Fourth Portuguese-Spanish Conference on Electrical Engineering*, July 1995.
7. Y. Fukuyama. Reactive tabu search for distribution load transfer operation. In *IEEE PES winter meeting*, Singapore, January 2000.
8. Y. Fukuyama and H. D. Chiang. Modern heuristic techniques for combinatorial problem. In *Proc. of IEEE FUZZ/IFES conference*, Yokohama, March 1995.
9. T. Hickey, Q. Ju, and M. H. Van Emden. Interval arithmetic: From principles to implementation. *Journal of the ACM*, 48(5):1038–1068, September 2001.

---

[1] High Tension Research group, Universidad del Valle

10. Y.J. Jeon, J.Ch. Kim, J.O. Kim, J.R Shin, and K.Y. Lee. An efficient simmulated annealing algorithm for network reconfiguration in large-scale distribution systems. *IEEE Transactions on Power Delivery*, 17(4):1070–1078, October 2002.

11. O. Lhomme. Consistency techniques for numeric csps. In *Proceedings of the 13th IJCAI, IEEE Computer Society Press*, pages 232–238, 1993.

12. Tobias Müller. Adding constraint systems to DFKI Oz. In *WOz'95, International Workshop on Oz Programming*, Institut Dalle Molle d'Intelligence Artificielle Perceptive, Martigny, Switzerland, 29 November–1 December 1995.

13. A. Neumaier. *Interval methods for system of equations*. Cambridge University Press, 1990.

14. H. Shirmohammadi and W. Hong. Reconfiguration of electric distribution networks for resistive line losses reduction. *IEEE Transactions on Power Delivery*, 4(2):1492–1498, April 1989.

15. G. Smolka. A foundation for higher-order concurrent constraint programming. In Jean-Pierre Jouannaud, editor, *1st International Conference on Constraints in Computational Logics*, Lecture Notes in Computer Science, vol. 845, pages 50–72, München, Germany, September 1994. Springer-Verlag.

16. C.T. Su and C.S Lee. Feeder reconfiguration and capacitor setting for loss reduction of distribution systems. *Elect. Power Syst. Res.*, 58(2):97–102, 2001.

Strasheela: Design and Usage of a Music Composition Environment Based on the Oz Programming Model

Torsten Anders, Christina Anagnostopoulou, and Michael Alcorn

Sonic Arts Research Centre, Queen's University Belfast, Northern Ireland
{t.anders, c.anagnostopoulou, m.alcorn}@qub.ac.uk

Abstract. Strasheela provides a means for the composer to create a symbolic score by formally describing it in a rule-based way. The environment defines a rich music representation for complex polyphonic scores. Strasheela enables the user to define expressive compositional rules and then to apply them to the score. Compositional rules can restrict many aspects of the music – including the rhythmic structure, the melodic structure and the harmonic structure – by constraining the parameters (e.g. duration or pitch) of musical events according to some numerical or logical relation. Strasheela combines this expressivity with efficient search strategies.

Strasheela is implemented in the Oz programming language. The Strasheela user writes an Oz program which applies the Strasheela music representation. The program searches for one or more solution scores which fulfil all compositional rules applied to the score.

1   Introduction

In computer aided composition (CAC), a composer creates music by communicating her or his musical intentions to her 'assistant', the computer. CAC addresses music mainly on the score level and in that way CAC differs from other areas of computer music such as sound synthesis or spatialisation. By using a CAC environment a composer formalises musical ideas or compositional problems and implements them in a computer program which outputs music in a symbolic representation. Diverse strategies exist to generate or transform music; examples include mathematical models (e.g. stochastics), models based on transforming existing data (such as spectral analysis data), or models implementing already existing compositional strategies (e.g. serial composition) [1].

To advance in the compositional process, the composer must not worry too much about low level programming detail. It is therefore highly desirable for the composer to express her intentions on a high level of abstraction. Consequently, CAC environments rely heavily on the expressive power of the underlying programming language and its programming concepts.

P. Van Roy (Ed.): MOZ 2004, LNCS 3389, pp. 277–291, 2005.

Different CAC environments are based on different programming concepts or paradigms. Often, an environment supports a specific paradigm particularly well and encourages the user to employ this paradigm. Other CAC environments support a combination of programming paradigms and the user may separately choose the adequate paradigm for each given sub-problem.

Most CAC strategies and programming paradigms are clearly different compared to the way in which musicians describe a musical style. Using a CAC environment a composer may control aspects of the pitch contour of some voice by deciding for a specific random distribution to generate the pitches. She may further shape the contour by multiplying the resulting pitch sequence with an envelope. Instead of using such a deterministic strategy – in which one process modifies the result of the previous process – musicians tend to describe music by a set of modular rules. A rule is not an algorithm to create a certain result. A rule often states merely a restriction on single notes and their parameters (e.g. duration or pitch) or mutual dependencies between the parameters of multiple notes. Such restrictions do not necessarily result in a single solution score. Instead, the restrictions reduce the domain of all possible scores.

The constraint programming paradigm presents a natural CAC approach in which the composer defines such modular rules restricting a score. In fact, during the last decade constraint programming has become an important strategy for CAC and several environments supporting constraint programming have been developed [2, 3, 4, 5, 6].

Virtually all existing constraint based CAC environments extend already established general CAC environments by constraint programming means. Perhaps surprisingly, most current environments come with their own specifically developed constraint solver. This article proposes a different approach by extending a state-of-the-art constraint programming language into a CAC environment. The programming language Oz [7] offers highly expressive constraint programming means in a multi-paradigm programming context which makes the language very interesting for CAC. The present article proposes Strasheela,[1] a CAC environment implemented in Oz.

The implementation of Strasheela takes advantage of Oz' multi-paradigm programming support. Besides constraint programming, Strasheela applies object-oriented programming, and higher-order functional programming. Strasheela's main data structure, the score representation, is defined by a class hierarchy. Many score object methods are higher-order procedures and expect procedures or method labels as argument. Compositional rules are expressed by constraints on score objects.

---

[1] Strasheela is also the name of a scarecrow in the children's novel *The Wizard of the Emerald City* by Alexandr Volkov (in which the Russian author retells *The Wonderful Wizard of Oz* by L. Frank Baum). Although Strasheela's brain consists only in bran, pins and needles, he is a brilliant thinker who loves to multiply four figure numbers at night. Little is yet known about his interest in music, but Strasheela is reported to sometimes dance and sing with joy.

Plan of the Paper. The following section presents an overview of Strasheela from a user's point of view. The Strasheela score representation is discussed in Sec. 3. Strasheela suggests expressive strategies to define compositional rules and to apply them to the score (Sec. 4). Strasheela predefines distribution strategies – in effect search orders – which are optimised for scores (Sec. 5). Many aspects of Strasheela are explained throughout the text by a single canon example which is finished in Sec. 6. Section 7 presents related work. The article concludes with a discussion of Strasheela's limitations (Sec. 8).

2   Strasheela Overview

Strasheela offers a means to create a symbolic score by formally describing it in a rule-based way. The resulting score is later performed by human musicians or a sound synthesis language to create the actual sound. The main objective of Strasheela is the creation of original music and not to replicate traditional musical styles. Having said that, a conventional example based on well-known textbook rules is more easy to communicate in a paper focusing on software design. All compositional rules discussed here are hence inspired by traditional counterpoint [8].

As an example, we assume that a composer wishes to use Strasheela to create a canon, a musical form in which several voices imitate each other in a rather literal way. The Strasheela user first instantiates a score data object and in doing so she predetermines certain aspects of the score. For the canon, the composer predefines the number of voices in the score and the number of notes in each voice. However, the composer leaves other aspects of the score undetermined. She may leave undetermined all durations and pitches of the notes, because she wants these parameters to satisfy a set of compositional rules she has in mind.

Possible rules include restrictions on the pitch succession in each voice (melodic rules), rules restricting the simultaneous pitch combinations (harmonic rules), rules on the sequence of durations in a voice (rhythmic rules), and a rule restricting the different voices to be similar such that they form a canon.

Each rule imposes some constraints on some score objects. For example, a melodic rule may restrict the pitch interval between two successive notes. However, a melodic rule will usually not only affect a single note pair but, for instance, all successive note pairs in all voices. Rules are therefore defined in a modular way: the rule definition is abstracted from its application to multiple score objects.

By instantiating the score data object, defining the compositional rules, and by applying the rules to the score, the composer states the constraint problem. A solution of the problem is a score which fulfils all the rules applied to it.

In Oz, a constraint problem is implemented by a search script, a procedure with the solution as its only argument [9]. The constraint solver of Oz finds one or more solutions for the script.

Strasheela outputs the solution score into multiple formats including the score format of several sound synthesis languages and common music notation.

The Strasheela user interface is the Oz programming language: a Strasheela user writes an Oz program which applies Strasheela's contributions to Oz – most of all its score representation.

3 The Score Representation

A general and powerful music representation is vital for the expressivity of Strasheela, because both the solution score and the problem definition are expressed using this representation. Much research has been done in the domain of music representation [10, 11, 12, 13, 14, 15]. The score representation of Strasheela combines ideas presented in the literature and in existing implementations of CAC environments.

3.1 Class Hierarchy

A musical score contains many different object types. Examples in conventional music notation include notes marking pitch and timing information, articulation signs, and staffs of five lines to organise notes in voices. Different musical styles may use different type sets. During the compositional process the composer may even introduce further types (e.g. roman numbers to sketch a harmonic progression).

The Strasheela score representation attempts to generalise this broad width of possible score information. Instead of implementing an enormous set of different types in an unrelated way, the representation defines the score data types as classes in a class hierarchy in the object-oriented programming sense. Figure 1 presents an example excerpt of the class hierarchy. Depicted are the relations between the classes used to represent timing information. Many of these classes are explained in subsequent sections. The user can extend the class hierarchy by her own classes if so desired.

Object-oriented programming in Oz is often stateful. Nevertheless, the Strasheela score representation is stateless.

3.2 Hierarchic Score Structure

Most existing score representations support the notion of score *events*. The instances of the event class produce sound when the score is played.

Many event attributes (such as start time or pitch) are specified by *parameters*. Strasheela defines parameters in their own class to allow the addition of information to the actual parameter value. For instance, parameters allow the composer to specify their unit of measurement (such as key-number or cent-value for pitch) which subsequently affects the score when it is transformed into an output format. Parameter objects are also important for the definition of specific search strategies (Sec. 5). Parameter values are the only predefined score data which the composer can constrain.

The class *note* is an event subclass. Besides other event parameters (e.g. start time) a note defines the additional parameter pitch. The class *element* is

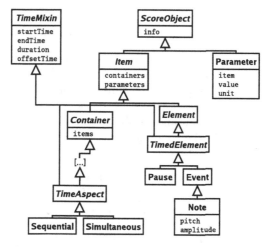

Fig. 1. Score class hierarchy. The excerpt shows timing related classes. The figure omits some classes for brevity, making some class names appear arbitrary (such as TimeAspect instead of TimedContainer)

a superclass of event. Instances of element subclasses (besides event) are silent when the score is played. Examples include the predefined class *pause* or a class representing an initialisation statement for some sound synthesis language.

Musicians rarely talk about single score events when talking about music. They talk about event groups such as motives, voices, rhythmic patterns, or chords. To express such concepts, Strasheela defines the class *container*. The superclass of both container and element is called an *item* in Strasheela. A container contains other items and so can represent groups of score objects. Data can be recursively nested to form a tree (e.g. to express a note in a motive in a melody, or a note in a chord in a staff).

Strasheela supports different hierarchies of different container types to express, for example, timing structure, grouping, harmonic information, or the bar structure. Multiple hierarchies can be combined in a graph in which different hierarchies share the same elements as leaves of their trees. As most of these container types depend closely on the music the user wants to represent, Strasheela predefines only abstract classes from which the user may derive her own classes according needs. Nevertheless, containers expressing a timing hierarchy are already predefined.

3.3   Hierarchic Timing Structure

Some score items have timing related parameters. For these objects, Strasheela explicitly represents the *start time, offset time, duration,* and *end time*. For all timed items, Strasheela implicitly constrains start time, duration, and end time (1). The offset time is an alternative means to express a pause in front of an item.

$$end_{\text{item}} - start_{\text{item}} = duration_{\text{item}} \tag{1}$$

Strasheela defines container classes whose instances constrain the timing of their contained items (Fig. 2). The items contained in a *simultaneous* object run in parallel with each other. The offset time of a contained item denotes how much the start time of the item is delayed. Equations (2) and (3) show the implicit constraints between a simultaneous object and all its contained items, n denotes the number of items in the container.

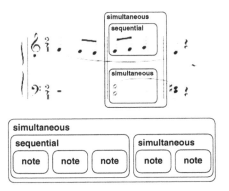

Fig. 2. The timing structure forms a tree with events as leaves, parameters are omitted (Béla Bartók. Mikrokosmos, No. 87)

$$\forall\, i \in \{1, \ldots, n\} : start_{\text{simItem}_i} = start_{\text{sim}} + offset_{\text{simItem}_i} \tag{2}$$

$$end_{\text{sim}} = \max(end_{\text{simItem}_1}, \ldots, end_{\text{simItem}_n}) \tag{3}$$

The items contained in a *sequential* object follow each other sequentially in time. The offset times of contained items specify pauses between the items (Equations (4) to (6)). Only the constraints (1) to (6) are implicitly applied to every score; further constraints are applied by the user.

$$start_{\text{seqItem}_1} = start_{\text{seq}} + offset_{\text{seqItem}_1} \tag{4}$$

$$\forall\, i \in \{1, \ldots, n-1\} : start_{\text{seqItem}_{i+1}} = end_{\text{seqItem}_i} + offset_{\text{seqItem}_{i+1}} \tag{5}$$

$$end_{\text{seq}} = end_{\text{seqItem}_n} \tag{6}$$

3.4   Application Programming Interface and Patterns

The application programming interface (API) for the score classes includes convenient constructors for complex scores, expressive score accessors as well as score transformers. For instance, the standard score constructor expects a shorthand representation of a score which consists of all score object initialisation methods nested according to the score hierarchy. Examples for typical accessors include a method which returns the item preceding some item in a container or a method which returns all items in the whole score which are simultaneous to some item. Many accessors and transformers are higher-order procedures. Such accessors include, for instance, a method which maps a user specified function to all objects in the score graph which fulfil some test function. With the help of this method, the user can, for example, collect the pitches of every second note in some voice to constrain this pitch list to follow some user defined pattern.

Strasheela predefines many pattern constraints which either constrain the order of list elements by unification, impose numeric constraints on list elements, or combine multiple sublists into an other list. For example, a simple order pattern repeats the first n list elements throughout the list in a circular manner; a more complex example unifies list elements according to some Lindenmayer system defined by the user. Numeric patterns constrain, for example, each list predecessor to be smaller then its successor, the maximum number in a list to occurs only once, or n list elements to be pairwise distinct.

4   Compositional Rules and Their Application

Oz predefines a broad width of constraints, for instance, for finite domain (FD) integers [9] and for finite sets of integers [16]. The Strasheela user applies constraints to score parameter values – which are usually FD integers but may be other constrainable data as well – to express restrictions on these parameters. For instance, a composer may express a melodic restriction which constraints the distance between the pitches of two consecutive notes to not exceed the interval of a fifth (7). The interval is measured in semitones, 7 denotes a fifth.

$$7 \geq |pitch_1 - pitch_2| \tag{7}$$

Yet, a *compositional rule* is usually more general as it holds more than only once. The Strasheela user therefore often encapsulates the constraints expressing a compositional rule into an Oz procedure. The user freely controls the *rule scope* by defining a control structure which accesses sets of score objects and applies the rule to them. Often – but not necessarily – the rule scope has a relation to the hierarchic nesting of the score. For example, a rule restricting a melodic interval may be applied to any consecutive note pair in any sequential container of a score.

Each application of this rule constraints a set of score objects which are inter-related in a uniform way: the pitches of a consecutive note pair in a sequential. Another rule may constrain sets of score objects which are inter-related in another uniform way, for example, the duration of some note and the durations of all its simultaneous notes. A *context* is the way how a set of objects is inter-related. Strasheela's score API predefines various context accessor methods which return, for example, all items in the score which are simultaneous to some given item. The user can also define her own context accessors. Using these accessors, the context for a rule as well as the control structure for the rule scope is usually defined in a convenient way.

Figure 3 illustrates the terms rule, context and scope graphically and shows how each rule imposes one ore more constraints between several score object sets. The example rule `RestrictMelodicInterval` (Fig. 3, a – Fig. 4 shows the Oz code) implements (7) as a procedure with the argument $note_1$. The preceding $note_2$ is accessed within the procedure. The rule is applied to all notes in two different voices which have a predecessor (Fig. 3, b).

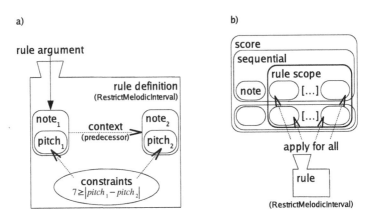

Fig. 3. Definition and application of a compositional rule. (a) A rule is a procedure which imposes constraints between the procedure arguments and often their contexts as well. (b) The rule scope is a set of score object sets to which the user applies the rule

```
proc {RestrictMelodicInterval Note1}
    Note2 = {Note1 getTimeAspectPredecessor($)}
in
    7 >=: {FD.distance {Note1 getPitch($)} {Note2 getPitch($)}}
end
```

Fig. 4. A melodic rule, defined as procedure

In Oz, a procedure is a first-class value which can be used as an argument to other procedures. Figure 5 shows how the scope of the rule `RestrictMelodic-Interval` (i.e. all notes which have a predecessor) is controlled. The method `forAll` applies the rule recursively to all score objects contained in `MyScore` for which the specified test function returns **true** – regardless of nesting depth.

There are situations in which a particular context of a score item is undetermined before search. For instance, simultaneous items are undetermined for most score items in case timing parameters (e.g. note durations) are found only during the search process. In such cases, standard accessors are unsuitable as they will suspend until the context is determined. Nonetheless, Oz supports the notion of constraining the validity of constraints and we can use this ability to constrain the context of an item even if we can not directly access this context.

```
{MyScore
 forAll(RestrictMelodicInterval
        test:fun {$ X}
                 {X isNote($)} andthen
                 {X hasTimeAspectPredecessor($)}
              end)}
```

Fig. 5. Application of the melodic rule

In Oz, the validity of a constraint is reflected into a truth value by a reified constraint [9]. A 0/1-integer – a FD integer with the domain $\{0, 1\}$ – represents the truth values *false* or *true*. Reified constraints can be used to state logical connectives. For example, the Strasheela user can express: the fact that two notes are simultaneous implies that the pitches of these notes must form a consonant interval (8). As 'isSimultaneous' and 'isConsonant' are both reified constraints, the user can express this implication even when simultaneous notes are undetermined before the search. The scope of the rule implementing (8) are all note pairs which are possibly simultaneous in the solution.

$$(\text{isSimultaneous}(note_1, note_2) \rightarrow \text{isConsonant}(note_1, note_2)) \leftrightarrow true \quad (8)$$

Whether two items are simultaneous or not is formalised by reified constraints on their respective start and end time (9). In an implementation of (9), the validity b is a 0/1-integer. Whether two notes are consonant is formalised in a similar way by reified constraints stating whether the interval between the pitches of two notes is in $\{$minor third, major third, fifth, $\dots$, octave + major third$\}$ (10).

$$((start_1 < end_2) \wedge (start_2 < end_1)) \leftrightarrow b \quad (9)$$

$$(|pitch_1 - pitch_2| \in \{3, 4, 7, 8, 9, 12, 15, 16\}) \leftrightarrow b \quad (10)$$

The rules discussed so far restrict local relations between score objects. However, to specify aspects of the musical form such as motifs and their relations, a rule context may also range over a longer time span. A simple example of this kind is a rule which constrains the musical form to a canon by a pair-wise unification of the note durations and pitches of two voices.

5   Score Distribution Strategies

Constraint problems in Strasheela involve often hundreds or more constrained variables resulting in a huge search space. An efficient search strategy is therefore crucial to make Strasheela useful for a composer.

Oz employs a complete search strategy which is often referred to as *propagate and distribute* [9]. Constraint propagation reduces the variables' domains by removing the values that cannot satisfy the constraints. When no further propagation happens, distribution decides for either some additional constraint on some variable or the complement of that constraint. That way, distribution restarts propagation. An important advantage of the Oz constraint programming model lies in the fact that this decision making process is fully programmable on a high level of abstraction: Oz allows to customise the search strategy according to the constraint problem.

Strasheela adapts this high-level means to define distribution strategies provided by Oz; the Strasheela user can easily define strategies to distribute score parameters. Such a distribution strategy has access to the whole score via each parameter, because the relations between an item and its parameters as well as a container and its contained items are bidirectional linked in the score representation. A distribution strategy aims to help constraint propagators to reduce the search space. To this end, a score distribution strategy often addresses with special care undetermined rule contexts. For instance, the constraints of a harmonic rule can only propagate and reduce the domain of note pitches after it is known which notes are simultaneous.

A few score distribution strategies are already predefined. A typical strategy first determines timing parameters, or determines parameters 'from left to right', that is in increasing order of the start times of their respective items. The latter strategy is explained in more detail in [17].

A distribution strategy not only effects efficiency. Also heuristics can be defined by distribution strategies, as the distribution strategy affects the order in which solutions are found. For instance, particularly useful for musical purposes are heuristics in which the distribution randomly decides in favour of a particular domain value.

6   The Canon Example

The above-mentioned rules established the starting point for a composer who extended the canon (Fig. 6) description to about 15 rules, many of which are inspired by [8].[2] The conjunction of all rules results in a complex search problem; the solution shown below is found in about 20 seconds (first solution found with a distribution strategy involving random on a 2GHz PC). However, a solution is found in only a single second in case some rule is excluded. Strasheela solutions can be output into several formats. Currently, the sound synthesis languages

---

[2] The composer controlled the rhythm (the canon starts and ends with long notes and note durations may change only slowly across a voice). She adjusted the melodic rules (only notes in c-major are allowed, the first and last pitch of the lower voice must be the fundamental, only jumps up a minor third are permitted) and extended the harmonic rule by voice-leading rules (passing notes are allowed, open parallels are not). The canon is changed into a canon in the fifth of the first n notes ($n = 10$ in Fig. 6). Perhaps the most important extension are rules which control the melodic contour, for example, which force the maximum and minimum pitch of each voice to occur only once.

Csound [18], SuperCollider [19], Common Lisp Music (CLM) [20], and the music notation software LilyPond [21] are supported.

Fig. 6. A canon example which applies about 15 rules

7   Related Work

Many constraint based CAC environments have been proposed [2, 3, 4, 5, 6]. This section discusses the Oz application COMPOzE and the environment PWConstraints.

7.1   COMPOzE

The composition system COMPOzE [22] generates a sequence of four-note chords to accompany multimedia presentations. The system expects as input a symbolic musical plan which consists of a harmonic progression and additional information. The harmonic progression is represented by harmonic functions in the tradition of the music theorist Hugo Riemann (e.g. $T s_3 D^7 T$). Additional information is used to restrict movements of single voices (e.g. "soprano melody shall move downward"). Besides this musical plan, COMPOzE's chord sequence output follows further compositional rules which are defined by the system and implement standard textbook rules on harmony.

COMPOzE represents music as a sequence of chords. Each chord consists of four notes and each note is represented by a FD integer denoting the pitch. The harmonic functions, voice movement restrictions and compositional rules are formulated as constraints on these pitches.

COMPOzE and Strasheela clearly have different goals. COMPOzE, on the one hand, formalises a certain sub-task of traditional music composition. COMPOzE solely constrains note pitches. The COMPOzE user adjusts the arguments of a predefined set of compositional rules applicable to four-voiced music.

Strasheela, on the other hand, does not predefine any general musical laws. Instead, Strasheela aims to provide the composer with a general tool to describe her own music by programming compositional rules from scratch. Strasheela offers means to represent and constrain music that is far more complex than a four-voiced chord progression. In particular, Strasheela supports polyphonic music where voices containing items such as notes, or chords run in parallel. More complex music is represented by further nesting of sequential and simultaneous containers. Besides note pitches, the whole timing structure and arbitrary additional parameters are constrainable.

7.2   PWConstraints and Score-PMC

PWConstraints [2, 6] is a library of the graphical programming language and CAC environment PatchWork [2]. PWConstraints consists of two main layers: a general constraint programming language (PMC) and an extension with special support for polyphonic music (Score-PMC). The Score-PMC user prepares in advance an arbitrary complex score to determine the rhythmic structure of the final result. She defines compositional rules which constrain score parameter relations (e.g. $7 \geq |\text{pitch}(note_1) - \text{pitch}(note_2)|$). The user states the scope of each rule with a pattern matching expression (e.g. a pattern like $[* \ note_1 \ note_2]$ applies a rule to all consecutive note pairs in the score). Within the rule definition, the user often accesses some score context (e.g. the pitches of simultaneous notes). PatchWork and PWConstraints are implemented in Common Lisp.

When I designed Strasheela, Score-PMC was one of the models I had in mind: Strasheela aims at being more general than Score-PMC without loosing efficiency. Important differences between the two environments are due to the differences of their underlying constraint solvers. PWConstraints, on the one hand, applies backtracking (with optional refinements such as forward checking or backjumping): a constraint checks the validity of constrained variables only *after* they are determined.[3] During search, the variables are determined in an order which was fixed before the search started. In Oz, on the other hand, constraint propagators prune the domains of constrained variables *before* their values are determined. During search, the distributor decides which variable to visit next only when it actually happens.

The Score-PMC user must fully predetermine the rhythmic structure of a score before the search starts. The program needs this information to deduce its static search order. Strasheela is more general: parameters which determine the rhythmic structure are constrainable like all other parameters. The Strasheela user may freely mix rhythmic rules with rules on, for instance, pitches, and rules which interrelate timing parameters and pitches. Score distribution strategies still allow an efficient search.

In the general language PMC, the domains of constrained variables consist of arbitrary data (e.g. ratios representing microtonal frequency proportions or nested lists representing whole musical sections). As constraints are only applied to determined variables, any Lisp function returning a boolean can serve as a constraint. In this respect, Oz is less expressive for the sake of efficiency. Constrained variables are quasi typed (e.g. FD integers or finite sets) and only specially defined propagators can constrain variables.

Score-PMC predefines several context accessors, but its design does not allow the user to define her own accessors. For example, to create a canon the user would wish to define an accessor for note sets which hold the same position in different voices, as this context is not predefined by Score-PMC. The pattern matching mechanism of Score-PMC to define the scope of a rule is convenient

---

[3] Forward checking rules complicate the situation, but most PWConstraints programs use plain backtracking.

mainly for melodic rules where notes occur in a sequential order. The Score-PMC user can not extend or change this mechanism, non-melodic rules are only expressible with the help of context accessors. Strasheela, however, allows the user to freely define new score accessors. The Strasheela user defines the scope of a rule by an arbitrary control structure. She could, for example, define her own pattern matching mechanism.

The polyphonic music representation of Score-PMC has a fixed hierarchic structure and a fixed set of score object types. In Strasheela, the hierarchic nesting is user defined and the class hierarchy is user extendable.

8   Discussion

The present paper argued that the Oz programming language is a highly suitable foundation for a computer aided composition (CAC) environment. The text introduced Strasheela, a composition environment implemented in Oz. Strasheela's design was outlined and the usage was shown in an application example.

Nonetheless, Strasheela is limited in some ways. Strasheela does not support arbitrary compositional rules, only score parameters are constrainable. In particular, the musical form is not freely constrainable as the hierarchic nesting of score containers and events must be fully determined before search. However, Strasheela allows to constrain the number of elements in a container by a 'trick': events with the duration 0 may be considered as non-existing.

Complex rhythms (e.g. nested tuplets) or complex microtonal music is best represented using fractions or real numbers for parameter values. The extendable Oz constraint model does support real-interval constraints. However, much more constraints are predefined for finite domain (FD) non-negative integers in Oz. Therefore, the predefined timing constraints (1) to (6) as well as related score API methods such as 'isSimultaneous' (9) are defined for FD integers and consequently the values of all timing parameters (i.e. all offset times, start times, durations and end times) are restricted to non-negative integers. As offset times are non-negative, they can only express pauses before items and not the overlapping of items.

Composers often want to formulate merely a preference instead of defining a strict rule. For instance, a composer might prefer small melodic intervals but still allow larger intervals. Also, composers wish to grade the importance of compositional rules such that less important rules might be neglected in an overconstraint situation. The Strasheela user may specify rule sets which allow the violation of rules a certain number of times or in certain situations using reified constraints. Also preferences (optionally graded in importance) can be expressed using best solution search: after a solution is found, further solutions are constrained to be better according to some user defined criterion. However, best solution search is often less efficient than searching for a single strict solution.

The score representation of Strasheela is rich and explicit. For instance, for every timed score item Strasheela introduces variables and propagators for four timing parameters. On the one hand, such an explicit representation makes a score description very convenient. For instance, both the definition of a rhythmical rule constraining item durations and a relation such as 'isSimultaneous' which constrains start and end times are straightforward. On the other hand, this rich representation causes the search script to consume much memory during search. Nevertheless, the Strasheela user may use recomputation – a technique which substitutes computer memory for computation time – to solve problems which would not fit into the available memory otherwise.

Despite these shortcomings, Strasheela realises a highly expressive CAC environment. The present paper explained how Strasheela represents a score, how the composer defines compositional rules and how she applies them to the score. Compositional rules can restrict many aspects of the music including the rhythmic structure, the melodic structure and the harmonic structure. Strasheela combines this expressivity with an efficient search strategy.

Acknowledgements

I am grateful to Mikael Laurson, Tobias Müller, Örjan Sandred, Chris Share as well as three anonymous reviewers for many comments on this text. I wish to thank the Oz community: many of my questions related to the present research were answered on the Oz mailing-list. This research was funded by a Support Programme for University Research (SPUR) studentship at Queen's University Belfast.

References

1. Roads, C.: The Computer Music Tutorial. MIT press (1996)
2. Laurson, M.: Patchwork. A Visual Programming Language and Some Musical Applications. PhD thesis, Sibelius Academy (1996)
3. Anders, T.: Arno: Constraints Programming in Common Music. In: Proceedings of the 2000 International Computer Music Conference. (2000)
4. Truchet, C., Assayag, G., Codognet, P.: OMClouds, a heuristic solver for musical constraints. In: MIC2003: The Fifth Metaheuristics International Conference. (2003)
5. Sandred, O.: OpenMusic. RC library Tutorial. (2000)
6. Rueda, C., Lindberg, M., Laurson, M., Block, G., Assayag, G.: Integrating Constraint Programming in Visual Musical Composition Languages. In: ECAI 98 Workshop on Constraints for Artistic Applications, Brighton (1998)
7. van Roy, P., Haridi, S.: Concepts, Techniques, and Models of Computer Programming. MIT Press (2004)
8. Motte, D.d.l.: Kontrapunkt. Bärenreiter-Verlag (1981)
9. Schulte, C., Smolka, G.: Finite Domain Constraint Programming in Oz. A Tutorial. (2004)
10. Selfridge-Field, E., ed.: Beyond MIDI. The Handbook of Musical Codes. MIT press (1997)
11. Dannenberg, R.B.: Music Representation Issues, Techniques, and Systems. Computer Music Journal **17(3)** (1993)

12. Wiggins, G., Miranda, E., Smaill, A., Harris, M.: Surveying Musical Representation Systems: A Framework for Evaluation. Computer Music Journal **17(3)** (1993)
13. Desain, P., Honing, H.: CLOSe to the edge? Advanced object oriented techniques in the representation of musical knowledge. Journal of New Music Research **2** (1997)
14. Dannenberg, R.B.: The Canon Score Language. Computer Music Journal (1989)
15. Dannenberg, R.B., Desain, P., Honing, H.: Programming language design for music. In Poli, G.D., Picialli, A., Pope, S.T., Roads, C., eds.: Musical Signal Processing. Lisse: Swets & Zeitlinger (1997)
16. Müller, T.: Problem Solving with Finite Set Constraints in Oz. A Tutorial. (2004)
17. Anders, T.: A wizard's aid: efficient music constraint programming with Oz. In: Proceedings of the 2002 International Computer Music Conference. (2002)
18. Boulanger, R., ed.: The Csound Book. Perspectives in Software Synthesis, Sound Desing, Signal Processing, and Programming. The MIT Press (2000)
19. McCartney, J.: Rethinking the Computer Music Language: SuperCollider. Computer Music Journal **26(4)** (2002)
20. Schottstaedt, B.: CLM. (`http://ccrma-www.stanford.edu/software/clm/`)
21. Nienhuys, H.W., Nieuwenhuizen, J.: LilyPond . . . music notation for everyone. (`http://lilypond.org/`)
22. Henz, M., Lauer, S., Zimmermann, D.: COMPOzE — intention-based music composition through constraint programming. In: Proceedings of the 8th IEEE International Conference on Tools with Artificial Intelligence. (1996)

Solving the Aircraft Sequencing Problem Using Concurrent Constraint Programming*

Juan Francisco Díaz and Javier Andrés Mena

Universidad del Valle, Cali, Colombia
Escuela de Ingeniería de Sistemas y Computación
{jdiaz, javimena}@univalle.edu.co
http://eisc.univalle.edu.co/

Abstract. In this paper we describe an application that solves the problem of aircraft sequencing in airports using a single runway. In this problem, the air traffic controller must compute a landing (take off) time for each plane in the *horizon* or airport. The cost is associated with the difference between the plane preferred time (for landing or taking off) and the time assigned to it. There is also a minimum separation time between planes that must be respected to avoid accidents. We have implemented an application using *Mozart* with finite domain constraints, GUIs to interact with the user, and a propagator with a simple, but very helpful operation to cut domains. The basis of the application is the engine that implements the model of the problem; it is easily extensible through the implementation of new distributors. This paper shows how the powerful features of *Mozart* could be exploited to implement practical applications.

1   Introduction

Upon entering within the radar range (radar horizon) of air traffic control (ATC) at an airport, a plane requires ATC to assign it a *landing time*, sometimes known as the *broadcast time* and also, if more than one runway is in use, assign it a runway to land.

The landing time must lie within a specified time window, bounded by an earliest time and a latest time, these times being different for different planes. The earliest time represents the earliest a plane can land if it flies at its maximum airspeed. The latest time represents the latest a plane can land if it flies at its most fuel efficient airspeed whilst holding (circling) for the maximum allowed time.

Each plane has a most economical, preferred speed, referred to as the cruise speed. The *preferred* or *target* time of a plane is the time it would land if it is required to fly at cruise speed. If ATC requires the plane to either slow down, hold or speed up, a *cost* will be incurred. This *cost* will grow as the difference between the assigned landing time and the target landing time grows.

---

* This work is supported in part by grant 298-2002 from Colciencias.

P. Van Roy (Ed.): MOZ 2004, LNCS 3389, pp. 292–304, 2005.

The time between a particular plane landing and the landing of any successive plane must be greater than a specified minimum (*separation time*) which is dependent on the planes involved.

Separation times depend on aerodynamic considerations. A Boeing 747, for example, generates a great deal of air turbulence (*wake vortices*) and a plane flying too close behind could lose aerodynamic stability. Indeed a number of aircraft accidents are believed to have been caused by this phenomena [7]. For safety reasons, therefore, landing a Boeing 747 necessitates a (relatively) larger time delay before other planes can land. A light plane, by contrast, generates little air turbulence; therefore, landing such a plane necessitates only a (relatively) small time delay before other planes can land. Planes taking off impose similar restrictions on successive operations, so we will only consider the landing case.

In this paper we describe a concurrent constraint programming application for solving the Aircraft Sequencing Problem (ASP) with only one runway. The ASP is about scheduling efficiently the landing (take off) times of planes at an airport, finding the solution at the minimum *cost*.

This application was developed in the context of the CRISOL[1] project; one of its aims is to build CCP performant applications for real-world problems. As our programming language we choose *Mozart* ([11]).

The rest of this paper is organized as follows: in section 2 we describe different distribution strategies for the ASP problem, that coupled with the branch and bound *Mozart* engine, allow us to find good solutions (optimal or close to the optimal) in a competitive way. In section 3, we describe one of the main aspects of this application: its architecture. It gives a big flexibility to the user: he can set a few parameters to specify a variety of behaviours of the search engine that allows the user to find the best solution in the time he has. In section 4, we show our first results for generic benchmark instances taken from [2] and for other (pad)instances mentioned in [4]. Finally, in section 5 we present some conclusions and future work.

2   The Implementation in `Mozart`

2.1   The Model

The input data of the problem (where it is assumed that costs grow linearly) is given as follows (where $i, j \in 1..P$):

P is the number of planes.
E_i is the earliest landing time for plane i.
L_i is the latest landing time for plane i.
T_i is the preferred landing time for plane i.
B_i is the cost per time unit for landing before the target time T_i for plane i.
A_i is the cost per time unit for landing after the target time T_i for plane i.
S_{ij} Minimum separation times between planes i and j if i lands before j.

---

[1] Constraints Research and Innovation for Software Solutions.

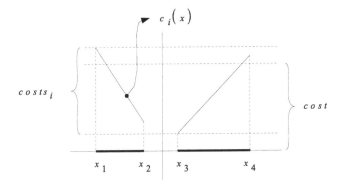

Fig. 1. Reference points for cost propagator and variables $costs_i$ and $cost$ where x_1 is the minimum value in t_i less than T_i, x_2 is the maximum value in t_i less than or equal to T_i, x_3 is the minimum value in t_i greater than or equal to T_i, and x_4 is the maximum value in t_i greater than or equal to T_i

The model used to specify the problem using constraint programming in *Mozart* is obtaining the minimum $cost$, following the constraints below:

$$t_i :: E_i \# L_i \tag{1}$$

$$(t_i + S_{ij} \le t_j \wedge m_{ij} = 0) \vee (t_j + S_{ji} \le t_i \wedge m_{ij} = 1) \tag{2}$$

$$cost = \sum costs_i \tag{3}$$

$$costs_i = c_i(t_i) \tag{4}$$

Where $c_i(x)$, the cost function for plane i landing at time x, is defined as follows (see fig. 1):

$$c_i(x) = \begin{cases} (T_i - x) \times B_i, & \text{if } x \le T_i \\ (x - T_i) \times A_i, & \text{if } x > T_i \end{cases} \tag{5}$$

The first constraint is used to model the fact that plane i must land in its time window. The second constraint models that the separation between every plane must hold. It is obvious that plane i can land before *or* (exclusive) after a plane j. The matrix m encodes a binary relation; if the plane i lands before the plane j then m_{ij} is 0; if the plane i lands after j then m_{ij} is 1. If we cannot assure that plane i must land before or after plane j, m_{ij} is undetermined. This matrix can be used to make some kind of preprocessing of the input data, and impose some redundant constraints. It is also assumed that $m_{ii} = 0$.

Every plane contributes particularly to the total cost of the solution. Plane i has an associated variable called $costs_i$ that is the cost this plane contributes to the total cost of the solution. If plane i lands before its preferred time T_i then the cost of landing plane i before T_i must be calculated using the penalty cost per unit B_i. Something similar occurs when plane i lands after its preferred time. This is modeled in the 3rd and 4th constraints.

Constraints 1, 2 and 3 were implemented directly in *Mozart* using its functions and propagators. Specially, there is a propagator called FD.disjointC that behaves exactly like constraint 2.

Constraint 4 could be implemented in *Mozart* with a thread waiting the value of t_i to be determined. Instead, we have implemented a propagator to take advantage of the additional information the problem provides, cutting the domains of t_i and $costs_i$ variables.

In order to model this problem, serializers and scheduling constraints could be used. However, these constraints are designed for problems in which choosing the minimum value for a variable is the best option. This is not the case of the ASP problem. Here it is probably better to try first some values (for variables) close to the target time.

Another problem when using *Mozart* serializers is that they are designed to set the same amount of time for each resource. This is not true for ASP because the separation time among planes (that is, the time a plane uses the runway) varies depending on the landing order.

2.2   Preprocessing

In [6–Section 5.2] we found some tips for preprocessing the input data; these tips help to know if a plane must land before another in an optimal solution. First, it is obvious that if, for example t_i :: 1#10 and t_j :: 11#20 then i lands before j, no mather the value of S_{ij} or S_{ji}. Note that FD.disjointC takes care of this preprocessing.

Second, if *all* of the following conditions are satisfied, then we can assure that i lands before j (i.e. $i \prec j$):

1. Plane i is earlier than plane j. More precisely $E_i \leq E_j$, $T_i \leq T_j$ and $L_i \leq L_j$.
2. The separation time between planes i and j is not longer than the one between planes j and i, i.e. $S_{ij} \leq S_{ji}$.
3. It is not more expensive (in terms of displacement of planes i and j) to make plane i land before plane j than the opposite. Mathematically speaking: $(A_i \geq A_j$ or $L_i \leq T_j)$ and $(B_i \leq B_j$ or $T_i \leq E_j)$.
4. Reversing the order making plane j land before plane i would not reduce the separation among plane i and other planes. If some third plane k is comparable to both i and j (i.e. $k \prec i, j$ or $i, j \prec k$) then we only need to check the separation in one direction; otherwise we check both. More precisely:

$$\forall k (i, k) \notin U \vee (j, k) \notin U, \quad S_{kj} \geq S_{ki}$$
$$\text{and } \forall k (k, i) \notin U \vee (k, j) \notin U, \quad S_{jk} \geq S_{ik}$$

where $U = \{(i, j) : m_{ij} = 0\}$.

The complexity of this algorithm is $O(n^3)$, but it makes the search of the optimal solution to be faster; however, in some cases it may impose several constraints hard to accomplish, making it harder to find a solution.

2.3   The Cost Propagator

For solving the problem we first tried to implement constraint 4 using the *Mozart* propagators. However, this option did not perform as fast as expected. In addition, in this implementation the use of reified propagators was necessary, but it was not successful because they only worked (reduced domains) when the search was very advanced. That is why we decided to create a propagator to cut domains of variables representing the cost of planes.

This propagator operates over variables t_i and $costs_i$. There are two ways to cut the domains: 1) cutting $costs_i$ based on the information of t_i, and 2) cutting t_i based on the information of $costs_i$.

There are three essential cases for both:

Case A. When $(\min(t_i) < T_i) \wedge (T_i < \max(t_i))$, that is, when the preferred time could be in the solution. In this case we must consider both, the penalty for landing before and the penalty for landing after the preferred time.

Case B. When $\max(t_i) \leq T_i$, that is, when any possible landing time is *before* the preferred time. Here, we only need to consider the penalty for landing before the preferred time.

Case C. When $T_i \leq \min(t_i)$, that is, when any possible landing time is *after* the preferred time. Here, we only need to consider the penalty for landing after the preferred time.

Cutting $costs_i$ Based on the Information of t_i: To carry out this type of propagation, the variable $costs_i$ must be expressed as a function of t_i.

Finding the maximum value of $costs_i$ is easy. For case B, $costs_i \leq c_i(x_1)$ can be imposed. For case C, $costs_i \leq c_i(x_4)$ must be used. For case A we must impose that $costs_i \leq \max(c_i(x_1), c_i(x_4))$.

Similarly, to find the minimum value of $costs_i$, the equations $costs_i \geq c_i(x_2)$ and $costs_i \geq c_i(x_3)$ must be used for cases B and C respectively. For case A we must impose that $costs_i \geq \min(c_i(x_2), c_i(x_3))$.

It is important to find the minimum value of $costs_i$ because it will help to cut branches in the branch and bound method. For example, if there are k planes, whose $costs_i$ variables have a minimum value μ, then $cost \geq k\mu$ must hold. This process is related to constraint (3).

Cutting t_i Based on the Information of $Costs_i$: In this case, t_i must be expressed as a function of $costs_i$.

$$(T_i - t_i) * B_i \leq costs_i \quad \Longleftrightarrow \quad t_i \geq T_i - \frac{costs_i}{B_i} \qquad \text{(for Case B)} \quad (6)$$

$$(t_i - T_i) * A_i \leq costs_i \quad \Longleftrightarrow \quad t_i \leq T_i + \frac{costs_i}{A_i} \qquad \text{(for Case C)} \quad (7)$$

For Case A we can use the equations 6 and 7 together.

Implementation and Stronger Propagation. The implementation has some "parameters" that can be defined in compilation time. The parameters are used because at first glance we do not know how good different propagation methods will be. The first parameter is to know if we want to propagate t_i based on the information of $costs_i$.

The second parameter determines how much of the stronger propagation must be done. There are three levels of stronger propagation:

Level 0 or Normal Propagation. It cuts the domain of t_i based on $costs_i$. It also sets the minimum value of $costs_i$ (if it is possible).

Level 1. It cuts the domain of $costs_i$ reducing its maximum value using the information of t_i.

Level 2. It does the same propagation of Level 1, and also executes the algorithm again if some of the crucial variables (t_i or $costs_i$) are changed.

Activation of these operations slows down the propagation process, but can cut complete branches of the search tree, speeding up the whole search process. We also know that in some cases it is better to search fast than "thinking" very much on how to cut domains. This approach tries to find some (semi)optimal points where propagation reduces domains while maintaining efficiency.

2.4   Distribution Strategies

Before trying to make a new distributor, we first tried to use the default *Mozart* distributors and we found the best performance was reached by the `splitMin` strategy. Although the performance was acceptable, it was not enough. That is why we decided to build our own distribution strategies.

Several distribution strategies have been implemented on t_i variables; the variable *cost* is ignored in all of them. We have built a generic distributor very similar to the *generic* distributor that is defined in `FD.distribute`, but it differs when selecting the value of the variable. Our distributor uses as arguments the number of the plane that we have selected according to the order, as well as variable t_i.

Strategy 1 - Modified Split. This strategy is based on the fact that SplitMin works well. However, we modified it so that it could select the "best half" for each plane time window.

Specifically, the strategy chooses variable t_i with the smallest domain. Then, if $T_i \leq mid(t_i)$ it tries first with $t_i \leq mid(t_i)$; otherwise, it tries with $t_i > mid(t_i)$.

Strategy 2 - Cost Acting as a Linear Function. This strategy tries to take advantage of the following cost propagator property: if all the possible values of plane i are on the left or on the right of T_i then the cost acts as a linear function. Then, the propagator can properly cut the domains and can determine easily and precisely the bounds of $costs_i$.

Choosing the t_i variable to be distributed is done according to an order defined by the following rules:

1. When $S_{ij} < S_{ji}$ (resp. $S_{ji} < S_{ij}$), t_i is better than t_j (resp. t_j is better than t_i).
2. When $S_{ij} = S_{ji}$ then t_i is better than t_j if $B_i + A_i < B_j + A_j$; otherwise t_j is better.

With this strategy, we try to distribute first the variable representing a plane generating the lowest waiting time due to turbulences. Ties are broken choosing the plane variable that seems more costly to move.

The value of the selected variable t_i is chosen in the following way (in order):

1. If the size of t_i is 2 then it takes the element nearest T_i.
2. If $T_i < \min(t_i)$ then it tries first with $t_i \le mid(t_i)$.
3. If $\max(t_i) < T_i$ then it tries first with $t_i > mid(t_i)$.
4. If $T_i \in t_i$ then it tries first with $t_i = T_i$.
5. If $B_i < A_i$ then it tries first with $t_i \le T_i$.
6. It tries with $t_i > T_i$.

The problem of this strategy is that it is not dynamic, that is, the order of the distribution of each variable is determined from the beginning. Then, we can not use new information about the domain of t_i variables as computation evolves.

Strategies 3 & 4 - Higher Penalty Strategy/Higher Expected Cost Strategy. These strategies are based on a greedy technique: when a variable is selected by the order function then it selects the value that implies the minimum local costs, i.e. the minimum $costs_i$. To select a variable, it tries to choose first the variable that seems to be the most expensive, because if we choose it later then the cost could be very high. Since it is very hard to know in the early stages of the search process if a variable is more expensive than other, we have made a very elaborate heuristic.

The heuristic consists of taking two measurements of the t_i variables. [2] One of the measurements is done by means of a function(k) that returns the expected cost of landing plane i in the worst case. The second measurement consists of adding the costs of not landing at the preferred time T_i, but before or after it, that is, adding B_i and A_i.

Using this information, measurements are taken into account in a special order to build strategies 3 and 4. For strategy 3, the variable with the highest adding $Sum_i = B_i + A_i$ between Sum_i and Sum_j is chosen. If they are the same, the variable with the highest k value is chosen. If the k value is the same for both planes, then the variable with the smallest domain is chosen.

Strategy 4 is similar, but it first takes into account the $k(t_i)$ values and then Sum_i values.

---

[2] At first, only one measurement was done but this value was often the same in many variables and hence it did not discriminate which variable was better.

The special cost function $k(t_i)$ is not related to $c_i(x)$, and is defined as follows:

1. Let $X \in t_i$ be the upper element less than T_i.
   Let $Y \in t_i$ be the lower element greater than T_i.
2. If $T_i \in t_i$ then $k(t_i) = 0$, .
3. If $(\min(t_i) < T_i) \wedge (T_i < \max(t_i))$ then
   $k(t_i) = \max((T_i - X) \times B_i, (Y - T_i) \times A_i)$.
4. If $T_i < \min(t_i)$ then $k(t_i) = (Y - T_i) * A_i$.
5. Otherwise, $k(t_i) = (X - T_i) * B_i$.

Once the variable t_i to be distributed is selected, we choose the value nearest T_i.

3   The Application and Its Implementation

The application has three main parts, each one independent from each other:

1. The Graphical User Interfaces (GUIs).
2. The ESASP (Engine for Solving Aircraft Sequencing Problem)
3. The distributors

The GUIs were designed to provide a good environment for solving, comparing, testing and showing the problems, solutions and some application issues. They are not designed only for the user but also for the programmer.

The ESASP is like an ADT that implements all the functions needed for solving the ASP. It consists mainly of the file reader, the definition (not implementation) of the distributors, the search engine and the solver.

The distributors implement the distribution logic for the program according to the explanation in Section 2.4.

3.1   The GUIs

Every time the user presses the Solve button, the program reads the file that contains the problem specification and then starts an execution environment (ESASP) that contains all the parameters the user has selected using the GUI showed in Fig. 2.

Once the ESASP has been initialized, the program shows a GUI like in Fig. 3 that initially shows the problem specification. When the user chooses to search a new solution, the program tries to find a better solution and if one or more solutions are found, then it shows the best of them. More generally there can be 5 types of answers that are showed on the top of the window:

– **No search has been done:** is showed when the user has not made any search.
– **Optimum solution:** is showed when the search tree has been explored totally and in the last search at least one (optimum) solution was found.

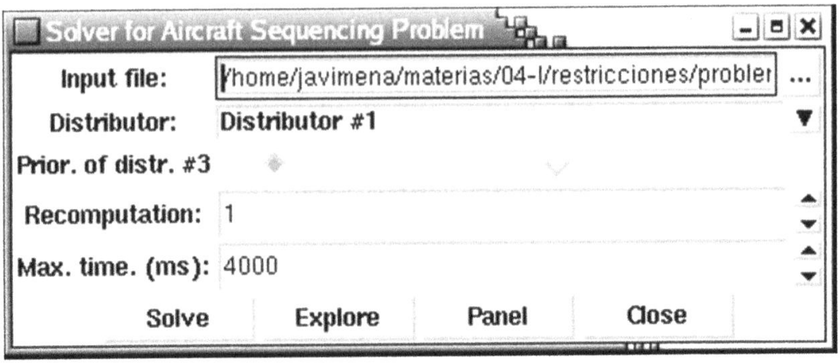

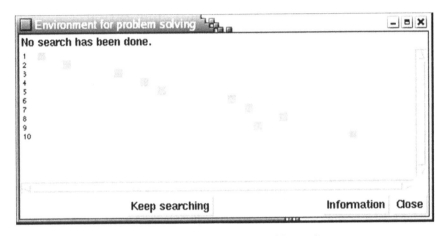

Fig. 2. GUI for configuration and control parameters

Fig. 3. Initial state for the problem solver

- **There are no more solutions:** is showed when the search tree has been explored, but no solution was found in the last search.
- **There has been found** n **better solutions:** is showed when n solutions have been found in the last search, but the search tree has not been explored totally.
- **There has not been found better solutions:** is showed when no solution was found in the last search, but the search tree has not been explored totally.

The program always shows the best solution found, its cost, the total execution time that has been used in the search, and the number of solutions found in the last search (if any).

Maybe the most interesting GUI is the one that handles the "cancelable" search. It is a window that shows the progress of the search. It has a cancel button that executes the StopSearch function (see Fig. 5) when it is pressed, and in another thread it calls the function SearchBestSolution (see Fig. 4) to find the best solution concurrently. This is interesting because its code executes

```
 1 proc {SearchBestSolution Engine NoSearch DeadTime Res?}
 2    proc {SearchNextSolution Found Counter Res?}
 3       if {IsFree NoSearch} then
 4          case {Engine next($)} of [S] then
 5             BestSolution := S
 6             {SearchNextSolution true Counter+1 Res}
 7          [] L then
 8             Res = L#Found#Counter
 9          end
10       else
11          Res = stopped#Found#Counter
12       end
13    end
14    NoStop BestSolution Sol
15 in
16    BestSolution = {NewCell nil}
17    thread Dead in
18       {Alarm DeadTime Dead}
19       {WaitOr Dead NoStop}
20       if {IsDet Dead} then
21          {StopSearch Engine NoSearch}
22       end
23    end
24    Res = {SearchNextSolution false 0}#Sol
25    Sol = @BestSolution
26    NoStop = unit
27 end
```

Fig. 4. The SearchBestSolution function

concurrently using *Mozart* threads, data-flow variables and timers, and the implementation is hidden from the GUI; it simply uses the functions defined by ESASP.

3.2   Engine for Solving the Aircraft Sequencing Problem (ESASP)

The ESASP is basically composed of 3 files: a) a file specification reader, b) an engine that encapsulates the functions of a generic ASP solver, and c) a generic distribution engine that replaces FD.distribute.

The problem of using the generic distributor of FD.distribute is that the call to the value function does not pass all the information we need about the chosen distribution variable. This is a problem for us, because in that function we need to know which variable was selected to choose a sound value properly. For example, when the variable t_i is selected, we need to know i to choose the value nearest T_i.

The real engine uses Search.object as its main search engine because it allows us to stop the search in any moment. The creation of the engine for solving ASP was easy; just a call to a function with the problem specification and some options. In this point it does the preprocessing, creates the specified

```
1 proc {StopSearch Engine NoSearch}
2    NoSearch = unit
3    {Engine stop}
4 end
```

Fig. 5. The StopSearch function

distributor with its parameters and creates a solver using a parameterized script, and a branch and bound constraint that says that the *cost* of a new solution must be better than that of the last solution.

In the earlier versions of the application, the preprocessing (creating the matrix M_{ij}) was done in the script because the boolean parameter received by `FD.disjointC` needed to be a `FD` variable. But this alternative uses a lot of memory, so we decided to make the preprocessing outside the solver, so that every time the space was cloned, only the changing information was cloned.

So, the matrix M_{ij} is created and initialized by the engine creator, and it is passed as argument to the parameterized distributor. In the moment of imposing the constraint (2) it checks if the value in M_{ij} is bound; in that case, it uses `FD.disjointC`. Otherwise (if M_{ij} is free) it uses `FD.disjoint` that does not require the parameter but does the same propagation.

ESASP provides one function called `SearchBestSolution` (see Fig. 4) that can be used to find a solution of any problem that uses `Search.object` with branch and bound. It executes the search unless the user calls the function `StopSearch` (see Fig. 5) or the time specified in `DeadTime` has been elapsed. `NoSearch` is a variable needed to avoid deadlocks; it is defined by the caller as a free variable and is used to communicate the threads that use the functions.

The `SearchBestSolution` function returns a tuple `State#Sol` where `State` is a tuple `S#F#C` containing information about the last search. `Sol` contains the best solution of the last search or `nil` if no solution was found. `S` can be either `stopped` if the search was stopped by the user or `nil` if there are no more solutions. `F` is `true` if solutions have been found in the last search, and `C` is the number of solutions found in the last search.

4   Results

Results are shown in Table 1. We have made all the tests of the application using a Pentium® III at 933 MHz with 256 MB of RAM running Gentoo Linux[TM] 2004.1.

Time for searching solutions for **airland** instances was set to 30 seconds approximately, while for **pad** instances was set to a minute. For each strategy we show the Cost of the Best Solution found (CBS) and the time (given in milliseconds) to find it (TBS). For some instances, the distributor could not find a solution in the elapsed time; we show that by using the symbol "–". For some instances, we don't know which the optimum solution is so we use the symbol "?".

Table 1. Comparison among our strategies

		Strat. #1		Strat. #2		Strat. #3		Strat. #4	
Problem	Optimum	CBS	TBS	CBS	TBS	CBS	TBS	CBS	TBS
airland1	700	700	360	700	260	700	6960	700	470
airland2	1480	1480	2750	1480	3330	2140	10	1720	220
airland3	820	3910	24200	820	5880	1980	50	820	230
airland4	2520	4400	18680	3240	2190	6780	120	3820	14870
airland5	3100	9150	160	4430	50	7620	520	7620	50
airland6	24442	24442	10	24442	10	24442	10	24442	10
airland7	1550	1550	130	1550	890	3974	160	3974	150
airland8	1950	4410	6520	3050	7760	2415	310	1980	5150
airland9	?	20149.97	14020	14951.68	1330	–	–	13432.76	15950
airland10	?	–	–	–	–	–	–	–	–
airland11	?	41341.52	27150	–	–	–	–	32763.05	8650
airland12	?	52226.3	22960	–	–	–	–	39825.21	14470
airland13	?	–	–	–	–	–	–	–	–
pad1	531.6121	531.6121	0	531.6121	20	531.6121	0	531.6121	0
pad2	995.9342	995.9342	12960	995.9342	4870	995.9342	53760	995.9342	790
pad3	2418.12	2886.1932	9730	–	–	2771.7053	36930	2419.3508	67150
pad4	3345.43	–	–	–	–	–	–	–	–
pad5	2424.68	–	–	–	–	–	–	–	–
pad6	3675	7180	23540	–	–	–	–	–	–
pad8	4820	15065	46680	–	–	–	–	–	–
pad10	6605	30610	4750	–	–	–	–	–	–

For **airland** instances, it was relatively easy to find at least one solution but in **pad** instances it was more difficult to find a solution. This might have happened because **airland** instances had a greater time-window for their planes, while in **pad** instances, some time-windows were very small. Also, **pad** instances had many airplanes whose landing times were very close. That could entail the preprocessing to be non-effective.

We cannot conclude that a strategy is better than the others because the results were very diversified. Anyway, we can execute concurrently the ESASP using all the distributors, and we would not have to spend much more time. It would be possible, indeed, to solve the problem using several computers with the distributed system that *Mozart* provides.

5   Conclusions and Future Work

We have shown that using simple problem-dependent distribution strategies is possible to build performant CCP applications for the ASP problem. In this aspect, our results are much better than those shown in [4] for constraint programming, and competitive with those found there using other techniques.

One of the main caveats of using CCP is memory consumption. However, this problem did not stop us from building a feasible application for this problem.

Now we are working in two ways: building more elaborate distribution strategies for the ASP problem, and extending the application for managing more complex ASP-like problems, as ASP with more than one runway as defined in [10].

References

1. Philippe Baptiste, Claude Le Pape, and Wim Nuijten. Incorporating efficient operations research algorithms in constraint-based scheduling. In *1st International Joint Workshop on Artificial Intelligence and Operations Research*, Timberline Lodge, Oregon, 1995.
2. J. E. Beasley. Or-library: distributing problems by electronic mail. *Journal of the Operations Research Society*, 41:1069–1072, 1990.
3. J. E. Beasley, M. Krishnamoorthy, Y. M. Sharaiha, and D. Abramson. Scheduling aircraft landings–the static case. *Transportation Science*, 34(2):180–197, 2000.
4. Torsten Fahle, Rainer Feldmann, Silvia Götz, Sven Grothklags, and Burkhard Monien. The aircraft sequencing problem. In *Computer science in perspective*, pages 152–166. Springer-Verlag New York, Inc., 2003.
5. Gyungwon Jung and Manuel Laguna. Time segmentation heuristic for an aircraft landing problem, March 6 2003.
6. M Krishnamoorthy and A T Ernst. Scheduling aircraft landings optimally. In *Proceedings of the 41st Annual Symposium of AGIFORS*, Sydney, Australia, 27 August – 1 September 2001.
7. J. Mullings. Trails of destruction. New Scientist, 1996.
8. A De Silva, G. Mills, J. Abela, and Krishnamoorthy Krishnamoorthy. Computing optimal schedules for landing aircraft, October 19 1995.
9. Antonio A. Trani, Julio Martinez, Hojong Baik, and Vineet Kamat. A new paradigm to model aircraft operations at airports: The virginia tech airport simulation model (vtasim). NEXTOR Research Symposium, November 13 2000.
10. Pim van Leeuwen, Henk Hesselink, and Jos Rohling. Scheduling aircraft using constraint satisfaction. In Marco Comini and Moreno Falaschi, editors, *Electronic Notes in Theoretical Computer Science*, volume 76. Elsevier, 2002.
11. Peter Van Roy and Seif Haridi. Mozart: A programming system for agent applications. In *International Workshop on Distributed and Internet Programming with Logic and Constraint Languages*, November 1999. Part of International Conference on Logic Programming (ICLP 99).

The Problem of Assigning Evaluators to the Articles Submitted in an Academic Event: A Practical Solution Incorporating Constraint Programming and Heuristics*

B. Jesús Aranda, Juan Francisco Díaz, and V. James Ortíz

Universidad Del Valle, Escuela de Ingeniera de Sistemas y Computacin,
Ciudad Universitaria - Melendez
{jesarana, jdiaz, jaortiz}@univalle.edu.co

Abstract. This article shows a practical solution to *The Problem of Assigning Evaluators to the Articles Submitted in an Academic Event*, a problem of combinatorial optimization. Apart from stating the problem formally and proposing a constraint model, the article describes the heuristics designed to find solutions. The application was developed using *Mozart*; different distribution strategies were implemented based on the already mentioned heuristics. The experimental partial results turned out to be competitive for real problems (180 articles, 25 evaluators).

1 Introduction

An academic event or congress consists of a series of conferences in which different research works or articles, previously referenced and selected by a Program Committee, are presented. These articles may cover different research areas, but they should be related to the main topic of the congress. Each representative of the Program Committee relies on a work group for the process of evaluating those articles.

The Program Committee receives the articles, and according to certain criteria including the strengths of the evaluators and the topics of the articles among others, assigns them for evaluation so that each article is evaluated by the maximum number of evaluators determined by the organizers of the event.

The quality of the solution (understood as the adaptation of it to all the distribution criteria) and the time taken to estimate it are critical aspects of the process. The first one minimizes the task of reassigning evaluators when they are not satisfied with the article assigned. The latter makes things easier for the Program Committee since it depends on time to test different solutions and choose the best one in quality. In the case of the organization of the Conferencia Latinoamericana de Informática (Latin American computing conference) of the

---

* This work is supported in part by grant 298-2002 from Colciencias.

P. Van Roy (Ed.): MOZ 2004, LNCS 3389, pp. 305–316, 2005.

CLEI [1], this process can take approximately three days and the solution found produces dissatisfaction among evaluators.

Therefore, it is interesting to have an application that allows us to find a solution that maximizes its quality (that is, a solution that minimizes the number of inconsistencies between assignation criteria and the real solution) as quickly as possible.

Based on what was previously stated, the design and construction of such an application was proposed. This application was developed using the Constraint Programming paradigm and the **Oz** language. As expected, the application of general mechanisms to find solutions was not very useful in real size entries. For that reason, problem-dependent mechanisms were designed and implemented. More specifically, different distribution strategies based on heuristics designed especially for the problem were implemented.

This article presents a formal description of the problem (Section 2), the most appropriate constraint model that we have found up to now (Section 3) and the heuristics designed to orientate the distribution strategies (Section 4). Finally, the results obtained (Section 5), a global description of the application architecture (Section 6) and the conclusions (Section 7) are presented.

2   Description of the Problem

According to the organizers of the **CLEI**, the process of distributing articles takes from 3 to 4 days. This is true for an entry of approximately 300 articles, 80 evaluators and 3 evaluations per article. The greatest difficulty lies in assigning enough evaluators to each of the articles complying with certain constraints the event involves (those constraints will be described later.) Most of the times, the article distribution results in many article assignations that do not comply with the constraints.

Considering that, the organization of the **CLEI** 2005 event, which will be held in Colombia in 2005, needs an application that supports the article distribution process, aiming to reduce the time the process takes and minimize the number of assignations that do not comply with the constraints set for the event.

The entry for the article distribution process in the academic event of the **CLEI** consists of the following data:

- **A set of articles or works:** The quantity of articles sent to an event as **CLEI** 2005 is approximately 300 from which the articles that will be presented in the conferences are selected.
- **The number of evaluations per article:** An article is reviewed by 3 evaluators; therefore, if there are 300 articles for the event, 900 evaluations would be necessary, and they would be done by the evaluators of the program committee.
- **A group of evaluators:** They are the program committee. Events as **CLEI** 2005 usually have, more or less, 80 members.

---

[1] Centro Latinoamericano de Estudios en Informática.

- **A set of constraints:** They are the requirements that should be met in any assignation of the articles received.

The constraints that should be taken into account when distributing the articles are:

- **Constraint 1** : The number of evaluations per article must be higher than or the same as the minimum required.
- **Constraint 2**: The number of evaluations per article must be less than or the same as the maximum required.
- **Constraint 3**: The number of articles assigned to each evaluator must be less than or the same as his capacity.
- **Constraint 4**: For each article, each of the evaluations should be done by a different evaluator.
- **Constraint 5**: The article's country must be different from the evaluator's country.
- **Constraint 6**: At least one of the main topics of the paper must coincide with a preferred topic stated by each one of the assigned evaluators.
- **Constraint 7**: The language of the paper must coincide with one of the languages each assigned evaluator masters.

The idea is minimizing the number of assignments that do not comply with the previous constraints during the assignment process. When it is not possible to assign an article complying with all the preferences, it is assigned considering the most important constraints, complying just with some of them. The organizers of the event may also consider that some preferences are mandatory and, therefore, a total distribution may not be achieved. In that case, the missing assignments are analyzed by the organizers of the event in order to find a solution.

Our application considers the factors mentioned, providing a solution to the distribution process.

3   Constraint Model of the Problem

The model developed to solve the problem is presented below.

- **Parameters**
  - m : Number of evaluators.
  - n : Number of articles
  - nT : Number of topics of the event
  - $minEP$: Minimum number of evaluators per article.
  - $maxEP$: Maximum number of evaluators per article.
  - cP_i : The country of article i, $\forall i = 1, \ldots, n$.
  - sP_i : The set of topics of article i, $\forall i = 1, \ldots, n$.
  - lP_i : The language in which the article i, is written $\forall i = 1, \ldots, n$.
  - cE_j : The country of evaluator j, $\forall j = 1, \ldots, m$.
  - sE_j : The set of topics the evaluator j masters, $\forall j = 1, \ldots, m$.

- lE_j : The set of languages in which evaluator j is willing to evaluate, $\forall j = 1, \ldots, m$.
- $capE_j$: The number of evaluations evaluator j is willing to do, $\forall j = 1, \ldots, m$.

- **Decision variables**
  - $dom_{i,k} = \begin{cases} j \text{ if the } k\text{-th evaluation of the article } i \text{ is assigned to evaluator } j, \\ 0 \text{ if no evaluator could be assigned} \end{cases}$
    $\forall i = 1, \ldots, n, \ k = 1, \ldots, maxEP$
  - c : Total number of evaluations assigned, in which $n * minEP \leq c \leq n * maxEP$.

- **Objective function**
  - $Maximizing \ c = |\{(i, k) : dom_{i,k} \neq 0, 1 \leq i \leq n, 1 \leq k \leq maxEP\}|$

- **Constraints**

  - Constraint 1:
    $$minEP \leq |\{(i, k) : dom_{i,k} \neq 0, 1 \leq k \leq maxEP\}|, \quad \forall i = 1, \ldots, n$$

  - Constraint 2:
    $$maxEP \geq |\{(i, k) : dom_{i,k} \neq 0, 1 \leq k \leq maxEP\}|, \quad \forall i = 1, \ldots, n$$

  - Constraint 3:
    $$capE_j \geq |\{(i, k); dom_{i,k} = j, 1 \leq i \leq n, 1 \leq k \leq maxEP\}|,$$
    $$\forall j = 1, \ldots, m$$

  - Constraint 4:
    $$(dom_{i,k_1} = dom_{i,k_2} = 0) \vee (dom_{i,k_1} > dom_{i,k_2}),$$
    $$\forall i = 1, \ldots, n, \quad \forall k_1, k_2 : 1 \leq k_1 < k_2 \leq maxEP$$

  - Constraint 5:
    $$\forall i = 1, \ldots, n \ \forall j = 1, \ldots, m$$
    $$[cP_i = cE_j \rightarrow (\ \forall 1 \leq k \leq maxEP : dom_{i,k} \neq j)]$$

  - Constraint 6:
    $$\forall i = 1, \ldots, n \ \forall j = 1, \ldots, m$$
    $$[sP_i \cap sE_j = \emptyset \rightarrow (\forall 1 \leq k \leq maxEP : dom_{i,k} \neq j)]$$

  - Constraint 7:
    $$\forall i = 1, \ldots, n \ \forall j = 1, \ldots, m$$
    $$[lP_i \notin lE_j \rightarrow (\forall 1 \leq k \leq maxEP : dom_{i,k} \neq j)]$$

4 Heuristics Designed to Orientate the Distribution Strategies

One of the most important factors that influences efficiency on the application is the distribution strategy. Usually, the distribution strategy is defined based on a variable sequence. When distribution is needed, the strategy selects one of the non-determined variables present in the sequence and distributes based on that variable.

Distribution strategies can be classified as follows:

- **Generic distribution strategies:** These are general strategies that do not depend on the problem and are defined in **Mozart** programming system. Some of them are: **first-fail** and **naive**.
- **Problem-specific distribution strategies:** In these strategies the programmer sets criteria to select the variables that will be distributed and their corresponding value. The criteria used in the strategy depend on the characteristics of the problem in order to speed up the distribution process.

In the development of our application, we used generic and problem-specific strategies. The results obtained with both kinds of strategies are presented later.

Problem-specific distribution strategies were implemented based on the following heuristics.

4.1 Heuristics in Variable Selection

In our problem, the variables to be distributed are the *article evaluations* $(dom_{i,k})$ and their values correspond to the assigned evaluator. In a solution, we expect all the variables to have an assigned value.

The selection of variables to be distributed was made using two heuristic functions:

- Heuristic function based on the *comfort* of the evaluators
- Heuristic function based on the *topics* of the article

Using those functions we expect to have an indicator of the difficulty to assign a value to each variable. With this information, the most difficult variable is selected.

Heuristic Function Based on the Comfort of the Evaluators. The comfort of the evaluator regarding a partial assignment is defined as the number of evaluations that he may still be assigned. The comfort of each evaluator is calculated dynamically as the difference between the maximum number of evaluations that he is able to do (cME_j) and the number of evaluations assigned in the partial assignment (cUE_j):

$$hEvaluator_j = cME_j - cUE_j,$$
$$\forall j = 1, \ldots, m.$$

Based on that, the $hComfort$ function is defined for each article as the addition of comforts of each of the possible evaluators of the article:

$$hComfort_i = \sum_{j:sP_i \cap sE_j \neq \emptyset} hEvaluator_j,$$

$$lP_i \in lE_j,$$

$$cP_i \neq cE_j,$$

$$j \neq dom_{i,k},$$

$$\forall k = 1, \ldots maxEP,$$

$$\forall i = 1 \ldots n,$$

Based on the values obtained by applying the heuristic function for each article, we choose to distribute one of the $dom_{i,k}$ variables of article i with the lowest $hComfort_i$ value. Intuitively, that means that we choose to distribute a variable representing that paper posing the greatest difficulty for finding a suitable reviewer.

Heuristic Function Based on the Topics of the Article. Again, the idea here is "calculating" the difficulty of evaluating an article. In this case, the heuristics that calculates the difficulty of evaluating article i is directly related to the main topics of the article.

Given any topic, t, its competitiveness ($cSubject_t$) is defined regarding a partial assignation of evaluators, as the difference between the remaining evaluators capacity for topic t ($oSubject_t$) and the number of article evaluations containing topic t that are still to be assigned ($dSubject_t$).

More exactly,

$$cSubject_t = oSubject_t - dSubject_t,$$

in which

$$oSubject_t = \sum_{j:1 \leq j \leq m, \{t\} \cap Subjects(Evaluator_j) \neq \emptyset} cME_j - cUE_j,$$

and

$$dSubject_t = \sum_{i:1 \leq j \leq n, \{t\} \cap Subjects(Article_i) \neq \emptyset} eN_i,$$

being eN_i the number of evaluations of article i still to be assigned (according to the current partial assignation).

The idea here is "estimating" the difficulty of evaluating an article($hSubject_i$). In this case, the heuristics that calculates the difficulty of evaluating article i is directly related to the main topics of the article:

$$hSubject_i = \sum_{t \in Subjects(Article_i)} cSubject_t,$$

Intuitively, $hSubject_i$ measures what our capacity to assign a reviewer to paper i is, given its main topics. We choose the variable with the lowest $hSubject_i$ value.

4.2 Heuristics When Choosing the Variable Value

Suppose that $dom_{i,k}$ is the variable chosen for distribution. And let $\{j_1, j_2, \ldots, j_{m_i}\}$ be the set of possible evaluators for article i. The j_l value that is first chosen for the $dom_{i,k}$ variable is the one that corresponds to the evaluator with more comfort in that moment:

$$hEvaluator_{j_l} \geq hEvaluator_{j_s} \forall s = 1, \ldots, m_i.$$

5 Results Obtained

Below we present the results obtained for problems of different sizes and using both models, but always the same set of data (taken from **CLEI** 1996).

In table 1, for each instance of the problem and for each distribution strategy, we show times (in seconds) obtained searching the first partial solution (using **searchOne**), number of non assignments **nns** (that is, the number of evaluations without an evaluator assigned at the end of the running) and its rate with respect to the total number of assignments required **nra** ($nra = n * maxEP$). Columns **ffs,hhbs,chbs** show results for the standard strategy (first-fail) and the two strategies that use heuristics based on the comfort of the evaluator and the heuristics based on the topics of the article, to select the variables. In both heuristic strategies the same function is used (based on the comfort of the evaluators) to choose the value of the variable to be distributed.

As it can be seen in the table above, the application performance in terms of efficiency in time and quality of the solution is better when using distribution strategies with heuristics.

However, it can not be said that one of the heuristics strategies is better than the other. And in terms of optimal solutions, it can not also be said that the solution found is always the optimum.

Table 1. Solution obtained for CLEI96 problem

Input Size		ffs			hhbs			chbs			nra
n	m	time	nns	%nns	time	nns	%nns	time	nns	%nns	
50	10	1	32	21.33	1	32	21.33	1.5	32	21.33	150
90	12	3	37	13.7	2	34	12.59	4	34	12.59	270
90	25	3	9	3.33	3	9	3.33	5	9	3.33	270
100	15	5	44	14.66	4	26	8.66	6	26	8.66	300
150	20	9	47	10.44	9	23	5.11	11	25	5.55	450
180	12	14	225	41.66	10	224	41.48	13	224	41.48	540
180	20	26	77	14.26	22	63	11.66	18	54	10	540
180	25	40	37	6.85	30	21	3.88	31	19	3.51	540

6   The Application

The name of the application created is CREAR. It is based on the model and strategies described above. Its architecture can be seen in Figure 1.

Three levels can be observed there:

- Presentation Level: It includes all functionalities that allow interaction between the program and the user.
- Application Level: It includes the program control and the main functionalities of the tool.
- Persistence or Storage Level: It includes the input and output files and the functionalities that allow their communication with the program.

In developing CREAR, besides **Oz** language, **Java** programming language was used, mainly at the presentation level. The description of each level is presented below.

Presentation Level. It includes the input reading and the presentation of results. It has the following modules:

- Data Capture Module: It includes the functionalities that allow to select input data, decide where to store output data, the constraints to be applied and the strategies that will be used to find the solution.

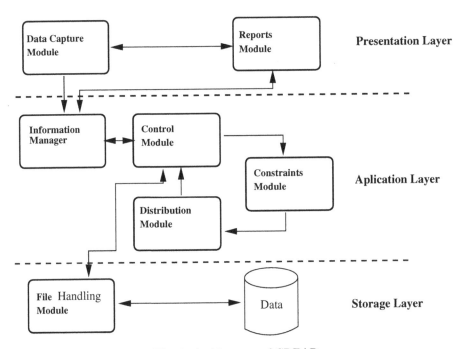

Fig. 1. Architecture of CREAR

- Report Module: It includes the functionalities that allow the program to show reports with statistics and interesting data of the solution found. These reports are fundamental for the organization of the event since, based on them, a final analysis which aims to lead to a better solution is done.

Application Level. It is here where solutions are to be found. It includes the following modules:

- Information Agent: It includes the functionalities that allow the communication between the interface and the driving force of the application so that they can work jointly.
- Control Module: It includes the functionalities that allow to ensure the system's integrity basically in the process of finding a solution.
- Distribution Module: It includes the different strategies that can be used to find the solution.
- Constraints Module: It includes all constraints to be considered.

Persistence Level. At this level, input and output data are stored.

- File Handling Module: It includes the functionalities that allow to read the input data of the problem and create the file with the solution.

6.1   Flexibility of Constraints

One of the most important characteristics of the application is the flexibility for imposing constraints.

Since in the problem entries are naturally over-constrained, the system lets the user choose the constraints he wishes to apply. The constraints that the user can choose are the following:

- Capacity Constraint: The number of articles to be evaluated must not exceed the capacity of the evaluator.
- Language Constraint: The language of the article must be one of the languages mastered by the evaluator.
- Country Constraint: The country of the main author of the article and of the evaluator must not be the same.

It should be observed that topic constraint is not optional since it is not convenient that an evaluator reviews a topic that he does not master.

6.2   Step by Step Solution

Another distinctive characteristic of the application lies in the possibility to find an incremental solution which disqualifies constraints as the solution is coming near.

To do that, the system allows to handle up to four steps as follows:

1. The system searches for a solution that meets the constraints chosen by the user. At the end, there may be still evaluations without an evaluator assigned.
2. The system considers those assignations that could not be done in the previous step and tries to do them taking into account the constraints chosen at that moment; generally these constraints are less than the ones in the previous step. At the end, there may be still evaluations without an evaluator assigned. This step can be repeated up to three times.

At the end of all steps it is possible that there may be not enough evaluations assigned to some of the articles; however, the system makes this number to be fairly reduced.

It is important to underline that the user may choose the number of steps and the constraints to be taken into account in each of them.

6.3   The Interface

The interface offers great flexibility to the user. It allows him to chose the constraints, steps, and the strategies to find the solution.

First of all, the interface lets the user determine the file with the input data of the problem and where the solution is to be stored. Based on what was previously said, the user can choose the strategy he wants to use to find the solution among the strategies described in Section 4.

After that, the system asks which constraints are to be applied (see Figure 2). Once the user has chosen them, he has to determine how many later stages will be tried (maximum 3), and which constraints are to be considered in each of them with a similar interface.

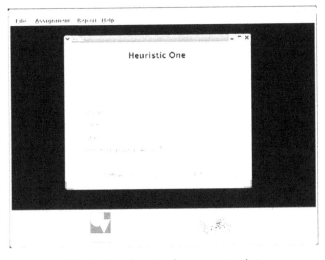

Fig. 2. Interface to choose constraints

Reports Evaluator X Capacity

	Evaluator's Name	Evaluator's Country	Real Capacity	Used Capacity	A\
Eval: 1	Jorge Santos	Arg	20	7	13
Eval: 2	Gustavo Rossi	Arg	30	26	4
Eval: 3	Claudia Bauzer	Bra	30	25	5
Eval: 4	Carlos Heuser	Bra	30	24	6
Eval: 5	Ana Salgado	Bra	30	24	6
Eval: 6	Vera Lima	Bra	30	24	6
Eval: 7	Ricardo Baeza	Chi	30	26	4
Eval: 8	Leopoldo Bertossi	Chi	30	26	4
Eval: 9	Christian Trefftz	Col	30	31	-1
Eval: 10	Tiberio Hernandez	Col	80	11	69
Eval: 11	Juan Francisco Diaz	Col	30	27	3
Eval: 12	Camilo Rueda	Col	20	15	5
Eval: 13	Claudia Roncancio	Ext	20	15	5
Eval: 14	Ignacio Trejos	Ext	30	29	1
Eval: 15	Ramon Puigjaner	Ext	30	26	4
Eval: 16	Jose Neira	Ext	20	14	6
Eval: 17	Marcelo Mejia	Ext	30	26	4
Eval: 18	Luis Trejo	Ext	30	26	4
Eval: 19	Manuel Ibarra	Ext	20	15	5
Eval: 20	Benjamin Baran	Par	10	2	8
Eval: 21	Adolfo Steiger	Ext	20	14	6

Print >>   Exit

Fig. 3. Report 1

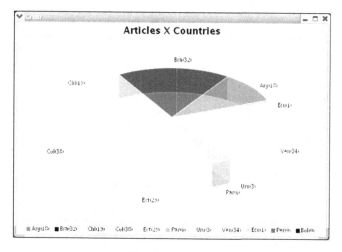

Fig. 4. Report 2

Once the solution is calculated, the system offers different options of reports, which are shown in Figure 3 and 4.

7   Conclusions and Further Works

This work shows the expressiveness of the CCP paradigm and the versatility of a programming language like **Oz** in developing applications that solve combinatorial optimization problems. Particularly, the ability to handle flexible constraints and to handle partial values was very important for building a flexible application with the ability to handle over-constrained problems and to perform iterative refinements of potential solutions.

Defining specific heuristics for the problem and the implementation of distribution strategies based on them are an important contribution of this work. The performance of the application in real problems was clearly superior using these strategies rather than generic distribution strategies.

One of the fundamental aspects in using CCP applications is the ability of the application to give an answer even when the entry is over-constrained. In this case, other important characteristics of our application were (1) modeling the problem as an optimization problem of just a CSP, (2) the flexibility in imposing constraints, and (3) the possibility of using constraints to increase the partially found solution.

Anyway, the possibility of using first class constraints is a characteristic that would give **Oz** more flexibility when facing over-restricted entries.

In a further work, we expect to integrate the application in current support systems like **WIMPE** [6] and **OpenConf** [10].

References

1. C. Castro and S. Manzano. (2001) Variable and value ordering when solving balance academics curriculum problem. In: Proc. of the ERCIM WG on constraints.
2. Juan F. Daz and Camilo Rueda. (2001) VISIR: Software de soporte para la toma de decisiones de vertimiento de agua en la represa del alto anchicay usando programacin concurrente por restricciones. Ingeniera y Competitividad. Vol 3, No. 2. Universidad del Valle, Cali (Colombia)
3. M. Henz and M. Muller. (1995) Programming in Oz. In G. Smolka and R. Treinen, Editors, DFKI Oz, Documentation Series. Mozart Documentation
4. Brahim Hnich, Zeynep Kiziltan and Toby Walsh.(2002) Modelling a Balanced Academic Curriculum Problem. In: Proceedings of CP-AI-OR-2002.
5. K. Marriott and P. J. Stuckey. (1998) Programming with Constraints: An Introduction. MIT Press, Cambridge, Mass
6. David M. Nicol. (2001) WIMPE: Web Interface for Managing Programs Electronically. http://www.crhc.uiuc.edu/ nicol//wimpe/wimpe6.1.html
7. C.Rueda and J.F. Daz and L.O. Quesada and C. Garca and S. Cetina. (2002) PATHOS: Object Oriented concurrent constraint timetabling for real world cases. In Proceedings XXVIII Conferencia Latinoamericana de Informtica, Montevideo, Uruguay
8. Christian Schulte and Gert Smolka. (2004) Finite Domain Constraint Programming in OZ. A Tutorial. Mozart Documentation
9. Peter Van Roy and Seif Haridi. (2004) Concepts, Techniques, and Models of Computer Programming. MIT Press
10. Zacon Group. (2004) OpenConf-Conference Manual Management System. http://www.OpenConf.org

An Interactive Tool for the Controlled Execution of an Automated Timetabling Constraint Engine[*]

Alberto Delgado[1], Jorge Andrés Pérez[1], Gustavo Pabón[3], Rafael Jordan[1],
Juan F. Díaz[2], and Camilo Rueda[1]

[1] Pontificia Universidad Javeriana - Cali
{albertod, japerezp, rjordan}@puj.edu.co, crueda@atlas.puj.edu.co
[2] Universidad del Valle
jdiaz@eisc.univalle.edu.co
[3] Central Planning Software
gustavo.pabon@centralsw.com

Abstract. Here we introduce *DePathos*, a graphical tool for a time-tabling constraint engine (*Pathos*). Since the core of *Pathos* is text-based and provides little user-interaction, finding an appropriate solution for large problems (1000-2000 variables) can be a very time consuming process requiring the constant supervision of a constraint programming expert. *DePathos* uses an *incremental solution* strategy. Such strategy subdivides the problem and checks the consistency of the resulting sub-divisions before incrementally unifying them. This has shown to be useful in finding inconsistencies and discovering over-constrained situations. Our incremental solution is based on hierarchical groupings defined at the problem domain level. This allows users to direct the timetabling engine in finding partial solutions that are meaningful in practice. We discuss the lessons learned from using *Pathos* in real settings, as well as the experiences of coupling *DePathos* to the timetabling engine.

1 Introduction

Combinatorial problems are ubiquitous in areas such as planning, logistics, scheduling and many others. One of these problems, university timetabling, refers to the scheduling of courses, lecturers and classrooms in such a way that several academic, administrative and resource constraints are satisfied. This task usually has to be performed at the beginning of each academic period. Constraint Programming (CP) has been used for modeling and solving this problem, as it naturally allows the expression of different types of conditions involved. Many solutions to this problem using CP technology have been proposed before (see

---

[*] This work was partially supported by the Colombian Institute for Science and Technology Development (Colciencias) under the CRISOL project (Contract No.298-2002).

P. Van Roy (Ed.): MOZ 2004, LNCS 3389, pp. 317–327, 2005.

Related Work, section 4.1). However, those proposals solve small size (albeit real) problems. Effectively handling timetabling for medium size universities (those having, say, at least 350 courses to schedule) poses a big challenge for CP technology. We believe that CP strategies must be complemented with tools giving the user clues as how to go about constructing a suitable solution in an incremental way. This is important since large timetabling problems tend to be over-constrained so that not every possible solution turns out to be acceptable in practice.

Pathos [9] is a timetabling application written in Mozart that has been used to successfully solve a problem of more than 1000 variables. A major obstacle in using *Pathos* is facing over-constrained situations. The front-end *DePathos* provides a systematic way to search for inconsistencies in these cases.

In our scheme the problem is partitioned in subproblems that are solved independently. Partitioning is done by the user following criteria relevant to the problem domain. This makes finding inconsistencies easier, as the user has more information and control over the data (constraints and variables) involved. This approach is also suitable when searching for approximate solutions that may not satisfy some of the constraints defined in the given problem, since it is possible to leave aside some elements of the input data.

The purpose of this paper is to describe a systematic approach for solving large timetabling problems in a real setting, using a constraint-based application. Ensuring consistency of the input data is one of the most difficult processes when solving this kind of problems. Automated mechanisms for guiding the search for inconsistencies are fundamental for the overall success of the scheduling process. We show how the systematic approach of *DePathos* helped us in solving complex timetabling problems.

The paper is organized as follows. In the next section the main features of the *Pathos* constraint engine are described. The process of running *Pathos* in a real setting is also discussed, showing the basic tasks involved and pointing out the factors that make the scheduling process difficult. Section 3 is devoted to *DePathos*, the developed solution for addressing some of the drawbacks of *Pathos*. Its components and main features are throughly explained, and some experiences in using *DePathos* are presented. We finally propose some directions for future work and also some concluding remarks.

2   *Pathos*: A Timetabling Constraint Engine

The variables used in *Pathos* are structures called *events*. Each event represents a session of a particular course (e.g., the first weekly session of Quantum Physics). Events keep information about the duration, the required resources, the location and the time slot in which the event will take place. The constraints modeling the problem can be categorized as follows:

- *Domain constraints*, used to determine the valid set of time slots for each event.
- *Basic constraints* over events, such as non overlapping constraints over events (called *no clash* constraints in [3]).
- *Non-basic constraints* extend basic constraints to groups of events. For instance, a condition stating that the lectures given by the same person cannot overlap.
- *Place constraints* are conditions on the location of an event. In *Pathos*, these constraints also take into account the required resources such as room capacity or particular teaching devices.

Pathos has been used for solving the timetabling problem at Universidad Javeriana - Cali. This problem is composed of approximately 1600 events, and has been solved in 46 seconds using an Intel Processor 900 MHz [9]. This performance refers only to the time taken by the constraint engine to find the first solution, and it does not include the time needed to eliminate inconsistencies in the input data, which was by far the longest process. This issue is analyzed in the following section.

2.1   Running *Pathos* in a Real Environment

In an ordinary execution of the system, the process of finding a schedule using *Pathos* could take between four and six weeks since the problem is usually *over constrained*. Usual sources of inconsistencies are small errors in stating resources or in asserting constraints related to needed resources. Because of the large number of constraints required for modeling the problem (around 17000 constraints), it is not easy to find such inconsistencies. Running *Pathos* comprises the following tasks:

Gathering of Data. The first step is to collect basic data: information about lecturers, courses to be offered, number and features of the available rooms, among others. This process has to handle both explicit and implicit information. The explicit information is extracted from well established sources like administrative policies and rules, curriculum and existing databases. In contrast, the implicit information is usually only known by the administrative personnel. Such information has to be precisely established by the programmer. While the explicit information can be easily extracted, gathering implicit information requires a more sophisticated process involving series of meetings between the programmer and the administrative personnel. The goal here is to state the constraints that must be satisfied, and to get an idea of which are the most important ones. In these meetings the programmer tries to explicit all conditions that are implicitly taken for granted by administrative people. The final result of this process is a XML-formatted input file for the constraint engine.

Initial Tests and Processing. The solving process begins by feeding the constraint engine with a problem constructed from the XML file obtained in the previous stage. Since a significant fraction (approximately 65%) of the constraints in the input data for *Pathos* are usually involved in some inconsistency, the bulk of the work rests on a debugging task. This process is time-consuming and is done with practically no guide, as the programmer must guess where the inconsistencies are and try to figure out how to correct them.

To make the debugging process easier, the input data is usually grouped by academic departments before being fed into the system. This is justified by the almost-disjoint nature of these subproblems. Within each department a further grouping by academic program is done. In most cases, however, these groupings do not provide enough information for finding inconsistencies. With no options left, a blind search over the input file is then performed. This *splitting* process is required because the system occasionally returns `fail` or is taking a long time trying to solve the given input. The splitting process has to be repeated many times until an appropriate solution is found. The result of this stage is a set of conflictive constraints.

Constraint Modifications. Once conflictive constraints are identified, it is necessary to negotiate them: in collaboration with administrative personnel, these inconsistent constraints are modified or eliminated, trying to satisfy as many constraints as possible. The changes in the constraints usually consist of augmenting or modifying weekly availability of certain rooms or resources needed for a given course. When inconsistencies are successfully corrected, the relevant output reports and database scripts are generated. Unfortunately, this rarely occurs in the initial runs of the system. The previous process is repeated several times.

2.2   Some Remarks Regarding the Process

The most salient disadvantage of the scheduling process is the human manipulation of the input data when looking for inconsistent data. This stage took a significant time of the overall project because modifications to the input file were done in an almost blind fashion. Most drawbacks in using *Pathos* are related to three issues:

– The monolithic structure of the input data.
– The process of manipulating the input data to search for inconsistencies.
– Communication with administrative personnel, i.e., what to do when an inconsistency is found.

Taking these issues as a starting point, we created a tool that solves the first issue in a simple way: adding a meaningful structure to the input data, based on the relationships and conditions present in the real problem. By augmenting the problem with such a structure, the manipulation of the input file is also tackled, as one could use such a structure as reference when debugging the input data. In relation with the last item, it is difficult to achieve substantial savings of the administrative work by means of an automated tool. This is due to the dynamic nature of the administrative work, where decisions are constantly changing based on many different factors. Nevertheless, the structure can serve as a common

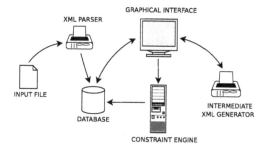

Fig. 1. Components of *DePathos*. The arrows represent the flow of information between them

place for programmers and end users. As pointed out in the next section, the reported tool improves the overall scheduling process by dealing with its most complicated task, the debugging process.

3   An Incremental Solution Approach

DePathos takes advantage of the hierarchical relations that underlies educational institutions to handle the timetabling process in an incremental way, as described next.

3.1   System Components

DePathos is composed of the following elements, shown in figure 1.

- A database, storing all information related to the scheduling process. This includes the input data, the solutions returned by the constraint engine and the modifications performed by the user.
- A XML parser that inserts the data representing the problem (described by a XML file) into the Database.
- A XML generator that outputs the data file for the constraint engine from the information in the database.
- A Graphical User Interface allowing the activation and deactivation of constraints, as well as configuration of some parameters for the solving process.
- The *Pathos* constraint engine.

The process of running *DePathos* can be summarized as follows. First, input data[1] is recorded into the database (using the XML parser) and loaded in the graphical interface. The user then configures and starts the incremental solution process using the graphical interface. As described in section 3.3, such a process requires multiple executions of the constraint engine. Input files (containing user

---

[1] It is assumed that such data was structured with a hierarchy in a prior process.

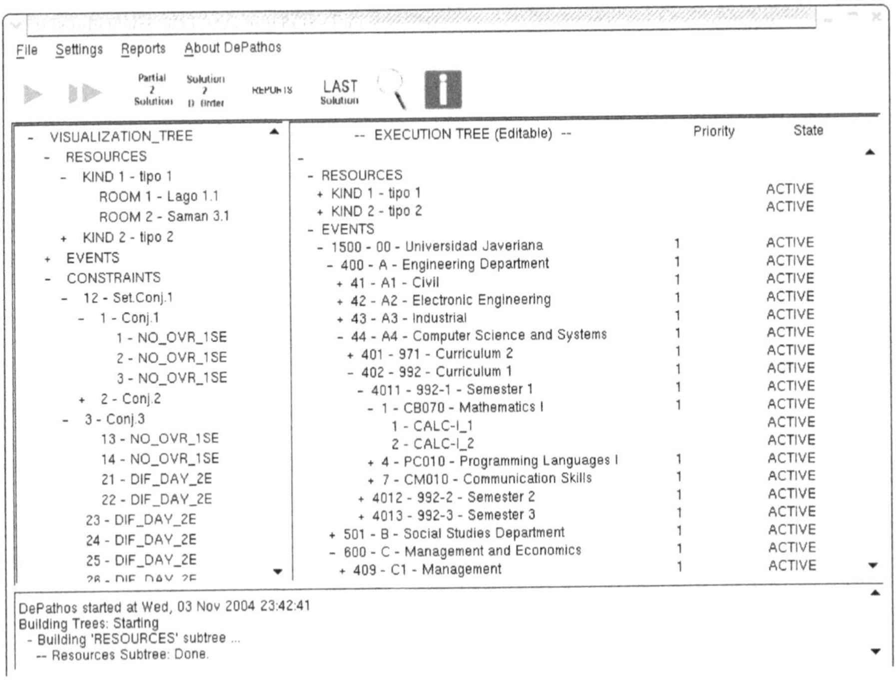

322   A. Delgado et al.

Fig. 2. Snapshot of the graphical user interface for *DePathos* before starting the incremental solution process

modifications and information in the database) for the engine are generated by the XML intermediate generator. When the incremental solution process stops, the user can either generate output reports from the solution or to perform some modifications.

It is important to remark that the integration between *Pathos* and *De-Pathos* is based on the XML interfaces and database connections provided by Mozart. In this way, a graphical interface developed in a programming language different from Mozart can be transparently combined with a program written in Mozart (*Pathos*). This turns out to be very useful when the user wants the application to be developed in a specific environment, such as a web-enabled one.

3.2   Establishing Hierarchies

The particular academic organization of an educational institution plays a fundamental role in *DePathos*. In this section we discuss how the solving process can take advantage of this organization.

For each event in the problem, *Pathos* attempts to assign a time slot satisfying every constraint over it. Thus *Pathos* can be seen as a constraint engine that only solves problems expressed in terms of events. However, a user would like to express the features and conditions of the problem more naturally. It is then necessary to create a layer above the constraint engine that abstracts away details of the engine from the user.

DePathos works as a tool for handling this layer. Besides the abstraction advantages mentioned before, *DePathos* supports the modeling of a timetabling problem in a set-based, hierarchical fashion, encouraging systematic thinking for solving it.

Consider the hierarchy depicted in the right hand side of figure 2. The whole university is modeled as a set containing three subproblems, corresponding to each one of the academic departments: Engineering (400-A), Social Studies (501-B) and Management and Economics (600-C). Each one of them is composed of several academic programs. The figure shows four different programs within the Engineering Department: Civil (41-A1), Electronic (42-A2), Industrial (43-A3) and Computer Science and Systems (44-A4). Note that each program has several subdivisions. For instance, the Computer Science and Systems Engineering program is divided in two curricula (401-971 and 402-992), and each curriculum is composed of several semesters and courses. Finally, at the lowest level in the hierarchy, each course is represented by its corresponding events. For instance, course "CB070 - Mathematics I" (inside curricula 1) has two events: "CALC-I_1" and "CALC-I_2".

In this way, an intuitive structure of subproblems can be obtained; its definition depends on unique features of the educational institution and on the desired level of detail. A salient feature of our approach is that it allows to include constraints over sets of events. Since *Pathos* does not consider these hierarchies, *DePathos* translates such constraints into constraints over events. In the next section we show how this hierarchical scheme can be combined with a systematic approach for finding inconsistencies.

3.3   Incremental Solution

The idea is to successively increase the size of the input data that is fed into the constraint engine, until all input data is considered. The process starts by considering a significant fraction of the hierarchy explained before –the *initial set*– which will be increased with a fixed number of subproblems (also extracted from the hierarchy) at each step of the process. The process is implemented in Algorithm 1. In this approach, a *subproblem* is a user-defined group of variables with their associated constraints, e.g., Mathematics in figure 2. A *consistency check* of a subproblem consists in running *Pathos* with the given problem. This process is represented in the algorithm with the isConsistent boolean function.

The parameters of the algorithm are the size of the initial set, the number of subproblems to be added in each step, the problem itself and an order relation over the subproblems inside the problem, respectively. In *DePathos*, this order relation is implemented by a user-defined priority over the elements in the hierarchy. *getSet* extracts a certain number of subproblems from a given problem and function *evaluate* checks consistency for a given set of subproblems. These functions are described in algorithm 2. Given two sets of problems A and B,

---

Algorithm 1 Incremental Solution Algorithm

IncSolution := **proc** (sizeInitSet, sizeAddSet, P, $\leq$)
Requires: sizeInitSet, sizeAddSet > 0, P is ordered w.r.t. $\leq$.
 1: setEval = $getSet(P, \leq, $ sizeInitSet)
 2: **if** *evaluate*(setEval, $\leq$) == **true then**
 3:    **while** $P \neq \emptyset$ **do**
 4:      $P = P - $ setEval
 5:      setToAdd = $getSet(P, \leq, $ sizeAddSet)
 6:      **if** *evaluate*(setToAdd, $\leq$) == **true then**
 7:        setEval = $Union$(setEval, setToAdd)
 8:        **if** isConsistent(setEval) == **false then**
 9:          return **failure**
10:      **else**
11:        return **failure**
12: **else**
13:    return **failure**
14: return **true**

Union (A, B) returns the set of all variables and constraints that are either in A or in B, including those constraints over both sets. Function $first(P, \leq)$ extracts the first element in P, according to the ordering relation $\leq$.

Termination of the incremental solution algorithm is guaranteed by P, which is the variant of the while loop. The same applies for *tempSet* in function *evaluate*. When the output is **failure**, the user is expected to modify (activate/deactivate) some elements in the problem using the graphical interface.

3.4   Visual Aids and Other Tools

DePathos allows the configuration of settings such as the maximum execution time allowed for each subproblem. *DePathos* also allows the user viewing and/or modifying constraint parameters, priorities and the state of the elements in the hierarchy.

DePathos provides visual tools (see figure 2). Two trees showing hierarchies are displayed. The left one (*visualization tree*) reflects the original problem in terms of resources, events and constraints during the whole process. Its purpose is to serve as a quick guide to browse the input data. This tree does not change during the process. Modifications of the input data are done on the *execution tree*, shown in the right hand side of the window. The content of the tree is continuously changing as the process progresses, taking into account user modifications and the current state of the problem.

3.5   Impact of *DePathos* in the Scheduling Process

In our tests it was clear that the size of the initial set and the number of subproblems added in each step are fundamental when trying to perform an efficient debugging process with *DePathos*. Consider a problem that is divided in a large

---

Algorithm 2 getSet and Evaluate functions

---

getSet := **proc** $(P, \leq, \text{numOfSets})$
Requires: numOfSets > 0, P is ordered w.r.t. $\leq$.
 1: $i = 0$, nSet $= \emptyset$
 2: **while** $i <$ numOfSets **do**
 3:     $f = \text{first}(P, \leq)$
 4:     nSet $= Union(\text{nSet}, \text{f})$
 5:     $P = P - \{f\}$
 6:     $i = i + 1$
 7: **return** nSet

evaluate := **proc** $(S, \leq)$
Requires: S is a set of subproblems, ordered w.r.t. $\leq$.
 1: tempSet $:= S$
 2: **while** tempSet $\neq \emptyset$ **do**
 3:     subSet $:= \text{first}(\text{tempSet}, \leq)$
 4:     tempSet $:= \text{tempSet} - \{\text{subSet}\}$
 5:     **if** isConsistent(subSet) $==$ **false then**
 6:        **return false**
 7: **if** isConsistent(S) $==$ **false then**
 8:     **return false**
 9: **return true**

---

number of subproblems. We found it too cumbersome to run the incremental solution by adding only one or a few sets in each step. Nevertheless, situations where it is necessary to add only one subproblem in each step are possible, like when the user is interested in catching a concrete source of inconsistencies.

On the other side, taking a large size for the initial set (about half of the number of subproblems) and adding about 10% of the total number of subproblems in each step, a solution was found faster than in the previous case. However, when inconsistencies were detected, finding the source of the problem in such a huge search space was not straightforward.

During our tests we distinguished two types of inconsistencies. Inconsistencies within a subproblem, mainly caused by some human error when defining constraints (or their associated elements) and inconsistencies caused by the interaction of subproblems, i.e., over-constrained situations. These inconsistencies were harder to find, since several subsets had to be considered. As we expected, such inconsistencies were related with the subproblem *DePathos* was considering at the moment, although the source of the inconsistency involved several other subproblems.

Using *DePathos*, we gain a concrete knowledge about a significant part of the inconsistencies in the input data. In contrast, when using *Pathos* alone the user had no clue at all to pinpoint the errors and inconsistencies. We believe that being able to distinguish the two kinds described above provides valuable help for the user. While the process of correcting inconsistencies was cumbersome, those "solvable" inconsistencies were easy to find and correct using *DePathos*, due to the visual aids it provides.

4   Conclusions

The modular implementation of *DePathos* allows the transparent replacement or modification of any of its components. For instance, a more efficient implementation of the constraint could be devised without affecting the behavior of the other components. Moreover, this design philosophy can be used in other constraint applications.

The whole development process of *Pathos* and *DePathos* has shown that building a constraint application is more complex than building an acceptable constraint program: as in any software development, the end user plays an important role. In our case, we showed how a stage of requirements elicitation for discovering implicit information about the problem was necessary. By expressing the problem in common terms, *DePathos* encourages the interaction between the constraint programmer and the end user.

In the choice of the parameters for the incremental solution process a trade-off between precision (or level of detail) and time performance must be considered. Bigger sets of subproblems in each step of the process allow a faster scheduling process but make the finding of inconsistencies difficult. An opposite selection of parameters can be time-consuming but it is more appropriate when searching for specific inconsistencies.

Inconsistencies can arise within a subproblem as well as in the union of several subproblems. *DePathos* can report some of the subproblems involved in the inconsistencies, although such subproblems may not be the only source of the inconsistencies. In this cases, the information *DePathos* provides guides the search for the conflictive elements in the problem.

Since finding a solution satisfying all constraints is hard, it is a common practice to accept partial or approximate solutions. *DePathos* makes the construction of such solutions easier by allowing deactivation of elements during the incremental solution process.

4.1   Related Work

The university timetabling problem has been studied from different perspectives, including operations research, simulated annealing [2], tabu search [1] and genetic algorithms [10]. Various timetabling systems using constraint technologies have been proposed (see [11, 8, 7, 5, 3, 12, 6]).

In [4], an incremental approach for scheduling timetables is proposed. However, such a proposal addresses the administrative problem of centralizing the information about timetables. In that case, as each department or section had its own method for building their timetables, the resources were not fully used and several timetable clashes arose. An incremental approach for centralizing the departmental timetabling procedures is then proposed. This takes into account the need of preserving the autonomous administration in each department. On the contrary, *DePathos* assumes a centralized scheduling process that considers all the departments and divisions in a University.

Acknowledgments. We would like to thank to the anonymous reviewers for their valuable comments that helped us improve this paper significantly. Luis Quesada, Carlos Olarte and Diego Linares also gave useful comments and suggestions.

References

1. Jean Paul Boufflet and Stéphane Nègre. Three methods used to solve an examination timetable problem. In *Practice and Theory of Automated Timetabling*. Springer, LNCS 1153, 1996.
2. M. A. Saleh Elmohamed, Paul Coddington, and Geoffrey Fox. A comparison of annealing techniques for academic course scheduling. In *Practice and Theory of Automated Timetabling II*. Springer, LNCS 1408, 1998.
3. Thom Fruhwirth and Slim Abdennadher. *Essentials of Constraint Programming*. Springer, 2002.
4. Simon Geller. Timetabling at the University of Sheffield, UK - an incremental approach to timetable development. In *Practice and Theory of Automated Timetabling*, 2002.
5. M. Henz and J. Wurtz. Using oz for college timetabling. In *International Conference on the Practice and Theory of Automated Timetabling*, 1995.
6. Kazuya Kaneko, Masazumi Yoshikawa, and Yoichiro Nakakuki. Improving a heuristic repair method for large-scale school timetabling problems. In *Principles and Practice of Constraint Programming*. Springer, LNCS 1713, 1999.
7. W. Legierski. Using Mozart for Timetabling Problems. In *Proceedings of the CPDC'01 Workshop on Constraint Programming for Decision and Control*, 2001.
8. Michael Marte. *Models and Algorithms for School Timetabling - A Constraint-Programming Approach*. Dissertation/Ph.D. thesis, Institute of Computer Science, LMU, Munich, 2003.
9. Gustavo Pabón and Carlos Rodriguez. Reingeniería de PATHOS (In Spanish). B.Sc. Thesis - Universidad Javeriana, Cali, 2003. Available at http://correo.puj.edu.co/japerezp/Crisol/.
10. D.C. Rich. A Smart Genetic Algorithm for University Timetabling. In *Practice and Theory of Automated Timetabling*. Springer, LNCS 1153, 1996.
11. C. Rueda, J.F. Díaz, L.O. Quesada, C. García, and S. Cetina. Pathos: Object-oriented concurrent constraint timetabling for real world cases. In *Proceedings, XXVIII Latin-American Conference on Informatics*, Uruguay, 2002.
12. D. Wasacz. Timetabling with CHIP. In *Proceedings of the CPDC'99 Workshop on Constraint Programming for Decision and Control*, 1999.

Author Index

Lecture Notes in Computer Science

For information about Vols. 1–3317

please contact your bookseller or Springer